PROVENCE CÔTE D'AZUR

Howard Rombough
Benoit Éthier
Hans Jörg Mettler
Bertrand Pierson

DDion

D1500688

ULYSSES
TRAVEL PUBLICATIONS
Travel better... enjoy more

| Series Director | English Editor | Cartography |
| Claude Morneau | Jennifer McMorran | André Duchesne |

Project Supervisor	English translation	Artistic Director
Pascale Couture	Côte d'Azur	Patrick Farei
	Andrea Szakos	Atoll Direction

Research and
Composition | Layout | Graphic Design
Côte d'Azur | Jennifer McMorran | Jean-François Bienvenue
Benoit Éthier | Pierre Daveluy |
Hans Jörg Mettler | | Photography
Provence | Collaboration | C. Simpson
Howard Rombough | Daniel Desjardins | Reflexion
Bertrand Pierson

The authors of Provence would like to thank: SNCF Grandes Lignes; Éric Cinotti and Pascale Noyer (SNCF Grandes Lignes Dép. Communication, Paris); Geneviève Canet (SNCF Marseille, Délégation au TER); Martin Stein, the Stein family and Mme Knigge (Avignon); Catherine Heuzé (Office du tourisme de Marseille); Bernard Brulas (Marseille); Mme Geneviève Foubert-Artioli (Marseille); Anne Igou and Delia Buffile (Arles); the Desjardins family (Arles); Fabrice Guisset (Villeneuve-lès-Avignon); Nicole and Alain Bellec (Avignon); Andrée and Jean-Pierre Pincedé (Château de Vergière, Saint-Martin-de-Crau); Lucille and Jacques Bon (Le Sambuc, Camargue); Olga and Henri Manguin (île de la Barthalasse, Avignon); Laurence Gurly (Vaison-la-Romaine); Aude and Jean-Loup Verdier (Vaison-la-Romaine); Martine Maret (Venasque); Gérard Roux (Gordes); Walter Lievens (Gordes); Vincent Bœuf (Gordes); Gabrielle Jugy and René Bergès (Beaurecueuil); John Lee (London); Brigit and Philippe Krenzer-Lievens (London); Lyndy and Sam Stout (London); Mme Jean Pierson and Lorette Pierson.
The authors of Côte d'Azur would like to thank Pierrette for her "technical" assistance and Clo for her friendly collaboration.

Distributors

AUSTRALIA
Little Hills Press
11/37-43 Alexander St.
Crows Nest NSW 2065
☎ (612) 437-6995
fax: (612) 438-5762

ITALY
Edizioni del Riccio
50143 Firenze-
Via di Soffiana
☎ (055) 71 63 50
Fax: (055) 71 33 33

U.S.A. :
Seven Hills Book Distributors
49 Central Avenue
Cincinnati, Ohio, 45202
☎ 1-800-545-2005
Fax : (513) 381-0753

CANADA :
Ulysses Books & Maps
4176 Saint-Denis
Montréal, Québec
H2W 2M5
☎ (514) 843-9882, ext.
Fax : 514-843-9448

NETHERLANDS and FLANDERS :
Nilsson & Lamm
Pampuslaan 212-214
Postbus 195
1380 AD Weesp (NL)
☎ 02940-65044
Fax : 02940-15054

GERMANY :
Brettschneider Fernreisebedarf
GmbH
D-8011 Poing bei München
Hauptstr. 5
☎ 08121-71436
Fax : 08121-71419

SPAIN
Altaïr
Balmes 69
E-08007 Barcelona
☎ (34-3) 323-3062
Fax : (3403) 451-2559

Other countries, contact Ulysses Books & Maps (Montréal), Fax : (514) 843-9448

Canadian Cataloguing in Publication Data
Howard Rombough, 1962-
    Provence, Côte d'Azur
    (Ulysses travel guides)
    Includes index.
ISBN 2-921444-37-2
1. Provence (France) - Guidebooks. 2. Riviera (France) - Guidebooks. I. Ethier, Benoit, 1958-
II. Mettler, Hans Jörg, 1948-   . III. Title. IV. Series.
DC611.P958H682 1995   914.4'904839   C95-940769-3

Everything is full-blooded. The food is full of strong earthy flavors... There is nothing bland about Provence...

Peter Mayle *A Year in Provence*

TABLE OF CONTENTS

LIST OF MAPS

Help make Ulysses Travel Guides even better!

The information contained in this guide was correct at press time. However, mistakes can slip in, omissions are always possible, places can disappear, etc. The author and publisher hereby disclaim any liability for loss or damage resulting from omissions or errors.

We value your comments, corrections and suggestions, as they allow us to keep each guide up to date. The best contributions will be rewarded with a free book from Ulysses Travel Publications. All you have to do is write us at the following address and indicate which title you would be interested in receiving (see the list at end of guide).

**Ulysses Travel Publications
4176 Rue Saint-Denis
Montréal, Québec
Canada H2W 2M5**

TABLE OF SYMBOLS

☎	Telephone number
⇄	Fax number
≡	Air conditioning
⊗	Ceiling fan
≈	Pool
ℜ	Restaurant
⊚	Whirlpool
ℝ	Refrigerator
C	Kitchenette
tvc	Colour television
pb	Private bath
ps or s	Private shower or shower
bkfst	Breakfast

ATTRACTION CLASSIFICATION

★	Interesting
★★	Worth a visit
★★★	Not to be missed

HOTEL CLASSIFICATION

Unless otherwise indicated, accommodation prices are for one room, double occupancy, during the high season.

RESTAURANT CLASSIFICATION

$	less than 100 F
$$	between 100 F and 250 F
$$$	more than 250 F

The restaurants in the guide are for a meal for one person, including tax and tip, but not including drinks.

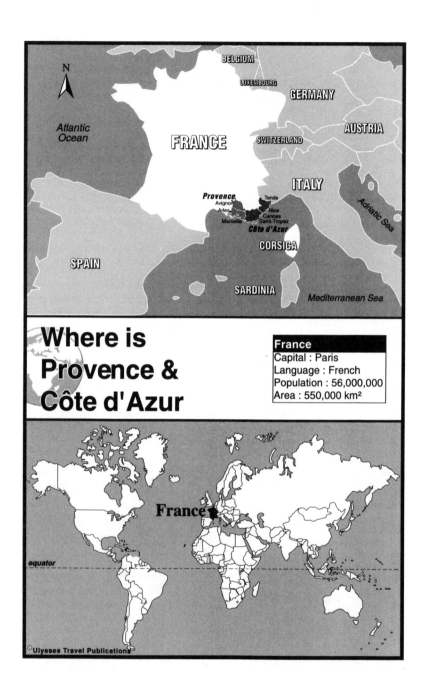

Where is Provence & Côte d'Azur

France
Capital : Paris
Language : French
Population : 56,000,000
Area : 550,000 km²

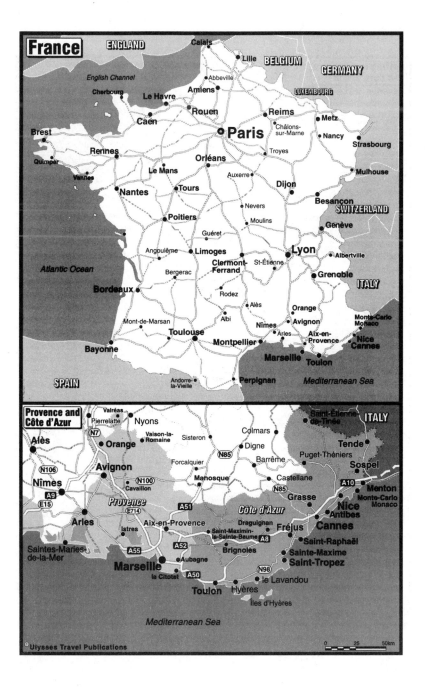

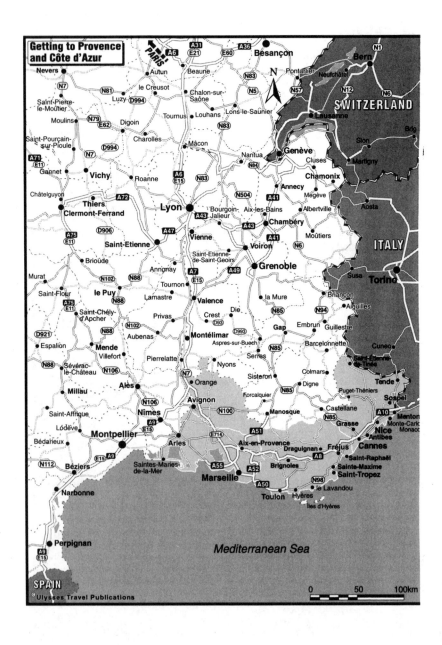

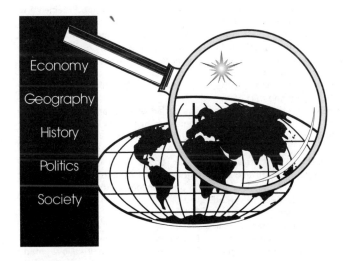

Economy

Geography

History

Politics

Society

PORTRAIT OF PROVENCE CÔTE D'AZUR

Provence Côte d'Azur is a land of contrasts. Its sunny climate and Mediterranean way of life offer something for everyone, no matter what your interests may be. Visitors will find sandy beaches on the Riviera, low plains in the Camargue, gently rolling hills in the Luberon and Vaucluse and steeper territory in the southern Alps.

The lively metropolitan centres on the coast differ sharply from the traditional villages, hidden paths and panoramic landscapes of the interior. There are an infinite variety of treasures to discover in Provence Côte d'Azur. Around every corner there seems to be another Roman monument, field of beautiful lavender or delicious meal of *bouillabaisse* or *ratatouille* just waiting to be claimed, inhaled and devoured.

Geography

The region is bordered by four distinct geographical features: the Rivière Rhône to the west, the Comtat Venaissin and southern part of the Alps to the north, the Italian border to the east and the Mediterranean Sea to the south. The administrative and economic region known as of Provence-Alpes-Côte d'Azur as a whole counts 31,436 km^2 and over four million inhabitants.

Provence Côte d'Azur is the most visited region in France, due to its fine weather, variety of natural beauty and historical sites, and of course, its Riviera attractions. Typically dry, hot summers are contrasted with unpredictable weather the remainder of the year. Winters can be harsh and cloudy in the mountainous areas, and mild along the coast. The Rhône valley and part of the coast are frequently hit by the mistral, the cold, violent wind coming from the north at speeds of up to 290 km/h.

In general, the land is characterized by an undulating topographical surface and a magnificient luminosity, as it is an area receiving a great deal of year-round sunshine. Provence Côte d'Azur is distinguished by three geographical areas: the **low plains** of the Comtat, Crau and Camargue at the Rhône basin; the **interior** with the calcareous plains of Provence, the hills of Provence and the mountains of the *Préalpes du Sud*; and finally, the rocky **coastline**, including the cliffs east of Marseille.

Low Plains of the Comtat, Camargue, Crau

These low regions next to the Rhône, (less than 250 m above sea level), are essentially alluvial plains. The Comtat and Camargue are muddy lands, while the Crau is pebbly. The narrow coastal plain is equally low and it forms a ribbon the length of the Mediterranean.

Interior

The homogeneous, yet puzzle-like series of hills, plateaus and basins (250 to 500 m) is dominated by a great limestone chain stretching east-west. The hills of Provence include the Alpilles, Lubéron, Sainte-Victoire and Sainte-Baume, and are primarily of sedimentary rock. The Maures and

Estérel range near the coast is of crystalline soil. From Mont Ventoux (1,909 m) passing by the Préalpes and reaching the Mercantour, the mountainous region rarely passes 3,500 m. They are strongly marked by rough mountain ridges and deep limestone valleys.

Coastline

The varied Mediterranean coast is distinguished by the low, sandy riverbanks of the west, and the rocky cliffs of the east. Among these are the impressive white coves around Marseille (the highest cliffs in Europe) and the red porphyry ledges of the Esterel.

■ Flora

The sunshine and favourable climate of Provence Côte d'Azur allow many interesting trees and flowers to grow in the region. Olive and oak trees are predominant in the lower regions, as both enjoy the limestone soil under altitudes of 700 m. The olive tree was introduced to the region by the Greeks 3,000 years ago, who called it "the tree of wisdom, abundance and glory".

Nowadays there are more than 50 varieties of olive trees; they grow to between five and eight metres and some reach 20 metres. Although they have a long life span, (centuries or even thousands of years), the olive tree's fruit is only good enough for picking for the first 15 years. The harvest is between November and January, depending on whether the ripe green ones or the mature black ones are desired. One thousand kilos of olives give 10 to 15 litres of oil. The first pressing yields the most sought-after virgin olive oil.

The holm oak (*chêne vert*) and the scrub oak (*chêne kermès*), both stubby trees, are seen throughout the region, including on hillsides slightly higher than those tolerated by the olive groves. Trees found on the plains or hillsides of the interior include pine (maritime, parasol and aleppo), the tall, distinctively shaped Cypress in their neat rows, plane, lotus, lime/linden (*tilleul*) sycamore and almond. Fields of lavender, displaying their violet flowers all summer long, are found in the hilly areas above 1,000 metres.

A great variety of fruit trees grow locally, principally peach, cherry, apricot, apple, pear and lemon. Carpentras and Cavaillon are renowned for their tasty melons. Asparagus, new potatoes, strawberries, mushrooms and dessert grapes are found as well. Vineyards, either in the Côtes de Provence area northeast of Marseille or Côtes du Rhône in the southern Rhône valley near Orange produce fine drinking wines, including fruity rosés, dry whites and the famous reds, Gigondas and Châteauneuf-du-Pape.

Herbs are abundant throughout the area, especially rosemary, thyme and savoury which grow wild. Basil, marjoram, summer savoury (*sarriette*) and tarragon are popular. A selection of these, called *herbes de Provence* are sold in markets, and used in cooking to enhance meat, fish and sauces. Many of these plants are used traditionally as herbal remedies or for medicinal purposes. Sage is meant to be good for fatigue and liver complaints, rosemary helps the respiratory system and thyme is said to be an aphrodisiac. Herbal teas or *infusions* from thyme, rosemary or laurel are meant to aid digestion. The Camargue is famous for its salt production, collected from the sea, pumped across huge salt tables, left to dry, then raked, washed and dried each September, it is ready later for the dinner table.

Flowers feature largely in the countryside, markets and gardens of Provence Côte d'Azur. Roses, jasmin and carnations are also cultivated professionally for the perfume market, traditionally centred in Grasse. An estimated 10,000 tons of flowers are treated there every year and it is said that for every four flacons of perfume which circulates throughout the world, three use the floral essences originating in Provence.

Worth seeing are the regional natural parks, like that of Camargue. Since 1970, the Camargue park protects 500 km^2 of fragile ecosystem, one which is unique in France because of its position at the mouth of the Rhône and Mediterranean.

■ **Fauna**

Hot, sunny weather, grassy fields and the sweet perfume of wild flowers are the perfect conditions for insect life in Provence Côte d'Azur. It's hard to mistake the music of the grasshoppers and crickets when night falls. Mosquitoes and blackflies are abundant in the Camargue and the Rhône valley. Toads, frogs and river bugs are found next to the rivers and streams, as are herons and even flamingoes.

The river banks in the Maures, Estérel and Rhône Valley are popular spots for amateur fishermen. Commercial fishing is centred on the seacoast, where crayfish, red mullet, John Dory, gilthead (*daurade*), monkfish, gurnard and scorpionfish are prized. Over-fishing of the sea has destroyed a large part of the marine-life, and pollution has killed off important marine plants.

It is thought that a number of places in the Mediterranean will soon be a new kind of dead sea.

The Camargue is also the only place in France where wild horses can be seen. They are small, but hardy, and are thought to have originallly arrived from Asia. They are born with a grey or berry-coloured coat - only later does it turn characteristically white. Beavers, otters, ducks, buzzards, game and as many as 400 species of rare birds are found in the protected regional parklands.

In the Luberon regional park, created in 1977, you'll find wild boar, the Bonelli eagle, and Grand Duke owl. Coastal conservation areas with an interesting variety of wildlife are located at Giens, Caraueiranne, Pradet, Bandol, Cassis and Estaque.

History

■ Prehistory

Provence owes a significant proportion of its rich history to the Greek and Roman presence in its early days. Greeks controlled the region for four centuries and the Roman's occupied it for five. However, the presence of human life in the region dates back nearly 900,000 years. Cut stone tools from this period have been found in a cave at Vallonnet, near Roquebrune. Remains of a 30-year-old Prehistoric man known as Grimaldi were found near Nice.

■ Greek and Roman Times

As the legend goes, near 600 BC, a ship from the Greek city of Phoceae in Asia Minor was returning from Spain when it stopped along the Provence coastline. At the same time, the chief of the Ligurians (habitants of the area) held a sumptuous banquet, to honour his daughter Gyptis. She had to choose a husband by offering a beautiful chalice to one of the numerous eligible bachelors from the region who had assembled for the occasion. Gyptis apparently had a taste for adventure and the unknown, for she chose the captain of the Phocaean sailing vessel who had been invited at the last minute. The man, Protis, married Gyptis and founded the first Greek city in Provence. It was called Massalia, present day Marseille.

Thereafter, Marseille became a strategic trading centre and stop-over for the Greeks. They brought pottery and wine with them, and returned with ships laden with lead from the Maures Massif and salt from the Etang de Berre. Indeed, the entrepreneurial Greeks were responsible for introducing the use of money, and the cultivation of olives and grapes. It wasn't an altogether peaceful time however, as the warring tribes of the Celto-Ligurians from north of the port often fought with the Greeks.

The Massaliotes called upon their Roman allies to help them in their battle with the Celto-Ligurians (181 and 154 BC). The Romans occupied the region from the Alps to the Rhône and defeated the Celto-Ligurians, having destroyed their base at Entremont. In 123 BC, the counsellor Sextius settled near the thermal waters of modern-day Aix-en-Provence, calling the camp Aquae Sextiae. From this base, he set out about to conquer the entire region, and it did indeed become the Roman territory La Provincia (hence the area's name Provence).

The region was intensely developed by the Romans over the next four centuries. Trade was important, and the techniques for the cultivation of olives and vines improved. The cities of Apt, Avignon, Carpentras, Glanum, Riez and Vaison-la-Romaine were created. Arles flourished, particularly after 49 BC when Caesar made it the capital of the province, having conquered Marseille which had remained independent. A sophisticated road network was built, including the *Via Agrippa* (the present day N 7) and the *Via Domitia* cutting across the country towards the Pyrenees, and linking it with Spain. Roman baths, theatres, arenas, triumphal arches, aqueducts and monuments covered the province. Some still exist to this day.

Caesar established his veterans at Arles, Béziers and Fréjus. Emperor Augustus added the new colonies of Avignon, Orange and Vienna. Local laws in 27 BC put the Alpes Maritimes region under direct control of the Emperor, while the rest of the land was lead by a governor and an assembly (based in Narbonne).

The decline of the region's prosperity struck in 250 AD, with the first of many invasions by the Barbarians. The area was divided and Arles held out the longest, finally surrendering to a Visigoth invasion in 476 (the same time as the fall of the Holy Roman Empire). Christianity, which of course had progressed slowly during the Roman times, played a greater role in everyday and political life. The monasteries of Saint-Victor in Marseille (413) and of Iles de Lérins thrived. Numerous invasions continued by the Visigoths, Burgundians, Ostrogoths and Franks. Provence eventually became part of the Frank Kingdom (536), though it kept a certain independence.

■ The Middle Ages

Provence managed to retain its independence from the eighth to twelfth century, despite wars and continued takeovers by emperors, princes and kings. The territory changed hands between the Saracens and the Emperor Charlemagne more than once, then it became part of the kingdoms of Provence-Viennois and Bourgogne Cisjurane, the second kingdom of Provence, the kingdom of Bourgogne-Provence and later the kingdom of Arles.

All the time though, local power was held by the counts of Arles and Avignon. Such authority and independence enabled Provence to develop economically. Its population grew steadily and Christianity developed.

■ The Counts of Provence

Provence was controlled by various counts of Barcelona from about 1200 onwards. Catalonia and Provence were great maritime trading partners and the new administrative connection was profitable. The most famous Catalan count was Raimond Bérenger V, renowned for his legislative work and cultural refinement. The lyrical magic of the troubadours flourished under his rule, as did Provençal Roman art, as seen in church architecture.

In 1246, the daughter of Raimond Bérenger married Charles of Anjou, who was the brother of the King of France, Saint Louis. As count of Provence and ruler of the Angevin dynasty, Charles the First (as he was now called) conquered the kingdoms of Naples and Sicily. Despite further flare-ups with Italy, Provence thrived, both commercially and legislatively. Marseille profited from the religious crusades

(1096-1270) and traded with the Middle East, Arabia, Africa, India and the Far East. Oranges, lemons, raisins, figs, sugar cane, carpets, glass, fabric, spices, precious stones, ivory and silver all entered its port.

Avignon became the *cité des papes* (city of the popes) between 1305 and 1376. Avoiding political troubles and violence in Italy, it was Pope Clément V who decided on the move. He was succeeded by Jean XXII, Benoît XII, and Clément VI (in 1341). They built a splendid Palais des Papes, which still dominates Avignon today. Clement VI and his court led a particularly extravagant life, worthy of a king, surrounded by finest artisans and feted by amazing entertainments.

Well-known counts of Provence included the great granddaughter of Charles the First, Queen Jeanne. She who sold Avignon to Clement VI in 1348. She ruled from 1343 to 1382, during a time when civil wars and political intrigue were rife. René d'Anjou (1434-1480), called the *bon roi René* (good King René), was much-admired for his appreciation for the arts and science. Both Jeanne and René were considered incapable leaders (much land was lost during their time in power, for example), but they had tremendous popular appeal. The great black pest killed off more than one-third of the Provençal population in 1348.

■ **Provence and the Kingdom of France**

By the end of the 15th century, Provence was primarily an agricultural region with an estimated population of nearly 400,000 people. It was controlled more by the *États de Provence*, than by René, a system which brought reasonable prosperity. After his death, René's nephew Charles III inherited the area. He died a year and a half later in 1482 without any offspring. King Louis XI of France became the count of Provence, and brought his forces in to quell any possible opposition. The region officially became a province of France in 1486.

The *États de Provence* established a law (existing until 1789), which decreed that the region would be an independent political entity separate from the kingdom of France. It marked the beginning of a power struggle between the local nobility against the royal power. It was as much a fight for cultural identity, including protection of the provençal dialect *Occitan* or *langue d'Oc*, as it was for political independence.

Louis XII created a parliament in Aix in 1501 in an attempt to strengthen his royal authority. The *Édit de Joinville* (1535) restricted the power of the *États de Provence*, and the *ordonnance de Villers-Cotterêts* (1539) stipulated that French was the region's official language, written and spoken. A century later, the meeting of the *États* were abolished under Richelieu (as elsewhere in France) and replaced by a less powerful community assembly (1636).

Provence was invaded twice in the first half of the 16th century, during the power struggles played out by François I and Charles Quint, leader of the Imperial troops opposing the monarchy and who sought refuge in the region. The second half of the 16th century was dominated by the wars of religion, which pitted Protestants against Catholics.

Noble rebels were called *sabreurs*, and the *Provençaux* who remained loyal to the crown, known as *canivets*. The people of Marseille were particularly vigilant in their resistance to the monarchy, so much so that Louis XIV abolished their municipal freedoms in 1660.

Early on in his reign, an intendant was installed in the area, which meant the virtual political integration of the region to the kingdom. However, political struggles continued.

The cities of Aix, Arles and Tarascon grew prosperous in the 18th century, as colonial trade flourished and brought new riches to Provence. It was a great period of architectural interest - many impressive *hôtels particuliers* were built to house the newly wealthy social class. The region nearly doubled its population in 300 years - 700,000 lived there at the end of the 1700s. Marseille was the largest trading port in the country. The region had a remarkably diversified economy - agriculture production (mainly olives and grapes) mixed with industry (leather goods, paper, soap and fabric).

■ Revolution

The re-installation of the *États de Provence* occurred in the 1770s, when an important political figure, Mirabeau became a prominent anti-monarchist. He led a delegation in Paris singing *la Marseillaise*, now France's national anthem.

Most *Provençaux* remained anti-revolutionary, though proudly independent. They demonstrated against the Revolutionary movement, and opposed the First Empire of Napoléon I. Provence was divided up into departments (Bouches-du-Rhône, Var and Basse-Alpes) in 1790, which officially ended the political-administrative homogeneity of the region. (In 1956, it was reunited as Provence-Côte d'Azur-Corse, nowadays Provence-Alpes-Côte d'Azur.)

At the beginning of the Second Empire, Nobel Prize winner Frederic Mistral (1830-1914) founded the *Félibrige*, a movement attempting to restore the *langue d'Oc* and local literature which was threatening to disappear. Economic, social and demographic forces were too strong for widespread success, yet Mistral's work did help to maintain traditional celebrations in the area. In August, 1944, Provence, having been occupied by the Germans, was liberated by Allied troops landing on the Maures coast.

■ History of Nice

Linked to Provence since the year 970, the *comté de Nice* decided in 1388 to give itself to Amédée VII, count of Savoie. At the time, Europe consisted of different duchies, counties and kingdoms (France was a kingdom), the territorial borders of which were constantly changing depending on the outcomes of the incessant warring going on between them.

It was not until 1860 that France definitively regained the *comté de Nice* by virtue of the treaty between Napoleon III and the king of Piémont-Sardaigne on March 24, 1860. Following the treaty, in April of the same year, a plebiscite was held which determined that 84% of *Niçois* were in favour of joining the kingdom of France.

There were however several times between 1388 and 1860 when the *comté de Nice* belonged to France, for example under Louis XIV or during the years following the Revolution. And then when Louis XI, King of France, took possession of Provence, the city of Nice and its surroundings were excluded. The object of several battles the *comté* changed hands many times, at one point part of the kingdom of France and at another part of the *duché de Savoie*. Following this it became part of the *Royaume Sarde* in 1718 when it was created. Its attachment to the Sardinian kingdom proved short-lived when the French Revolutionary armies retook possession of this territory in 1793, where it remained French until 1814, at which point Napoleon I abdicated and was exiled to the island of Elbe. Following the departure of the Emperor, Nice ended up as part of the Piémont-Sardaigne kingdom. It was only in 1860 with the Treaty of Turin, that Emperor Napoleon III regained Nice and the Savoie in exchange for an alliance with Piémont intending to assure France's support of Italian unity.

■ **History of Monaco**

The history of Monaco differs very little from the history of Provence. It begins at the end of the 12th century when the Genoese nobles were divided into two camps, the *Guelfes* and *Gibelins*, in a dispute over who was in charge. More details can be found in the Monaco chapter, see p 225.

Politics and Administration

Provence and Côte d'Azur are terms commonly used in tourism. However, they don't actually have a political or administrative significance, per se.

In 1790, one year after the French Revolution, the nation was divided into 95 *départements* which included about 36,000 communes (cities, villages,

etc.). In 1960, President Charles de Gaulle divided France into 22 administrative regions in order to run the country effectively. The administrative region **Provence-Alpes-Côte d'Azur (PACA)**, as it exists today, was established in 1972 during the presidency of Georges Pompidou. PACA comprises six *départements*: Alpes-de-Hautes-Provence (01), Hautes-Alpes (05), Alpes-Maritimes (06), Bouches-du-Rhône (13), Var (83) and Vaucluse (84).

This guide covers just four of the departments which form PACA: the Vaucluse, the Bouches-du-Rhône, the Var and the Alpes-Maritimes. However, the portraits which follow concern the six departments making up PACA.

In 1982, President Mitterand of the Socialist Party (elected in 1981 and re-elected in 1988 for another seven-year term) reinforced an existing law permitting regional power by introducing a new law decentralizing existing administrative structures. At the moment, regional power is divided among three political bodies:

● *préfets* (prefects proposed by the Prime Minister but nominated by the President of the Republic), who are representatives of the national government and are responsible for applying its laws; *conseillers généraux* (general councillors elected by popular vote for a six-year period) who are members of the *conseil régional* (regional council) and represent their departments;

● *maires* (mayors) and *conseillers municipaux* (muncipal councillors), (both elected by popular vote for a period of six years), who are responsible for the administration of each commune (collection of property and housing taxes, local development, etc.).

• *présidents des régions* (regional presidents) and *conseillers régionaux* (regional councillors) who are responsible for the interests and well-being of their region.

Despite this structure, real political power lies in the hands of the departments and the communes. Generally, the mayor represents the political majority of the commune. Regional bodies only receive a share of land taxes, property taxes, business taxes and car licensing fees. Their budget mainly goes towards spending on regional investments. Therefore, regions have some power, but nowhere near the political autonomy enjoyed by Swiss cantons, for example. France, has made efforts to decentralize towards the regions, but has not become a federation in the Canadian sense.

The importance of each commune can be highlighted by an interesting phenomenon: candidates for the mayors' seats in large cities might be politicians who already play important roles in national politics in Paris but who don't have any previous attachment to the area in which they are running. Local electors often vote for these political personalities hoping that their city will later obtain operating budgets which are higher than the norm, because of the prestige of these nationally recognized mayors.

PACA is a region mainly led by the conservative right-wing (RPR - *Rassemblement Pour la République*) and conservative centre-right (UDF - *Union de la Démocratie Française* and the PR - *Parti Républicain*). Nevertheless, the Bouches-du-Rhône and especially its principal city Marseille, support the Socialist party as well as the Communist party.

During the late 80s, the extreme right gained popularity in the area. The campaign platform of Jean-Marie le Pen and his party campaigned on what many considered a racist platform, telling voters that their region was invaded by Arab foreigners.

Economy

Provence-Alpes-Côte d'Azur is one of France's major tourist regions, due particularly to the cachet of the Cannes-Nice-Monaco-Menton coastline. The area is also extremely fertile: agriculture and flower production is particularly important. Additionally, the region exploits its industrial, business and technological research capabilities, though industry is less-developed here in comparison to the national average.

The region is an important transport crossroads with the port of Marseille (the most important in the Mediterranean) and two airports at Marseille and Nice. Over the centuries the region developed important relations with the Middle East, Africa and Asia: 20 % of its imports come from these three areas and 10 % of its exports end up there. Otherwise, the region maintains solid relations with its European Union member nations. Trade is particularly buoyant with Italy, PACA's most important trading partner. Italy represents 20 % of its exports and 17 % of its imports.

■ Agriculture

With more than 660,000 ha, PACA encompasses 2.3 % of the national agricultural surface area. The agricultural lands are quite diversified, for the region experiences different climates and types of soil. Arable land is in short supply along the seacoast, but it is nevertheless fertile and perfect for growing fruits and vegetables. This area is also known for its greenhouses, for flower cultivation. The excellent irrigation which characterizes the Bouches-du-Rhône provides the right conditions for vegetable farms and fruit orchards. The marshy wetlands of the Camargue produce a significant quantity of rice.

Vineyards producing grapes for wine-making and eating, plus orchards (olive, cherry, apricot, peach, fig trees) dominate a large region forming a band stretching from the Bouches-du-Rhône/Vaucluse border along the Durance Valley all the way to the eastern limit of the Var department. In the heart of the region, particularly in the area historically known as the Comtat Venaissin, is a vast plain where cereals, fodder and vegetables are cultivated. The territories of the Alpes du Sud, the Rhône delta and the Estérel are not suitable for agricultural production. However, they are ideal for growing herbs and aromatic plants (lavender, sage, thyme, rosemary, basil) which has made Provence famous the world over. Herb production represents 1,500 businesses spread over a territory of nearly 12,000 ha. Fragrant fields of lavender and its derivative lavandin are characteristic of this region.

The region grows the largest amount of flowers in all of France. Over 1,200 businesses occupying 1,800 ha of land cover the coastal areas of the Var and the Alpes-Maritimes.

The number of people employed in the agricultural business fell by two-thirds over the last 40 years. At the start of the 1980s, a little more than 60,000 worked in this sector. Agricultural businesses tend to be smaller here than in the rest of France: the average holding is 15 ha compared to 29 ha elsewhere. Farming properties are particularly small in the Alpes-Maritimes, with an average of 11.2 ha and even more so in the Var, with an average of 7.7 ha. However, these businesses generally benefit from high revenues, particularly those growing flowers, fruits and vegetables.

With the exception of the Alpes-Martimes and the Var, the PACA territory benefits from large irrigable areas.

■ Viticulture

For more than two thousand years, the vines and olive trees have marked the Provençal landscape. Vines occupy more than 100,000 ha in Provence, meaning 16 % of the region's agricultural area and 11 % of France's vineyards. 20,000 people are employed in the wine business and the average vineyard measures 6 ha, which is close to the national average of 5.5 ha. The majority of the vineyard owners are members of one of the region's 174 cooperative caves (associations).

The dynamic Provençal wine industry tries to specialize more and more in order to offer consistently better wines. Despite the constant reduction in surface area devoted to growing grapes, the number of vineyards carrying the coveted "*appellation d'origine contrôlée*" (A.O.C.) tag has actually grown. Wines with these three words on its label must be made solely from grapes harvested in the stated domaine. They are subject to specific quality controls, including the composition of different varieties of grapes which makes up each particular cellar's unique wine.

Over the last 25 years, the number of A.O.C. wines has increased to the point where it now represents two-thirds of over-all production. Meanwhile, the output of so-called *vins de table* (table wines; most are perfectly drinkable for everyday purposes) has decreased. At the moment, sixteen *appellation d'origine contrôlée* wines exist, thus assuring the deserved acclaim of Provençal wines.

Fresh, young Provençal rosés are much admired and they marry so well with the region's Mediterranean cuisine; of course quality reds and whites are abundant. Amongst the many fine wines in this region, two reds from the Côtes du Rhône area in the Vaucluse are justly renowned throughout the world: Châteuneuf-du-Pape and Gigondas. Also in the Vaucluse, Côtes du Ventoux and Côtes du Luberon wines are easily found and just as easily quaffed! Four A.O.C. wines are produced in the Bouches-du-Rhone: Côtes de Provence, Côteaux dAix, Palette and Cassis. The Var produces the very good Bandol, Côtes de Provence and Côteaux Varois wines. There are just a few small wine-makers in the Alpes-Maritimes, a number with fine reputations such as the Bellet wines.

■ **Livestock Farming**

The vast grassy areas found in the alpine departments, the Vauclusian hills, the Alpilles and the large marshlands of the Camargue are used principally for sheep farming. Raising sheep is one of the agricultural triumvirate (along with olives and wine) which exists in the Mediterranean area for more than 2,000 years. Currently, 3,600 enterprises share the raising of 60,000 ewe mothers.

Cattle raising takes up a large part of the mountainous region of the Hautes-Alpes and the low-lands of the Crau and Camargue. Pig farming is concentrated in the Bouches-du-Rhône. This industry is currently in decline, due to European over-production causing the drop in prices. Game farming is handled mainly by large enterprises who produce primarily heavy fowl and chickens for the skin.

■ **Fishing**

Fishing is not an important economic activity in the region, as is commonly thought. In one year, the 1,500 fishermen between Marseille and Menton produce on average 20,000 tons of fish. Around 90 % of this catch comes from the Bouches-du-Rhône, the rest is from the Var and Alpes-Maritimes. Sardines represent half of this production; the rest is divided among bass, mullet, rascasse and octopus. These fish are commonly found on restaurant menus in the region. Other types of fish come from the Atlantic where the catch is much more varied.

■ **Industrial Sector**

Over the years, the industrial sector has developed around two different poles. The first forms a strong, technologically-advanced sector of French and international groups including Exxon, British Petroleum, Arco, IBM and Texas Instruments. These businesses are involved in petroleum, ship building, aeronautics, steel manufacturing and electronics.

The second pole includes a multitude of small and middle-sized businesses producing goods ranging from hand-crafted items to consumer goods such as food items, clothes, leather goods, furniture and construction materials.

Such development is the result of an important burst of industrial activity in the region between 1950 and 1974. Port industries including ship building, oil refining, petrochemical development and upgrading port services in Marseille (the Étang de Barre area) and Toulon, enjoyed the greatest growth. Since this time, this sector is in decline due to aging installations and failure to keep up with new research. Certain countries have rapidly industrialized and grabbed PACA's part of the market, notably in the oil refining, petrochemical, ship building and aeronautics sectors. The secondary sector has lost 100,000 jobs since 1975.

Many ship building yards closed their doors in the 1980s. The disused sites were transformed with governmental assistance into industrial zones. Despite their growth, the number of jobs have diminished. Today, the region counts 100 industrial zones, of which 40 % are in the Bouches-du-Rhône.

PACA suffered important job losses between 1975 and 1990. The situation was further aggravated in the early 1990s when the world-wide economic recession hit the region, and the rest of France.

■ Housing

Building construction has played an important part in the local economy. In 1974, it employed 166,000 people. From 1990, this number fell to 124,000, which is 8.4 % of the total number of the region's employed, and 38 % of the secondary sector jobs. Today, the sector has declined once more and suffered considerable losses of profit and jobs. The reasons are twofold: the economic recession of 1991-1993 and the saturation point for new building construction along the coast. The construction sector exploded during the 1980s along the Riviera, where every available piece of land was bought by speculators and prices sky-rocketed. Inevitably, sites where too built-up, over-populated and not always aesthetically pleasing. The end result is many places along the coast have unfortunately lost their charm.

■ Energy Sector

The energy sector involves 19,000 jobs of which more than half work in the Bouches-du-Rhône. Jobs are found in coal mining (the Houillères de Provence mine feeds a thermic power station producing 2.5 billion kilowatt hours of power), oil refining and natural gas. Nearly one third of the yearly natural gas production in France, 27 megatons, comes from the Fos and Étang de Berre refineries in the Bouches-du-Rhône. Hydro electric power is supplied by a number of stations concentrated in the Alpine area which produce nearly seven billion kilowatt hours.

■ High-Tech Industries

A vast network of high-tech industries cover the region and are often complementary enterprises serving one another. This series of poles establish the structure of the economic development of the region and are its driving force.

Six technological poles link the territory. They are, from west to east:

• "l'Agroparc" Avignon-Montfavet, site of the Institut National de la Recherche Agronomique (INRA), which is concerned with agricultural and food issues;

• the Manosque-Cadarache pole, specializing in the nuclear sector;

• "l'Europôle" in Aix-en-Provence, occupying 8,000 ha on the Arbois plateau, and specializing in electronics;

• the multi-purpose Marseille-Provence pole;

• the Toulon-Var pole, specializing in instrumentation and weapons manufacture

• the multi-purpose Nice-Sophia-Antipolis pole, a French version of California's Silicon Valley.

These technological poles share a common goal: research and innovation. They participate in realizing the region's great technological potential and are an important source of jobs. Additionally, they attempt to attract large business investment, thereby enforcing the strength of the Mediterranean arc, stretching from Valence in the west to Lombardy in Italy in the east. Plans are to enlarge this arc so as to include the technology bases of Gênes in Italy and Barcelona in Spain.

The region is the second most important in France in terms of research. Around 9,000 researchers work here, which is 10 % of all in the country.

In just 20 years, the Sophia-Antipolis technological park in the

Alpes-Maritimes has become the largest in Europe with over 700 bureaus represented.

People

Provence-Alpes-Côte d'Azur has around 4.5 million people. The region is the most urbanized in France after the Paris area. Nearly 90 % of its inhabitants, around four million, live in large cities and their suburbs.

Before 1840, the population was spread reasonably uniformly across the six departments making up the PACA region. This equilibrium changed dramatically from 1936 onwards with industrialization, the strong growth of the tourism sector and the massive influx of retired people tempted here by the favourable climate. So today the greatest population densities are found in communities along Mediterranean coast: people have left the *arrière-pays* (inland countryside) for the pleasant conditions next to the sea.

There are some exceptions. Some large coastal cities have suffered a population exodus from the centre towards the suburbs. An example is Marseille, which has lost nearly 100,000 inhabitants since 1975. An improved road network, a better quality of the environment and in particular, the more affordable house and land prices contribute to this effect.

The number of people choosing the sunny Provençal climate in which to have second homes has sky-rocketed. Their number has more than quadrupled since 1962, moving from 97,000 to 400,000 in 1994. The most sought after area for Parisians and wealthy

Europeans looking for a comfortable vacation home is the Lubéron in the Vaucluse. Since the 1990s, the Alpilles area around St-Rémy-de-Provence and les Baux has become increasingly popular. Elsewhere in the PACA region, certain pockets of the Alpes-Maritime region are favoured by the same crowd. Housing prices in Cannes and in neighbouring Côte d'Azur villages are unbelievably elevated. However, real estate is most expensive in Monaco, due to lack of space and its allure as a tax haven.

For a long time, the Provence-Alpes-Côte d'Azur was the most sought after region in France by property seekers. Now however, it is in second place after the Languedoc-Roussillon (southwest France) because of housing costs. In 1962, after Algeria achieved independence from France, PACA's population increased dramatically: hundreds of thousands of *pied-noirs* (French nationals working in the former north-African colony) returned and settled in the area. As well, during the period of strong economic growth in the 60s and 70s, tens of thousands of north-African workers (Algerians, Moroccans and Tunisians) found work in local industry and construction. Following the wave of Islamic fundamentalism in North Africa in the mid-90s, the pressure to immigrate to this region of France is strong. This is despite tough new French legislation restricting entry into the country.

The region has also welcomed immigrants from other Mediterranean cultures: Italians, Spaniards, Portuguese. Well-off northern Europeans (primarily Dutch, Belgian, German and Swiss) have also made the region their place of permanent residency. At the moment, around 375,000 foreigners reside in the region. This is 8.7 % of the population and comparable to the average found in other French regions. This group is found primarily in the Bouches-du-Rhône and the Alpes-Maritimes.

Culture

The region's varied culture is a colourful tapestry weaving together rich heritage, language, traditions, customs and folklore.

Its great artists have recorded its natural beauty for centuries, perhaps none more famously than the post-Impressionist painter Cézanne. Though critical opinion varies, Cézanne is considered by many as the precursor to Cubism. Braque, Derain and Dufy were enchanted by the strange volumes of the cliffs and viaducts of the Estaque coastline north of Marseille. Their colourful, fragmented interpretations on canvas spawned the Fauve movement. Early 20th century painting turned darker and fractured as social and political troubles struck world-wide: Cubism was born. Simultaneously, a number of artists have made their mark on the region - great painters such as Matisse, Picasso, Chagall and Léger moved here to take advantage of the extraordinary light, landscapes and favourable climate.

The region is also home to *l'École de Nice* (School of Nice), with such artists as Klein, Arman and César. The movement is now in its third generation. Today, Nice and the surrounding area has become an important centre for artistic creation. Countless museums, small and large, attest to this vibrant artistic activity.

However, PACA has established an international reputation for its marvellous arts festivals. The Avignon theatre and dance festival and the Aix-en-Provence music and opera festival are two well-established annual events. Both go off in the summertime and attract performers and avid spectators from around the world. See list of major festivals p 44.

The most famous festival of all must surely be the Cannes Film Festival, held every May. Now more than 50 years old, the Cannes festival is internationally recognized as the place for industry insiders to buy new films for their domestic markets, while an excited public can get in some good star-gazing. During the two-week festival period, the famous sea-side boardwalk known as the Croisette and the beach below become awash with producers, directors, actors and actresses of various levels of talent and fame.

Clearly, culture is strongly anchored in this region and plays an unparalleled importance in its development. Now, more than ever, PACA's artistic life is flourishing despite real and threatened budget cut-backs due to the economic recession of the early 90s.

■ Heritage

The Provence-Alpes-Côte d'Azur region possesses a monumental heritage and its history is extremely rich. Architecture in particular is exceptional. Architectural sites dating back to prehistoric times are to be found here. Amateur art historians can easily make a voyage back in time to discover a splendid variety of monuments, archaeological collections and museum to thrill the imagination. Their travels will take them from Prehistory to present-day, passing by Antiquity, the Middle Ages and the Renaissance.

Happily, since the beginning of the 20th century, France deploys greater and greater efforts to protect its heritage, which was damaged by numerous wars and years of neglect. A law was passed in 1913, then a decree in 1924, which enforced the protection and respect for the nation's cultural heritage. This welcome vigilance means that today over 30,000 sites are protected in France. PACA contains 1,500.

Recent efforts have strengthened further this national policy. In 1983, an urban code was adopted in order to assure a greater protection of those sites already under the watchful eyes of conservationists. For example, special authorization must be granted to build around the perimeters of listed sites, so as to protect the historic and aesthetic character of the entire area. Conservationists regret that more wasn't done sooner in order to prevent hideous building sites from going up in the past few decades, many of which have blighted PACA's natural beauty.

The main architectural sites in the region are:

Prehistoric and Antiquity Sites: Found in the Haut-Pays of Nice (Mont Bego, Fontanalba, Vallée des Merveilles) and along the coast (Terra Amata, the Lazaret grotto in Nice). Triumphal arch and Mausoleum near Saint-Rémy de Provence; the Salien d'Entremont site near Aix-en-Provence. Other areas include the megalithic sites of the Haut-Var, Estérel, Grasse and Vence.

Roman Sites: The amphitheatre and triumphal arch in Orange; the agglomeration of monuments in Arles (including Amphitheatre, Arena, Thermal Baths and Cryptoportiques Arcade beneath the Forum); the Puymin and Villasse sites in Vaison-la-Romaine; the "trophy" of Turbie; the thermal baths of Cimiez near Nice; the monuments of Fréjus (Arenas, theatre, aqueduc and gilded Gate).

Middle Ages: sites and ruins are found all over the region, including the Middle Ages villages of Antibes, Eze, Villedfranche, Menton, Vence, Saint-Paul, le Castellet, etc.; monuments include Saint-Honorat on the Iles de Lérins, the Verne in Colobrières. Ecclesiastical sites from this period are remarkable and include the Cistercian Abbeys known as the "trois soeurs" (three sisters): Sénanque (near Gordes), Silvercane (near la Roque d'Antheron) and Thoronet, plus innumerable churches and cathedrals existing in the villages and cities of the region (Saorge,Moustiers-Sainte-Marie,Digne, Saint Maximin-la-Sainte-Baume, latter parts of the Venasque Baptistry, Saint-Victor Abbey in Marseille). Château-fortresses including Brignoles and Tarascon.

Renaissance: countless remarkable monuments from this period include grand private mansions called *hôtels particuliers*, châteaus at Gordes, Entaigues, etc., residences known as bastides in the coastal region of Toulon and La Ciotat, homes in the city centres of major communities such as Avignon, Aix-en-Provence, Marseille, Toulon and Nice, military installations such as Fort Carré in Antibes, the Arsenal in Toulon, Fort Saint Nicholas in Marseille. Churches in the Baroque architectural style, showing a Genoese influence, are found in the Nice area around Menton, Sospel, la Turbie, etc.

The *belle époque*: this style took hold in the second half of the 19th century, leaving sumptous villas all along the Mediterranean coastline: Hyères, Cannes, Menton, Maures, Marseille. These charming villas capture a variety of styles: eastern (Neo-Moorish), English (Neo-Gothic) or Italian (Neo-Baroque).

Twentieth Century: Passing by influences of Art Nouveau and Art Deco, a number of striking contemporary structures have been built in our era, among them the Palais des Festivals in Cannes, the Chagall museum, the Acropolis theatre in Nice, Le Corbusier's high-rise neighbourhood in Marseille, and most recently the headquarters for the Bouches-du-Rhône in the outskirts of Marseille, completed in 1994.

■ Medieval Art

The Middle Ages gave us two important architectural movements: Romanesque and Gothic.

Romanesque Art in the PACA region was influenced by two sources. The first came from Arles (the ecclesiastical centre at the time), which was the birthplace for Art Provençal (sometimes called *Art Rhodanien* in French, after the Rhône river nearby). The second came from Lombardy, Italy, and was known as Art Alpine.

In the 12th century, Arles experienced an economic, legal and cultural renaissance. From this point on, artists of the period were influenced by art of Roman times. Their style became known as Art Roman Provençal or Provençal Romanesque. This meant in church architecture, the predominant lay-out was a simple crucifix shape, usually with just a single nave, broken barrel-vaulted ceiling and balanced with tall double arches resting on pillars. Windows were rare; their tops were simple half-circle shapes.

Art Roman Alpine is more evident in the areas bordering Italy - the eastern part of Provence-Alpes-Côte d'Azur, and was developed from a base in the former ecclesiastical province of Embrun (still the best place to see this style today). However, this style was often adapted to the Provençal Romanesque form, particularly in architecture found farther west. So, in Fréjus, Grasse and Vence, cathedrals have a basilica design, with three naves and Lombardy arches. Finally, the Haute-Provence represents an area mixing these two artistic styles: *Art Rhodanien* predominates, but mixes with a number of other native influences.

Gothic Art is not well represented because of the duration and the strong presence of Romanesque architecture in the region. It arrived here much later - first thanks to the Angevins French dynasty and later by the Popes in Avignon. On top of that, it appeared in a simplified form: *Gothique Méridional* (Southern Gothic), characterized by churches with wide and low single-naves, a choir without ambulatory, and walls resting on supports. The finest example of this unique Gothic style is found in the Dominican basilica of Saint-Maximin-la-Sainte Baume.

■ **Language and its Dialects**

The historical language of this region is called *langue d'oc*. It is a language with different dialects and modifications according to the area where it is spoken. *Langue d'oc* is a blend of neo-Latin tongues. It has less in common with French than with Catalan (which it merged with before the 15th century), with Italian, Spanish and even Portuguese. The geographic boundaries amongst these dialects never coincided with the political-administrative boundaries. In general, two poles exist: the *sud-occitan* (southern occident) or *rhodano-méditerranéen* (*Rhone-Mediterranean*) and the *nord-occitan* (northern occident) or *rhodano-alpin* (Rhone-Alpine).

Today, the *langue d'oc* is spoken only by older citizens of the region. Throughout its history, the language has always been threatened. In 1539, François I made French the country's official language. Afterwards, in 1561, Italian became the official language of the county of Nice. In the middle of the 16th century, French spelling was used for the *langue d'oc*. Such incidents meant the language became little more than a patois or regional dialect, less and less used in the 20th century. However, for the past few years, there seems to be a new interest in the *langue d'oc*. Some regions are reclaiming its use in daily life: on radio and television, as well as on street and place names.

Occident literature has known two periods of glory during its history: the troubadour period (between the 11th and 13th century) and in the 19th century. The work of the troubadours was marked by Christian, Jewish, Arab and Oriental influences. Their subject matter was infused with either eroticism or religion. In the 19th century, the occident language experienced a renaissance with the publication of a Provençal-French dictionary. Most importantly however, the new passion of the *langue d'oc* was due to the poetry and prose of Frederick Mistral. He founded the Félibrige literary movement, which promoted the use of the local dialect, and many poets followed in his footsteps. Mistral himself was a champion of the celebration of Provençal traditions and culture. He received the Nobel Prize for Literature and he became not only a local, but national hero.

Cuisine

Provençal cuisine, with its Mediterranean roots, is one of the healthiest in the world, so you might just return from your trip in better shape than when you arrived. The region has an estimated 300 days of sun every year, which provides the ideal climate for the impressive variety of fresh fruits, vegetables and herbs grown locally. The Provençal people, perhaps unwittingly, follow a low-fat diet - foods are cooked in olive oil rather than butter; while milk and cream are uncommon.

The Mediterranean coast is an excellent source for quality fish and seafood, while in-land, sheep, mutton and some beef are raised. Tomatoes, olive oil and garlic are the three staples which turn up in any number of dishes. These are the key ingredients for the sauce accompanying poultry, fish and vegetables known as *à la provençale*.

One of the best-loved dishes is **bouillabaisse**. This golden-coloured soup is made from a mix of at least four or five fish, including red mullet (*rouget*), conger eel (*congre*), monkfish (*baudroie*), gurnard (*grondin*), seabreem (*loup-de-mer*), scorpionfish (*rascasse*) and John Dory (*saint-pierre*). They are cooked rapidly so that the flavour of the fish doesn't disappear; the delicious stock owes its special

taste to the harmonious balance of tomatoes, onions, saffron, sage, fennel, olive oil and orange peel, and sometimes white wine or brandy. Some chefs add crab, crayfish, mussels and tiny shrimp. Mandatory accompaniments are crusty baguette, grated Gruyère cheese and *rouille* (a piquant sauce made from garlic, red peppers, olive oil and saffron). Traditionally, the tender pieces of poached fish are served in a separate bowl from the soup. Opinions differ as to the classic bouillabaisse, so may just be forced to try a few!

Provençal soups are often intended as meals in themselves, served with just wine and French bread rubbed with garlic. *Pistou* is made from summer vegetables and vermicelli pasta, with basil, olive oil, tomatoes and garlic. The delicious *bourride,* is a fresh bouillon made from Mediterranean fish and with *aïoli* sauce (a garlic, olive oil and egg yolk mayonnaise) whisked in just prior to serving. The *revesset* soup is a green bouillabaise thanks to the addition of Swiss chard, fresh spinach and sorrel leaves. Others include *aigo boulido, aigo sau d'iou*, and the *soupes au baton* (so-named because the concoction is stirred with a small laurel branch or *baton*).

Aïoli is also the name for an ages-old local dish from the *arrière-pays*, or back-country area in from the Riviera coast. Poached salt cod or whatever fresh fish catches the chef's eye in the market on any particular day is matched with large serving dishes of steamed vegetables such as artichokes, broad beans, carrots, zucchinis and sweet potatoes. A heaping boil of garlicky aïoli sauce accompanies this feast. Plates of sun-dried tomatoes and herbs go well with this dish as well.

Another favourite Provençal dish known worldwide is **ratatouille**, the flavourful mix of eggplants, zucchinis, tomatoes, onions, peppers, basil and garlic, all stewed in olive oil. It is served hot as a main dish, cold as a starter salad during the warm summer months or as a *farci* - a stuffing for large tomatoes and green or red peppers. Gourmet supermarkets from Tokyo to New York now sell superior-quality ratatouille frozen or canned.

Countless varieties of fresh fish are found along the coastline between Marseille and Martigues. The latter seaport is known for its *poutargue*, a type of "white caviar" made from salted lump fish (*mulet salés*). Marseille introduced to the rest of France, the marriage of small shell fish such as mussels, cockles (*clovisses*), winkles and small crabs (*favouilles*), with fresh pasta dishes.

Ratatouille

Serves 4

6 tbsp extra virgin olive oil
2 eggplants (*aubergines*), unpeeled and chopped
6 ripe tomatoes, seeded and chopped
1 sliced onion
1 green pepper, sliced in thin strips
1 red pepper, sliced in thin strips
2 zuchinnis (*courgettes*), sliced
2 garlic cloves, crushed
salt and ground pepper
1 tablespoon *Herbes de Provence*
1 bay leaf

1) In a large covered sauce pan, fry the sliced onion in the olive oil over medium heat until they are transparent.
2) Add the unpeeled chopped eggplant, salt, and cover. Gently cook for 15 minutes.
3) Add the strips of green and red peppers, then the chopped tomatoes, crushed garlic, herbes de provence and bay leaf. Salt and pepper to taste.
4) Cover and simmer for one hour. Remove the lid when the ratatouille is nearly cooked to allow excess liquid to evaporate.
5) The dish should resemble a chunky vegetable stew. It can be served hot as a main course, or better yet, cold as a starter with a glass of Provençal rosé and fresh baked bread.

Sheep and especially mutton (notably the Sisteron lamb) are appreciated for their succulent flavour. *Gigot d'agneau* (leg of lamb), perhaps prepared with garlic, anchovies and rosemary, is a favourite Sunday lunchtime meal with Provençal families, whereas *daube* is reserved for special occasions. It's no wonder, considering that the best *daube*, a simple but tasty lamb or beef stew made with red wine, garlic and local thyme, parsley and bay leaves has to be marinated overnight and allowed to cook slowly for at least three to four hours.

Pieds et paquets (feet and packets) is Marseille's contribution to the world of culinary curiosities. It consists of lambs' trotters nestled next to seasoned bacon, salt pork, garlic, onion and parsley wrapped carefully in lemon-scented tripe. The **saucisson d'Arles** (dried beef and pork sausage) has a long reputation. The region's cuisine makes use of its game birds, young rabbit, and wood thrush *(grives)*, snipe *(bécassines)* and plover *(pluviers)* are still hunted. Truffles (**truffes**) from Tricastin, knick-named black diamonds by Brillat-Savarin due to their rarity and high cost, are sold in the impressive market at Carpentras and in the area.

Local sheep and ewe farms produce many distinctive, often crumbly, regional cheeses made from sheep and ewe's milk such as *bossons, brousses* (similar to *fromage frais)*, *cashats, macérés,* and *picodons*. Be sure to try the **banon** - a chèvre served fresh or ripe, wrapped in oak leaves and much more flavourful.

It is no wonder the region is called "the garden of France" - 20 % of France's fruit and vegetables come from Provence. The valley of the Durance river is one of the largest orchard and vegetable-growing areas in France, and the Vaucluse grows the most dessert grapes in the country. Figs from Solliès, almonds from the Aix-en-Provence area

and oranges, lemons and citrons (*cédrats*) from the Alpes-Maritimes are renowned. Other locally-grown fruits are Charenton, honeydews and watermelons, apricots, cherries, peaches and strawberries. Olive trees (*oliviers*) provide the prized first-pressed virgin olive oil, as well as luscious green and mature black eating ones. A simple treat is **tapenade**, a purée made with crushed olives, anchovies, capers and olive oil. Delicious on toasted bread or accompanying fish or white meat.

Sweet specialities from the region include almond cakes (*caladons*), crunchy biscuits (*Villaret*), croissants with pine nuts (*pignons*), chocolates called *tartarinades* from Tarascon, candies made from a base of almond paste (*calissons*) from Aix, macerated fruits (*fruits confits*) from Apt, Digne, Valréas and Grasse, nougat from Saint-Tropez, and a velvety butterscotch candy (*berlingots*) from Carpentras. Lavender or rosemary honey from the Vaucluse are irresistible.

Marseille is the production centre for the liquorice-flavoured alcohol Pastis. Provence Côte d'Azur wines are generally light and fresh and make ideal accompaniments for the fish and vegetable-based local cuisine. The Côtes-de-Provence, Cassis, Gigondas and Châteauneuf-du-Pape are particularly good. The sweet dessert wine Beaumes-de-Venise comes from Vaucluse and is wonderful with local pastry, fresh fruit or just on its own.

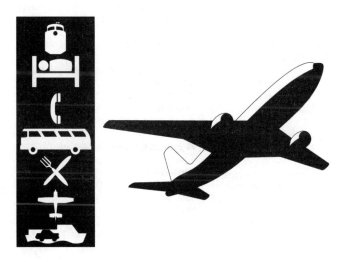

PRACTICAL INFORMATION

This section is intended to provide you with all the information you will need to prepare for your trip to Provence Côte d'Azur.

Entrance Formalities

■ Passport and Visas

North Americans must have a valid passport to enter France. Residents of the European Union and of Switzerland are not obliged to carry their passport with them, but must have a valid national identity card.

Canadians and Americans are admitted without a visa for stays of up to three months.

In additions, all travellers, except members of the European Union and of Switizerland, must have an ongoing or return ticket.

As these regulations are subject to change at any time, we recommend that you verify them with the French embassy or consulate nearest you before leaving on your trip.

Customs

Canadians over the age of 18 are allowed to bring back into the country one litre of spirits containing over 22 % alcohol, two litres of wine, as well as 200 cigarettes (or 100 cigarillos, 50 cigars or 250 g of tobacco).

Tourists from the European Union or Switzerland are allowed to bring back 1.5 litres of alcohol, 4 litres of wine and 300 cigarettes (or 150 cigarillos, 75 cigars, or 400 g of tobacco).

Embassies and Consulates

■ **Foreign Embassies in France or Provence - Côte d'Azur**

There are no embassies in Provence or Côte d'Azur, as they are located in Paris. Some countries have consulates in the area.

Belgian Consulate
5 Rue Gabriel Fauré
06 Nice
☎ 93 87 79 56

British Embassy
33 Rue du Faubourg-St-Honoré
Paris 75383
☎ 42.66.91.42

British Consulate
24 Av. du Prado
Marseille 13006
☎ 91.53.43.32

Canadian Embassy
37 Avenue Montaigne
75008 Paris
☎ (1) 44 43 29 16

Délégation Générale du Québec
66 Rue La Boétie
75016 Paris
☎ (1) 45 02 14 10

Swiss Embassy
142 Rue de Grenelle
Paris
☎(1)49 55 67 00

Swiss Consulate
13 Rue Alphonse Karf
06 Nice
☎ 93 88 85 09

United States Consulate General
12 Bd. Paul-Peytral
13286 Marseille
Cedex 6
☎ (33) 91.54.92.00

■ **French Embassies Abroad**

Australia
French Consulate
492 St. Kilda Rd.
Melbourne, Victoria
3001
☎ (03) 820-0921

Canada
French Embassy
2 Elysee
Place Bonaventure
Montréal, Québec
H5A 1B1
☎ (514) 878-4381-87

French Consulate
130 Bloor St. West
Suite 400
Toronto, Ontario
M5S 1N5
☎ (416) 925-8044

Great Britain
French Consulate General
1 Cromwell Place
London, SW7
☎ (0171) 581-5292

United States
French Embassy
4101 Reservoir Rd. NW
Washington D.C., 20007
☎ (202) 944-6000

French Consulate
10990 Wilshire Boulevard
Suite 300
Los Angeles, CA, 90024
☎ (310) 479-4426

French Consulate
934 5th Ave.
New York, NY, 10021
☎ (212) 606-3621

 Tourist Information

■ **Abroad**

Australia
BNP Building - 12th Floor
Castlereagh Street
Sydney NSW 2000
☎ (2) 231 52 44
fax (2) 221 86 82

Belgium
Maison de la France
21, Avenue de la Toison-d'Or
1060 Brussels
☎ (2) 513 73 89
fax (2) 514 33 75

Canada
Maison de la France
30 Saint Patrick Street
Suite 700
Toronto, Ontario
M5T 3A3
☎ (416) 593 4723
⇄ (416) 979 7587

Maison de la France
1981, Avenue McGill College
Bureau 490
Montréal, Québec
H3A 2W9
☎ (514) 288-4264
⇄ (514) 845-4868

Great Britain
Maison de la France
178 Picadilly
London W1V 0Al
☎ (44) 171 493 6694
⇄ (44) 171 493 6594

Netherlands
Maison de la France
Prinsengracht 670 - 1017 KX
Amsterdam
– (31) 20 620 3141
⇄ (31) 20 620 3339

Switzerland
Maison de la France
2, Rue Thalberg
1201 Geneva
☎ (41) 227 328 610 or 227 313 480

Maison de la France
Bahnofstrasse 16 Postfach 4979
CH 8022 Zurich
☎ (41) 211 30 85
⇄ (41) 212 16 44

United States of America
Maison de la France
9454 Wilshire Boulevard
Suite 975
Beverly Hills, CA 90212-2967
☎ (310) 271-7838
⇄ (310) 276-2835

Maison de la France
676 North Michigan Avenue
Chicago, IL 60611-2819
☎ (312) 751-7800
⇄ (312) 337-6339

Maison de la France
2305 Cedar Springs Road - suite 205
Dallas, Texas 75201
☎ (214) 720-4010
☎ (214) 720-0250

Maison de la France
444 Madison Avenue
New York, NY 10022
☎ (212) 838-7800
⇄ (212) 838-7855

■ **In Provence Côte d'Azur**

You will have no trouble finding all the tourist information you need in Provence Côte d'Azur. Most villages and towns have a *syndicat d'initiative* (tourist office) to provide visitors with information. Throughout the guide the telephone number and address of the tourist office in each area is provided.

Entering the Country

■ **By Plane**

Most overseas visitors to Provence either arrive in Paris and continue their voyage south by plane or by high-speed train (TGV), or fly directly to the airports in Marseille or Nice.

International flights land at Paris Roissy Charles de Gaulle Airport, though a few charter flights may land at Paris Orly Airport. A few charter airlines are also using Lyon Satolas airport - overseas visitors may pick up the TGV to Avignon-Marseille from the SNCF train station connected to the terminal.

Charles de Gaulle Airport
Information ☎ 28 62 22 80

Orly Airport
Information ☎ 49 75 15 15

To reach the centre of Paris from Charles de Gaulle or Orly airports, a number of transportation options are available:

1) Car Rental

2) Taxi (from 40 min to 75 min, depending on traffic; between 180 F and 250 F from Charles de Gaulle and between 120 F and 180 F for Orly)

3) Rapid transit system (**RER**) to the city centre, then continue by the RATP-run Métro underground transportation system or by taxi. RER tickets cost between 40 F and 50 F, take about 45 minutes, and leave every 15 minutes throughout the day. **RATP** also provides a direct Roissybus service running between Charles de Gaulle and Place de l'Opéra, (35 F) and a Orlybus service running between Orly and Denfert Rochereau Métro station (30 F). Both run every 15 minutes throughout the day.

4) Air France bus service, direct to Étoile-Arc de Tiomphe (from Charles de Gaulle airport, 45 F) or Invalides and Montparnasse (from Orly airport, 35 F).

Flights to Provence and the Côte d'Azur from Paris leave from Orly Airport, situated south of the capital. This poses transportation headaches for passengers arriving from abroad at Roissy Charles de Gaulle airport north of the city. Expect either a long journey on the RER and Métro across town or a very expensive taxi ride. Many visitors prefer to spend a day or more in Paris.

French airlines Air France, Air Inter, AOM and TAT offer regular flights to Avignon, Marseille and Nice throughout the day. Flights last about one hour and ten minutes. Contact your travel agent or the airlines directly for details.

Nice Airport
Information ☎ 93.21.30.30

Avignon-Caumont Airport
Information ☎ 66.70.08.59

Marseille Airport
Information ☎ 42.89.09.74
Reservations ☎ 91.91.90.90

Once in Avignon, Marseille or Nice, a number of car rental agencies offer a variety of automobiles and package rates. Prices for car rental vary considerably - some of the best deals are available only if booked from abroad ahead of time for a period of a week or more. However, some local agencies are able to beat the prices of the multi-national groups and so they are worth investigating. Listings of car rental agencies are located at the beginnning of the appropriate chapters.

■ **By train**

Avignon is conveniently just four and a half hours away from Paris by the high speed TGV train. Marseille is five and a half hours by the TGV, which continues into the Côte d'Azur (stopping at Toulon, Hyères, Saint-Raphaël, Cannes, Antibes and Nice). A new TGV station opened in late 1994 at Paris' Roissy Charles de Gaulle airport, allowing overseas visitors the opportunity to travel directly to Provence without the hassle of entering the French capital city. Of course, you'll have to coordinate the arrival time of your plane with the train departure so that you depart the same day.

Others might enjoy the opportunity to rest and see a few of Paris' sites and will choose to travel south after a few days. TGV trains leave regularly (as many as 11 a day), seven days a week

from Paris Gare du Lyon (fewer trains depart from Roissy Charles de Gaulle airport). Reservations are not necessary in off-peak times, though reductions, called Joker fares, are available to all who book two weeks or one-month in advance. Reservations for Joker fares are only made in France, and you are obliged to stick to the day and time indicated on the ticket once it is purchased. Timetables are available from any French SNCF train station, SNCF boutiques and travel agents.

SNCF Information
☎ (1) 45.82.50.50

Alternatively, major European cities including Brussels, Geneva, Barcelona and Rome are connected to the important Provençal centres by direct trains. From Avignon, Marseille and Nice, the **regional SNCF train service TER** (Transport Express Régional) provides a dependable and comfortable service to smaller towns in the area. The region is well-served by buses, run by private operators.

■ **By car**

A major road network, including efficient expressways, links Provence-Côte d'Azur to Paris, northern Europe, Italy and Spain.

Avignon is at least an eight hour drive from Paris (722 km) by the Autoroute du Soleil A 7-E 15 expressway. Marseille is nine hours from Paris and is on the A 7-E 714 expressway. Nice is accessible by A 8-E 80 and A-10 expressways. Along the coast however, traffic is quite heavy during holiday periods (July and August weekends, Winter and Spring student school breaks, for example) and can add another couple of hours to your journey.

Be sure to carry some French currency with you for the toll booths (*péages*) on the larger expressways. French roads are in great condition but you pay for them! Credit cards are accepted.

Gasoline is more expensive in France than in North America: one litre of *essence* (gasoline/car petrol) costs about 6 F (about double the Canadian price and triple the American price).

Health

No vaccinations are necessary before entering France. Health services are excellent.

■ Illnesses

It is highly unlikely that you will encounter any serious illnesses during your stay. Food, excessive drinking and climate can cause various problems, so take the necessary precautions.

There are a significant number of AIDS cases - the region is the second most affected area in France after Paris. As in other places, cases of venereal diseases are known. It is therefore wise to take necessary precautions.

■ The Sun

In spite of its benefits, the sun can cause numerous problems. Always wear sunscreen to protect youself from the sun's harmful rays. Many of the sunscreens available on the market do not provide adequate protection, so before setting off on your trip, ask your pharmacist which ones are truly effective against the dangerous rays of the sun. Overexposure to the sun can cause sunstroke, symptom of which

include dizziness, vomitting and fever. Cover yourself well and avoid prolonged exposure, especially for the first few days of your trip, as it takes a while to get used to the sun. Even once you are used to the sun's intensity, moderate exposure is best. Wearing a hat and sunglasses can help shield you from the harmful effects of the sun. Lastly, don't forget that sunscreens are most effective when applied 20 to 30 minutes before exposure to the sun.

■ The First Aid Kit

A small first aid kit can help you avoid many difficulties. It is best to prepare it carefully before setting off on your trip. Make sure you take along a sufficient supply of all perscription medicines you take regularly, as well as a valid prescription in case you lose them. Other medicines, such as Imodium or its equivalent (for intestinal disorders and diarrhoea) may be purchased before leaving, but are available in local pharmacies. In addition, adhesive bandages, disinfectant, pain relievers, antihistamines, condoms and medicine for stomach upsets may be purchased before leaving but they are also readily available throughout Provence Côte d'Azur.

Insurance

■ Cancellation Insurance

Your travel agent will usually offer you cancellation insurance when you purchase your airplane ticket or vacation package. This insurance guarantees reimbursement for the cost of the ticket or package in case the trip has to be cancelled due to serious illness or death. Travellers with no health problems are unlikely to require such protection, and should weigh its advantages carefully.

Theft Insurance

Most homeowner's insurance policies in North America cover some personal possessions, even if they are stolen abroad. In order to file a claim, you must have the police report. Depending on what is covered in your policy, it is not always necessary to take out additional insurance. European travellers, on the other hand, should make sure their policies protect their property in foreign countries, as this is generally not the case.

Life Insurance

Many credit cards offer life insurance when used to buy plane tickets. In addition, many travellers have a life insurance policy already. In these cases it is not necessary to obtain life insurance coverage.

Health Insurance

This is without question the most useful kind of insurance for travellers, and should be purchased before leaving. Look for the most complete coverage possible because health care costs in foreign countries can add up quickly. When you buy your policy, make sure it provides adequate coverage for all types of potentially costly medical expenses, such as hospitalization, nursing services and doctor's fees. It should also include a repatriation clause in case necessary care connot be administered on site. In addition, as you may have to pay upon leaving the clinic, you should check your policy to see what provisions it includes for such cases. During your stay in Provence,

you should always keep proof that you are insured on your person, as it will save you a lot of trouble if you are unlucky enough to require health care.

Climate

Provence has a Mediterranean climate, characterized by a hot, dry summer period, very little rain (less than 60 rainy days) and therefore lots of sunshine.

Temperatures reach as high as 35° C in the summer, though 30° C is more common. In the winter, the climate is mild along the coastline and temperatures rarely dip below 10° C. However, the villages of the *arrière-pays* (inland countryside) are often cooler in the winter, especially those on exposed areas around the Vaucluse and Luberon hills. April and October tend to be the wettest months, with short, heavy outbursts of rain as well as lighter showers lasting a few days.

Conditions are ideal in late May and throughout June, when temperatures of around 26° C and abundant sunshine predominate. Plants, flowers and fruit trees are in full bloom and the roads are generally clear of vacationers. September is pleasant, with a favorable climate. The sea water is still warm at this time for those holidaying by the coast. In contrast, July and August are the high tourist season in Provence. Europeans are on vacation at this time and it is necessary to reserve well in advance for accommodation. Some of the more popular towns are over-crowded and getting around by car takes more time and patience.

The famous Mistral wind hits Provence throughout the year. This ferocious wind lasts for a day or even days at a time, and can blow up to 100 km an hour.

■ **Packing**

Much depends on the type of trip planned and during which season you travel. During the winter, when temperatures are fresh, be sure to bring a wool sweater, raincoat, jacket or overcoat and appropriate footwear. For the hot summers, pack loose, light cotton clothing. A sweater for air-conditioned rooms and high altitudes, plus a light windbreaker or raincoat might also prove useful. For active types, a bathing suit, solid walking shoes and appropriate hiking apparel (rucksack for supplies, sun hat) are advised. Of course, sunglasses, sun cream and hat are necessary to prevent sunstroke.

Casual wear is acceptable in most cafés and restaurants, although good standards of dress are observed everywhere. During the warmer months it is acceptable to wear shorts and T-shirts in outdoor cafés and fast-food places. However, they are not appropriate in fancier restaurants for the evening, when gentlemen wear trousers and perhaps a light-weight sports-jacket and women wear trousers, skirts or dresses. Only the top, chicest restaurants demand jacket and tie for men, and appropriate dress for women.

Safety and Security

You should take the same precautions in Provence as you would anywhere else. Keep your passport, traveller's checks and credit cards with you at all times. avoid bringing valuables to the beach, but if you must, keep an eye on them. Store valuable objects and papers in your hotel room if it is equipped with a small safe or at the hotel reception.

You should pack a copy of your passport and your intinerary, as well as a list of the serial numbers of your traveller's checks. If ever the originals are lost or stolen, knowing their reference numbers will make it much easier to replace them.

Although Provence Côte d'Azur is not a dangerous region, it has its share of thieves, especially in the places most frequented by tourists. A certain degree of caution can save you a lot of trouble. Don't keep your luggage or bags on the seat of your parked car in clear view; avoid showing the contents of your wallet when paying for a purchase. Conceal your traveller's checks, passport and some of your cash in a money belt. Remember, the less attention you attract, the less you risk being robbed.

■ **Car Theft**

It may be hard for a North American to imagine the huge risk that exists in Southern France of having objects stolen from your car. Drivers would be wise to take the following precautions:

● Never leave your luggage in an unsupervised car. Thieves need only five minutes to get what they want without any trace. Car door locks are no secret to these professional pilferers.

● Above all do not leave anything visible that might have any value: bags, jackets. The lock might be picked in hopes that the jacket contains a wallet.

• If you must keep your luggage in your car be careful when stopping for gas or for fast-food. Place the car where you can see it constantly. In the city pay for a parking lot, and choose a spot near the attendant.

• Always leave the glove box wide open, to avoid the supposition that your camera might be inside.

In general leave your bags at the hotel while you are sightseeing, even if you have checked out. The reception desk will usually keep them for you. Finally always remember that whatever precautions you've taken, you could still be robbed and avoid carrying too many valuables with you.

Mail and Telecommunications

You can buy stamps at any post office, and also at the major hotels. Airmail is collected on a daily basis.

You'll have no trouble finding public telephones. Some still operate with coins but most use cards; these cards, known as *télécartes*, are available at the post office and tabacs and cost 40 F for 50 units.

To call Provence Côte d'Azur from Canada and the United States, dial 011 33, then the local number. (For Paris-Ile-de-France region, dial 011 33 1, then the local number.) From most European countries, dial 00 33, then the local number.

Discount rates are available at certain times of the day. In Canada, the cheapest time to call is between 6 PM and 8 AM EST; in Switzerland and Belgium, between 8 PM and 8 AM and all day Sunday.

Direct Dial numbers

To call these places from Provence Côte d'Azur dial the code followed by the area code and local number:
• Canada and the United States: 001
• Belgium: 19 32
• Great Britain: 19 44
• Netherlands: 19 31
• Switzerland: 19 41
• Paris: 16 1

In addition, most hotels offer fax and telex services, as do all post offices.

Transportation

■ Roads

Roads in Provence Côte d'Azur are well-maintained and extensive. Apart from the highways, there are a number of *routes nationales* (several lanes) and *routes départementales* (two lanes), which extend even to the smallest village, perched on a cliff-side. Many smaller roads are very narrow and winding, which can be somewhat disconcerting. Local residents, accustomed to these conditions, often drive very quickly. Some visitors might prefer to use the public parking spaces and parking lots which are conveniently located at the entrance to many villages, then explore the area on foot.

Watch out for the numerous speed bumps (*dos d'anes* - or donkey's backs) on the roads both near and in the cities, which serve the laudable purpose of slowing down traffic to protect pedestrians.

A Few Tips

Drivers License: North American and European drivers licenses are valid in France.

The Highway Code: North Americans are advised that at intersections, priority is given to cars arriving on the right, regardless of which driver arrived first. However, major roads are served by round-abouts and cars within them always have priority. Therefore, wait for the way to completely clear before entering the round-about.

The use of seat belts is mandatory in France.

Maximum speed limit on highways is 130 km/h.

Service Stations: Most service stations on highways are open 24 hours a day, others are generally closed at night.

A road map will make it easier for you to find your way around Provence. The detailed maps published by either Michelin or Institut Géographique National (IGN) are recommended. They identify even the smallest back-roads in the Vaucluse and Luberon hills for example, and will prove very useful.

■ Car Rentals

All international car rental agencies have branches in the region. Most are represented in the airports and around the main train stations. Throughout this guide, we'll do our best to provide you with the names and addresses of car rental agencies in the region. You'll find this information in the "Finding Your Way Around" section of each chapter.

All you need to rent a car in Provence is your driver's license. You must, however, be 21 years of age or older.

If you rent a car upon arrival, expect to pay around 250 F per day (unlimited mileage) for a compact car. Better value deals are always offered for periods of a few days or a week. If you rent a car for a longer period, check with your travel agent before departing to find out if economical rental packages are available.

■ Motorcycle and Scooter Rentals

The idea of travelling the region's roads on a motorcycle or a scooter appeals to many people. A number of agencies specializing in the rental of this type of vehicle exist and are found in the "Finding Your Way Around" section of each chapter. Note that by law you are required to wear a helmet.

■ Public Transportation

The cities and towns of Provence are served by a growing network of buses. Local tourist offices will provide up-to-date schedules and details.

■ Hitchhiking

Hitchhiking is a popular means of transportation, especially for young people. It is a pleasant way to get around and meet people. However, follow the same safety measures that you would anywhere else in the world if you choose to hitchhike.

■ Taxis

Private taxis are another way to get around the area, and are practical for short journeys. However, it is an expensive mode of transportation if you are trying to get from one area to the next. Expect to pay around 12 F per kilometre, low tariff. There is a supplement for luggage.

Taxis are easily found at airports and near train stations and hotels. Taxi stands are found throughout the larger cities like Avignon, Aix-en-Provence, Marseille and Nice.

■ Boats

Many private operators offer sea shuttle services regularly between the coastline and neighbouring islands. One in particular is the service linking Marseille and la Ciotat. In all cases, check prices before boarding.

Pleasure boat rental, with or without skipper, is also possible.

Money and Banking

The local currency is the French Franc (F), equal to 100 centimes. There are 5, 10 and 20 centime pieces in circulation, as well as the 1/2, 1, 2, 5, 10 and 20 F coins and 20, 50, 100, 200 and 500 F bills. When this guide went to press in July 1995, the exchange rates were as follows:

1 $Can	3,42 F
1 $US	4.75 F
1 DM	3.43 F
1 £Sterling	7.85 F
1 $Aus	3.51 F
1000 lira	3.01 F
100 pta	4.06 F
100 Dfl	3.8 F

For easier on-the-spot reference, all prices in this guide are quoted in French francs.

■ Banks

Banks usually offer the best exchange rates if you're converting foreign currency into francs. Most banks in Provence Côte d'Azur are open Monday to Friday from 8:30 AM to noon and from 2 PM to 4:30 PM

■ Foreign Exchange Offices

You can also exchange money at foreign exchange offices. In the larger centres, some are open late at night and on weekends. Be sure to check both the exchange rate and the commission charge, before accepting a transaction (banks usually offer a better deal).

If banks and foreign exchange offices are all closed, you can always exchange money at one of the major hotels, though the rates won't be nearly as good.

■ Credit Cards and Travellers' Cheques

Visa and Mastercard are the most accepted. Even in large tourist centres, many places don't accept American Express and Diners card. Shops, restaurants and hotels in small towns and villages don't always accept credit cards so check ahead. You will usually have no trouble paying by travellers' cheque.

Accommodation

There is no shortage of good accommodation in Provence, no matter what your budget and taste. From vacation villages and *gîtes ruraux* (rental houses) to inviting *chambres d'hôtes* (bed and breakfasts) and luxury hotels, the choice is large and varied.

In this guide, we have listed what we believe to be the best accommodations in each category. The prices quoted were in effect when this guide went to press, and are clearly subject to change at any time. Unless otherwise indicated, these rates apply to one double room for two people per night. Each listing also includes a complete address, telephone number and fax in order to assist you in making reservations from home. It is strongly advised to reserve accommodation ahead of time, especially during the summer season. The best places, particularly those with an unique location or special charm, should be booked well in advance.

All accommodation listed in this guide has been personally-inspected by the authors. In an effort to recommend accommodation with a high level of comfort, local character and friendly welcome, chain hotels and establishments on major roads or near noisy areas are not included.

■ Luxury Hotels

There are several luxury hotels in the region, plus a number of manor-style establishments in the countryside. These three and four-star hotels meet all the international standards of comfort and convenience. Some have that little added plus - local character.

■ Small and Medium-Sized Hotels

There are a large number of small and medium-sized hotels and inns scattered throughout Provence Côte d'Azur. Most are independently owned, so the welcome and service are highly personalized. These are often as well-located as the luxury hotels (near important places of interest, with lovely views, etc.), but are more of a bargain.

■ Furnished Lodgings and Residential Hotels

These are two very similar options. In both instances, guests stay in fully-equipped (kitchenette, refrigerator, dishwasher, etc.) studios or apartments. Residential hotels have some of the characteristics of traditional hotels, such as private bathrooms, televisions and telephones, but are usually located in large, private homes. Local tourist offices supply comprehensive listings of this sort of accommodation. Inquire about reservation requirements, as some of these places are only available by the week.

■ *Gîtes Ruraux* and *Chambres d'Hôtes*

The *Gîtes de France* association proposes hundreds of *gîtes* and *chambres d'hôte* in Provence. This type of accommodation enables visitors to get to know local people; it is common in villages and practically non-existent in the larger city centres.

Some *gîtes* are independent units, while others adjoin the owner's residence. they are completely furnished and equipped with appliances. As a general rule, *gîtes* are rented by the week, but a few also offer weekend rates. *Chambres d'hôtes* are bed and breakfast accommodation in the owner's home, breakfast included.

All of these establishments must meet certain specific standards of quality before being listed in the association's annually-updated listings book *Gîtes Ruraux*, available in travel bookshops along with *French Country Welcome*. A number of Provence's Gîtes de Prestige finest *chambres d'hôtes* are listed here.

■ **Camping**

There are loads of campgrounds throughout the region, and the variety of services offered is staggering. Camping is illegal on unauthorized terrain.

 Restaurants and Fine Food

Provence Côte d'Azur is overflowing with good places to eat, so you can enjoy excellent food wherever you go. Provençal cuisine is famous throughout the world, making this one of the best reasons to visit here. In addition, international cuisine is represented (Oriental, African, Arabic) for visitors searching for something exotic.

As a general rule, restaurants are open from noon to 3 PM and from 7 PM to 10 PM. In the large city centres, you can eat even later, especially during the high season. A few serve dinner only, starting at 7 PM, and most are closed one day a week. We strongly recommend therefore, that you make reservations, especially at the height of the tourist season. At the same time, ask if the restaurant accepts credit cards, as this is not always the case.

In this guide, we have tried to provide you with the best possible selection of restaurants, for all budgets. Each listing includes the restaurant's telephone number, which will make it easy for you to call for reservations. The prices quoted are intended to give you an idea of the cost of a meal for two people, tax and tip included, but without

drinks. Furthermore, throughout France, tax and service are included in the prices on the menus.

An escalating price system operates in French cafés. Drinks at the *comptoir* (bar counter) are cheaper than drinks consumed sitting at tables inside the café, which are in turn cheaper than drinks consumed on an outside terrace. In other words, for the same drink, customers pay a few francs more for the pleasure of being served on a beautiful terrace.

■ **Provençal Cuisine**

The Mediterranean location influences every Provençal meal. Dishes are typically based on a *cuisine de la terre* - literally, cooking from the earth. Good restaurants, whether basic or fancy, always make propitious use of the regions fresh produce. So sun-ripe tomates, olive oil, garlic and wonderful fragrant herbs like thyme, rosemary, sage and basil constitute the fundamentals of many recipes. Lamb, fresh fish and an impressive variety of vegetables form the main dishes, while local chèvres, hand-picked fruits and Provençal wine accompany them.

Curiously, there are very few indiginous fish, despite the fact that the bouillabaisse de Marseille is famous the world over. Sea-perch (*loup*) and rascasse are local fish, and figure predominantley amongst the six or seven types necessary for an authentic bouillabaisse. But as there are restrictions on the amount of fish which may be caught (and water pollution seems to have killed off the rest), the price of bouillabaisse is consequently high. Many fish served on menus (particularly shell-fish) comes from the Atlantic coast of France.

■ Drinks

The licorice-flavoured alcohol **pastis** is one of the most famous local apéritifs. The two well-known brands are Pernod and Ricard and you will no doubt hear the expression in bars "*Donnez-moi un Pernod*" (Give me a Pernod).

Another popular apéritif is a **kir** - a glass of white wine with a touch of cassis (black currant) liqueur. A kir royale substitutes champagne for white wine.

There is no locally-made beer. The most common beers served in the area are Heineken, Carlsburg and Kronenberg. They are often available on tap. A **panaché** is a mix of beer and fizzy lemon soft drink.

The sunny, dry weather has made Provence an important wine producer. Try the famous Côtes du Rhône (including the delicious reds Châteauneuf du Pape and Gigondas), Côtes du Ventoux, Côtes d'Aix and Côtes de Provence. The region produces a significant quantity of rosé wine. It is drunk fresh and often as an apéritif.

In restaurants, it is wise to order local wines by the *pichet* (small clay pitcher). They are usually light and fresh and offer good value. Most restaurants offer a wide selection of French wines from other regions (Bordeaux, Burgundy, Alsace, Loire), but often at relatively elevated prices.

Entertainment

■ Night Life

All sorts of nocturnal activities exist in the region. Larger city centres, notably Avignon, Marseille, Aix-en-Provence, Nice and Monaco offer theatres, concerts, nightclubs and discotheques. Otherwise, the smaller towns and villages are very quiet at night. In these areas, the liveliest evening event can be a drink in a local café or impromptu concert in a village square.

Summertime is festival season in France, and a number of music and theatre perfomances are held throughout the area. As well, local communities put on traditional entertainments at this time, usually centred around local history or folklore. Tourists are very welcome at these events.

Local newspapers are the best source of information concerning up-to-the-minute concerts, plays and films. Keep an eye out for free entertainment listings papers such as *Tik Tak* in Marseille (it also covers the Aix-en-Provence area); *7 jours 7 nuits* for Côte d'Azur and flyers posted in bars, restaurants and local shops.

■ Festivals and Events

There are an astounding number of events, festivals and processions in Provence every year. The major ones are listed here and explanations for most appear in the appropriate chapters which follow; tourist offices provide details of exact dates and times, plus news about local events.

January

● Exhibition of Santons and Crèches (throughout Provence, villages display the traditional clay figurines and elaborate Nativity scenes)
● Messe des Truffes (Richerenches, Sun following Jan 17, mass celebrating the truffle harvest)

February

- Carnival (Aix-en-Provence, Marseille)
- La Chandeleur (Marseille, Candelmas procession from the Saint-Victor Abbey)

March/April

- Feria Pascale (Arles, Easter Weekend, bull fights, parades)
- Bouvine Pascale (Saintes-Marie-de-la-Mer, Easter weekend, rodeos)
- Festival de Musique à Saint-Victor (Marseille, music in Saint-Victor Abbey)

May

- Fête des Gardians (Arles, May 1, games, parades in traditional costume)
- Pélerinage des Gitans (Saintes-Maries-de-la-Mer, May 24-25, gypsy folklore celebration)
- Festival de la Bande Dessinée (Orange, comic book festival)
- Foire aux Agneux et aux Asperges (Gillon, fair celebrating lamb and the asparagus harvest)
- Pèlerinage de la Saint-Gens/Fête Provençale (Monteux, traditional pilgrimage and festival, around May 15)
- Fete de la Transhumance (Saint-Rémy, Mon of Pentecost, procession of sheep through the streets)

June

- Fête de la Tarasque (Tarascon, last weekend in Jun, parade)
- Fête de la Saint-Jean (folklore celebration: Vaison-la-Romaine, Beaumes-de-Venise, Pernes-les- Fontaines, Sault, Maubec, Allauch, and with fireworks, Monteux, late Jun)
- Foire des Potiers (Malaucène, Cadenet, potters fairs)
- Fête du Melon (Monteux, festival celebrating the melon harvest of the Comtat Venaissin plain)

- Festival de Quatuors à Cordes (string quartet concerts in Fontaine-de-Vaucluse, Roussillon, Goult, La-Roque-d'Anthéron, Jun-Sep)

July

- Festival International d'Art Lyrique et de Musique (Aix-en-Provence, world-class music and opera festival)
- Rencontres Internationales de la Photographie (Arles, major photography exhibitions, talks and workshops)
- Festival d'Avignon (Avignon, international theatre and dance festival, including "Off" program of alternative events, until early Aug)
- Festival International de Jazz (Salon-de-Provence, jazz festival)
- Festival Marseille Méditerranée (Marseille, dance, theatre, music)
- Festival des Iles (Marseille, theatre on the islands of Frioul, Château d'If, Ratonneau and Pomègues)
- Fêtes de Sainte Madeleine (Sainte-Baume, folklore celebration, 21-22 Jul)
- Fêtes d'Arles - La Pégoulado (Arles, folklore celebrations, dance, music)
- Festo Virginienco (Saintes-Maries de la Mer, Festival of the Virgin celebrations)
- Les Chorégies (Orange, music festival, Jul-Aug)
- Nuits Théatrales et Musicales de l'Enclave (Grillon, Richerenches, Valréas, Visan, theatre and music events throughout the summer in the Enclave des Papes area)
- Festival Passion (Carpentras, music and theatre festival, Jul-Aug)
- Festival de Gordes (Gordes music and theatre festival)
- Festival de la Sorgue (Isle-sur-la-Sorgue, music festival)
- Les Vendredis Folkloriques, les Samedis Taurins, Les Kiosques à Musique (Cavaillon, concerts, Jul-Aug)

●Festival du Sud-Luberon (La-Tour-d'Aigues, danse, theatre, music, art, Jul-Aug)

August

●Fête de la Véraison (Châteauneuf-du-Pape, medieval fair, early Aug)
●Grande Cavalcade Provençale (Aubagne, late Aug)
●Festival Provençale (Séguret, including wine festival, late Aug)
●Fête des Vins (Bédoin, wine festival)
●Fête de l'Éte et du Cheval (Malaucène, summer festival, early Aug)
●Fête de la Lavande (Sault, lavender harvest festival)
●Musique d'Été and Rencontres Méditérranéennes Albert Camus (Lourmarin, music festival and writers' gathering)
●Festival (Abbaye de Sénanque near Gordes, concerts and exhibitions)

September

●Fête des Vins (Cassis, tastings, Provençal dances, early Sep)
●Les Prémices du Riz (Arles, 800-year old rice harvest celebration, bullfights, rodeos, parades)
●Fête des Olives Vertes (Mouriès, late Sep, olive harvest festival, parades, mass, brocante fair)
●Fête des Vendanges (Entrechaux, Ventoux wine harvest festival)

October

●Pélerinage (Saintes-Maries-de-la-Mer, Sunday closest to Oct. 22, traditional pilgrimage procession)
●Festival de Musique Sacrée (Marseille, sacred music concerts played in the Saint-Victor Abbey, continuing to Dec)

●La Fiesta des Suds (Marseille, music, dancing, folklore from southern cultures held in the docks area)

November

Christmas traditions (continuing to mid-Jan throughout Provence:
●Santons clay figurine fairs, theatrical representations of the Nativity scene called pastorales)
●Baptême du Côtes-du-Rhône Primeur (Avignon, first tastings of new Cotes-du-Rhône wine)

December

●Messe de Noël (traditional Provençal Christmas Midnight Mass, Dec 24, throughout the region, service with live Nativity scenes at Les Baux-de-Provence, Allauch near Marseille, Séguret, Villedieu)

 Shopping

If you love shopping and beautiful boutiques, you'll be in heaven in the Provençal cities of Avignon, Aix-en-Provence and Marseille and on the Côte d'Azur in Nice, Monte-Carlo and Cannes. Leading French and European names in perfume, crystal, watches, haute couture and leather goods are found here. The major department store Galeries Lafayette has a branch in Marseille and in Nice. These cities are popular tourist destinations, and some prices might be higher than elsewhere. Of course, bargains can always be found.

Shops are generally open Monday through Friday from 9 AM to 1 PM and from 3 PM to 7 PM, and on Saturday from 9 AM to 5 PM In addition to the major shopping streets, there are shopping centres in the suburbs of the larger cities.

Tourists can be reimbursed for the French sales tax paid on articles sold in most large shops. The system, called *détaxe*, is only available if you spend more than 2,000 F in one shop, on the same day. Forms are available from shops and travellers are reimbursed only after leaving the country.

Typical souvenirs from the region include *Savon Marseillais* (soap), sachets of *Herbes de Provence*, olive oil, *santons de Provence* (small painted clay figurines representing Provençal daily life), pottery, and of course, wine. There are outdoor markets in most places each week. These are great places to people-watch and pick up some souvenirs.

Public Holidays

1 January	New Years Day
Variable	Good Friday
Variable	Easter
1 May	Labour Day
8 May	Armistice Day 1945
Variable	Ascension Day
Variable	Pentecost (Pentecôte)
14 July	Fête Nationale
15 August	Assumption Day
1 November	All Saints Day
25 December	Christmas Day

General Information

■ Time Zone

Provence follows Central European time, which is one or two hours ahead of Greenwich Mean Time (GMT), depending on the season. There is six hours difference between Québec and Ontario, New England and the Eastern United States. The farther west you go, the greater the time difference. This means Western Canada and the United States, behind are nine hours.

■ Electricity

Local electrictiy operates at 220 volts AC (50 cycles), so tourists from North America will need to bring along an adaptor with two round pins and a converter for their appliances.

Visitors from Great Britain will only need an adapter with two round pins.

■ Women Travellers

Women travelling alone should not encounter any problems. On the whole, women are treated with respect and harassment is relatively rare. Off course, a certain amount of caution is required; for example, women should avoid walking alone through poorly lit areas late at night.

■ Weights and Measures

France uses the metric system.

■ Weather

For up-to-date weather reports:
☎ 36 68 02 13 (Vaucluse) or
☎ 36 68 02 84 (Bouches du Rhône)

■ Emergency Telephone Numbers

Ambulance or Medical Emergency (SAMU/Service Aide Médicale d'Urgence):   ☎ 15
Police: ☎ 17
Fire: ☎ 18

OUTDOOR ACTIVITIES

Befitting its exceptional climate and varied landscape, Provence Côte d'Azur offers active types a vast selection of outdoor activities. Provence Côte d'Azur rises from sea-level along the mighty Mediterranean coast to more than 1,900 m (6,232 feet) at the top of Mont Ventoux. With such extraordinary geographical differences, all types of activities are possible, from swimming and windsurfing to downhill skiing and hang-gliding.

In order to give you an overall idea of what is available, we have included below a summary of the most popular outdoor activites. In subsequent chapters, each of which is devoted to a specific region, the addresses listed in the "Outdoor Acitivities" section will enable you to obtain further information.

Two useful addresses will provide specific information about your favourite sport:

Chambre Départementale de Tourisme (Sports et Loisirs de Vaucluse)
La Balance-Place Campana
P.B. 147
84008 Avignon Cedex
☎ 90 86 43 42
⇄ 90 86 86 08

Comité Départemental du Tourisme (Sports et Loisirs de Bouches du Rhône)
6 Rue du Jeune Anacharsis
13001 Marseille
☎ 91 54 92 66
⇄ 91 33 01 82

Hiking

The region is ideal for everything from gentle walks along country paths to serious hiking through steep, rugged terrain. No matter your level of fitness, one thing is certain: the scenery is always remarkable and the chance to see countless unusual species of plant and wildlife awaits you.

Professional hikers and Sunday strollers are spoiled. In the Vaucluse a number of marked trails are available for varying levels of expertise. Easy hikes are found in the plains of the Enclave des Papes (Papal Enclave) around Valréas, around the wine centre of Châteauneuf-du-Pape, and through low-lying fields and along the rivulets of the Comtat Venaissin area. Only slightly more challenging are the well-marked trails through the glorious hills of the Dentelles de Montmirail. As in most areas, the tourist offices here in the charming villages of Séguret, Gigondas, and Sablet provide specially-prepared maps for visitors wishing to discover their region on foot. The tourist office in Vaison-la-Romaine is particularly well equipped to answer questions and provide maps.

For many visitors, Provence means one thing: the cliffside villages and fields of lavender in the Luberon. Countless pathways, backroads and professionally-prepared hiking trails make their way throughout this most beautiful of areas. Much of the Luberon is a Regional Natural Park and is carefully managed by experts who have published numerous guides for visitor about its trails, flora and fauna.

The Bouches du Rhône benefits from its position facing the sea. Here, amateur explorers are invited to discover the Camargue region at the delta of the Rhône river. Nature lovers are spoilt here too - most of the Camargue is also a Regional Natural Park where unusual wildlife (most famously, pink flamingoes) roam at will. Along the coast east Marseille, the rugged fjords known as les Calanques offer serious hikers some trails worthy of an all-day outing.

Inland, hikers may choose from the lovely Alpilles around the tourist centres of Saint-Rémy and les Baux (relatively easy, though rugged trails looking over sun-drenched countryside), or better yet, the exceptional variety of trails in Cézanne's beloved area: Montagne Sainte-Victoire and Saint-Baume Massif area southeast of Aix-en-Provence.

Due to the risk of forest fires, certain trails are systematically closed during the summer, so ask at the local tourist office before heading out.

The Vaucluse regional government publishes an excellent brochure with a map and details of hiking trails in the area. Though written in French, the map and suggested routes are easy to understand. Write ahead for a copy of the *"Memento de la Randonnée Pédestre en Vaucluse"* from the Chambre Départementale de tourisme de Vaucluse (address above).

Specific information on hiking in the Vaucluse can be obtained from:

Comité Départemental de la Randonnée Pédestre
63 Rue César Frank
84000 Avignon

In the Bouches-du-Rhone, contact:
Comité Départmental de la Randonnée Pédestre
La Batarelle Haute - Bât. D1
I, Impasse des Agaces
13013 Marseille

■ **Sunstroke**

Long sections of some trails are exposed to the sun, with no shady spots in which to take refuge. The risk of sunstroke is therefore considerable and threatens all hikers enjoying their favourite outdoor activity. Cramps, goose bumps, nausea and loss of balance are the initial syptoms. If these symptoms arise, the victim should be moved quickly into the shade, fanned and given something to drink.

To avoid this problem, always wear a hat and arm yourself with a good sunscreen. You are also stongly advised to go hiking early in the morning during the particularly hot summer days. No matter what season, wear thick and sturdy shoes and dress appropriately.

■ **What to bring**

On each excursion, your backpack should contain the following objects: a water bottle, a pocket knife, an antiseptic, bandages (both adhesive and non-adhesive), scissors, aspirin, enough food for the trip and, during the summer, sunblock and insect repellent.

 Bicycling

A good way to discover the villages and countryside is by bicycle. This mode of transportation (called *cyclotourisme* or *randonnées à velo* in French) permits visitors take their time to appreciate the history, sights and smells of Provence and to create personalized circuits according to taste and whim. Often, hotels, inns and bed and breakfasts have bicycles for guests' use, so don't hesitate to ask. For serious exploring, especially along difficult routes, a mountain bike is recommended.

Professional cyclists from around the world take part in the annual Tour de France in July. Visitors to Provence Côte d'Azur can watch this passionate event, as the nation-wide route runs through the region (tourist offices and the local press will announce where and when the cyclists are expected).

For a calender of cycling events and list of local organisations, contact:

Ligue de Provence de Cyclotourisme
Jacques Maillet
15 La Trévaresse
13540 Puyricard
☎ 42 92 13 41

For the Vaucluse, contact:

Comité Départemental du Vaucluse de Cyclotourisme
Roland Gabert
4 chemin des Passadoires
84220 Piolnec
☎ 60 29 62 10

For the Bouches du Rhône, contact:

Comité Départemental des Bouches du Rhône de Cyclotourisme
Pierre Flecher
Les Prevenches B 12
36 Avenue de Saint Barnabé
13012 Marseille
☎ 91 34 89 92

Mountain Biking

What better way to discover Provence's hidden treasures than by mountain bike (known as VTT or *vélo tout terrain*)? The summer heat and many hills to climb in the Vaucluse, Luberon, Alpilles and Montange Saint-Victoire areas are bound to discourage some, however. You must be in good physical condition to enjoy this sport in these places.

The Vaucluse regional government publishes an excellent brochure with a detailed map of routes and their level of difficulty throughout the department. Portions of some of the routes are easy enough for bicyclists as well as mountain bike cyclists. Write ahead for the "*Memento de la Promenade et Randonnée Cyclotouriste/VTT en Vaucluse*" from the Chambre Départementale de Tourisme de Vaucluse (address above).

For other information about mountain biking in the entire Provence region, contact:

Comité Départemental de VTT
Chez Stanis Kowalczyk
5 rue de Bretagne
13117 Lavéra
☎ 42 81 59 05

Boating

Visitors are offered various programs of activities involving excursions at sea and rentals of all sorts of boats. Based obviously on the Mediterranean coast, a number of places in major sailing harbours offer the budding sailor an entire range of possibilities. Inquire at local tourist offices for details about local water-oriented events, including races and regattas. Otherwise, contact:

Comité Départemental de Voile
Base de Tholon
18 Boulevard de Vallier
13500 Martigues
☎ 42 80 12 94

Regional Nature Parks

Provence benefits from the Parc Naturel Régional du Luberon (120,000 ha/296,400 acre) across the Vaucluse and Alpes-de-Hautes-Provence departments and the Parc Naturel Régional de la Camargue (72,000 ha/324,000 acres) in the Bouches-du-Rhône. The organizations managing these two parks are responsible for preserving, and at the same time promoting, the natural surroundings. They also organize all sorts of activities ranging from guided walking tours, envrionmental festivals and museum visits.

Centre de Ginès
Centre d'Information du Parc Naturel
Pont de Gau
13460 Les Saintes Maries de la Mer
☎ 90 97 86 32
(information only)

Mas du Pont de Rousty
Pont de Rousty
13200 Arles
☎ 90 97 10 40

(Camargue park museum and marked nature trail, 12 km southwest of Arles on the D 570, see p 135)

Maison du Parc du Lubéron
1 Place Jean Jaurès
84400 Apt
☎ 90 74 08 55
(information, museum and shop)

Fishing

The region's rivers and ponds are favourite spots for those loving *la pêche* (fishing). Trout, salmon and eel are the most common species. Sea-fishing is possible along the Mediterranean coast, from the ports such as Cassis, La Ciotat and Marseille (tourist offices provide details). Local regulations must be observed, so contact the associations before casting off.

A third type of fishing, called *pêche à pied* (literally: fishing by foot) takes place in Provence along the sandy rivers of the marshy Camargue region, where tiny mollusks known as tellines (like mussels but much smaller) are gathered by hand. Prepared with garlic and parsley, these tasty critters are served as an hors d'œuvre in the area.

In the Vaucluse contact:

Fédération Départementale de Pêche
5 Boulevard Champfleury
84000 Avignon
☎ 90 86 62 68

In the Bouches du Rhône contact:

Fédération Départementale de Pêche
Espace La Beauvallée - Hall B
Rue M. Gandhi
13084 Aix-en-Provence
☎ 42 26 59 15

Horseback Riding

There are numerous stables scattered throughout Provence. Horses with or without guides are available for visitors some of the more than 50 *centres équestres* (equestrian centres) in the region. Riders often spend a few days exploring the hills and plains of Provence, but please note, only those with experience at high altitudes, on isolated terrain, and in variable climatic conditions (storms, fog, heat and cold) should attempt this sort of holiday.

The Vaucluse regional government publishes an excellent brochure for horseback riders, including a map with suggested trails, addresses of stables, and useful information. To receive the "*Memento de la Randonnée Equestre en Vaucluse*" write to the Chambre Départementale de Tourisme de Vaucluse (address above).

Also in the Vaucluse:

Comité Départemental d'Equitation
René François
Chemin Saint Julien
30133 Les Angles
☎ 90 25 38 91

In the Bouches du Rhone contact:

Comité Départemental des Sports Equestres
M. Girard - Les Décanis
Chemin de Collaver
13760 Saint-Collaver
☎ 42 57 35 42

Horseback riding is one of the most popular ways of discovering the Camargue and its wildlife, without disturbing them. Contact the **Association Camarguaise de Tourisme**

Equestre at the Centre de Ginès, Pont de Gau (address above).

Rock Climbing

With so many clliffs and sheer rocky surfaces in the region, Provence is ideal rock climbing (escalade) territory. This can be a dangerous sport and is therefore for professionals only. It shouldn't be attempted without the right equipment nor proper training.

In the Vaucluse, the main sites are at Buoux, the Dentelles de Montmirail and the Colline Saint-Jacques (Cavaillon). Contact:

Comité Départmental de la Montagne et Escalade
7 Rue Saint-Michel
84000 Avignon
☎ 90 25 40 48

In the Bouches du Rhône, the number of sites, of varying difficulty, is astounding. The favourite spots are Sainte-Victoire, the Calanques (a vertiginous climb above the turquoise sea), Sainte-Baume and the Alpilles. Contact the very helpful Daniel Gorgeon at:

Comité Départemental Mont-Alp-Escalade
5 Impasse du Figuier
13114 Puylobier
☎ 42 66 35 05

Golf

Why not combine sight-seeing with a few rounds on a local golf course? Numerous 18-hole courses cover Provence, plus a choice of 9-hole and practise grounds are offered. The Comité Départemental du Tourisme Bouches du Rhône publishes an excellent colour guide to the 11 courses in its department (in French but easy to understand, free, address earlier in this chapter).

Swimming

Provence isn't just villages perched on the sides of cliffs and wonderful hiking trails. It's also a region with streams, rivers and crystal-clear ponds worthy of a refreshing dip on a warm day. More than 20 spots are officially available for *baignade* (swimming) in the Vaucluse and are tested annually for water quality (A for good, B for average, C for water that may be occassionally polluted). Telephone the DDASS (*Direction Départementale des Affaires Sanitaires et Social*) health department for an up-to-date water quality report: ☎ 90 27 70 00. Lifeguards are not on duty at every swimming site; safety is therefore the responsibility of each swimmer.

In the Bouches du Rhône, the sand and pebble beaches of the Camargue next to the Mediterranean, including the Saintes-Maries-de-la-Mer area, offer an extensive choice of swimming spots. In Marseille, the municipality carefully reclaimed land from the sea in the late 80s, so that today the Prado Beaches are one of the most popular summer desitinations for locals and visitors. A full range of water activities are available, though sun-tanning and swimming are still the favourites here (see p 179).

Nudist beaches (*plages naturistes*) are found at Martigues (Plage de Bonnieu),

Salin de Giraud in the Camargue (Plage de Piemanson, known as Plage d'Arles) and at the Sugiton Calanque near Marseille (one hour walk from the Luminy parking area).

 Windsurfing

The best windsurfing is at the south end of the Prado Beaches in Marseille (see p 179) and at Saintes-Maries-de-la-Mer. Equipment hire and lessons are available.

 Scuba Diving

The hidden water gorges of the Vaucluse, particularly along the Albion river (linking to terrestrial sites Fontaine de Vaucluse, Canyon de la Nesque and Plateau d'Albion), are unique diving spots for scuba divers. They are dangerous and only professionals have access to them. Contact:

Comité Départemental de Spéléologie de Vaucluse
Musée Requien
67 Rue Joseph-Vernet
84000 Avignon

The limestone basins with colourful plant and marine life along the Mediterranean attract professional divers from around the world. The coast offers scuba divers some of the finest conditions in Europe. Underwater prehistoric caves have been found, notably the Grotte Cosquer in July 1991. Here, 37 m below the surface, Henri Cosquer discovered a cave with paintings in charcoal or magnesium oxide dating from between 10,000 and 20,000 years. Divers must be experienced and licensed, otherwise a number of groups offer day and half-day lessons (including a first dive). Details from:

Comité Régional des Sports Sous-Marins
24 Quai de Rive Neuve
13007 Marseille
☎ 91 09 36 31

 Snorkelling

Unlike scuba diving, little equipment is required for snorkelling - a mask, a snorkel and a pair of flippers. Anyone can take part in this sport, which is a good way to discover the area's "hidden" (i.e. underwater) treasures.

 Hunting

Killing animals for sport is a controversial subject for many people. Nevertheless, rabbit, *gibier* (game) such as partridge and duck, as well as larger animals including wild boar and deer, have been hunted for hundreds of years in the region. For many locals, hunting is a question of tradition and survival: these animals provide food for the tables of the most humble farmhouse as well as the finest restaurants. The hunt is strictly controlled and is open between the second Sunday in September until the last day of February. Details from:

Fédération Départementale des Chasseurs de Vaucluse
Le Concorde
Centre d'Affaires de Cap-Sud
84000 Avignon
☎ 90 89 89 97

Fédération Départementale des Chasseurs de Bouche du Rhône
Quartier Maleverny
13540 Puyricard
☎ 42 92 16 75

 Tennis

Many hotels, as well as public sports complexes, have tennis courts. Equipment is usually supplied or can be rented in most instances.

  Canoeing and Kayaking

Though most water ways in Provence aren't suitable for this sport, there is one exception. The scenic Sorgue river in the Vaucluse is a favourite spot for canoeing and kayaking enthusiasts.

For an exciting accompanied trip down the Sorgue from Fontaine-de-Vaucluse to Isle-Sur-la-Sorgue, including lively commentary, contact:

Michel Melani, Kayak Vert
84800 Fontaine-de-Vaucluse
☎ 90 20 35 44

Lessons for individuals and groups contact:

Club de Canoë-Kayak Islois
La Cigalette
84000 Isle-Sur-La-Sorgue
☎ 90 38 33 22 or 90 20 64 70

Other details from:

Comité Départemental de Canoë-Kayak
Jean-Pierre Claveyrolle
HLM Les Comtamines 3, No 106 EGI
Route d'Avignon
843000 Cavaillon
☎ 90 71 32 53

 Hang-gliding

Suspended by an airfoil at 2,500 m in the sky, hang-gliding is an exciting alternative to land-locked sports. In the Vaucluse, the most popular organisations arranging flights are centred around Mont Ventoux and in the Luberon. In the Bouches du Rhône, the Montagne Sainte Victoire and Sainte-Baume Massif area are favoured.

For detailed information regarding sites and their conditions, training courses and hang-gliding schools, contact:

Ligue de Vol Libre de Provence
c/o A. Keller
2 rue Émile Guigues
03200 Embrun
☎/⇄ 92 43 53 71

Association Vaucluse Parapente
Maison IV de Chiffre
26 Rue des Teinturiers
84000 Avignon
☎ 90 85 67 82

  Downhill and Cross-Country Skiing

Though not exactly the French Alps, down hill skiing (*ski alpin*) is offered on two runs from Mont Ventoux during the winter season. Call ahead to confirm ski conditions; equipment hire and lessons are available.

Mont-Serein (7 ski runs, 7 km long, restaurant): ☎ 90 63 42 02

Chalet Reynard (2 ski runs, 3 km long): ☎ 90 63 16 54 (Comité Départemental de Ski)

Cross-country skiing is limited to the forests around Mont Ventoux (details from the Comité Départemental de Ski, ☎ 90 63 16 54).

Ballooning

For a completely different perspective on things, why not see Provence from the air? A company in the Bouches-du-Rhône arranges ballooning trips in the region (1,400 F per person for a half day, including around one hour in the air and a glass of Provençal wine after the flight). Contact:

Ulysse Aventure
Jacques Massemin
B.P. No 17
13570 Barbentane
☎ 90 95 53 28
⇄ 90 95 54 50

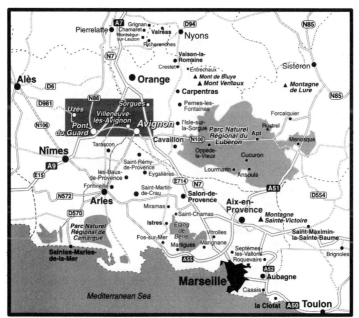

AVIGNON:
GATEWAY TO PROVENCE ★★

T he historic city of Avignon is the classic starting point from which to discover the riches of Provence. Famous now for its impressive *Palais des Papes*, or pope's palace, annual summer theatre festival, and superb museums, Avignon is popularly known by every French-speaking school child who has sung *Sur Le Pont d'Avignon* (On the Avignon Bridge), a reference to the 12th century structure actually named Le Pont Saint-Bénézet.

Avignon has been a human settlement since neolithic times. In the fourth century BC, the Cavares Celto-Ligurian tribe formed a community here and by the second century BC it was a trading post for the Massaliotes native to the region. During the Roman occupation of Provence (for four centuries starting in 123 BC) the town was called Avenio and was prized due to its strategic position on the left bank of the Rhône. The 35 m high plateau, le Rocher des Doms, with its strategic views over the river, the Île de la Bartélasse and the surrounding countryside, was the focal point of Avignon's development.

After the fall of the Holy Roman Empire in 476 AD, through to the end of the 10th century, Avignon was occupied by several peoples, and was the scene of power struggles and bloody battles. Barbarian tribes, including the Goths and the Franks sought control of the region.

Better times came during the 11th and 12th centuries, when Avignon enjoyed virtual independence from the rest of Provence. In the 12th century, Provence was split in two and ruled by the Count of Toulouse and the Catalan Count of Barcelona. However, from 1136 Avignon was impartial - it had its own governing council, *le consulat* and a military force, much like an Italian city-state of the period.

Avignon's greatest glory was from 1309 to 1417, when it became the *Cité des Papes*, the popes' city, a name which has stuck to this day. Avoiding feuds in Rome, the Pope Clement V decided that Avignon would become the centre of the Christian world. It was a natural choice, as the Papal rulers had already designated a large portion of Provence as their territory in 1274, called the Comtat Venaissin. Additionally, at the time of Clément V's arrival, Avignon was geographically closer to the heart of the Christian world than Rome. In all, seven popes lived in Avignon. The town prospered remarkably for over one hundred years, as kings, princes, intellectuals, artists, papal administrators and families of cardinals all made Avignon their home.

In 1481, at the death of Charles III, the nephew and sole inheritor of the *bon roi* René d'Anjou who died a year earlier, Louis XI of France became Count of Provence. He annexed Provence once and for all to the kingdom of France in 1486 as the absolute monarchy based in Paris had no use for a free-minded southern partner.

So, for a century and a half local institutions were removed, and with them Provence's right to self-government. However, Rome continued to administer Avignon. The prosperous town therefore remained a foreign parcel of land within the French kingdom (and stayed that way until the Revolution).

The French monarchy coveted Avignon, and tried to take control of this precious jewel — Louis XIV occupied the town from 1663-67 and again in 1689-90, while Louis XV took hold of it from 1768-74. Avignon finally submitted and became part of France (along with the Comtat Venaissin) by a decree in the *Assemblé National* on September 14, 1791. However, it wasn't until February 19, 1797 that Pope Pious VI consented to give Avignon away in the Treaty of Tolentino.

The town continued to prosper during the 19th century, thanks to its role as an important agricultural and artistic centre. It became the leading area for ceramic manufacture and silk and fabric weaving. The famous Provençal printed fabrics, heavily commercialized today, are local reproductions of the lovely so-called Indian prints imported from the east during this period. Architecture of a religious, administrative and private nature, which flourished in the 17th and 18th centuries, continued, though at a slower pace. Many remarkable mansions *hôtels particuliers* are of particular interest. Although Avignon's population stands at 91,475 today, the greater metropolitan region holds 170,000.

 Finding Your Way Around

■ **By plane**

Avignon is served by the Avignon-Caumont airport handling daily flights (one hour from Paris, for

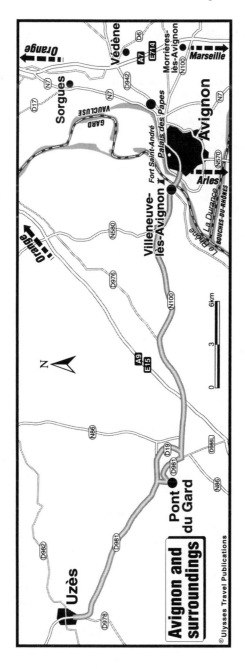

Avignon and surroundings

© Ulysses Travel Publications

example) from across the country, contact *Air Inter* for details.

■ By train

Avignon is conveniently just four and a half hours away from Paris by the high speed TGV train. TGV trains leave twice daily, seven days a week, from Paris' Gare du Lyon and Charles de Gaulle airport. Reservations are not necessary in off-peak times, though reductions, called Joker fares, are available to all who book two weeks or one month in advance. Reservations for Joker fares can only be made in France, and you are obliged to stick to the day and time indicated on the ticket once it is purchased. Timetables are available from any French SNCF train station, SNCF boutiques and travel agents.

■ By car

Avignon is at least eight hours drive from Paris (722 km) by the **Autoroute du Soleil A7 - E15** expressway. However, traffic is quite heavy during holiday periods (July and August weekends, February school break, for example), and can add another couple of hours to your journey. Arriving from the north on the A7 - E15, carry on the A7 after Orange (the E15 veers towards Nîmes), and follow the signs for Avignon by taking the D225 or N100, both of which lead directly into the city centre. From the Côte-d'Azur and the southeast, the N7 leads directly into Avignon. From Marseille take the A7 north and connect with the N7 north into the city. Be sure to carry some French currency with you for the toll booths (*péages*) on the larger expressways. French roads are in great condition but you have to pay for them!

Car rental

The major car rental agencies are located next to the main SNCF train station, to the right upon leaving the station.

Avis
34 Bd St Roch
☎ 90.82.26.33

Budget
2A Av Monclar
☎ 90.87.03.00

Europcar
2A Av Monclar
☎ 90.82.49.85

Hertz
4 Bd Saint Michel
☎ 90.82.37.67

 Practical Information

■ Tourist Office
41 Cours Jean Jaurès
84000 Avignon
☎ 90.82.65.11, ⇄ 90.82.95.03

A good starting point to pick up free maps, information and details about special events, including the theatre festival.

■ Parking

Avignon is a historic city with winding streets, many of which are narrow or pedestrian only, so parking can be a problem within the walled city centre. Paying for underground parking lots alleviates some of the problem — the most convenient one is next to the Palais des Papes *(access by following* signs from *Rue de la République* and *Place de l'Horloge; 900 places; open 24 hours a day)*. Otherwise, it is advised to park just outside the ramparts, along its perimeter, or in the parking lot on avenue Monclar, situated between the Gare SNCF and Gare Routière train stations.

■ **Banks**

All the major French banks are found in the city centre, most along the Rue de la République. Hours are the following: Mon to Fri 8:30 AM to noon, 2 PM to 4 PM Most have foreign exchange desks, often offering a better deal than the independent exchange offices. Check both the exchange rate and the commission fee charged.

■ **Post Offices**

Cours Kennedy
☎ 90.86.78.00
Mon to Fri 8 AM to 7 PM
Sat 8 AM to noon

 Exploring

■ **Suggested Excursions**

Impressive **panoramic views** ★★ of Avignon, Mont Ventoux, the Luberon and Alpilles mountain ranges can be had from both Fort Saint-André and the Tour Philippe le Bel. A good flea market is held every Saturday, in the parking lot next to Place Charles David and Avenue Charles de Gaulle. From Avignon, cross the Pont Daladier bridge and follow the signs for Villeneuve, then turn right onto Avenue Gabriel Peri for the centre.

Pont du Gard ★★★

Don't miss the chance to see the 2,000 year old Pont du Gard, the highest aqueduct-bridge built by the Romans. Constructed in 19 BC, it was used to transport water from the rivers and valleys nearby, all the way to Nîmes. It functioned right up until the Middle Ages, and was restored under Napoléon III (1843-1846). Made from beautiful blond stone, the aqueduct is 49 m 75 m high (at low water periods) and consists of three levels of arches - six at the bottom, 11 in the middle and 35 on top. Today, one can drive across it, picnic nearby, swim around it and even hire a canoe or kayak. Over 2,000,000 million people visit it annually - it's crowded during the summer months, but plans to build a state-of-the-art information centre have been temporarily scrapped and the place somehow retains an untouched, natural charm. *(Directions: Twenty km west of Avignon on the N 100, then either the D 19 or D 981 for 2 km, both circle northwestwards to the Pont du Gard.)*

Uzés ★

Another 16 km finds you in this lovely medieval town, which like the Pont du Gard, is really no longer in the Provence department, but in the Gard. No matter, because you can easily spend an interesting afternoon discovering the quaint streets of Uzés, which has been heavily restored. Start at the Place aux Herbes, with its pretty colonnaded buildings and fountain, then head into the side streets. From the Place du Duché, you can admire the town hall and visit the Palais du Duché *(entry charge)* with its curious mix of architectural styles and panoramic view... Another fine view of the surrounding country

The Popes At Avignon

Avignon is the artistic centre it is today thanks to the remarkable cultural growth in the town during the popes' presence there in the 14th century. At the beginning of the century, Italy was torn apart by rival families, each vying for power. Pope Clément V, the former archbishop of Bordeaux, sought refuge from these turbulent times and moved to the region in 1309. His successor, from 1316-1334, Jean XXII (former Bishop of Avignon) confirmed once and for all the town's role as centre of the Christian community. He also contributed to the area's reputation for fine wine - the château (now abandoned), in the famous wine-producing village Châteauneuf-du-Pape, was his summer residence.

However, it was during the reign of the former Cistercian monk Pope Benoît XII (1334-1342) and his cultured successor Clément VI (1342-1352) that Avignon really developed. What is now known as the "old palace" was built under the Benoît XII on the site of the former bishops' residence. The "new palace" was built afterwards and corresponded to the more advanced tastes of Clément VI. He apparently didn't care about costs - the finest craftsmen were sent from Italy and the rest of Europe to complete his palace.

Today the palace's refined sobriety reminds us more of a fortress than an official residence. For good reason. Houses and narrow streets pushed right up against the monument and looting in the area was rife. It was not until February 1, 1404 (under Pope Benoît XIII) that the area in front of the palace was completely cleared away, leaving the impressive pedestrian square we see today.

During Clément VI's reign the population of Avignon reached 100,000 people. Pilgrims from around the Christian world made their way to Avignon. It became an intellectual centre, attracting poets, writers and artists to the area and young people to its university. The finest craftsmen, including cabinet-makers, tailors and silversmiths, set up shops. As the local economy took off, Avignon became a financial and business centre. Architects from around Europe constructed elegant Gothic houses for the cardinals and nobles built wonderful mansions.

In 1348, the reigning countess, Queen Jeanne, sold Avignon to Clément VI for 80,000 gold florins. It is said that Jeanne relinquinshed the town so as to be absolved by the Pope of the accusation that she assassinated her first husband. Urbain V (1352-1370) succeeded Clément VI. The impressive ramparts circling Avignon today were rebuilt during this time.

Avignon's glory didn't last forever. With the troubles abating in Italy, Pope Grégoire XI returned to Rome on September 13, 1376, where he reinstated it as the Pope's official residence the following year. He died in 1378, at which time the Great Schism erupted. Bowing to public pressure, the Vatican elected Urbain V, the first Italian Pope in over a century. A number of cardinals rebelled against the decision and fled to Avignon. They voted Clément VII (1378-1394), followed by Benoît XIII (1394-1408) as their popes. In the past the population had been 100,000, now there were only 5,000. Supported by France, Spain and Naples, the pair would be known as *les anti-papes*, or anti-popes. Afterwards, Avignon was ruled by papal administrators up until the Revolution (1790).

side may be had from the pastoral Promenade Jean-Racine (named after the playwrite who spent a year here), next to the 17th century Cathédrale Saint-Théodorit with its original gilded organ. *(Directions: From Avignon, take the N 100 to Pont du Gard, then take the D 19 to Uzés.)*

Please see other chapters for details about other excursions which can be started from Avignon:

Orange see p 78
Hills and villages of the Luberon see p 102
Camargue see p 133
Vaison-la-Romaine see p 80
Arles see p 128
St-Rémy-de-Provence see p 121

The residence of seven popes and two anti-popes during the 14th century, the **Palais des Pâpes** ★★ (1) *(adults 27 F, last ticket sold 45 min before closing; guided tours upon request, extra charge; open everyday except Dec 25 and Jan 1; Jan to end of Mar and Nov and Dec, 9 AM to 1:45 PM and 2 PM to 6 PM; Apr to mid-Aug and Oct, 9 AM to 7 PM; mid-Aug to end of Sep, 9 AM to 8 PM; Place du Palais)*, or popes' palace, dominates Avignon with its majestic towers and façade. The

vieux palais, or old palace, was built by local architect Pierre Poisson for Pope Benoît XII (1334-1352) with a distinctly Cistercian soberness. Clément VI (1342-1352) seamlessly added his *nouveau palais*, or new palace, in a similar Gothic, though more luxurious, manner (architect: Jean de Louvres). Nowadays visitors follow a map and discover cloisters, chapels, public reception rooms, private apartments, kitchens and even prisoners' chambers. Be sure to see the remarkable frescoes by Matteo Giovanetti in the Chapelle du Consistoire representing the lives of Saint John the Baptist and Saint John the Evangelist.

The palace fell into disrepair following the popes' departure for Rome, it was at one point used as a barracks for Napoleon's armies, and it would have been demolished had it not been for the intervention of the French state's historical monuments service. Part of the palace has been used as a convention centre, and since 1947, the main courtyard is used by the theatre festival in the summer. The palace interiors are sparse and are of most interest to those fascinated by the popes' reign in France. Otherwise, admire this historic monument from the vantage point of the **Place du Palais** ★ (2) in front, created in 1404, or from the **Rocher des Doms ★ (3)** with its marvelous panorama.

The **Cathédrale Notre-Dame des Doms ★★ (4)** *(Place du Palais, Rocher des Doms, ☎ 90.86.81.01)* is a simple 12th century Romanesque church where the popes officiated. Originally constructed beween 1140 and 1160, with later additions (14th and 15th century primarily), the cathedral holds the tomb of Jean XXII and one thought to belong to Benoît XII. Note the 13th century stone altar, and the chancel with its 12th century marble pontif's chair and superb painted cupola above.

The **Remparts (5)**, or ramparts, 4.3 km stone walls circling the city were completed in 1370, and were designed to protect Avignon from invaders during papal times. Twelve towered gates lead into the city, including the Porte de la République (the entrance for Cours de Jean Jaurès, Rue de la République, Place de l'Horloge and the Popes Palace).

The **Pont Saint-Bénézet ★★ (6)** *(Oct to Mar, Tue to Sun 9 AM to 5 PM; Apr to Sep, open everyday 9 AM to 6:30 PM; closed Dec 25, Jan 1 and May 1)* otherwise known as the Pont d'Avignon bridge was constructed of wood from 1177 to 1185, and rebuilt in 1226 in stone. Legend recalls that in 1177 a young shepherd Bénézet was instructed by an angel to build a bridge on the Rivière Rhône. The bishop of Avignon agreed to provide the money necessary if the boy could lift a stone so heavy that 30 men couldn't move it. Bénézet miraculously carried the stone all the way to the banks of the Rhône, on the site of the first arch. Needless to say, the community supported Bénézet's ambitious project with money and manpower. The bridge stretched across to the Île de la Barthelasse, though now just four of the original 22 arches remains and the bridge ends in the middle of the river.

The **Place de l'Horloge (7)** at the top of Rue de la République leading to the Pope's Palace is touristy and a popular spot for street musicians and beggars. Under the shade of large plane trees, you'll find a row of mediocre restaurants with boards advertising menus written in a plethora of languages. Young waiters and waitresses stand in front of these terraces trying to entice passersby. The Hotel de Ville, or city hall, and theatre are here, both solid examples of mid-19th century architecture, plus, of course, a 14th century clock tower.

The **Église Saint Pierre ★ (8)** *(Sat 10 AM to noon, Sun 8:30 AM to noon; Place Saint Pierre, ☎ 90.82.25.02)* is a 14th and 15th century church with amazing 16th century carved wooden doors depicting the Virgin Mary, the Angel of Annunciation, Saint-Michel and Saint-Jérome. The interior includes paintings and floral scenes set in gilded wood panelling typical of the 17th century, a scultped stone pulpit from the 15th century, and a stone retable in the small south chapel dating from early 1500.

Musée Calvet ★★ (9) *(Closed for renovation, partial re-opening in 1995 but check beforehand; 10 AM to noon and 2 PM to 9 PM, closed Tue and public holidays; 65 Rue Joseph Vernet, ☎ 90.86.33.84)* is one of France's finest small public museums. It presents a mix of prehistoric, Greek and Roman antiquities with paintings, sculpture and *objets d'art* from the Renaissance to this century. French, and in particular, Avignonnais, painting

1. Palais des Papes
2. Place du Palais
3. Rocher des Doms
4. Cathédrale Notre-Dame-des-Doms
5. The Remparts
6. Pont Saint-Bénézet
7. Place de l'Horloge
8. Église Saint-Pierre
9. Musée Calvet
10. Palais du Roure
11. Musée Lapidaire
12. Place Saint-Didier
13. Église Saint-Didier
14. Rue du Roi René
15. Rue de la Messe
16. Rue des Teinturiers

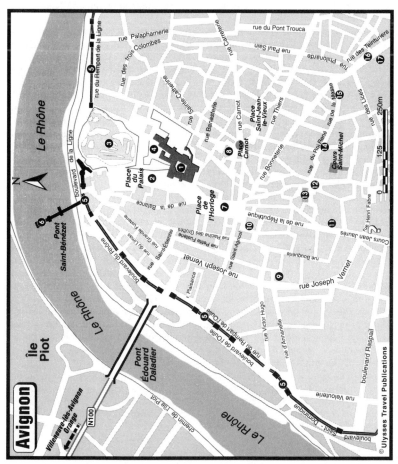

© Ulysses Travel Publications

are well represented. As well, there is a large and important collection of wrought-iron dating from the Middle Ages. It is situated in the pretty 18th century mansion, l'Hôtel de Villeneuve-Martignan.

The **Palais du Roure (10)** *(Museum visit upon request or free guided tour Tue 3 PM; 3 Rue Collège du Roure, ☎ 90.80.80.88)* provides an interesting inside look at bourgeois Provençal life while visiting the private residence (beautiful furniture and fabrics, local oil paintings) of the last owner Jeanne de Flandreysy-Espérandieu, who lived here from 1909 until 1944. The building, l'Hôtel de Baroncelli-Javon, built in 1469, is the former mansion of a wealthy Florentine banker. Nowadays, it also houses a library devoted to the history and literature of Provence. The interior courtyard, with Gothic door, fig trees, a curious collection of iron bells hanging on the walls and four authentic *pots d'Anduze* (wonderful glazed clay pots made locally for over a century), is an oasis of calm in the centre of Avignon. According to a commemorative plaque, Jeanne de Flandreysy-Espérandieu saved the building "gave it a soul and welcomed illustrious hosts".

Walking along the narrow streets in Avignon's historic neighbourhoods is one of the city's greatest pleasures. The city is divided by the north-south axis Cours Jean-Jaurès and the Rue de la République, which date from the 1850s. Unfortunately these are busy commercial streets with little charm. However, the stunning baroque façade of the **Museé Lapidaire (11)** *(free admission Nov to Apr, charge May to Oct; Tue to Sun 10 AM to noon and 2 PM to 6:27 PM; 127 Rue de la République, ☎ 90.85.75.38)* is worth noting. Once a 17th century Jesuit

chapel, it now houses a collection of precious stones and archaeological artifacts.

The most interesting streets are found in the **Vieille Ville** (old town), on either side of the Rue de la République and the Place de l'Horloge (pick up a free Avignon map from the tourist office). Much of this labyrinth area of roads is pedestrian only, and a number of architectural wonders can be found amongst the commercial hustle and bustle.

Starting at the peaceful **Place Saint Didier (12)**, by exploring the **Eglise Saint Didier ★ (13)** *(open during services only)*. This simple church in the Provençal Gothic style was built in the 1350s. A large nave, contains late 14th century frescoes and a charming stone altarpiece depicting the Carrying of the Cross, yet it is popularly known as Notre-Dame du Spasme (Our Lady of the Spasm). You'll understand why when you see the figures' shocked expressions.

Next, head east, along **Rue du Roi René ★ (14)** for a look at a trio of superb 17th and 18th century *hôtel particuliers* or mansions. The austere Hôtel d'Honnorate de Jonquerettes at number 12 dates from the 18th century, and faces the pretty Hôtel de Fortia de Montréal, built a century earlier. A masterpiece awaits you on the corner at number seven — the elaborate Hotel de Berton de Crillon (1649), now it is offices.

Still continuing eastwards, Rue du Roi René leads into the narrower, winding **Rue de la Messe (15)** and a pair of beautiful *hôtel particuliers*. Turn right onto **Rue des Teinturiers ★★ (16)**. You'll find yourself in the neighbourhood once used by manufacturers of the famous provençal prints called *indiennes* in the 18th century. The road is lined with plane trees and follows the meandering Rivière Sorgue — even a few of the abandoned water-wheels used by the *teinturiers* (clothdyers) can still be seen. This relaxed area has a couple of bar/cafés, two boutiques and a print shop and is frequented by artsy laid-back locals. It is pretty at night and not crowded. At number eight you'll find the charming 16th century **Chapelle des Pénitents Gris ★ (17)** *(Wed to Mon, 8 AM to noon and 2:30 PM to 6 PM, closed Sun afternoons, Tue and public holidays).*

 Outdoor Activities

■ **Mountainbiking/Hiking**

The Vaucluse department tourist office, located outside of the city centre, provides maps and information about walking tours, mountainbiking and hiking. (Avignon's tourist office will point you in the right direction too.)

Comité départemental de Tourisme
La Balance, place Campana
BP 147
84008 Avignon Cédex
☎ 90.86.43.42

Transhumance
BP 9
84004 Avignon
☎ 90.95.57.81
By mountain bike (VTT - *vélo tout terrain*) or by foot, this group organizes tours of the Avignon area. Initiation tours, full-day or several-day tours (around the Dentelles de Montmirail, Vaucluse mountains or Luberon park) are also arranged. Equipment can be rented.

Two businesses offering bicycle rentals by the hour or the day:
Velomania
1 Rue de l'Amelier
☎ 90.82.06.98

Alain Blache
11 Avenue Monclar
☎ 90.85.56.63

 Horseback Riding

Equestion Centre and **Avignon Pony Club**
Ile de la Barthelasse, chemiin du Mont Blanc
☎ 90.85.83.48

■ **Other Activities**

For details about golf, swimming pools, tennis, squash, or even ice-skating, call Avignon sports hot line, better known as the Municipal Sports Service
☎ 90.85.22.58.

 Accommodation

Foyer International YCJG - YMCA *(80 F to 120 F, bkfst; 7 bis, Ch. de la Justice, 30400 Villeneuve,* ☎ *90.25.46.20)*. 200 beds, in dormitory, shared rooms and individual accommodation. Half and full board available. Closed annually December 25 to January 2.

Hôtel Provençal *(220 F, bkfst 23 F, ps; 13 Rue Joseph-Vernet, 84000 Avignon,* ☎ *90.85.25.24,* ⇄ *90.82.75.81)*. Simple, clean rooms (a few need refreshing) with small bathrooms. No elevator. Good location.

Hôtel Mignon *(200-250 F, bkfst 25 F; ps, tv, ☎; 17 Rue Joseph-Vernet, 84000 Avignon, ☎ 90.82.17.30, ⇄ 90.85.78.46)*. Cute hotel with character, basic rooms but considering the central location, good value. Breakfast room.

Hôtel Danieli *(390-490 F, bkfst 35 F; pb, tvc; 17 Rue de la Républic, 84000 Avignon, ☎ 90.86.46.82, ⇄ 90.27.09.24)*. Cheery rooms (though lacking local charm) and friendly reception staff in this centrally-located hotel on the city's bustling commercial street. Breakfast room, bar, parking in paid public underground car park 200 metres away.

Hôtel Palais des Papes *(280-580 F, bkfst 35 F; ℜ, pb, ☎, tvc; 1 Rue Gérard-Philippe, 84000 Avignon, ☎ 90.86.04.13, ⇄ 90.27.91.17)*. Comfortable hotel with Gothic interior, recommended more for its ideal location next to the Palais des Papes than for the somewhat cold welcome from the front desk staff.

L'Anastasy *(300-350 F, bkfst; no credit cards; ≈, tel; Île de la Barthelasse, 5 km north, turn immediately right off the Pont Daladier bridge from Avignon ☎ 90.85.55.94, ⇄ 90.82.94.49)*. A warm welcome awaits you at this attractive *chambre d'hôte* (bed and breakfast) run by the local personality Olga Manguin, the former owner/chef of an Avignon café and her husband, Biquet, grandson of the influential Fauvre artist Henri Manguin. A copious breakfast is served on the shaded patio in warm weather, surrounded by a beautiful garden, in this pearceful country atmosphere (though it is just 15 minutes from the centre of Avignon). Four simple rooms, two without private bathroom. Olga prepares evening meals upon request

(100 F per person) and offers one-week Provençal cooking courses several times a year (accommodation included, call or write for details). Tricky to find - follow Chemin des Poiriers and l'Anastasy is on your left 50 metres after Distillerie Manguin.

Hôtel des Agassins *(450-750 F, bkfst 75 F; ≡, ≈, ℜ, pb, tel, tvc; lieu-dit "Le Pigeonnier", 84130 Le Pontet)* A hacienda-style modern hotel, fully-equipped for business clients and tourists. Though next to a busy thoroughfare, the hotel is sheltered by fir trees and the 25 rooms face a courtyard garden and swimming pool. Comfortable but it lacks authentic Provençal feel.

Hôtel d'Europe *(610-1,450 F, bkfst 90 F, garage 50 F; ≡, ℜ, pb, tel, tvc; 12 Place Crillon, 84000 Avignon, ☎ 90.82.66.92, ⇄ 90.85.43.66)* Beautiful old 17th century *hôtel particulier* belonging to Provençal nobility, converted into a hotel in the 18th century. Noted personalities, from Napoléon to Charles Dickens have stayed here. 50 good-sized, renovated rooms, and friendly service.

La Mirande *(1,300-1,900 F, bkfst 95 F, garage 80 F; ≡, ℜ, ☉, pb, tvc; 4 Place de l'Amirande, 84000 Avignon, ☎ 90.85.93.93, ⇄ 90.86.26.85)*. Stunning former cardinal's palace, transformed in the 18th century by the celebrated architect Mignard into a mansion (one of 100,000 castles in France that are registered historical monuments), and now recently entirely restored by architect Gilles Grégoire and interior decorator François-Joseph Graff. Considered one of the most beautiful hotels in France: the 19 bedrooms and one apartment, restaurant, breakfast salon, bar, covered inner courtyard and terrace are impeccably designed with a harmony of colours, fabrics and antiques, befitting a *hôtel particulier* of the period. The owners, the Stein family, are considered *'mecenats'* by the Avignonnais for their work. Situated at the foot of the Palais des Papes, this is relaxed luxury at its finest.

 Restaurants

Le Jujubier *($, no credit cards; Mon to Fri for lunch only, and dinner during Theatre Festival in July; 1 Rue Pétramale - 14 Rue du Roi René, 84000 Avignon, ☎ 90.86.64.08).* "La cuisine de Provence comme jadis" and it's true! Marylin and Marie-Christine spent six months researching the old provençal recipes and recreate them here, ingredient by ingredient, in their pleasant restaurant in a quiet street near the bustling centre. Cold zucchini soup with basil; quails with herbs, and a sublime honey ice-cream with lavender. Excellent value and a warm welcome.

Les Félibres *($; Mon to Sat 11 AM to 6:30 PM, closed in August; 14-16 Rue du Limas, 84000 Avignon, ☎ 90.27.39.05).* Delightful bookshop specializing in Provence, interior design, gardening and cooking, and, more importantly for foodies with weary feet, a tearoom. Locals swear that this is the spot for the best pastry in town: rich chocolate cake (35 F), mixed fruit gratin with crême anglaise (30 F). Light meals are served and Les Félibres also sells wine, teas and gifts for the home and table. Note the plaque on the wall on Rue du Limas opposite, marking the extraordinary high water level of the Rhône, Nov. 4 1840.

Simple Simon *($; Tue to Sat, 11:45 AM to 7 PM; 26 Rue Petite Fusterie, 84000 Avignon, ☎ 90.86.62.70).* An authentic British flavour in the heart of Provence. Not such a bad idea when the savoury tartes, salads and English treats such scones, lemon curd tart or trifle (summer-time only) are so well-prepared. Cosy interior, small outside terrace, smiling waitresses.

Woolloo Mooloo *($; Tue to Sat; 16 Rue des Teituriers, 84000 Avignon, ☎ 90.85.28.44)* Long and narrow cafe, with old tables and rough cement walls, attracting an arty crowd. A curious mix of Caribbean and American cuisine (trout with curried vegetables and white rice, 62 F; apple crumble 25 F).

La Fourchette *($$; Mon to Fri; 17 Rue Racine, 84000 Avignon, ☎ 90.85.20.93)* Menu 145 F (110 F without entrée). Forks on the wall and ceiling set the scene for this smart restaurant styled like a country inn and much liked by locals. Fish emphasis. Beef *daube* with macaroni gratin; grilled saumon with puréed potates and sorrel.

L'Isle Sonnante *($$; Tue to Sat; 7 Rue Racine, 84000 Avignon, ☎ 90.82.56.01).* Menu at 130 F (lunch) and 185 F (dinner) only. Fresh room with pretty porcelain and oak bar with brass fittings. One of the best restaurants in Avignon, and the creative menu says it all: red fish terrine with tomato *coulis*, rabbit filet with a Nyons olive purée stuffing; *dorade* filet in puff pastry, with mint-flavoured *fervettes*. Excellent cheese and desserts. Highly recommended.

Fabrice *($$; Wed to Sun; 3 Boulevard Pasteur, 30400 Villeneuve-lès-Avignon, ☎ 90.25.52.79)* A new restaurant worth crossing the Pont Daladier into historic Villeneuve (follow Avenue General Leclerc, turn right at Avenue Pasteur), for a fresh, modern twist to Provençal cuisine. Young chef Fabrice Guisset did his military service in Paris, cooking for Edouard Balladour, Finance Minister at the time. He works wonders with local produce - such as courgettes, eggplant and flavourful tomatoes in his deliciously simple vegetable terrine with tapenade vinaigrette; pistou soup with chèvre croutons, or smoked tuna with crispy artichokes and asparagus. The dining room, with a subtle coral-coloured nautical look, is in the house where his grandfather once lived. Friendly, attentive service; pleasant patio. Menus at 130 F and 180 F.

Entertainment

■ Bars

Woolloo Mooloo (see restaurants above)

La Tache d'Encre *(open everyday, until 3 AM during the Theatre Festival; 22 Rue des Teintuiers, 84000 Avignon, ☎ 90.85.46.03, ⇄ 90.85.97.32).* Restaurant at the front (lunch and dinner) and funky bar behind, this place attracts a sympathetic young crowd. Changing art exhibition every month.

■ Theatre Festival

For those who wish to sample the latest dance, musical and dramatic creations from around the world, some daring, some classic, then the *Festival d'Avignon* is for you. Created in 1947 by Jean Vilar, the Avignon festival attracts 120,000 people a year, from early July to early August. Advance programs are available as of mid-March, final programs, as of mid-May. *(Contact the festival office 8 bis, Rue de Mons, ☎ 90.82.67.08 for information or call ☎ 90.86.24.43 for bookings from mid-Jun).*

Since the 60s, an alternative event called le Festival Off (mainly young French theatre groups performing in the streets) has taken place at the same time. Programs are available from mid-May: send a SAE (16 F) to Avignon Public Off, BP 5 - 75521 Paris cedex 11 ☎ (1) 48.05.20.97.

Shopping

Les Halles *(Tue to Sun, 6 AM to 1 PM; Place Pie).* Modern, covered farmers market with local produce, meats and fish. Wonderful selection of seasonal fruits - cherries, apricots, plums and peaches freshly picked in the region. The perfect place to prepare a picnic - sliced meats, breads, cheeses, olives and wines are all available.

La Trapézienne *(Tue to Sun 7:30 AM to 8 PM; 22 Rue Saint Agricole, 84000 Avignon, ☎ 90.86.24.72)* Good quality pastry shop, selling local candy specialities, including *cailloux, calisson d'Aix*, plus savoury items including *fougasse crattelons*. Its speciality is *Gateau Trapézienne* (mousseline cream in a fine brioche).

Mouret Chapelier *(Tue to Sun 9:30 AM noon and 2:30 PM to 7 PM, Mon 2:30 PM to 7 PM; 20 Rue des Marchands, ☎ 90.85.39.38).* The only hat-maker in France classed as a Historical Monument for the Louis XVIth shop design.

L'Autre Côté (*10 AM to noon and 2 PM to 7 PM, closed Sun and Mon in low season, open Mon afternoon mid-Jun to late Sep, open Sun during Theatre Festival; 21 Place Crillon, 84000 Avignon,* ☎ *90.86.37.66,* ⇄ *90.27.05.97).* Quality reproductions of old Provençal pottery, in rich blue, green and yellow glazes. The charming owner Martine Fouga is helpful.

Hervé Baum (*Tue to Sat; 19 Rue Petite Fusterie, 84000 Avignon,* ☎ *90.86.37.66,* ⇄ *90.27.05.97).* Long-established antiques shop, one of the best in Avignon, includes objects for the garden and decorative items. A wonderful, personal selection by Baum, includes pieces from a few francs to few thousand francs. The owner also displays at Isle-sur-la Sorgue on weekends. Other antiques shops are found on Rue Petite Fusterie, parallel to Rue Joseph Vernet (for smart fashion shops).

La Memoire du Monde (*Mon to Sat 9 AM to 7 PM; 26 Rue Carnot and 16 Rue de la Bonneterie, 84000 Avignon,* ☎ *90.82.47.93).* Good selection of literature, theatre and travel books.

Droguerie - Vannerie (*10 AM to noon and 2 PM to 7 PM; closed Sun, Mon AM; 33 Rue Bonneterie, 84000 Avignon,* ☎ *90.86.13.66).* Bargain shop which sells Savon de Marseille from the only real soap manufacturer left producing this body and laundry shop. Beware of expensive imposters in trendy tourist shops elsewhere!

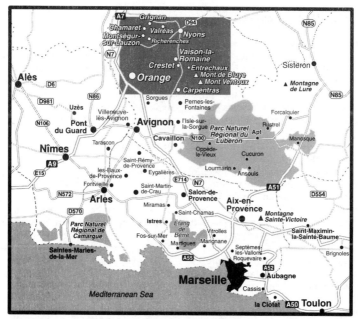

THE HAUT COMTAT VENAISSIN ★★

he area once known as the Comtat Venaissin covered most of the present-day Vaucluse department. The northern part of this scenic area is highly enjoyable for many visitors to Provence, for it provides a rich history, a varied landscape and many small towns to explore without the crowds of tourists.

The Comtat Venaissin grew during the popes' installation in Avignon, from 1305 to 1376, and during the reign of the anti-popes, known as the Great Schism, 1378 to 1409. Carpentras was purchased in 1320 and made capital of the county, a distinction held by Pernes-les-Fontaines since 968. Carpentras was later made the seat of the *États du Comtat*, similar to the *États de Provence*, which were local administrative assemblies.

Pope Jean XXII bought the rights to the town of Valréas with Richerences in 1344, and the towns of Visan (1344) and Grillon (1451) were added later. This explains why a small part of the northern Vaucluse, surrounded on all sides by the Drôme department, exists today as a small enclave. In 1348, Pope Clément VI bought Avignon from Queen Jeanne, but the city remained independent from the Comtat Venaissin. Much later, Louis XIV in 1662-1663 and in 1688-1689 and Louis XV between 1768 and 1774 occupied the region and tried to annex the Comtat Venaissin to France. It finally surrendered, along with Avignon, on September 14, 1791.

The area surrounding the town of Orange has its own unique history. Known as Arausio, the town was a

Roman military colony following Caesar's conquering of Provence in 50 BC. From 35 BC, a typical Roman city took shape, including roads, houses, shops, and monuments. Today, visitor's can still marvel at Orange's famous amphitheatre, triumphal arch and temple.

During the 15th century, this small enclave within the Comtat Venaissin became the Principauté d'Orange, or principality, having passed from the houses of Baux, to Chalon, to William of Nassau and Stathouder of the Netherlands in 1529. The principality enjoyed a number of privileges. It had an important university, and due to its liberal spirit, it harboured many protestants during the wars of religion. During the war with Holland and its leader William III of Nassau, Louis XIV occupied Orange (1662) and destroyed the citadel, its fortifications and ramparts. Today the Dutch Royal Family retains its historical name of Orange-Nassau.

 Finding Your Way Around

■ **By car**

The Upper Comtat Venaissin is serviced by a good road network. From Paris in the north and Avignon or Marseille in the south, the **N 7** highway passes through Orange, while the **A 7 - E 15** Autoroute du Soleil freeway passes right next to it. Vaison-la-Romaine is a good-sized town with a number of accommodation and eating choices, and is a practical starting point to discovering this entire area (though it is quiet in the off-season). The scenic Dentelles de Montmirail hills (including villages such as Séguret and le Barroux) and Mont Ventoux are easy drives

away. Vaison-la-Romaine is at the crossroads of the **D 975** and **D 977** (from Orange) and the **D 938** from Carpentras. Renting a car in Avignon or Marseille is the most practical way to explore the smaller villages which are inaccessible by rail.

■ **By train**

Gare SNCF
Avenue Fréderic Mistral
☎ 90.34.17.82
Daily service between Avignon and Orange; transfer at Avignon for connections to larger centres including Aix-en-Provence, Arles and Marseille.

■ **By bus**

Gare Routière
Cours Pourtoules
Regular, though infrequent service to the surrounding area.

 Practical Information

■ **Tourist Offices**

Orange
5 Cours Aristide Briand
84100 Orange
☎ 90.34.70.88 ⇄ 90.34.99.62
(A tourist office annex is open Apr to Sep at Place des Frères Mounet.)

Vaison-la-Romaine
Place du Chanoine Sautel
84110 Vaison-la-Romaine
☎ 90.36.02.11

Carpentras
170 Allée Jean-Jaurés
84200 Carpentras
☎ 90.63.00.78 ⇄ 90.60.41.02

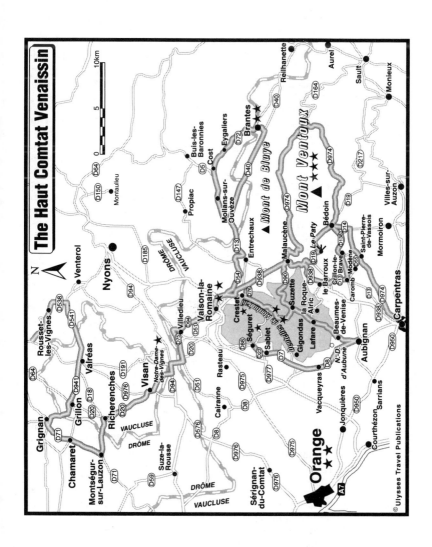

The Haut Comtat Venaissin

© Ulysses Travel Publications

Exploring

■ **Orange** ★★

Faced with so many interesting sites and villages to explore in Provence, Orange is sometimes pushed aside. A couple of hours are usually all that are awarded this town of 28,000 inhabitants — a glimpse of the Roman Théâtre Antique and a drive past the Arc de Triomphe and then on to more exciting things. While Orange admittedly lacks the elegance of Avignon and Aix, the character of Marseille or the breathtaking scenery of the Luberon hills, the town does hold unexpected pleasures and a longer visit is merited. It possesses charming small squares, with animated cafes under the leafy shade of tall plane trees, a pleasant old town with narrow streets and a lively Provençal market every Thursday. Live musical performances (opera, recitals, jazz and rock), as well as films on a giant screen, take place all summer long at the open-air Théâtre Antique and should not be missed.

The **Théâtre Antique** ★★★ *(adults 20F, reduced rate 20 F, includes admission to the Musée d'Orange; Apr 1 to Oct 4 open everyday 9 AM to 6:30 PM; Oct 5 to Mar 31 open everyday 9 AM to noon and 1:30 PM to 5 PM; closed Dec 25 and Jan 1)*, Orange's most famous monument, is the only Roman theatre in Europe with its stage wall intact. It dates from the early first century AD, when a great variety of performances took place, uniquely during the daytime. From the exterior, the great wall is 103 m long and 37 m high. Inside, the stage wall has five tiers, with stage supports on the upper two levels and decoration on the others.

If you think the statue of the Emperor Augustus above the Porte Royale, or royal doorway looks reconstructed, you're right. It was found during excavations of the theatre in 1931, and though all its bits and pieces were stuck together it somehow looks off-balance. The stage, 61.2 m long and 13.2 m wide, was made of wood. It once had a decorated roof. During Roman times, the privileged class sat on movable seats on each side of the stage in an area known as the *parascenia*. Behind them, 9,000 spectators sat on the stone tiers (the *cavea*) which is divided in three parts and linked by underground galleries with large entrances. The ruins of a temple and one of only three existing Roman gymnasiums in the world are found to one side of the theatre.

Nowadays, when visiting Orange during the summer months, try to catch one of the evening performances in the theatre and hear how fine the acoustics really are. Thank goodness Louis XIV was sensitive enough to preserve the stage wall which he called "the prettiest wall in my kingdom" when he gave orders to destroy Orange's citadel and ramparts nearby, in the 17th century.

Along with the theatre, the **Arc de Triomphe** ★★, or triumphal arch, built between 21 and 26 AD, is classed by UNESCO as a historical monument. It does not actually commemorate any military triumph, but instead once marked the entrance to the Roman town of Arausio (now Orange) and testifies to the great deeds of the soldiers of the 2nd legion who founded it in 36 BC. The north side of the three-arched monument is the best preserved — on it can be found panels of weapons, naval spoils, objects of worship and engraved inscriptions. The

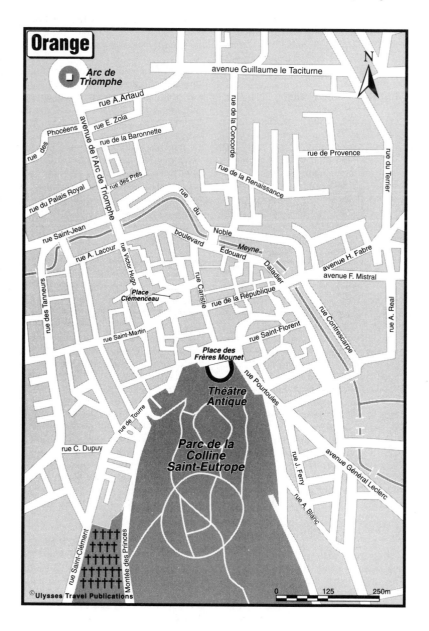

Orange

Arc de Triomphe

avenue Guillaume le Taciturne

rue A.Artaud

rue E. Zola

rue des Phocéens

avenue de l'Arc de Triomphe

rue de la Baronnette

rue de la Concorde

rue de Provence

rue du Terrier

rue du Palais Royal

rue des Prés

rue de la Renaissance

rue Saint-Jean

rue du Noble

rue A. Lacour

rue Victor Hugo

boulevard Édouard Daladier

Meyne

avenue H. Fabre

avenue F. Mistral

rue des Tanneurs

Place Clémenceau

rue Cariste

rue de la République

rue Contrescarpe

rue A. Real

rue Saint-Martin

rue Saint-Florent

Place des Frères Mounet

rue de Tourre

Théâtre Antique

rue Pourtoules

rue C. Dupuy

Parc de la Colline Saint-Eutrope

rue J. Ferry

avenue Général Leclerc

rue A. Blanc

rue Saint-Clément

Montée des Princes

0   125   250m

© Ulysses Travel Publications

rectangular mass is 19.57 m x 8.5 m x 19.21 m and the central arch is eight metres high. Underneath the vaulted roof, notice the ceiling decorated with hexagonal boxes.

■ Châteauneuf-du-Pape

Everyone appreciates a summer home, even popes. During his stay in Avignon in the 14th century, Pope Jean XXII had a château built in this community which henceforward was called Châteauneuf. Subsequent popes had vines planted in the pebbly land surrounding their getaway residence and a quite drinkable wine was made. Due to the popes' and their prelates' demanding tastes, a great wine was born. The area's wine first received attention outside of the area in the 18th century. It has been regarded as one of the world's great wines since 1929, when it was granted the title *appellation d'origine contrôlée* Châteauneuf-du-Pape which places severe procedures on the growing and production. Nowadays nearly seven million bottles, about half of the total production, are exported. Châteauneuf-du-Pape is the only French wine authorized to be made from 13 different types of grapes *(for wine festivals see p 94; details about Châteauneuf-du-Pape vineyards, visits and tastings, contact Comité de Promotion des Vins de Châteauneuf-du-pape, 12 Avenue Louis Pasteur, 84230 Châteauneuf-du-Pape, ☎ 90.83.72.21, ⇄ 90.83.70.01).*

■ Vaison-la-Romaine ★★

Visitors get three towns for the price of one when visiting Vaison-la-Romaine. This charming place of great archaeological importance is divided by the Ouvèze river — on the right bank lies the old Roman site as well as modern-day Vaison, while on the left

bank, built up against a rocky hillside, is the *Haute Ville*, or upper town, dating from the Middle Ages.

The Celt tribe known as the Voconces inhabited the area since the Iron Age, and a settlement called Vasio on the spot of present day Vaison became an administrative and political capital. Following the occupation of Provence by the Romans in the first century BC, the Voconces became their allies after local wars (58-51 BC). During the first century AD, Vaison became a well-structured Roman town, with shops, a theatre, residential streets, and water arriving from a nearby aqueduct.

After Provence was divided in 1125, Vaison belonged to Raymond V, Count of Toulouse. He promptly built a château on the right bank hillside overlooking the Ouvèze. During the 13th century, following the Wars of Religion, the population abandoned the plain and moved to the Haute-Ville (just below the château), where they were protected from invaders. By the 17th century, times became relatively more peaceful, and Vaison's citizens returned to the lower plain across the Ouvèze. Although records of Vaison-la-Romaine's reconstruction date as far back as the 15th century, it wasn't until 1848 that the town received state financing for archaeological work. Serious excavations began in 1907 (the Puymin area) and in 1934 (the Villasse area).

Remarkably the archaeological sites of the **Roman Cities - Puymin ★★ and Villasse ★** *(adults 34 F, children 12 F, students 20 F, combined ticket for both sites, plus the Musée d'Archéologie and the Cathédrale and Cloître; Jun to Aug, open everyday 9 AM to 12:30 PM and 2 PM to 6:45 PM; Mar to May,*

Sep and Oct, open everyday 9:30 AM to 12:30 PM and 2 PM to 5:45 PM; Nov to Feb, Wed to Mon 10 AM to noon and 2 PM to 4:30 PM, closed Tue, closed Dec 25 and Jan 1) were only discovered this century and they provide a clue as to why the Roman town of Vasio was nicknamed *urbs opulentissima*, or very opulent city. As these two areas are ruins, it is important to pick up a descriptive map at the tourist office beforehand in order to fully explore the area. Puymin *(opposite the tourist office, entrance at the corner of Rue Burrhus and Rue Bernard Noël)* is more interesting since the remains of the buildings are in better shape allowing the complexity of Roman life to unfold before your eyes.

The first area after entering Puymin is the villa of the wealthy Massii family, note the inner courtyard, reception rooms, kitchen and lavatories. A large part of the house is still buried underneath the modern city - it is thought to have covered 2,000 m^2. Following this was a colonnaded promenade, called Pompeii's Portico, leading to a series of narrow houses which were rented at the time. Behind the wooded area is the **Musée d'Archéologie**, an archaeological museum which holds many objects (jewellery, tools, ceramics), friezes and most noteworthy, marble statues of the emperors Claude, Domitien, Hadrian, and the latter's wife, Sabine, all found on the site.

Beyond the museum, along a rising pathway, is the first century AD **Roman theatre**. Similar in design to the theatre at Orange, this one is smaller and has lost its stage wall. About 7,000 spectators could sit here, on 32 rows of seating, split by three principal stairways. It has been heavily reconstructed, and is now the site of theatrical and musical performances in the evening during the summer months (contact the tourist office for a *Les Nuits d'Été* program).

The Villasse area (entrance opposite the Place Burrhus parking lot, by the Tourist Office) consists of the ruins of two large residences (House of the Dolphin, House of the Silver Bust) divided by the so-called Colonnade Road and Road of Shops, and a public hot springs bath.

Cathédrale   Notre-Dame-de-Nazareth and **Cloître ★** *(same hours as the Roman ruins, except closed Oct to Apr, noon to 2 PM)*. The cathedral and cloister were completely rebuilt in the 12th and 13th centuries on the site of a 6th century church. Vaison's cathedral is a marvellous example of Provençal Romanesque architecture. From the exterior, standing in front of the east apse, you'll notice the monument actually rests upon remains (column drums, pieces of entablature) of an original Gallo-Roman basilica. The square bell-tower is oddly off-centre. Inside, six bays and aisles are supported by square pillars. The nave's cylindrical vaulted ceiling and cupola above the last bay were 12th century additions. Note the marble altars — the one in the north apse is thought to be 6th century.

Through a separate entrance on the north side, visit the pretty barrel-vaulted cloister. Like the cathedral, it too was completed between 1150-1160 and restored at the end of the 14th century. The columns supporting the arches facing the interior courtyard are remarkably sculpted; interesting artifacts (sarcophagus, inscriptions in stone, statues) line the surrounding galleries.

People intrigued by ecclesiastical architecture will want to take the extra trouble to visit the **Chapelle Saint-Que-nin** *(visit only by prior arrangement with the tourist office; from Avenue Général de Gaulle, turn left onto Avenue Saint-Quenin, 500 m on the left)*. Built during the second half of the 12th century in the Provençal Roman-esque style, the nave was recon-structed between 1630 and 1636. Its curious feature is the unusual triangular apse and its fine decoration (fluted half columns with Corinthian capitals), notably the joyful frieze. Saint-Quenin was a Vaison bishop in the 6th century.

The **Pont Romain** is a Roman bridge linking the Grand Rue to the upper town. Nearly 2,000 years old, the modest bridge is 17 m wide and seven metres high. Its parapet was ripped apart during a flash flood in 1616, and rebuilt afterwards. The embankment was destroyed by a German bomb in 1944 and the bridge's vault shaken. The flood of September 1992 destroyed the parapet a second time. Following renovations costing 2.5 mil-lion francs the bridge is now open again. Locals remark that it is slimmer — the architects followed the bridge's original design.

The **Haute Ville** ★★, or upper town can be reached by turning right after cross-ing the Roman bridge and entering by a ramp on the left. By car, cross the Ouvèze by the Pont Neuf, and follow signs indicating the parking lot for the Château. The *Vaissonnais* moved from the right bank of the Ouvèze to the upper town next to the Château during the 13th century, when they were threatened by ruthless invaders. A walk through the narrow, cobble-stone streets (most prohibited to cars), is like stepping back in time. Coming from the Roman bridge, look for the **Place des Poids**. The only real remains of 14th century architecture are sections of

rampart walls and two arched gates. Note the beautiful façades of the houses, which date from the 16th to the 18th centuries and the belfry with the 17th century wrought-iron cage.

The pretty **Place du Vieux Marché** with its plane trees, fountain and small cafe, was the location for a weekly market which lasted from 1483 through to the 19th century. Along the Rue de l'Eveché visitors will discover the deteriorating Palais Épiscopale, Hôtel de Taulignan, the Chapelle Pénitents-Blancs and the Hôtel Fabre de Saint-Véran. The church at the end of the Rue de l'Église (the interior is not open to the public) was built in 1464, with later additions. Good views can be had from the tiny, attractive square in front of the church.

The Upper Town is dominated by the ruins of the Château built by the Count of Toulouse, Raymond V, in the late 12th century (access by foot only, a steep climb). It became a papal fortress when the Comtat Venaissin passed into the hands of the popes in 1274. From the 16th century onwards, its was restored for comfort, yet was aban-doned in 1791 during the Revolution. The Château's prime interest today are the fine views over Vaison-la-Romaine and the region to be had from the foot of the crumbling monument (visitors are not permittes inside.)

■ The Dentelles de Montmirail ★★

This pretty hill range with deep valleys southeast of Vaison-la-Romain provides some of the prettiest scenery in all of Provence, equal in beauty to the Luberon. The jagged, limestone rock formations with pointed peaks indeed resemble lace fabric (hence the name in French, *dentelle* means lace). Many charming villages appear to miraculously hang from the sides of rocky cliffs, and the narrow roads are perfumed with the sweet smells of the yellow *genêt* (gorse or woodwaxen), aromatic plants and fresh pine trees. Late spring and early summer are particularly enjoyable when the fruit trees and flowers blossom. An entire day or more could be spent simply touring the back-roads, stopping at a few of the picturesque villages. Alternatively, the Dentelles de Montmirail is a walker's paradise (the Vaison-la- Romaine tourist office will supply information and maps for hikers). The highest point is Mont Saint-Amand (734 m), and most of the many signposted pathways are not too taxing.

Suggested Route:

From Vaison-la-Romaine, head south on the D 938 (direction Carpentras) for about five km. Turn right onto the D 76 to visit the charming, untouched village of **Crestet ★**. Here you'll find the pretty Église Saint-Sauveur dating back to the 11th century (with a working fountain dating from 1787 in front), a private château (belonging to the bishops of Vaison-la-Romaine until the Revolution), and some wonderful views. Near the spot where you leave your car is an old municipal covered wash basin, with a tinkling drainage gutter running past stone steps and beautiful wild flowers. Higher up a few pedestrian streets twist and turn. The front doors of homes meet the road, some seem abandoned. There are no shops, cafes or businesses. A local historian, Charley Schmitt, has written a guide about the village's history *Mieux Connaitre Crestet, Village Vauclusien* which is available for 45 F in local bookshops and from the author's home which is sign-posted on the road.

Return to the D 938, and turn right onto the D 90 at **Malaucène** (10 km), whose busy principal road is bordered with plane trees. The stretch of the D 90 road between Malaucène and Beaumes-de-Venise, passing by Suzette, as well as the very narrow D 90A to La Roque Alric, must be one of the most beautiful routes in Provence. Wonderful views of the Dentelles and its vineyards greet you at every turn (as does the heady citrus perfume of wild thyme, and more *genêt* and pine trees).

At **Suzette** you'll find an attractive church and a fine view over the rolling hills. If you've braved the twisted D 90A, you'll discover the small community of **La Roque Alric** perched on the cliff-side, with a wooden cross high up on the top of the hill. Back on the D 90, you'll pass by **Beaumes-de-Venise**. The excellent sweet Muscat *vin doux* or dessert wine is produced from the grapes grown in the neighbouring sun-blessed vineyards.

Now follow the D 81, leading onto the D 8 north towards Vacqueyras. Here you will pass the 9th - 10th century Chapelle Notre-Dame d'Aubane. Past Vacqueyras, turn right onto the D 7 for **Gigondas**. The area produces the celebrated red Côtes du Rhône Cru or vintage Gigondas wine, considered the finest in the area. Numerous properties as well as a co-operative are open for tasting *(information from the tourist office, Place du Portail, 84190 Gigondas, ☎ 90.65.85.46)*. The town dates from the Middle Ages. It has the ruins of a château and good views from the church terrace looking over the impressive landscape. Inside the Église Saint-Catherine (11th century) are three interesting statues in gilded wood — the parish patron saints Cosme and

Damien, and the Notre Dame des Pallières.

Carrying on north on the D 7, you'll hit the village of **Sablet**, calm and peaceful, and taking the road on the right, (D 23) the popular town of **Séguret ★**. It is a centre for craftsmen and artists, and its pretty narrow cobbled streets, 12th century church, belfry (14th century) and Mascarons Fountain are well looked after. However, its official designation (along with a number of other towns) as "the prettiest village in France" means it is crowded on weekends and during the summer. A number of tourist shops and the special parking lot for cars and buses below the town attest to Séguret's popularity with visitors, so it is best to visit during the week. From Séguret take the D 88 north, and connect with the D 977 back to Vaison-la-Romaine.

■ Mont Ventoux ★★★

A day trip by car to the top of this mountain (the highest in Provence, 1912 metres) is for all those who enjoy spectacular views. From Vaison-la-Romaine, take the D 938 south (direction Carpentras) to Malaucène. In the village, turn left at the road indicating D 974 Mont Ventoux. The D 974 is a well-kept, scenic (naturally it is steep and twisted at times!) road (26 km) leading directly to the summit from the north face. **Commanding views ★★★** as far as the Alps to the northeast and Marseille to the south can be had from the top. Two viewing tables explain the important geographical sites, and a weather station, observatory, ugly television antenna and small chapel are nearby. Please note: fog and heat haze can diminish the view, plus heavy winds mean it can be quite cool at the summit. The upper part of the D 974 is closed in bad weather, (such as the possibility of heavy snow in the winter).

Continuing on the D 974 from the summit, the pine-bordered road is dotted with a few picnic tables and a **ski station** *(for information about ski conditions, rentals and prices telephone the Chalet d'Accueil du Mont Ventoux ☎ 90.63.49.44)*. Near the bottom scenes of civilization appear again - restaurants, cafes and inns. **Bédoin** is a pretty village with tree-shaded roads and a Jesuit church from the early 18th century.

The D 19 from Bédoin passes a panoramic stop called Le Paty and connects with the D 938 taking you north to Vaison-la-Romaine or south to Carpentras. An alternative route which is worthwhile taking is the small D 138 which can be reached by passing through the centre of Bédoin and turning right, in a westwards direction, towards the hilltop town of **Crillon-le-Brave**. This village is named after a soldier who served under Henri IV, who was born at Murs, lived in Avignon and had a château here. Nowadays the village has come alive thanks to a four-star country inn, the Hostellerie de Crillon-le-Brave (see p 91), owned by a Canadian group, and a very good simple restaurant at its base. Remains of ramparts and the Église Saint-Romain (12th to 14th centuries) are the sole interest here, apart from the wonderful views.

A confusing series of roads takes you back to the D 938 and the town of **Le Barroux**. Try following the D 138 south from Crillon-le-Brave, and turn right onto the D 55 leading you to the hamlets of St-Pierre-de-Vassols, Modène and then Caromb. The D 55, D 21 and better yet D 13 (north) lead to the D 938. The massive fortress-like Le

Barroux **Château** *(adults 20 F, reduced fare 10 F; May, Jun and Oct, open everyday 2:30 PM to 7 PM; Jul to Sep, open everyday 10 AM to 7 PM;* ☎ *90.62.35.21)* dominates the landscape. Built in the 12th century and rebuilt in the 16th, the château fell into ruins after the revolution. After restoration work began in 1929, it was burnt by the German army in 1944. The view and the château's interesting design are worth noting, though as it is under restoration again, there is little in the way of furniture or objects inside.

■ **Mont Bluye ★**

A second excursion from Vaison-la-Romaine, around the scenic Mont Bluye and the Toulourenc River valley is recommended, as it is an area of great natural beauty. Unspoilt by man, it is a chance to visit more charming villages perched on hillsides amongst a rugged landscape. Three kilometres south of Vaison on the D 938 (direction Carpentras), turn left onto the D 54 to **Entrechaux** where there is the 10th century Chapelle Notre-Dame-de-Nazareth, 9th century Chapelle Saint-André and 11th century Chapelle Saint-Laurent, *(Tourist Office Place du Marché,* ☎ *90.65.63.95)*.

Take the D 13 through Entrechaux, and take note that as you cross the Toulourenc River and into the Drôme department the road becomes the D 5. Carry on through Mollans-sur-Ouvèze, following the D 5 for six kilometres in the direction of Buis-les-Barronies, but turn right on the smaller D 72 road at the tiny hamlet of Cost. The scenic D 72 leads eastward past Eygaliers, (a village known for its production of *tilleul*, lime/linden), and rises sharply, as you approach Brantes.

Perched 600 metres high on a craggy cliff, **Brantes ★★** seems like a village forgotten by time. One basic hostelry greets visitors, otherwise there are no businesses. A couple of narrow streets (access by foot only) lead to a small **chapel ★** which faces the valley. Like a hidden jewel box, it is adorned with freshly painted trompe-l'oeil arches, oil paintings, three hanging copper candelabra and statuary. Nearby, is the pottery workshop of Jaap Wieman and Martine Gilles. The husband and wife team have produced lovely earthenware (floral and fruit patterns in pink, yellow and pale blue, for example) here for 20 years and now supply a shop in Paris. A small showroom *(call ahead:* ☎ *72.28.03.37,* ⇄ *75.28.18.61)* is open to the public - a dessert plate is a mere 160 F but you can spend much more!

Twist down the D 136 from Brantes and turn right onto the D 40 (west). This is a delightful **16 kilometre valley drive ★** along the winding tree-lined banks of the Toulourenc. Locals swim and fish for trout in the river; the peace and quiet of the area is perfect for cycling, walking and horseback riding. You have now circled back and will pick up the D 5 again. Turn left, towards Entrechaux and the D 938 for Vaison-la-Romaine or Carpentras.

■ **The Enclave des Papes ★**

This small parcel of land seemingly inserted in the Drôme north of Vaison-la-Romaine is in fact part of the Vaucluse. The principal city of Valréas was bought from the king of France by Pope Jean XXII in the 14th century. The area remained papal territory, part of the Comtat Venaissin, until formation of departments at the time of the Revolution in 1791. The four communities of Valréas, Richerences, Visan and

Grillon agreed to remain loyal to their Provençal origins and joined the Vaucluse. Today, the area's economy is supported by light industry, sheep farming, agriculture (notably tomatoes, melons, asparagus), very good Côtes du Rhône wine and in certain wooded areas that typically French delicacy — truffles.

From Vaison-la-Romaine, take the D 51 north and after two kilometres turn right onto the D 94 for **Villedieu** (another four kilometres). This sleepy village of 550 people has a pretty shaded square with large plane trees and a fountain (drinks and coffee from the Bar du Centre are served here). On foot, cross through the impressive stone gate in the old rampart wall and walk up to the 12th century church. Its simple interior features a small circular glass window above the altar with a luminescent red cross, and a couple of oil paintings (one from the 17th century portrays a particularly menacing devil).

Driving through Villedieu, take the D 75 which becomes the D 51 to the D 20. Follow the D 20 into the popes' enclave (the road turns left and for a few hundred metres becomes the D 94, take the first right to regain the D 20). Just before the town of Visan, turn right down a small road which is signposted Notre-Dame des Vignes. Hidden amongst fir trees stands a remarkable chapel - an oasis of ecclesiastical tranquility in the middle of nature. Fully-restored and classified as a historical monument by the French state, **Chapelle Notre-Dame des Vignes ★** dates from the 13th century. The vaults were restored in the 17th century with painted trompe-l'oeil florettes, the newly-restored wood-panels of the altar glisten with gold leaf. The chapel has been a site of hermitage for nuns since 1490. It was closed earlier this century, but is now taken care of by two nuns. Mass is held every Friday at 6 PM during the summer, and a popular retreat takes place every Sep. 8. *(Tue, Thu to Sat, 10 AM to 11:30 AM and 3 PM to 6 PM, Wed 3 PM to 5:30 PM, Sun 3 PM to 6 PM, closed Mon, closes at 5 PM in winter).*

Carry on the D 20 for 10 kilometres, passing through Visan, until you reach **Richerenches.** Note the stone ramparts which still surround the old part of the city, and particularly the heavy gate studded with iron nails and the interesting square clock tower above. An important truffle market takes place here Saturday mornings from November to March.

At the end of the town, turn left onto the D 18 (which becomes D 71B) for **Montségur-sur-Lauzon.** Officially located in the Drôme, this village of 800 people is mentioned here because on the hilltop in the centre of Montségur-sur-Luzon is a curious primitive **chapel,** (dating from 958) next to the ruins of a 12th century château. The square belfry is topped by an unusual feature — a small cupola in stone. Inside, note the strange tank-like structure discovered in the wall on the west side of the original 10th century nave. Historians don't know if it was a druid altar, sacrificial tomb or primitive baptismal font. Skeletons were found under the heavy stones covering the floor — a reminder that up until the Revolution, parishioners were buried in the church upon request. The Montségur-sur-Lauzon chapel is open for exhibitions, concerts and visits, throughout the year, generally in the afternoons *(check first with the Tourist Office at Grignan,* ☎ *75.46.56.75).*

Take the D 71 north, past Chamaret to **Grignan.** Again, we're officially in the

Drôme, but you should not miss a chance to visit one of the finest chateaux in Provence. Grignan is a lively town with a bank, post office, cafes and businesses which encircle the elevated château and 16th century church (note the 17th century retable and organ). Unlike so many chateaux in the region, the **Château de Grignan** has been beautifully restored and possesses a fine collection of period furniture, paintings and *objets d'art (adults 25 F, reduced rate 15 F, includes obligatory guided visit; open everyday 9:30 AM to 11:30 AM and 2 PM to 5:30 PM; Jul and Aug until 6 PM; Nov to Mar closed Tue, closed Dec. 25 and Jan. 1;* ☎ *75.46.51.56).*

From Grignan, take the D 941 to Grillon and Valréas. The former capital of the popes' enclave, **Valréas** is today its principal city *(Tourist Office, Place A. Briand, 84600 Valréas,* ☎ *90.35.04.71).* Housing the *Hôtel de Ville,* or city hall, the **Château de Simiane** ★ is the former residence of the grandchild of Madame Sévigné. It was restored by her husband, Louis de Simiane, in the early 18th century and today you may visit the reception rooms, library and archives and admire its paintings and furniture *(free admission, Sep to Jun with guided visit, Mon to Sat 3 PM to 5 PM; adults 20 F, Jul and Aug, including two-hour guided visit of the town and its monuments; Wed to Mon 10 AM to noon and 3 PM to 7 PM; Place A. Briand,* ☎ *90.35.00.45).*

The **Église Notre Dame de Nazareth** ★ *(open everyday 10 AM to noon and 2 PM to 6 PM)* appears to have been built upon a 11th century church and transformed in the 15th century.

■ **Carpentras**

Carpentras lies in the flat, fertile land known as the Comtat plain, equidistant from Vaison-la-Romaine (28 km), Orange (24 km) and Avignon (23 km). It has always been a market town, and has suffered numerous invasions and was occupied many times. Greeks and Phocaeans came here to buy local products including wheat, honey, sheep and goats. It was a colony under Julius Caesar (the Roman commemorative arch at the south end of the city still remains intact). Ramparts were constructed during the period of invasions and the bishops sought refuge on the high ground at Venasque. Burgundians, Ostrogoths and Franks successively occupied Carpentras until the 12th century when the region was controlled by the Count of Toulouse.

It became part of the newly created papal territory Comtat Venaissin in 1229. For one hundred years, local unions and bishops disputed for control of the city. It became the capital of the Comtat in 1320, and a second ring of ramparts was built to keep out pillagers. Capentras had a period of relative prosperity during the 17th and 18th centuries, during which time many public buildings were restored and private *hôtels particuliers* built. A sizeable ghetto harbouring Jews who fled to this papal land following persecution in France in the 14th century existed until the 19th century.

The **Porte d'Orange** ★, or Orange Gate was built when Pope Innocent VI, realising that the old Roman ramparts were too slender, called for a new stone defensive wall to surround Carpentras (1357 to 1379). Most of it was destroyed in the 19th century, but this heavy gate still remains.

Cathédrale Saint-Siffrein ★ *(Place Générale de Gaulle, ☎ 90.63.08.33)* was built on the site of a 12th century romanesque cathedral, and shows a diversity of architectural influences owing to the fact that it was built over a span of 100 years (1405-1519). The ensemble is essentially late southern Gothic. A striking *Glory* in gilded wood by the famous local sculptor Jacques Bernus (1650-1728) is located in the chancel. Note the delicate wrought iron railing with eight candle braces on the nave balcony which leads to the bishops' apartments. The elaborate Flamboyant Gothic sculpted south entrance is called the *Porte Juive*, or Jewish door, because it was used by Jews who had converted to Catholicism.

The **Arc Romain ★** *(Place d'Inguimbert)*, or Roman arch was built during Augustus' reign in the 1st century AD to commemorate the Roman victory over the barbarians. The east side facing the Palais de Justice (courthouse) represents two chained prisoners. It is only Roman ruin left in Carpentras.

The **Musée Comtadin-Duplessis ★** *(adults 30 F, reduced fare 20 F, includes all four museums; Nov to Mar 10 AM to noon and 2 PM to 4 PM; Apr to Oct 10 AM to noon and 2 PM to 6 p.m; enter by the Bibliothèque Inguimbertine 234 Bd Albin-Durand, ☎ 90.63.04.92)* houses two inviting museum collections in a pleasant 18th century *hôtel particulier*, with garden. The Comtadin museum (ground floor) presents an important collection of local folklore, including furniture and unusual items such as bird decoys, cattle bells

and figures. The Duplessis museum (first floor) has oil paintings (14th to 16th century) of local figures, including canvases by the Carpentras native Joseph Duplessis (painter to Louis XIV) and some period furniture.

The **Synagogue ★★** *(Mon to Thu 10 AM to noon and 3 PM to 5 PM, Fri 10 AM to noon and 3 PM to 4 PM, closed during holidays; Place de la Mairie, ☎ 90.63.39.97)*. Though the Place de la Juiverie was almost entirely destroyed in the 19th century, the synagogue has kept most of its original components. Located in the centre of the old *carrière*, the synagogue was built between 1741 and 1743 by architect Antoine d'Allemand. Its facade does not differ from those of neighbouring houses because of a very strict regulation prohibiting all exterior decoration and too large dimensions. The lower medieval part where the *mikva* and the bakehouse are situated has a monumental staircase leading to the worship hall. This place of worship has two levels, the assembly hall with its tabernacle, and the platform gallery with the *tebah*, or officiant's gallery.

Inside the 18th century **Hôtel-Dieu ★** *(10 F; Mon, Wed and Thu 9 AM to 11:30 AM; Place Aristide-Briand, ☎ 90.63.10.72)*, or hospital, hides a pharmacy dating from 1762 which is still completely intact. Note the painted panelling by Duplessis, the remarkable collection of earthenware jars (from Italy, Montpellier and Moustiers), and some brass and glass containers. Also visit the chapel and grand staircase. Let's hope that this is the only hospital visit during your trip to Provence.

Outdoor Activities

 Hiking

The Comtat Venaissin region is ideal terrain for walking and hiking. The most remarkable walks are found in the beautiful hills of the Dentelles de Montmirail. Serious hikers will be thrilled with the well-marked trail GR 4 which winds through this area, past Crestet, Séguret and Gigondas. At least three days is suggested to complete the entire circuit of 55 km. For a guidebook and details, contact the hiking association:

Cîmes et Sentiers
Vaison-la-Romaine
☎ 90.36.02.11

The tourist office in Vaison-la-Romaine publishes a very good guide in French called *Inventaire des Chemins et Drailles du Massif des Dentelles de Montmirail* which describes the trails of the Dentelles de Montmirail.

Several groups arrange guided walks through the hills of the Dentelles de Montmirail, as well as in the Mont Ventoux area:

Vaison-la-Romaine
Rando-Ventoux
Centre Régional de la Randonnée
Buisson
☎ 90.28.95.61

 Horseback Riding

Orange
École du 1er REC
Route du Parc
☎ 90.51.63.85

This riding school arranges accompanied horseback riding tours of the area.

Vaison-la-Romaine
Rando-Ventoux
Centre Régional de la Randonnée
Buisson
☎ 90.28.95.61
This group arranges guided tours on horseback through the hills of the Dentelles de Montmirail, as well as in the Mont Ventoux area.

Le Crestet
Centre Équestre "Les Voconces"
☎ 90.36.24.46

Carpentras
Ranch de l'Etalon Blan
Chemin de Sève
Entraigues
☎ 90.83.17.68
Tours on horseback are arranged at this ranch, which is also a pony-breeding centre.

 Mountainbiking

Orange
Le Club de Cyclotourisme
48 cours Aristide Briand
☎ 90.34.08.77
This association organizes bike tours of the area every Saturday afternoon.

Gigondas
Détroit Evasion Sportive
Eric Neuville
☎ 90.36.03.57
This association rents mountain bikes, and upon demand organizes guided bike tours of the Dentelles de Montmirail.

Accommodation

■ **Orange**

Hôtel Arcotel *(170 F without shower, 220 F with shower, bkfst 25 F; ☎, pb in some rooms; 8 Place aux Herbes, 84100 Orange, ☎ 90.34.09.23, ⇄ 90.51.61.12)* Excellent location on a charming square with a large plane tree. The 19 rooms in this old building are modern, though basic; each is well-equipped and clean. Parking is in the hotel's private courtyard.

Hôtel Le Glacier *(250-260 F, bkfst 30 F; ☎, pb, ≡, tv; 46 Cours Aristide Briand, 84100 Orange, ☎ 90.34.02.01, ⇄ 90.51.13.80)* The 30 tasteful, good-sized rooms are regularly renovated and each has a modern bathroom. Although the hotel is on a noisy road, all but two rooms face the back and look onto rooftops and neighbours' terraces. Le Glacier has been in the Cunha family for three generations and a friendly, warm welcome greets everyone.

Hôtel Arène *(310 F with shower, 410 F with bath, bkfst 40 F; pb or ps, ≡, ☎, tv; Place de Langes, 84100 Orange, ☎ 90.34.10.95, ⇄ 90.34.91.62)* Considered by many as the best hotel in Orange, each of the 30 rooms is eclectically furnished. Some have small balconies overlooking the pretty square (directly behind the *Hôtel de Ville*, city hall). The helpful owner, Danielle Coutel, offers personal advice on the best restaurants in the area, and is responsible for those little things that matter - home-made jams with breakfast, flowering window boxes outside. Private parking garage.

■ **Sérignan-du-Comtat**

Hostellerie du Vieux Château *(360-800 F, bkfst 40 F; pb, ☎; Route de Sainte-Cécile les Vignes, 84380 Sérignan-du-Comtat, ☎ 90.70.05.58, ⇄ 90.70.05.62, closed one week in late Dec and one week in Feb)* Large and fresh individually-decorated rooms, each with a modern bathroom, this inn is more expensive than similar establishments. Madame Truchot is very friendly and takes care of all your requirements. The excellent restaurant is popular at lunch and dinner-time with locals. This pretty village has a handsome 17th century *hôtel particulier* next to the 18th century Église Saint-Etienne, with a typical wrought-iron cage belfry housing three bells each dating from different periods. Serignan is eight kilometres north of Orange, at the crossroads of the D 43 and the D 976.

■ **Vaison-la-Romaine**

Hôtel Burrhus *(240-320 F, bkfst 29 F, garage 30 F; ps or pb, tv in some rooms, ☎; 2 Place Montfort, BP 93, 84110 Vaison-la-Romaine, ☎ 90.36.00.11, ⇄ 90.36.39.05, closed Nov. 15 to Dec. 15)* 24 simple and cheery rooms (10 at 250 F are brand new). A few look onto the square which can be noisy during the summer, but they have wonderful views of the *Haute Ville*, or upper town and its château. In good weather breakfast is taken outside on a shaded terrace. Excellent value and highly-recommended for the friendly welcome and down-to-earth charm of its young manager Laurence Gurly.

Hôtel de Lis *(350-580 F, bkfst 29 F, garage 30 F; pb, ☎, tv; same address and telephone as Hôtel Burrus above)* The more elegant sister hotel next to

Hôtel Burrus (check-in there first) has 10 large, newly-refurbished rooms decorated in understated good taste. Breakfast in your room or at the Burrus.

L'Éveché *(360-400 F, bkfst incl., no credit cards; ps, one room with pb, ☎, salon with tv; Rue de l'Éveché, 84110 Vaison-la-Romaine, ☎ 90.36.13.46, ⇄ 90.36.32.43)* In a restored 16th century house in the heart of the medieval *Haute Ville*, or upper town, this charming *chambres d'hôte* (bed and breakfast) has four comfortable rooms decorated in Provençal fabrics, with cool clay-tile floors, white walls and some antiques. Small modern bathrooms. Breakfast is taken on a private terrace full of flowers and plants, that overlooks the town. Nice touches include thick towels and locally-made perfumed soap. Pleasant welcome from the owners, Aude Verdier and her architect husband Jean-Loup. Popular with foreign tourists, so book early.

■ **Crillon-le-Brave**

Clos St. Vincent *(340-430 F, one cottage 700 F for two people, 800 F for four, no credit cards, bkfst incl.; ≈, salon with tv, 84410 Crillon-le-Brave, ☎ 90.65.93.36, ⇄ 90.12.81.46)* Highly-rated bed and breakfast with five tasteful rooms with wood beams in a fresh Provençal style. Thick feather duvets are provided in the winter, and cool cotton quilts in the summer. The smell of fresh rosemary scents Françoise Vazquez's home. A delicious breakfast of home-made jams and breads is served on one long table and evening meals are available if Françoise is notified a day ahead (130 F, wine and apéritif included). The high season is often booked months in advance.

Hostellerie de Crillon-le-Brave *(750-1150 F, bkfst 75 F, half-board* add 260 F per person; ≈, ℜ, pb, ☎, tv; Place de l'Eglise, 84410 Crillon-le-Brave, ☎ 90.65.61.61, ⇄ 90.65.62.86, closed Jan to Mar)* Five-year-old hotel with Canadian owners, entirely decorated in provençal prints (everything from the waiters' waistcoats to the wall coverings) with pretty reading rooms, professional service, and an un-stuffy attention to detail. Remarkable views of Mont Ventoux and the Dentelles de Montmirail. There are 20 rooms, plus apartment suites, in four different buildings. The very good but pricey restaurant has a wood burning fireplace for the cooler months and a lovely stone terrace surrounding a small fountain open in the summer (popular with smartly-dressed locals for Sunday lunch). The wonderful charm of an English country-inn.

■ **Villedieu**

Château de la Baude *(480 F, bkfst incl., no credit cards; ≈, tennis, ☎, tvc, billiard room; La Baude, 84110 Villedieu, ☎ 90.28.95.18, ⇄ 90.28.91.05)* After spending over two years restoring a 12th century fortress, Chantal and Gérard Monin opened this luxury bed and breakfast in 1994. Three rooms and two two-bedroom duplex suites *(680 F for four people)* are designed in a fresh Provençal style. Peaceful natural setting with a friendly welcome.

■ **Brantes**

L'Auberge *(100-125 F, bkfst 25 F; 84390 Brantes, ☎ 75.28.01.68)* Very basic rooms with wash basin only, (shower and toilet in the hall). Chosen for its friendly, end-of-the-world atmosphere, in this charming cliff-side village 600 metres above the Rivière Toulourenc valley. Lunch and dinner meals are available for an unbeatable 55 F and a special Sunday lunch for 110 F.

■ **Carpentras**

Hôtel du Fiacre *(195-370 F, bkfst 35 F, garage 30 F; ps or pb,* ☎, *tv; 153 Rue Vigne, 84200 Carpentras,* ☎ *90.63.03.15,* ⇄ *90.60.49.73)* is a serene 18th century *hôtel particulier* with a calm inner courtyard where breakfast is served. Helpful, smiling staff. Despite the old-fashioned decoration in the bedrooms, this is a good address in a town which otherwise doesn't have much reliable accommodation away from busy roads.

 **Restaurants**

■ **Orange**

La Roselière *($, menus at 80 F and 130 F; closed Wed and Thu PM; 4 Rue du Renoyer, 84100 Orange,* ☎ *90.34.50.42)* Rustic restaurant with a small shaded terrace on a quiet street corner, near the Cathédrale Notre-Dame and the Hôtel de Ville (city hall). Items are market fresh — grilled eggplant, fillet of fresh cod and roasted rabbit for example. Casual and friendly.

L'Aïgo Boulido *($-$$; 20 Place Sylvain, 84100 Orange,* ☎ *90.34.18.19)* Attractive Provençal decor complements this popular restaurant specializing in regional cuisine, such as chicken breast stuffed with *tapenade* (olive paste), half baby chicken prepared with an onion and orange-zest chutney, roast sea bass with macerated garlic cloves. Lunch menu 70 F, dinner 95 F and 120 F. Try to book a table in the front

room, or the terrace if you don't mind the noise of cars passing by on the street next to it.

Le Parvis *($$; 3 Cours Pourtoules, 84100 Orange,* ☎ *90.34.82.00)* One of Orange's fanciest restaurants, serving updated Provençal classics from its chef J. M. Berengier. Most dishes succeed, such as snails in filo pastry pockets with a tomato *coulis*, grilled red mullet, nougat with fresh strawberries, though portions are small and sauces are unexciting. Four menus from 98 F to 192 F are all good value. Service is efficient though reserved.

Le Garden *($$; 6 Place de Langes, 84100 Orange,* ☎ *90.34.64.47)* Well-situated restaurant on a peaceful square, a variety of local dishes are offered, including rabbit terrine, salmon on a bed of fennel with a dill sauce, fillet of pork seasoned with rosemary. Warm *amuse-gueules*, or tongue-teasers, start the meal, while home-made *tuilles* (curled wafer-thin almond cookies) accompany some desserts. Young waitresses try hard, but are not very professional. Menus at 140 F and 170 F.

Au Goût du Jour *($$; 9 Place aux Herbes, 84100 Orange,* ☎ *90.34.10.80)* Near the Théâtre Antique and facing the pretty Place aux Herbes, the fresh grey and apricot interior of this small (eight tables) restaurant welcomes guests with a well-considered menu. The long, thin slices of roast duck in its own juices with Provence honey is delicious, the rabbit pie with fresh herbs, tasty. Good value. The *Menu Surpris* includes four courses for 99 F.

■ **Vaison-la-Romaine**

Le Batleur *($-$$, set menu 118 F; closed Sun PM, Mon and Oct; 1 Place Théodore Aubanel, 84110 Vaison-la-Romaine, ☎ 90.36.28.04)* Tasty family cooking, includes its specialty rack of lamb with almond stuffing. Completely renovated after closing for six months following the tragic flooding of the nearby Rivière Ouvèze in 1992. Reasonably-priced wine list.

Auberge de la Bartavelle *($$; closed Mon; Place-sur-Auze, 8410 Vaison-la-Romaine, ☎ 90.36.02.16)* Chef Richard Cayrol's creative menu takes its inspiration from southwest France. Recently, the 120 F menu included ravioli in truffle juices, cod in a light saffron-flavoured cream sauce and warm chocolate terrine. Fresh herbs are used liberally, dishes are presented as a festival of colours. Menus at 120 F and 150 F are excellent value all things considered. A Ulysses favourite.

■ **Séguret**

Le Mesclun *($$; Apr to Sep open everyday, closed Mon in the off-season; Rue des Poternes)* A cosy restaurant down a pretty stone road in the village, serving delicious meals made from local products such as linguini pasta with herbs and chèvre, roast lamb with almonds and prunes, and for dessert, cheesecake with red berries. Menus at 145 F and 170 F. Outdoor terrace with magnificent panoramic views.

■ **Crillon-le-Brave**

Restaurant du Vieux Four *($-$$; set menus only: closed Mon and Jan to mid-Feb; 60 F weekday lunch, 110 F evenings and Sunday lunch, no credit cards, located in the village below the hotel, ☎ 90.12.81.39)* Country-style restaurant opened in 1993, replacing the village's bakery. Wonderful Provençal specialties include salmon fillet with leek and basil sauce, thyme-scented lamb, and grilled eggplant with a tomato *coulis*. Fresh desserts. Popular with locals who know good food and good value, so reserve ahead.

■ **Carpentras**

Blue Alexandra *($; Sun and Mon until 7 PM, open every day and night during Carpentras festival, last 2 wks in Jul; 20 Rue David Guillabert, 84200 Carpentras, ☎ 90.60.50.40)* Relaxing tearoom/cafe serving delicious home-made cakes (pear and raspberry crumble 21 F, chocolate cheesecake 21 F) and light lunches (salads, omelettes) with wine, cider and beer.

Le Marijo *($; 73 Rue Raspail, ☎ 90.60.42.65)* A cheery place welcoming locals, students and tourists who come for the reliable if unremarkable Provençal dishes such as fish soup, followed by either *pieds et paquets à la Marseille* (lambs' trotters and stuffed lambs' tripe) or steak with *tapenade* (olive paste) plus cheese or dessert for 80 F. Menu Gourmand 110 F.

Le Vert Galant *($$; lunch menu 95 F, dinner menu 170 F; closed Sat lunchtime and Sun; 12 Rue Clapies, 84200 Carpentras, ☎ 90.67.15.50)* A pleasant rustic decor (candles and dried flowers on the tables, oil paintings by local artists on the walls) greets customers at one of Carpentras' better restaurants. Elaborate selections include filet of roast duckling, kale stuffed with *escargots*, good cheeses and a sublime citrus fruit pie for dessert.

Entertainment

Sorry night-hawks, but the Upper Comtat Venaissin is a quiet place and visitors are hard-pressed to find evening entertainment in the area. Young revellers looking for nightclubs and cosmopolitan bars with the latest music will have to check out larger centres.

Evenings in this area are spent in restaurants and local cafes. Indeed, in most of the towns and villages, the liveliest event at night is a performance by a local musician in a bar or cafe. In these cases, flyers posted in the area announce dates and times.

The exception are the many local **festivals of culture and tradition** which take place every year, particularly in the summertime. The best known take place in the spectacular 2,000 year old outdoor Roman theatre in Orange: **Les Nuits d'Été du Théâtre Antique** ★ *(opera and ballet, plus classical and popular music, Aug,* ☎ *90.51.89.58)* and the **Chorégies d'Orange** ★ *(classical music and opera, Jul-Aug,* ☎ *90.34.24.24).*

Wine-lovers will enjoy the colourful festivities in Châteauneuf-du-Pape:
Le Saint-Marc named after the wine-makers protector, the Saint-Marc celebrations include a street procession, tastings and a dinner; Apr. 25;
La Fête de la Véraison ★ weekend-long activities drawing thousands of people to celebrate the moment when the grapes turn red and mature - tastings, local crafts, open-air entertainment, mass in Saint-Théordoric chapel; first weekend of Aug;

Le Ban des Vendages the day of the beginning of the grape harvest is announced publicly during a big supper; Sep.

Shopping

■ Vaison-la-Romaine

Lanchier-Avias *(Tue to Sun 7:30 AM to 8 PM, closed 1 PM to 1:30 PM in off-season; Place Montet,* ☎ *90.36.09.25)* Good pastry shop run by the same family for three generations. Specialties are *pavé* (fruit tart with almond paste and local honey), and *croquantes* (crunchy almond biscuits). Pastries are made with freshly-picked local fruits.

Lou Canesteou *(closed Sun PM and Mon; 10 Rue Raspail, 84110 Vaison-la-Romaine,* ☎ *90.36.31.30)* Vaison's finest cheese shop, offering a good selection of locally-made chèvre including *Banon* (wrapped in oak leaves), *picadon* and *cachat.*

■ Carpentras

Jouvaud *(Rue de l'Évêché, 84200 Carpentras,* ☎ *90.63.15.38,* ⇄ *90.63.21.62)* Classy pastry and gift shop. A few tables for tea and cake are provided if you can't resist the extraordinary cakes, pastries and chocolate. Nougat made with lavender honey is its specialty. The store also sells unique gift items.

R. Clavel *(Rue Porte d'Orange, 84200,* ☎ *90.63.07.59).* Fifth generation chocolate and sweet shop which claims the world record for making the largest *berlingot* candy.

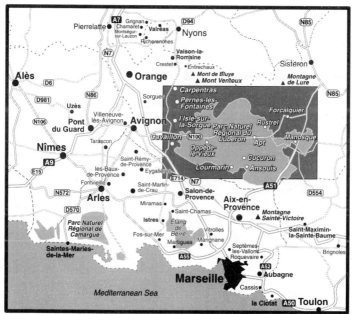

THE PLATEAU DU VAUCLUSE
AND THE LUBERON ★★★

For many visitors and residents alike, this pretty region represents the heart of Provence. It is blessed with an unparalleled and varied natural beauty: gentle rolling hills, impressive gorges, and fertile plains.

There have been inhabitants here since the Paleolitic (10,000 BC) period. The Celt and Ligurian peoples occupied the territory from the 4th century BC onwards – the ruins of their communities (known as *oppida*) have been found in the area. It was a time when druid priests were respected religious leaders, preaching immortality and reincarnation. The Celts were superstitious and believed that certain shepherds possessed supernatural powers, such as

the ability to read signals and hear voices from the earth and the sky. Their interpretation of natural phenomena protected their flocks of sheep and helped crops to thrive. They prepared magic potions from plants and herbs to ward off sickness and evil forces, and believed witches (male and female) existed to wreak havoc on the world.

The Romans settled here following the creation of their new colony in 118 BC, but little is known of their stay. The area was greatly influenced by a fervent wave of Christianity in the region in the late Middle Ages, through to the 10th century and religion played an essential role for a number of centuries. Churches and priories were built, as were the three masterpieces of

Cistercian architecture: the Sénanque, Silvacane and Thoronet abbeys (each built during the 12th century). During the same time, the Vaudois religious movement gained popularity and divided the population. Today the Vaudois would be classified as a fundamentalist religious sect. It was begun in the late 12th century by a wealthly Lyon merchant Pierre Vaud (or Vald), who fled his hometown after his movement was excommunicated by Pope Lcius III in 1184. The movement's leaders, Barbes or Beards, were lay preachers whose members renounced material possessions and strictly followed the Gospels. They retaliated against organized religion, and congregated secretly in members' homes. Most were peaceful farmers, though some historians note that some Vaudois went so far as to raze churches.

Many Vaudois settled in the Luberon region in the 15th century, which had been devastated by the plague and pillaging. Wealthy landowning nobles and the priories and abbeys welcomed the opportunity to have the area re-peopled and culitivated again. However, the Vaudois were persecuted during the Reformation movement, when Inquisitors were appointed throughout France to capture "heretics", mainly Lutherans. In 1545, troops of François I were sent to the region to eliminate the Vaudois who had settled primarily in the Luberon. Supported by the Baron of Oppède, president of the parliament of Aix and led by Captain Polin, forces left Pertuis on April 16 of that year and destroyed 11 villages in six days. Nearly 3,000 were murdered, hanged or burned at the stake. Thousands sought refuge in the hills and isolated areas of the Vaucluse plateau or escaped into Italy.

The following centuries were relatively more peaceful, yet still marked by violence. As elsewhere, the 19th century saw economic growth. The region's agricultural importance was recognized, and an infrastructure (artisans, small commerce) supporting the needs of the local population emerged.

Nowadays, this area is untouched by the industrialization common in areas with towns and cities of greater importance. Agriculture is the main economic activity. Here, the noble professions of farming and sheep-herding continue to reign. Farmers work independently and rarely possess more than 30 hectares of land each. While driving or walking through the area you will notice the variety of things grown. Two items predominate: vineyards in the valleys and lavender fields in the drier, higher areas.

Some villages seem to have been untouched for centuries. They are typically perched on the sides of the calcerous cliffs. Houses and activity now, as then, appear to centre around each village's church and château. However, both the Vaucluse plateau and the Luberon have changed since the 1970s when wealthy Parisians and Europeans bought second homes here. The residences and swimming pools of actors, politicians and industrialists are discretely hidden down silent paths, behind cyprus trees and alarmed gates. The invasion has had a positive effect – in 1977 the Parc Naturel Régional du Lubéron was created. The 120,000 hectare (296,400 acre) area became a conservation area where strict building restrictions are imposed with the goal of preserving its fragile eco-structure and natural beauty.

Many of the newcomers are writers, artists or artisans who respect the land

and wish to keep the area undeveloped. Tourism now plays an important role in the local economy and is the sole livelihood for many owners of hotels, restaurants and shops. Countless articles in the press and media attention on this particular region of Provence since the 80s have brought coach-loads of tourists from as far away as Australia and Japan. If at all possible, we suggest you travel in the early autumn, or best of all in May or June. Though you might miss the violet splendour of the fields of lavender in July and August, the fruit trees and flowers in bloom make for fantastic scenery and accommdation is easier to find.

 Finding Your Way Around

■ By plane

Marseille is the closest international and national airport; otherwise daily flights arriving from Paris and other French cities land and depart at Avignon-Caumont Airport.
Marseille Airport
☎ 42.78.21.00
Avignon-Caumont Airport
☎ 90.81.51.15

■ By car

Due to the number of interesting small villages in relatively isolated spots, a car is necessary to fully explore the region properly. (A good selection of car rental agencies is found in Avignon and Marseille.)

The Vaucluse plateau is 40 kilometres east of Avignon and 15 kilometres east of Carpentras. By car, take the N 100 (signposted "Apt") past L'Isle-sur-la-Sorgue and enter the area from the south (turn left onto the D 2 north for Gordes; turn left onto the D 4 north for Roussillon). Alternatively, from Avignon take the D 942 to Carpentras and either continue on this road for the Gorges de la Nesque; or take the D 4 south for Venasque, and a scenic, though circuitous, route leading to Gordes and Roussillon from the north.

The westernmost part of the Luberon is 40 kilometres east of Avignon. Three direct routes are possible, depending on your final destination. For villages in the north Luberon, including Oppède-le-Vieux, Ménerbes, Lacoste, Bonnieux and Apt, take the D 100 east from Avignon (signposted "Apt") and turn where indicated. Alternatively, for the same villages, you may take the N 7 east from Avignon. After 11 kilometres, carry on the same highway (the N 7 turns sharply for Salon-de-Provence, which you don't want) which is now the D 973 (signposted "Cavaillon"). After four kilometres, avoid the turn for Cavaillon and carry on the same highway which is now the D 22 (signposted "Apt"). The D 22 connects with the D 100 after 18 kilometres.

A third option, useful for destinations in the southern parts of the Luberon, is to continue on the D 973 circling Cavaillon. The D 973 follows the banks of the Durance River towards Lourmarin, Cucuron and Ansouis.

■ By train

The closest train stations serving the Vaucluse Plateau and the Luberon are in Avignon and Orange. Visitors arriving by TGV from Paris who only plan to travel in this area of Provence should therefore arrange car rental in Avignon.
Gare SNCF Avignon ☎ 90.82.50.50
Gare SNCF Orange ☎ 90.34.01.44

■ By bus

Larger towns in the area are served by regular, though infrequent, bus service. However, this is not a recommended way to see the Vaucluse plateau and the Luberon, because the most scenic spots and the interesting sites and monuments are often very far from places connected by bus service. Only those visitors who plan to stay in one area for a number of days should consider using a bus to get to their destination, from say, the SNCF train station in Avignon. In general, there is no bus service after dark. Details from the Avignon bus station; tourist offices can also provide details.

Gare Routière Avignon - ☎ 90.82.07.35

Practical Information

Many village tourist offices offer informative guided tours lasting one or two hours and some provide local guides upon request. This is an excellent area for cycling and walking – if these activities interest you contact the closest tourist office to obtain special maps and information about equipment rental.

■ Tourist Offices

Plateau du Vaucluse and Northern Luberon

Fontaine-de-Vaucluse
Chemin de la Fontaine
84800 Fontaine-de-la- Vaucluse
☎ 90.20.32.22 ⇄ 90.20.21.37

Gordes
Place du Château
84220 Gordes
☎ 90.72.02.75 ⇄ 90.72.04.39

L'Isle-sur-la-Sorgue
Place de l'Église
84800 L'Isle-sur-la-Sorgue
☎ 90.38.04.78

Pernes-les-Fontaines
Place de la Nesque
84210 Pernes-les-Fontaines
☎ 90.61.31.04 ⇄ 90.61.33.23

Venasque
Place de la Mairie
84210 Venasque
☎ 90.66.11.66

Cavaillon
79, Rue Saunerie
84300 Cavaillon
☎ 90.71.32.01 ⇄ 90.71.42.99

Apt
Place Bouquerie, BP 15
84400 Apt
Tel 90.74.03.18 ⇄ 90.04.64.30

Bonnieux
7, Place Carnot BP 11
84480 Bonnieux
☎ 90.75.91.90 ⇄ 90.75.92.94

Roussillon
Place de la Poste
84220 Roussillon
☎ 90.05.60.25

South Luberon

Lourmarin
Avenue Philippe de Girard
84160 Lourmarin
☎ 90.68.10.77

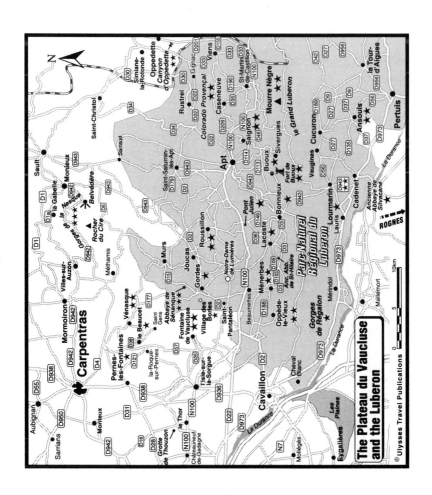

The Plateau du Vaucluse
and the Luberon

© Ulysses Travel Publications

Curcuron
Mairie Rue Léonce Brieugne
84160 Curcuron
☎ 90.77.28.37

Exploring

■ The Plateau du Vaucluse ★★

Two enchanting villages lie at the base of the Vaucluse plateau in the Comtat plain: L'Isle-sur-la Sorgue and Pernes-les-Fontaines. Canals run peacefully through both sites, making these places pleasant stopping points before entering the nearby mountainous region.

L'Isle-sur-la-Sorgue ★★

L'Isle-sur-la-Sorgue is graced by a shallow canal system fed by the Sorgue River and is knicknamed the *Venise du Comtat* (the Venice of the Comtat). The first settlers here were fishermen and they have since played a role in the town's history. In the early 13th century, Raimond Bérenger VII granted the L'Isle-sur-la-Sorgue fishermen the exclusive right to fish in the Sorgue, from its source to the Rhône. Nowadays, a *Roi de la Sorgue* (King of the Sorgue) is elected once a year. The town's street names betray its fishy past – Rue de l'Anguille (eel), Rue de l'Écrevisse (crayfish) and Rue de la Truite (trout) for example.

You'll notice many waterwheels still in operation, reminders that L'Isle-sur-la-Sorgue was an important producer of silk in the 17th century and manufacturer of paper in the 19th century. The old city with its canals, streets shaded

by plane trees and elegant buildings is best discovered on foot.

Église Notre-Dame des Anges ★ *(Mon to Fri 10 AM to noon and 3 PM to 6 PM; Place de l'Église)* is a *collégiale* or collegiate church with a rich 17th century baroque interior, including a large ornate glory in gilded wood representing the assumption and coronation of the Virgin Mary.

Hôtel Dieu *(free admission, must see concierge first, 10 AM to noon and 2 PM to 6 PM; ☎ 90.38.01.31)* Like the hospital in Carpentras, this 18th century building has an interesting pharmacy with decoration painted by Duplessis and a fine collection of earthenware pots from Moustiers.

L'Isle-sur-la-Sorgue is an antique lovers paradise every Saturday and Sunday, year-round, when the entire town becomes an **antique and flea market ★**. This is the place to buy original glazed pottery jars in mustard yellow and green – for the same price as you find in shops elsewhere selling mass-produced reproductions. Many local people come here for Provençal furniture and objects for the home and garden. Whether you spend a little or a lot, the festive atmosphere in the streets is unbeatable (see p 117).

Pernes-les-Fontaines ★

Pernes-les-Fontaines is so-called because this town is dotted with 36 old fountains. Once the capital of the papal territory Comtat Venaissin (968-1320), Pernes became an important community following the installation of the representatives of the counts of Toulouse (called *Sénéchaux*) in the château in 1125. Ramparts were built during the 15th and 16th centuries to protect the townspeople from plunderers, the Vaudois and carriers of the plague.

Only the rampart gates remain today (the walls were destroyed in the 19th century) – the most striking is the 16th century **Porte Notre Dame** ★ *(Quai de Verdun next to the Nesque river)*. At this spot, note the **Fontaine Cormorant** (built in 1761 and named after the bird ontop) and the **Pont Notre** with the 16th century chapel apparently stuck on one side. Across the river, is the old **château** of the counts of Toulouse, just the castle keep and wrought-iron cage bell tower remains. The sober **Église Notre Dame de Nazareth** stands next to the square of the same name and dates from the 11th century.

The Pernes tourist office provides a free map giving the names and dates of the fountains. Beware - don't drink the water from the Fontaine de la Lune (of the moon) opposite the 14th century Porte St-Giles. Legends says it makes people *lunatique*, or crazy!

Venasque ★★

Venasque is positioned on top of a steep-sided rocky crag overlooking the Nesque valley and Carpentras plain. This strategic location made Venasque the ideal second residence for the bishops of Carpentras, who came here (6th through to the 11th centuries) to escape Barbarian invasions in Carpentras. Nowadays, this charming village is worth a visit for its pretty streets, marvellous views and historical interest.

Most interesting is the **Baptistère ★★** *(guided tour adults 10 F, children under 12 free; Thu to Tue 10 AM to noon and 3 PM to 7 PM; next to Église Notre-Dame)* considered to be the oldest religious building in the region,

and some say, in all of France. Its origins are not clear. Legend indicates that a pagan building occupied the site during Roman times and that a sanctuary was built here in the 6th century (Merovingian period) by Saint-Siffrein de Lérins, who was consecrated Bishop of Venasque before 542 AD. The stone building was rebuilt in the 12th century and used as an episcopal funeral church. Its structure follows the Greek cruciform design: four semi-circular vaulted apses face a central square, with a hollow basin used most likely as a baptismal font. The north apse is the oldest, its slender columns came from Roman temples.

Le Beaucet ★

Near Venasque, lies the picturesque village of **Le Beaucet** (one-way road D 39 south), which is perched on a cliff-side and dominated by the ruins of a 12th century château (built for the Carpentras bishops). Unfoturnately, the 80 steps linking the village to the château are usually closed due to falling rocks or landslide, though you can see the ruined castle-keep, four walls of a chapel, cisterns and the draw-bridge. A popular pilrgrimage in memory of the 12th century hermit Gens Bournareau has taken place in the area at midnight every 16th of May since the 15th century. Gens was sainted for his miraculous ability to bring rain to the dry valley. During the pilgrimage, the hermit's statue is carried from the church in his birthplace of Monteux (near Carpentras) to the Saint-Gens Hermitage 15 kilometres from Le Beaucet. Relics of Saint-Gens are found in the Hermitage and the natural spring (*fontaine*) supposedly discovered by the hermit is marked along a pathway. An important artisans workshop is found at Le Beaucet, which holds internships promoting conservation and crafts techniques *(information from Monsieur H. Morel, Les Ateliers du Beaucet, Centre Internationale de Formation en Métiers d'Art, 84210 Le Beaucet, ☎ 90.66.10.61).*

Fontaine-de-Vaucluse ★★

South of the village of Roque-sur-Pernes on the D 57, and just seven kilometres from L'Isle-sur-la-Sorgue along the D 25 lies Fontaine-de-Vaucluse. By following on foot the Chemin de la Fontaine pathway next to a pretty canal, past the tourist office and T-shirt vendors, you arrive at the famous natural spring which is the origin of the Rivière Sorgue. Set amongst a lush gorge, the fountain is the most powerful in France and fifth in the world (it pumps out 630 million cubic metres of water a year on average). Winter and particularly the spring are the most spectacular times to see the fountain in action - 90 cubic metres of water gush out every second and pour down the river bed. During the summer, when the spring is low, you see a calm, deep blue basin and can appreciate the surrounding sheer cliff, eroded and sculpted by the powerful water. Divers have plunged as far as 205 metres below the surface (the German Hasenmeyer in 1983) and exploratory measuring instruments have been dropped, but the spring's origin remains a mystery. Speleologists have discovered a complex under-water network in the limestone rock, aided by rain and melting snow from Mont Ventoux and the Vaucluse plateau in the springtime.

A strong word of caution: Fontaine-de-Vaucluse is extremely crowded in the summer months and the souvenir stands along the Chemin de la Fontaine give the village an unfortunate touristy spirit, much like the worst aspects of the otherwise spectacular Niagara Falls.

Gorges de la Nesque ★★★

The Gorges de la Nesque is a spectacular canyon 400 metres deep, carved into the Vaucluse plateau. Once inhabited by Paleolithic man, Celts and Ligurians, then by the Romans, the gorges offer marvelous panoramic views, unobstructed by evidence of modern man. A short half-day drive around an irregular circular route may start at either the village of Villes-sur-Auzon in the west or the town of Sault in the east.

Turn back along the D 1 and after two and a half kilometres catch the D 942 towards **Monnieux**. The village's Saint-Pierre church is Romanesque with later additions, and the ruins of a 12th century watch tower can be seen. Carry on the D 942 for 20 kilometres back to Villes-sur-Auzon. This is the most impressive section of the Gorges de la Nesque. Along the twisty, steep road you will pass a viewpoint (marked "Belvédère") overlooking the rock known as the Rocher de Cire (872 metres) and drive under three short tunnels.

■ Gordes and the Petit Luberon ★★

The Petit Luberon is indeed smaller, though no less spectacular, than the Grand Luberon mountain range due east. A number of typical Provençal towns perched on the cliff-sidse are found north of the Petit Luberon.

Gordes ★

One of the best known of these towns is Gordes. Its blond drystone houses are arranged precariously around the edge of the Vaucluse plateau facing the

Luberon hills. Panoramic views of both Gordes and the Luberon hills in the distance are best from the viewpoint on the D 15 before entering the village. Gordes was once a centre for the pre-Roman primitive peoples called the Vordeuses and hence the village's name (it has nothing to do with gourds!) Worth discovering are the pretty drystone houses dating from the 16th to 18th century and cobble-stone pathways which encircle the Place du Château and the 18th century Église Saint-Firmin. The community has been spoiled by the influx of wealthy people owning second homes in the area and by tourism. For the most part, Gordes' restaurants and accommodation are over-priced and over-rated.

The massive Renaissance **Château de Gordes** (1525-1541) with prominent circular towers was once a 12th century fortress. The long dining room on the first floor has an immense stone fireplace more than seven metres long with an ornate chimney. Upper floors house the distinctive bold geometric works by the late op-art painter Victor Vasarély in the **Musée Vasarely** *(adults 25 F, reduced rate 15 F; Jul and Aug, open everyday 10 AM to noon and 2 PM to 6 PM; Sep to Jun, closed Tue;* ☎ *90.72.02.89).*

Classified as a historical monument, the **Village des Bories** ★ *(adults 25 F, reduced rate 15 F, children free; open everyday 9 AM to sunset; follow the signposted road at the junction of D 15 and D 2, south of Gordes,* ☎ *90.72.03.48)* is a hamlet of curious shaped drystone shelters with peaked roofs. Though the building technique was derived from neolithic period structures, most of the *bories* date from the 16th to the 19th century. They were usually used as shelters by shepherds and hunters and are found throughout

the region. Yet as is visible here, self-sufficient communities lived in *bories*. Five groups of habitations, which include sheep pens, ovens for baking bread, and two-tiered living quarters with everyday objects such as wine vats and eating utensils are on display.

Set in a verdant vale next to a field of lavender, the **Abbaye de Sénanque** ★★★ *(adults 14 F, reduced rate 10 F; Mar to Oct, Mon to Sat 10 AM to noon and 2 PM to 6 PM, Sun and Catholic holidays afternoons only; Nov to Feb, Mon to Fri 2 PM to 5 PM, Sat and Sun and school holidays 2 PM to 6 PM; Mass Sun 9 AM, Mon to Fri noon; 4 km north of Gordes on the D 177,* ☎ *90.72.05.72)* is one of the most remarkable monuments in Provence. Founded in 1148, the abbey is an exceptional example of austere Cistercian architecture. Its plan is based on a combination of squares and circles within squares. Though still an active Cistercian abbey, the public may visit the fully-restored 12th century buildings. There is a bookstore and a gift shop selling honey and lavender essence made at the abbey, plus the Sénancole liqueur invented by the monk Marie Maurice. Because of Abbaye Sénanque's importance, it is crowded during peak times.

Roussillon ★★

Rousillon is a splendid village perched high amongst the striking ochre quarries and rich green pine forests in the surrounding Fées valley. The ochre industry thrived in the late 19th century, reached its peak in the 1920s when 40,000 tons a year was quarried and is now no longer in operation. The ochre pigment is produced by separating then grinding the iron-oxide deposits in the earth to a dry powder.

It is used in paint, cosmetics, food colouring (it's non-toxic) and plaster. As you'll see, Roussillon's houses are tinted with the rich ochre earth in hues ranging from pale yellow to rich red, while their doorways and windows are colorfully painted.

A couple of cafes face the shaded village square, the Place de la Mairie, next to the town hall. A pretty pathway from this square winds up under an attractive bell tower (once a fortified gateway) with a typical wrought-iron bell cage, and leads to the simple Romanesque Église Saint-Michel. Follow a pathway behind the church to discover wonderful panoramic views facing north toward Mont Ventoux and the Alps. Other good viewpoints greet visitors at every turn.

Cavaillon

This town, famous for the delicious melons grown nearby in the Rivière Durance valley, lies at the edge of the Comtat plain at the approach to the Petit Luberon. As Cavaillon stands at the crossroads of such major roads as the D 973 from Avignon and Aix-en-Provence, the D 938 from L'Isle-sur-la-Sorgue, Pernes-les-Fontaines and Carpentras and the A 7 from Marseille, you are liable to circle around the town at some point in your trip. With so many interesting areas to visit in the region, there is no need to penetrate into Cavaillon if your visit to Provence is limited. Incidently, the true Cavaillon melon is not a cantaloupe which it closely resembles but the smaller, rounder and sweeter charentais, with a smooth pale green outer skin.

■ The Petit Luberon South

A cluster of pretty villages in the Petit Luberon, south of the N 100, manage to retain a natural charm and are less frequented than popular places farther north, such as Gordes, Roussilon and L'Isle-sur-la-Sorgue.

Oppède-le-Vieux ★★

A tiny community built on the peak of a rocky crag 12 miles east of Cavaillon on the D 176, Oppède-le-Vieux appears hidden amongst overgrown vegetation and pine trees. Access to the old village is by a well-marked pathway, leading up to the church and farther on the ruins of a Middle Age château, from which there are good panoramic views. Once abandoned, the hamlet has been slowly restored since the 1950s. Work has focused primarily on a few mansions dating from the 15th and 16th century and more recently, the pretty 12th century church. There is little activity in Oppède, so enjoy the peaceful village square and cobblestone roads. The village once suffered a bad reputation, because the château belonged to Baron Maynier who authorized the massacre of the Vaudois people in 1545 (see p 96).

Ménerbes ★★

Passing along the D 188 at the junction of the D 103, lies Ménerbes. Built on a hilltop, it was the capital for the Protestant movement during the Wars of Religion in Provence in the 16th century. After the fall of other Protestant communities in the Luberon, the movement resisted French forces for over five years in the late 1580s before surrendering. Nowadays, visitors can see the 14th century church, imposing 12th to 15th century citadel and discover the magnificent old houses and charming cobblestone streets. Ménerbes is the birthplace of the Republican poet Clovis Huges, and the artist Nicholas de Staël lived in one of the village's two châteaux.

Lacoste ★

Lacoste, six kilometres east of Ménerbes on the D 109, is famous as the home of the writer of erotic works, including *120 Days of Sodom* and *Justine*, Donatien-Alphonse-François, the Marquis de Sade. He fled a scandal in Paris caused by his libertine ways to his grandfather's château at Lacoste in 1771. He was imprisoned and condemned to death following later escapades and died in the Charenton asylum near Paris. The magnificent château (dating from the 11th century) is now owned by a professor who has been restoring it for more than three decades *(visits on weekends can be arranged by contacting the owner, M o n s i e u r   A n d r e   B o u ë r, ☎ 90.75.80.39).*

Lacoste has a number of sloping cobbled streets and pretty blond limestone houses, (though a few are in a state of sad disrepair), spanning out from the main street Rue Basse. It is happily less frequented than other towns in the area. A striking view of Bonnieux across a valley can be had from the east side of the village.

Bonnieux ★

Bonnieux is a pretty village with tiers of terracotta roofed houses tumbling down a cliff-side over the Calavon valley. It occupied a strategic position on the principal route between Italy and Spain during the Roman occupation of Provence. During the Middle Ages, the town moved up the hill to its actual site. Ramparts and towers were built

during the 13th and 14th centuries to keep out marauding tribes (some ruins remain). The Catholic *Bonnieulais*, as village's residents are called, held a certain animosity towards their Protestant neighbours in Lacoste. Some beautiful 16th, 17th and 18th century mansions remind us that Bonnieux was once a prosperous place, when the Comtat Venaissin belonged to the Popes. Many bishops chose Bonnieux as their place of residence from the 14th century until the Revolution and it therefore received special privileges. The town hall (Rue de la Mairie) occupies the former 18th century residence Hôtel de Rouville.

Visit the **Musée de la Boulangerie** *(adults 10 F, reduced rate 5 F, children free; Jun to Sep, Wed to Mon 10 AM to noon and 3 PM to 6:30 PM; Oct to May, Sat, Sun and holidays only; 1 2   R u e   d e   l a   R é p u b l i q u e, ☎ 90.75.88.34)* to discover the machines, techniques, posters and history of bread baking plus a surprising collection of different types of loaves in a former bakery.

A 12th century Romanesque church called simply the **Vieille Église**, surrounded by beautiful cedar trees dominates the upper ground *(follow 86 stone steps; contact the Tourist Office to visit inside)*. There are **good panoramic views ★** from the small park, once the church's cemetery, looking north towards Gordes and Rousillon. The so-called new church (1870s) is found at the lower end of Bonnieux, and has four 16th century paintings in the primitive style representing the Passion and originating from the old church.

Don't miss the small Roman bridge *(six miles north of Bonnieux on the D 149, next to the N 100)* crossing the Calavon river. Built in the year 3 BC in cut stone without the use of mortar, the **Pont Julien** ★ is still in good condition. Its three arches span 70 metres.

■ **The Grand Luberon ★★**

Apt

Apt is an important commercial centre, serving the entire Grand Luberon area. It is famous for the lively Saturday morning provençal market (Place des Martyrs-de-la-Résistance), where you can buy a mesmerizing array of local products, including hand-made pottery. The town and its neigbouring communities are renowned for their colourful hand-made ceramic tiles (called *carreaux d'Apt*) and pottery (see shopping page 118), fruit jams and *confits* (delicious preserved fruits). Apart from these pleasures, Apt is not of great interest to the tourist, as recent buildings have blotted the landscape.

The **old town**, surrounded by its old stone walls, has a few fountains, chapels and houses from the 16th, 17th and 18th centuries and, next to the Cathedral on the Rue des Marchands, a beautiful clock tower built in the 16th century. A chapel in the 12th and 14th century **Cathédrale Saint Anne** *(Tue to Sat 9 AM to 11 AM and 4:30 PM to 6:30 PM, Sun 9 AM to 11 AM; Place de la Cathédrale)* was added in 1660 after a visit here by Anne of Austria during a pilgrimage; note as well the 1st and 11th century crypts and the treasury. The comprehensive **Musée d'Archéologie** *(adults 10 F, reduced rate 5 F, children free; Oct to May, Mon and Wed 2 PM to 5 PM, Sat, 10 AM to noon; Jun to Sep, Mon to Sat 10 AM to noon and 2 PM to 5 PM, Sun 10 AM to noon; 4 Rue de l'Amphithéâtre, ☎ 90.04.74.65)* contians a good collection of items dating from prehistory and Gallo-Roman times,

the remains of a Roman theatre, as well as a fine selection of Apt and Moustiers ceramics.

The **headquarters of the Parc Naturel Régional du Luberon** ★ is based here *(Sep to Jun, Mon to Sat 8:30 AM to noon and 2 PM to 6 PM; Jul and Aug, closes at 7 PM; Oct to Easter, closed Sat; 60 Place Jean Jaurès, ☎ 90.04.42.00)*. This is the place to pick up information about the many fascinating hiking trails and/or to book guided walking tours throughout the Luberon hills. Interesting exhibitions occur every year, based on regional themes, plus a permanent display in a cave-like setting describes the evolution of fossil life. For nature lovers, the gift shop offers an excellent selection of books on the Luberon and its walking trails, wildlife, and history.

Rustrel and the Colorado ★★

Ten kilometres northeast of Apt is the tiny village of Rustrel (along the D 22) which was once the centre for ochre production one hundred years ago, and just prior to that an important iron ore industry. A 17th century château houses Rustrel's town hall. The main interest today is the nearby **Colorado Provençal ★★**. Lying south of the D 22 road, between Rustrel and the hamlet of Gignac by the Dôa river, are a number of pathways leading to this incredible series of rust-coloured rocks jutting towards the sky in strange configurations, ochre quarries and numerous viewing points. Here, more than ever, one understands why the multi-coloured ground is called *terres d'ocres, de sang et d'or* (earth of ochre, blood and gold). The Colorado is reached on foot only, but the paths are clearly marked. The highlight is the cleverly-named Cheminées de Fées (Fairies Chimney). The Roussillon Tourist Office sells for 30 F an informative booklet called *Circuits de Découverte du Colorado Provençal* by local expert, François Morénas.

North of Viens, along a twisty, narrow road (D 201) past the pretty **Oppedette Canyon ★★**, is a village seemingly perched at the end of the world. Called **Oppedette**, it was once a Ligurian community before the Roman occupation of Provence. Not much is here — stone houses, a tiny cafe and a small 12th century church (closed to the public). The perilous gorges along the Calavon river surrounding the village once sheltered Protestants fleeing persecution during the Wars of Religion.

In the hills of the Grand Luberon, south of Apt and the N 100, rests the charming village of **Buoux ★**. It possesses a château now owned by the Parc Naturel Régional du Luberon and an 18th century church.

The rugged surrounding area is full of grottos and steep cliffs rising above the jagged Aigue Brun river. It is popular with professional rock climbers. Amongst the gorges nearby is **Fort de Buoux ★★** *(adults 10 F, reduced rate including children 5 F; open everyday from sunrise to sunset; follow the signs along the D 113 south of the village, cross over a bridge after a holiday camp — there is a car park next to the path leading to the fort which is accessible by foot only, ☎ 90.74.25.75; wear suitable shoes)*. On top of the plateau are the ruins of a 14th and 15th century fort. The ruins of ramparts, an old village, fortress walls and a Romanesque chapel can be seen. Note the curious stone silos dug into the ground, a hidden stone staircase and along the pathway, numerous tombs built into the rock face. The site has been a natural defense since prehis-

tory; it was a Protestant stronghold in the 16th century but was destroyed in part soon after.

Saignon ★★

Saignon is a peaceful spot overlooking the Calavon valley with a very pretty Romanesque church called Notre-Dame, opposite the town hall, château ruins, a pottery workshop, and a tinkling fountain next to a charming small hotel/restaurant on the village square. In other words, this is a fine place to stop for a couple of nights and discover the Luberon's sites and walking trails. (Just don't tell too many people — Saignon is not over-run with visitors.) Hikers will enjoy climbing up to the **Mourre Nègre ★★** (1,125 metres), the highest peak in the Grand Luberon. Magnificent panoramas of the entire Vaucluse area greet you at the top (small car park four kilometres south of Saignon, access by foot along the marked GR 92 path).

Lourmarin ★

The **picturesque road D 943 ★★** between Bonnieux and Cadenet winds through the Aiguebrun Valley, between the Petit and Grand Luberon. Surrounded by vineyards, olive and almond trees, lies the village of Lourmarin. Livelier than its neighbours, you'll find a few cafes, bars, shops selling regional specialties and a couple of good restaurants. Locals like to point out that Nobel Prize winner Albert Camus lived and wrote here (he is buried in Lourmarin's cemetery). Needless to say, with all this activity amongst such a pleasant setting, Lourmarin is popular with tourists during peak periods.

Apart from a Romanesque church, a temple and the pretty streets with their fountains, Lourmarin's principal site is the 15th-16th century **château** ★ *(adults 30 F, reduced rate 25 F, children free; Oct to Jun, open everyday guided tours at 11 AM, 2:30 PM, 3:30 PM and 4:30 PM; Jul to Sep at 11 AM, 11:30 AM and every half hour 3 PM to 6 PM; Nov to Jun, closed Tue;* ☎ *90.68.15.23).* One wing is occupied by the École des Beaux Arts d'Aix-en-Provence, but visitors are offered an informative guided tour through the interesting Renaissance part with curious staircases, beautifully furnished apartments, a music room and two large stone fireplaces.

Rognes

The village of Rognes is 14 km south of Lourmarin *(ten minutes from the Silvercane Abbey)* along the D 543. The village's 17th century Église de l'Assomption contains some celebrated altars (unfortunately it is often closed).

Curcuron

Seven kilometres east of Lourmarin along the D 56 is Curcuron. This is a peaceful village with an interesting clock tower and stone gate (remains of a 16th century defensive wall) and some attractive houses. A magnificent 17th century retable above the altar and a life-size painted wooden statue of Christ, bound and pierced with thorns, rest in the 12th-14th century **Notre-Dame de Beaulieu** ★ church. Lower down, next to a cafe, is a large rectangular water basin (called l'*Etang* or pond, and rather cloudy!) prettily bordered by tall plane trees.

Ansouis ★★

Further east is the village of Ansouis *(tourist information from the Hôtel de Ville,* ☎ *90.09.96.12,* ⇄ *90.09.93.48),* which has a splendid private 12th century residence well worth visiting for its collection of 17th and 18th century furniture, Flanders tapestries and pretty façade. The **Château d'Ansouis** ★ *(guided tour adults 30 F, reduced rates 25 F, 20 F and 15 F, children free; Apr to Oct, open everyday 2:30 PM to 6 PM; Nov to Mar, closed Tue, Jul 14 and Aug 30, additiional tour at 11 AM;* ☎ *90.09.82.70)* has been occupied by the De Sabran family since it was built eight centuries ago. Otherwise, this charming village has pretty streets, a wrought-rion bell tower built into a 16th century building and the 13th century Église Saint-Martin attached to the château's ramparts.

■ The Rivière Durance Valley

Running west to east, parallel to the Petit and Grand Luberon is the Durance River and a number of villages along its banks. The Durance often floods in the spring and a canal network is now in place, producing electricity and irrigating the plain. Many parts of this area lack the natural beauty of the nearby Luberon hills, as power stations and industry have taken over. However, there are a number of sites of interest. Starting from the west, near Cavaillon, lovers of steep, treacherous drives will be satisfied by a ten kilometre twisty one-way road across barren hills *(difficult access - head for the hamlet of Vidauque just east of the D 31 side-road and turn right up a steep incline on a narrow road D 30. This leads past two peaks, called the Tête des Buisses and Trou-du-Rat, and eventually looks over the Durance river and winds down to the major D 973 road).*

For hikers, the **Gorges de Régalon** ★ (marked on the D 973 road between Cheval-Blanc and Mérindol, park on the right and follow the indicated path past an informative panel describing the site's history and geological importance) provides a fascinating short walk, though it is dangerous in wet weather.

A plaque commemorating the slaughter of the Vaudois is found on top of a hill overlooking **Mérindol**, a village which was destroyed along with many others in 1545 and rebuilt in the 17th century. South of Lourmarin and Cadenet, across the Durance River, lies one of the region's three Cistercian abbeys. The design of the **Abbaye Silvacane ★** *(adults 27 F, reduced rate 18 F, children free; Oct to Mar, Wed to Mon 9 AM to noon and 2 PM to 5 PM; Apr to Sep, open everyday 9 AM to 7 PM; with occassional closure in Aug at 5 PM when classical music concerts are held, call for details; ☎ 42.50.41.69)* resembles the sobre beauty of the slightly older Abbaye Sénanque near Gordes. Built between 1175 and 1230, it is less well preserved and is no longer a working abbey, but is owned by the state department of Historical Monuments. Still, a visit through the cloister, extremely high barrel-vaulted church and into the monks quarters is worthwhile.

 Outdoor Activities

Outdoor enthusiasts are advised to stop at the headquarters of the Luberon Regional Natural Park for a gamut of helpful information from its welcome service and shop. This includes guide books on hiking trails in the area and the Luberon by car, thematic brochures about plant and animal life, and details about guided walks. Otherwise, tourist offices provide information about activities and services organised by local groups.

Parc Naturel Régional du Luberon
60 Place Jean Jaurès
BP 122
84400 Apt
☎ 90.04.42.00 ⇄ 90.04.81.15

 Hiking

This region has something to please everyone - from idyllic paths to challenging hills. Because much of the region is protected by legislation permitting development, nature lovers may admire unique species of flora and fauna here, in addition to wonderful panoramic views. The tourist office in Lourmarin publishes a brochure regarding four marked trails in the South Luberon *Les Sentiers Promenades du Sub Luberon*. Similarly, the Venasque tourist office publishes a brochure outlining a number of walks (between 2h30 and 7h duration) in this lovely area. Guided visits of the Gorges de la Nesque with commentary are organized in July and August by the Sault tourist office.

Serious hikers will enjoy the following trails (Topo-Guides on sale in bookshops provide exact details): **GR 4** (Mont Ventoux to Vaucluse Plateau), **GR 9** (Mont Ventoux to Vaucluse Plateau and the Grand Luberon), **GR 91** (Mont Ventoux to Fontaine-de-Vaucluse), **GR 6-97** (Vaucluse Plateau to Petit Luberon and the Gorges de Régalon), **GR 91** (Mont Ventoux), **GR 92** (Grand Luberon), **GR 97** (Luberon).

Horseback Riding

Apt
L'École du Cheval
Quartier de Roquefure
☎ 90.74.37.47
Equestrian centre and pony club organizes tours in the area on horseback.

Bonnieux
Randonnées du Luberon
Col Pointu
☎ 90.04.72.01
Guided tours on horseback.

Malaucène
Les Écuries du Ventoux
Quartier des Grottes
☎ 90.65.29.20
This *gîte* (farmhouse) arranges tours on horseback (plus hiking tours, private swimming pool).

Saignon
Centre Équestre de Tourville
Quartier des Gondonnets
☎ 90.74.00.33
Lessons as well as guided tours on horseback.

Lourmarin
Les Cavaliers du Gilbas
Lourmarin
☎ 90.68.39.59
Lessons as well as guided tours on horseback.

 Mountain Biking

Bedoin
Midi Cycles
☎ 90.65.63.63
Mountain bike rental, and guided tours of the area on demand.

Mormoiron
G. Aubert
☎ 90.61.83.90
Monsieur Aubert organizes an exciting two day mountain bike circuit in the Gorges de la Nesque, as well as a descent of Mont Ventoux.

Lourmarin
Freestyle
Rue du Temple
☎ 90.68.10.31
Mountain bike rental, with or without guide, plus trips organized for groups.

 Downhill Skiing

■ **Mont Ventoux**

Mont Serein (north face of Mont Ventoux, 1400 m to 1900 m)
☎ 90.63.42.02
Ski school, equipment rental, seven runs in the wintertime; grass skiing in summertime. Chalet restaurant for the complete après-ski sensation.

Chalet Reynard (south face of Mont Ventoux, 1420 m to 1640 m)
☎ 90.61.84.55
Smaller version of the above, with four short runs.

 Cross-country skiing

Cross-country skiing is limited to the forests around Mont Ventoux (details from the Comité Départemental de Ski, ☎ 90.63.16.54).

Golf

Saumane (Fontaine de Vaucluse)
International Golf & Country Club
☎ 90.20.20.65
Practice greens, 18 hole course.

  Canoeing and Kayaking

The scenic Sorgue river in the Vaucluse is a favourite spot for canoeing and kayaking enthusiasts.

Michel Melani, Kayak Vert
84800 Fontaine-de-Vaucluse
☎ 90.20.35.44
Exciting guided trip down the Sorgue from Fontaine-de-Vaucluse to Isle-Sur-la-Sorgue, with commentary.

Club de Canoë-Kayak Islois
La Cigalette
84000 Isle-Sur-La-Sorgue
☎ 90.38.33.22 or 90.20.64.70
Lessons for individuals and groups.

 Accommodation

■ **L'Isle-sur-la-Sorgue**

La Meridienne *(250-350 F, no credit cards; pb, ≈; Aux Fontanelles, Chemin de la Lône, 84800 L'Isle-sur-la-Sorgue,* ☎ *90.38.40.26,* ⇄ *90.38.58.46)* Each room in this pleasant bed and breakfast run by Muriel Fox (a photographer from Avignon) and Jérôme Tarayre (a former doctor in Paris) has a small terrace, a pretty garden and a swimming pool. Quiet, peaceful location (off the N 100 south of Isle-sur-la-Sorgue).

La Pastorale *(150-350 F, no credit cards; pb, locked garage; Route de Fontaine de Vaucluse, Les Gardioles, 84800 Lagnes,* ☎ *90.20.25.18)* The friendly couple, Elisabeth and Robert Negrel, recently moved from Paris and converted this pretty stone farmhouse into a bed and breakfast, next to fields and a small road. The bedrooms are spacious and comfortable, but simply furnished. Breakfast, served in a pretty clay-tiled room includes home-made jams and very good coffee. Monsieur Negrel has a small antique/knick-knack shop next door. Well-situated (at the D 24 and D 99 crossroads, between the N100 and Lagnes village) for trips to L'Isle-sur-la-Sorgue and Fontaine-de-la-Vaucluse.

Mas de Cure Bourse *(320-520 F, bkfst 45 F;* ℜ*,* ≈*,* ☎*, tv; Route de Caumont-sur-Durance, 843800 L'Isle-sur-la-Sorgue,* ☎ *90.38.16.58,* ⇄ *90.38.52.31)* Chef Françoise Donzé's well-acknowledged talents in the kitchen are the first reason to come to this hotel, formerly an 18th century inn. Along with husband Jean-François, a banker, the colourful Donzé gave up her job as a chemist and started the hotel in 1980. 13 pleasant bedrooms in the Provençal style, ideal for families. Patio and garden, seminar and reception facilities.

■ **Pernes-les-Fontaines**

L'Hôtel Hermitage *(320-400 F, bkfst 40 F; pb,* ≈*,* ☎*, tv; Route de Carpentras, 84210 Pernes-les-Fontaines,* ☎ *90.66.51.41,* ⇄ *90.61.36.41)* Don't be put off by the busy road out front — this 20-room hotel faces its own large, leafy park and is a haven of tranquillity. This former residence of Captain Dreyfus, is decorated with Provençal furniture. Rooms are attractively renovated; breakfast or drinks may be taken on a stone terrace. Unbeatable value.

Saint-Barthélémy *(200-300 F, no credit cards; pb or ps; 84210 Pernes-les-Fontaines,*☎ *90.66.47.79)*A bed and breakfast in a restored 18th century stone house, once the residence of Baron Quiquerant, a royalist who fled to Russia during the French Revolution. The five rooms – four with showers one with bath – are rather plain. The real pleasure here is the enclosed garden with flowering laurel trees, and breakfast on the terrace, shaded by a large weeping willow tree. Swimming is possible in a small waterfall with private spring nearby. (From Pernes, take the D 1 direction Mazan for two kilometres, then turn right on the Chemin de la Roque).

Mas La Bonoty *(275-320 F, bkfst 38 F; pb,* ≈*,* ℜ*,* ☎*; Chemin de la Bonioty, 84210 Pernes-les-Fontaines,* ☎ *90.61.61.09,* ⇄ *90.61.35.14)* The peace and quiet of a restored farmhouse set in a low plain with a good restaurant (see p 115) and eight comfortable rooms lend this hotel a real country inn atmosphere. Large pool and terrace. Guests are warmly received like one of the family. Good value. (From Pernes, take the D 28 to the village of Saint Didier, turn left on the Chemin de Barraud, leading to Chemin de la Bonioty.)

■ **Venasque**

La Maison aux Volets Bleus *(315-385 F, no credit cards; pb, mini-bar; closed Nov 15 to Mar 15; 84210 Venasque,* ☎ *90.66.03.04,* ⇄ *90.66.16.14)* If you have ever dreamed of the ideal bed and breakfast, this might be it. Five tasteful rooms (one with two bedrooms) are freshly decorated with Provençal prints and have bathrooms with pretty tiles. Breakfasts are served on a long, narrow terrace with gorgeous clear views of

the Vaucluse hills. The large front room has the same view a stone fireplace, local bric-a-brac, dried yellow wildflowers hanging from the ceiling and tons of books on Provence. The owner Martine Maret is a former chef and a warm, generous host — she'll suggest the best places to buy local chèvre, Provençal fabrics and olive oil. Evening meals for 120 F without wine (recently roast rabbit, melon with Muscat and cheese feuilleté) if arranged in advance. They are served on a second terrace next to a fountain and flowering plants. Cats on the premises.

Auberge La Fontaine *(five fully-equipped apartments at 700 F, bkfst 50 F;* ☎*,* ⇄*, minitel, pb,* ℂ*, tvc,* ℜ*; Place de la Fontaine, 84210 Venasque,* ☎ *90.66.02.96,* ⇄ *90.66.13.14)* Former businessman Christian Soehlke has been the host/chef of this comfortable inn for 20 years. Each large apartment is two or three-storied, has a small balcony, is decorated differently (modern, Provençal, country-style) and can accommodate families of four. Meals are served in the dining room or the informal bistro (see p 115).

■ **Fontaine-de-Vaucluse**

Auberge de Jeunesse *(45 F, bkfst 20 F, meals 50 F; Chemin de la Vignasse, 84800 Fontaine-de-Vaucluse,* ☎ *90.20.31.65)*. Located just outside Fontaine-de-Vaucluse, towards Gordes. Closed Nov. 15 to Feb. 15. FUAJ (YHA) membership card necessary.

■ **Gordes**

La Gacholle *(490-600 F, half-board for two people 890 F to 1,050 F, bkfst 54 F;* ☎*, pb, tv, mini-bar,* ≈*,* ℜ*; closed Nov 15 to Mar 15; Route de Murs,*

84220 Gordes, ☎ *90.72.01.36,* ⇄ *90.72.01.81)* A friendly spot from which to visit the Luberon, thanks to comfortable rooms (some are a bit dated), an unparalled view of the hills and valley, excellent Provençal cuisine and above all, the smiling, considerate welcome by Gerard Roux and his team, who are equally professional and personable. Reasonably priced for an area with inflated prices. Nine of the 12 rooms have valley views, some with private terrace. The talented new chef Bruno Chastagnac works wonders with local fresh fish, produce, herbs and olive oil. Tennis court and pretty swimming pool.

Ferme de la Huppe *(500 F, bkfst 50 F; pb, ℜ, ≈, ☎, mini-bar; RD 156 - Les Pourquiers, 84220 Gordes,* ☎ *90.72.12.25,* ⇄ *90.72.01.83)* Pretty stone farmhouse in the Luberon valley with a landscaped garden and shaded terrace next to the pool, just south of Gordes. Eight attractive rooms (some in the 18th century building, others in a new wing) and rustic-style restaurant. The owners, the Konnings family, have created a friendly, relaxed atmosphere.

Les Bories *(600-1900 F, bkfst 74 F; pb, ℜ, ≈, tvc, ☎, minibar; Route de l'Abbaye de Sénanque, 84220 Gordes,* ☎ *90.72.00.51,* ⇄ *90.72.01.22)* For those fed up with cute Provençal prints and country furnishings, try one of the 18 luxuriously-appointed rooms in this hillside hotel which has more in common with the Côte d'Azur than the Luberon. A charming new manager in 1994 is making great strides with the young staff (mainly student interns) and restaurant, which indeed, is a restored stone *borie*. Each bedroom has terrific views over pine-tree studded hills towards Gordes. Tennis court, incredible indoor marble swimming pool.

■ Lacoste

Relais du Procurer *(500-700 F; ≈, pb, tv, ☎; Rue Basse, 84710 Lacoste,* ☎ *90.75.82.28,* ⇄ *90.75.86.94)* Luxury bed and breakfast in a 17th-century stone house right in the middle of this pretty village. Well-equipped and furnished rooms, though a few are a bit dated for some people's tastes. A narrow outdoor swimming pool, surrounded by four walls, is found off an upper floor.

■ Bonnieux

L'Hostellerie du Prieuré *(500-590 F, bkfst 40 F, ℜ, ☎, pb; closed Nov 5 to Feb 15; Rue J-B Aurard, 84480 Bonnieux,* ☎ *90.75.80.78,* ⇄ *90.75.96.00)* A lovely hotel with character in a former 18th century abbey. 10 comfortable rooms, a charming dining room in the old kitchen with an open hearth and a pretty garden/terrace for breakfast. Note the delightful models of Paris theatre interiors illuminated in a display case under the bar in the sitting room. Restaurant menus at 146 F and 206 F. Too bad the welcome is rather aloof.

■ Saignon

Auberge du Presbytère *(300 F, bkfst 45 F; ℜ, pb; closed Nov 15-30; Place de la Fontaine, 84400 Saignon,* ☎ *90.74.11.50,* ⇄ *90.04.68.51)* A number of the ten tasteful bedrooms have terraces and views of the Luberon, others overlook the fountain. (You'll find a stack of books instead of a television next to your bed!) Well recommended for the pleasant welcome and peaceful atmosphere. Drinks can be taken in the bar or on the terrace next to the fountain (11 AM to 1 PM and 4:30 PM to 8 PM).

■ **Lourmarin**

Villa Saint-Louis *(250-350 F, no credit cards;* ☎*, tv, pb; 35 Rue Henri de Savournin, 84160 Lourmarin,* ☎ *90.68.39.18,* ⇄ *90.68.10.07)* Old *gendarmerie* (police station) and once a *relais de poste* (roadside inn), this charming 18th century house gets our vote as one of the best bed and breakfasts in Provence. Run by the exhuberant Bernadette Lassallette and decorated with extraordinary taste by her husband Michel (a professional decorator). Bedrooms are filled with antiques and objects collected over the years from flea markets, plus a bohemian mix of fabrics, paintings and furniture. Each has a fireplace and equipped bathroom; there is a pretty terrace and garden. The breakfast room has a kitchenette for client's use. Bicycles are lent to guests to explore the region.

L'Hostellerie du Paradou *(170-230 F, bkfst 30 F; pb,* ℜ*; closed Nov 15 to Dec 15, restaurant closed Thu, Sep to Jun; Route d'Apt, Trouée de la Combe, 84160 Lourmarin,* ☎ *90.68.04.05,* ⇄ *90.68.33.93)* Eight simple rooms (no telephone or television) in a peaceful garden setting with trees, next to the scenic D 943. Restaurant meals are served in a pretty glassed-in veranda and on a shaded terrace (menus at 100 F and 145 F, trout with almonds, beef daube). Discreet, friendly welcome. Good value.

■ **Ansouis**

Le Jardin D'Ansouis *(230-290 F, no credit cards; pb; Rue du Petit-Portail, 84240 Ansouis,* ☎⇄ *90.09.89.27)* A very pleasant bed and breakfast with two rooms, decorated with good taste by the caring Arlette Rogers. Breakfasts are a treat – eggs, croissant and bread, delicious home-made jams and local honey are served on a terrace next to the wonderful garden. Dinners served if guests indicate in advance (between 50 F and 200 F including wine).

 Restaurants

■ **L'Isle-sur-la-Sorgue**

Le Jardin du Quai *($-$$; Thu to Tue, closed Tue PM; 4 Avenue Julien-Guigue, 84800, L'Isle-sur-la-Sorgue,* ☎ *90.38.56.17)* This delightful restaurant is a favourite with the antique dealers from the nearby markets on the weekend and it's easy to see why. A pretty shaded garden and a fresh interior decorated with amusing bric-a-brac, is the setting for some of this town's best food. Recent wonders included delicious fried red fish fillets, lamb chops with rosemary and superb desserts (cheesecake, rhubarb and plum pie). Sunday lunch menu is 110 F. Everything is home-made and the service is friendly and efficient. Located next to the SNCF train station.

Le Caveau de la Tour de l'Isle *(Tue to Sun 9 AM to 1 PM and 3 PM to 8 PM, closed Sun PM; 12 Rue de la République, 84800 L'Isle-sur-la-Sorgue,* ☎ *90.20.70.25)* At the back of this charming old-fashioned vintner (excellent selection of local bottles and knowledgeable, friendly staff), is a tiny *bar à vins,* where customers may try a glass of wine over a plate of *tapenade* (olive paste), chèvre or *cavier d'aubergine* (eggplant purée) and toasted bread.

■ **Pernes-les-Fontaines**

Le Troubadour *($-$$; Wed to Sun, lunch and dinner; 56 Rue du Troubadour, 84210 Pernes-les-Fontaines;* ☎ *90.61.62.43)* Very good authentic Provençal specialties including bouillabaisse and game, in a rustic atmosphere. Three menus: lunch (Wednesday-Friday, 60 F), *menu gourmet* (90 F) and *menu gourmand* (130 F). Friendly, professional service.

Mas La Bonoty *($-$$, Chemin de la Bonioty, 84210 Pernes-les-Fontaines,* ☎ *90.61.61.09,* ⇄ *90.61.35.14)* The farmhouse restaurant of this peaceful hotel serves good local cuisine at reasonable prices — menus at 145 F and 195 F. *(From Pernes, take the D 28 to the village of Saint Didier, turn left on the Chemin de Barraud, leading to Chemin de la Bonioty).*

■ **Cavaillon (Cheval Blanc)**

Alain Nicolet *($$-$$$; closed Sun PM and Mon in off-season; Route de Pertruis, BP 28, 84460 Cheval Blanc;* ☎ *90.78.01.56,* ⇄ *90.71.91.28)* A fine gourmet restaurant in a stone country house, emphasizing beautifully-prepared fresh seasonal products. During warmer months, diners may eat on the shaded terrace with beautiful unobstructed views of the countryside. Professional service and a pleasant welcome from Mireille Nicolet. Menus at 170 F, 215 F and 350 F.

■ **Cabrières-D'Avignon**

Le Bistrot à Michel *($$; Jan, Wed to Sun; Jul and Aug, Wed to Mon; Grand Rue, 84220 Cabrières-D'Avignon,* ☎ *90.76.82.08)* Once a quiet village bistro run by the welcoming Bosc family, the Bistrot à Michel has become a trendy spot which is popular with Parisians and North Americans thanks to recent media attention. Fortunately, it still serves very good food using fresh ingredients, such as a warm tomato and tuna tart, fillet of cod or *pieds et paquets.* Amusing cartoons and old movie posters cover the walls. Pricey. Menus at 100 F (salad, dessert, glass of wine - weekday lunch only) and 160 F (two courses plus cheese or dessert).

■ **Venasque**

Auberge La Fontaine *($$; Place de la Fontaine, 84210 Venasque,* ☎ *90.66.02.96,* ⇄ *90.66.13.14)* Good meals served in the first floor rustic dining room include nice touches like thick home-made bread and delicious *tapenade* served while pondering the menu. Monthly music recitals with dinner. The informal bistro on the ground floor is ideal for lunch (both restaurants are closed from mid-November to mid-December.)

■ **Gordes**

Les Vordenses *($$; closed Wed; Les Goges, 84220 Gordes,* ☎ *90.72.10.12,)* A pleasant restaurant in the valley below Gordes run with great care and professionalism by a young couple. Provençal specialties with a game menu in the winter. Happily, a light lunch menu for hot summer days is offered. Appropriately called *Menu Petite Faim,* items such as tomato, chèvre and basil salad (50 F) and zucchini flan with basil (45 F) are listed. Good wine list with local bottles. Shaded terrace.

■ **Bonnieux**

Le Fournil *($$; Tue to Sun; 5 Place Carnot, 84480 Bonnieux,* ☎ *90.75.83.62)* Situated on a pleasant square with a fountain in the village centre, Guy Malbec and Jean-Christophe Lèche offer delicious and inventive twists to Provençal classics, such as a cold pistou with mussels and cockles, a lamb flan with eggplant, braised hake with violet artichokes, warm chocolate cake with pistachio sauce. A choice of menus (112 F, 148 F and 158 F). Terrace in the summer.

Henri Tomas *($; 7 and 9 Rue de la République, 84480 Bonnieux,* ☎ *90.75.85.52)* The jovial Tomas offers his specialty tart galette Provençale and other sweet things in his pastry shop in the front, and a tearoom in a couple of rooms behind which date from the 12th century and were once used as a press-house producing olive oil. Perfect for a cup of steaming hot chocolate in the cooler months. Situated opposite the Musée de la Boulangerie.

■ Saignon

Auberge du Presbytère *($-$$; Place de la Fontaine, 84400 Saignon,* ☎ *90.74.11.50,* ⇄ *90.04.68.51;dinner only, closed Nov 15 to 30).* The restaurant in this delightful village proposes a set menu for only 145 F including two courses, cheese and dessert. Drinks can be taken in the bar or on the terrace next to the fountain *(11 AM to 1 PM and 4:30 PM to 8 PM).*

■ Viens

Le Petit Jardin *($-$$; Thu to Tue, dinner only; Village centre, 84750 Viens,* ☎ *90.75.20.05)* A typical village cafe (open all day) with a cosy restaurant behind serving no-nonsense classics like *salade chèvre chaud* and *confit de canard.* The 115 F menu is an unbeatable value. Recently, it included

mushroom terrine, roast lamb, cheese, dessert and a carafe of Côtes de Luberon wine. Service next to the stone hearth in the winter, or in the beautiful garden in the summer. Worth dropping by to meet Muguette, the colourful hostess.

■ Lourmarin

L'Oustalet de Georges *($-$$; Tue to Sun, closed Sun PM; Avenue Philippe-de-Girard, 84160 Lourmarin,* ☎ *90.68.07.33)* A definiite emphasis on fresh, provençal items (pistou soup, cod fillets with olives) in an old roadside house. Good three course lunch menu (105 F, weekdays only) includes a salad selection dressed with local olive oil or a fish terrine to start , and a fine *tarte du jour* to finish.

Michel Ange *($$; mid-Jun to mid-Sep open everyday; mid-Sep to mid-Jun Thu to Tue, closed Tue PM; Place de la Fontaine 84160 Lourmarin,* ☎ *90.68.02.03)* A cheery Mediterannean theme runs through this restaurant (formerly Maison Ollier) in the village centre. Clay-tile floors, Tuscany colours and lots of fish and pasta dishes. Menus at 108 F, 158 F plus a *Menu Dégustation* for 258 F.

Le Braséro *($; closed Mon, Tue lunchtime and Oct; 9 Rue de l'Église, 13840 Rognes,* ☎ *42.50.17.63)* No awards for its interior, but Le Braséro serves the best pizza (35 F - 50 F) in the entire region — the chèvre and basil should win the awards. Also pastas, salads and full menus. *Rognes is 14 km south of Lourmarin (10 min from the Silvercane Abbey) along the D 543.*

Entertainment

■ **Festivals**

As in the Comtat Venaissin, the Vaucluse and the Luberon are rural areas with spectacular natural beauty but little nightlife. Visitors are here to soak up the region's rich history, to explore the countryside and its charming villages by foot and car and enjoy the delicious local food and wine. Evenings are not spent in the disco or at a smokey jazz club because there aren't any. But there are beautiful sunsets and great food to linger over.

There is one big exception: summertime is festival time in France and all of Provence is alive with festivals celebrating the region's culture, history and traditions. Major festivals in the Upper Comtat include:
Festival de Gordes jazz, classical music and theatre; mid-Jul to mid Aug;
Festival de Quatuors A Cordes in Fontaine-de-Vaucluse, Roussillon, Goult string quartet concerts, Jun to Sep;
Fête de la Lavande in Sault lavender festival, Aug;
Fête des Vendanges in Entrechaux Wine harvest festival, Sep;
Festival du Sud-Luberon in La Tour-d'Aigues dance, theatre, music, Jul;
Rencontres d'Été in Apt historians and writers events, Aug;
Festival International de Folklore in Cavaillon Fridays, Jul and Aug;
Chansons Françaises in Cavaillon music concerts, Saturdays, Jul and Aug;
Les Kiosques à Musique d'Été in Cavaillon Sunday afternoons, Jul and Aug;
Musique d'Été and **Rencontres Méditerranéennes Albert Camus** in Lourmarin Music and writers event, Aug.

 Shopping

■ **L'Isle-sur-la-Sorgue**

Les Délices du Lubéron *(270 Avenue Voltaire-Garcin, 84800 Isle-sur-la-Sorgue, ☎ 90.38.45.96)* A good selection of the best Provençal food products, including olive oils, *tapenade*, herbs, nougat and candy.

Antique Markets

The entire village becomes an antique and flea market on weekends (arrive by 10 AM to find parking space during the summer). Try to bargain — start at 15 per cent off the asking price and hope to get a 10 per cent reduction. The choice is happily varied in taste, quality and price — here are some of the best spots to check out:

Espace Béchard *(1 Avenue Charmasson, Route d'Apt, ☎ 90.38.25.40)* Eleven professional dealers with quality furniture and objects.

L'Isle Aux Brocantes *(Passage du Pont, 7 Avenue des 4 Otages, ☎ 90.20.69.93)* Over 35 dealers in a sheltered antiques village atmosphere, with a strong mix of big and small items, including antique pottery and linens. Chez Nane, a busy restaurant/tearoom is found at the back *(weekends only, ☎ 90.20.69.93)*.

Xavier Nicod *(9 Avenue des Quatre-Otages, ☎ 90.38.07.20)* An eclectic selection of antiques and amusing objects chosen with a good sense of humour by Nicod and his wife.

Le Quai de la Gare *(opposite the SNCF train station, ☎ 90.20.73.42)* An interesting mix of antiques and brocante dealers in a pleasant gallery, offering furniture, mirrors, *objets d'art*, etc.

■ **Venasque**

Atelier de Faïence *(mid-Mar to mid-Oct, Thu to Tue 10 AM to 7 PM; Place de la Fontaine, 84210 Venasque, ☎ 90.66.07.92)* Pretty and original blue and white pottery in primarily geometric patterns, created by the friendly and sweet Anne Viard-Oberlin.

■ **Apt**

Dumas *(Tue to Sat 8:30 AM to noon, 2 PM to 7 PM; 16 Place Gabriel Péri, 84400 Apt, ☎ 90.74.23.81, ⇄ 90.74.63.59)*. Though you can find newspaper and magazine kiosks in the larger villages, it's hard to find a book-shop with a good selection of fiction and non-fiction works in the entire Luberon area. Here's the place for biblophiles!

Jean Faucon *(Mon to Fri 8 AM to noon and 2 PM to 6 PM, Sat 9 AM to noon and 3 PM to 6 PM, closed Sun; 12 Avenue de Libération, 84400 Apt, ☎ 90.74.15.31)* Six generations of Jean Faucon's family have been making traditional Aptware. Each ceramic piece (from plates to pots and tobacco jars) uses local earth and a special technique to achieve the fine waves of yellow, red, green, brown and white. This pretty shop displays these refined and beautiful items to their best.

■ **Sault**

André Boyer *(Mar to Jan, Tue to Sun 9 AM to noon, 2 PM to 6 PM; 8490 Sault-de-Vaucluse, ☎ 90.64.00.23, ⇄ 90.64.08.99)* The Boyer family has been making the region's finest nougat and delicious macaroon almond biscuits from this charming shop (you can't miss it in the village centre) for over 100 years. André, great-grandson of the founder Ernest, continues to follow the traditional methods of preparation — his nougat is made from local almonds and lavender honey.

■ **Goult**

Pitot *(Mon to Sat 9 AM to noon and 2 PM to 6 PM; signposted directly off the N 100 at Ponty, near Goult, 84220 Goult, ☎ 90.72.22.79)* Inspired by 18th century Aptware, Antony Pitot creates a fine white earthenware covered in typical solid mustard yellow or rich green glazes. These are not the repro-ductions you see all over the region, but original pieces as Pitot makes his own moulds sold only at his studio.

■ **Notre-Dame des Lumières**

Edith Mézard *(open everyday, 3 PM to 6:30 PM; Château de l'Ange, 84220 Lumières, ☎ 90.72.36.41, ⇄ 90.72.36.69)* Beautiful embroidered clothes for men and women, as well as a wonderful selection houses linens (sheets, pillow cases and bed covers, serviettes and tablecloths, bath towels). Flowers, poems and initials are stitched by hand onto the finest quality linens and cottons. The cool, contemporary boutique was designed by Jacqueline Morabito and fits in surprisingly well with Mézard's tiny château-residence in Lumières, next to the village of Goult. Orders are taken.

■ **Lourmarin**

L'Ange Bleu *(Tue to Sun 3 PM to 7 PM; 25 Rue Henri de Savonin, 84160 Lourmarin, ☎ 90.68.01.58)* Charming Flemish gentleman Ignace Morreel sells a good selection of antiques – regional and otherwise.

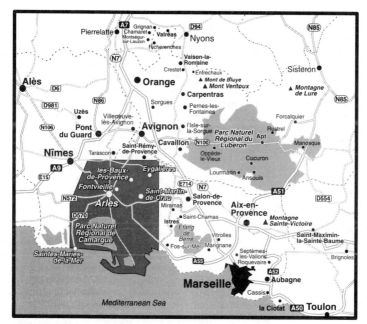

THE ALPILLES, ARLES AND
THE CAMARGUE ★★

This surprising area provides a bit of everything – world famous Roman ruins, beautiful scenery untouched by man, quiet Provençal villages and stylish towns. Welcome to an important part of the French department known as the Bouches-du-Rhône.

The Alpilles is an impressive chain of white jagged limestone hills situated 25 kilometres south of Avignon, circled by three interesting towns: Saint-Rémy-de-Provence, Tarascon and Arles, plus a number of quiet villages. West of the Alpilles lie fields of golden wheat, to the north are orchards and due south is the Crau, a dry pebbly plain. Bordering the Crau and extending all the way to the Mediterranean Sea is the Camar-

gue. This is the delta of the Rhône and much of the wet marshland is a regional park. Here rice and salt production and fishing are the main activities. Indigenous white horses roam and, somewhat remarkably, colonies of pink flamingoes live peacefully.

Before the stone age, the waters of the Rhône and the Durance rivers flowed into a huge gulf leading to the sea. Over thousands of years, the sea level lowered and earth deposits carried by the rivers' currents accumulated and formed small islands. Eventually, a landscape resembling that of today was created, allowing habitation in the area. Land was still being reclaimed as late as the 4th century – a considerable portion of the Camargue didn't exist until then and is naturally-formed reclaimed land.

Paleolithic man lived in the region, followed by the Celto-Ligurian tribes, then the Greek Phoecaeans. (The natural history museums in Arles, Saint-Rémy-de-Provence and Baux contain interesting artifacts from these times.) Great progress and growth occured during Roman times, when Augustus Caesar stationed members of his 6th battalion in Provence.

After Marseille, Arles was perhaps the most important Roman settlement in the entire region. It was a great trading centre linking the sea to inland communities following the construction of a canal linking Arles to the Golfe de Fos west of Marseille. Remains of the Roman arena, amphitheatre, baths and rampart walls with round towers can be visited today.

The region remained relatively calm from the 15th century onwards as political and economic life continued to focus on Aix and Marseille. Its inhabitants carried on doing what they knew best — namely looking after the orchards, vineyards and olive groves, existing here since Greek times, tending sheep north of the Alpilles, and raising cattle and horses in the Camargue. Though Arles was no longer in the limelight, it was still a commercial centre with a growing merchant-class. As a result, elegant buildings and *hôtels particuliers* were constructed there and in Saint-Rémy-de-Provence.

Among the many writers and artists who have lived here and immortalized the landscape and its people, three stand out. Frédéric Mistral, the poet and founder of the *Félibrige* movement to promote the Provençal language was born and lived in Maillane, north of Saint-Rémy. Alphonse Daudet, another native author to the region, wrote the famous satire *Les Aventures de Tartarin* in which he ridiculed the residents of Tarascon and *Lettres de mon Moulin*. Finally, Dutch painter Vincent Van Gogh spent two years (1888-1890) of his life in Arles and at the Saint-Rémy asylum, the St-Paul-de-Mausole Monastery, before committing suicide in Auvers-sur-Oise near Paris three months later.

The world's social press carefully scrutinizes the comings and goings of famous personalities who have second residences here, among them model turned boutique-owner Inès de la Fressange, singer Charles Aznavour and designer/restaurateur Sir Terence Conran. Saint-Rémy's most famous part-time resident is Princess Caroline of Monaco, who in 1991 was offered a 99-year lease on a 17th century stone farmhouse by Count Jacques Sénard.

 Finding Your Way Around

The area is bordered by the Rhône and Durance rivers, due south of Avignon and serviced by good roads and the regional French SNCF train network.

■ **By train**

Trains from SNCF's regional service TER run throughout the day from Avignon and Marseille to stations in Arles, Saint-Rémy and Tarascon.

■ **By car**

From Avignon take the D 571 south for Saint-Rémy and Baux (25 km); take the D 570 south for Arles (34 km); take the D 970 south for Tarascon (23 km).

Saintes-Maries-de-la-Mer at the southern tip of the Camargue is 72 km south on the D 570.

The major towns lie about 60 km from the Marseille Marignane airport. For Saint-Rémy-de-Provence and Tarascon (a further 16 kilometres), take the **A 7 - Autoroute du Soleil** north to Cavaillon, then head west on the **D 99**. For Arles, take the **A 7 - Autoroute du Soleil** north to Salon-de-Provence then head west on the **N 113 - E 80**. For Saintes Maries-de-la-Mer, follow directions for Arles, then take the **D 570** south (a further 38 km).

 Practical Information

■ **Tourist Offices**

Saint-Rémy-de-Provence
Place Jean-Jaurès
13210 Saint-Rémy-de-Provence
☎ 90.92.05.22 ⇄ 90.92.38.52

Arles
Esplanade Charles de Gaulle
13200 Arles
☎ 90.18.41.20 ⇄ 90.93.17.17

Tarascon
59 Rue des Halles
13150 Tarascon
☎ 90.91.03.52 ⇄ 90.91.22.96

Baux
Ilot "Post Tenebras Lux"
13520 Les Baux-de-Provence
☎ 90.54.34.39 ⇄ 90.54.51.15

Saintes-Maries-de-la-Mer
5 Avenue Van Gogh
13732 Les Saintes Maries-de-la-Mer
☎ 90.97.82.55 ⇄ 90.97.71.15

 Exploring

■ **Saint-Rémy-de-Provence ★**

Extensive archaelogical work began on the Roman ruins of **Glanum (1)** *(adults 24 F, reduced rates 13 F and 5 F; Apr to Sep, open everyday 9 AM to 7 PM; Oct to Mar, open everyday 9 AM to noon and 2 PM to 5 PM; guided tours possible if arranged in advance; two kilometres south of Saint-Rémy-de-Provence on the D 5, ☎ 90.92.23.79)* after World War I and continues today. Historians believe the Phoecaeans settled first on this site as far back as the 6th century BC. Visitors now can distinguish (barely at times) a real Gallo-Roman city dating from 30 BC to 10 BC amongst the ruins — a large thermal bath with a number of rooms, a long avenue with residences, a temple and a natural spring. Barbians destroyed the city in the 3rd century AD and a new community developed around present-day Saint-Rémy.

Two important monuments can be seen today next to the Glanum site: a **triumphal arch** and a **mausoleum** collectively called the **Antiques ★★ (2)** *(free admission)*. The arch dates from 6 BC, is decorated with reliefs commemorating Caesar's defeat of Gaul and is missing a top level. The scultpure work is particularly well-executed. The well-preserved 19-metre high mausoleum was built around 30 BC.

Not far from the Glanum ruins is the **Monastère Saint-Paul de Mausole ★ (3)**. The painter Vincent Van Gogh checked himself into the clinic here during the last year of his life (1890). In a peaceful, wooded setting, you may visit the pretty 12th century colonaded **cloître (4)**, or cloister next to the Romanesque

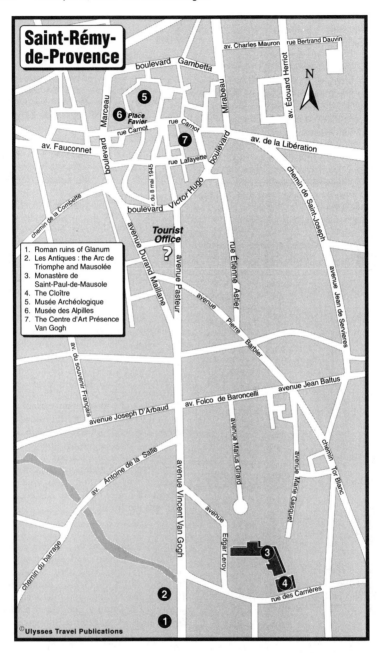

Saint-Rémy-de-Provence

av. Charles Mauron rue Bertrand Dauvin

boulevard Gambetta

av. Édouard Herriot

N

Marceau

⑤

⑥ *Place Favier*

rue Carnot rue Carnot

Mirabeau

boulevard

⑦

av. Fauconnet

boulevard

av. de la Libération

rue Lafayette

rue du 8 mai 1945

Victor Hugo

chemin de la Combette

boulevard

chemin de Saint-Joseph

avenue Durand Maillane

Tourist Office

?

avenue Pasteur

avenue Jean de Servières

rue Étienne Astier

1. Roman ruins of Glanum
2. Les Antiques : the Arc de Triomphe and Mausolée
3. Monastère de Saint-Paul-de-Mausole
4. The Cloître
5. Musée Archéologique
6. Musée des Alpilles
7. The Centre d'Art Présence Van Gogh

avenue Pierre Barbier

av. du souvenir Français

avenue Jean Baltus

av. Folco de Baroncelli

avenue Joseph D'Arbaud

avenue Marius Girard

avenue Marie Gasquet

chemin Tor Blanc

av. Antoine de la Salle

avenue Vincent Van Gogh

avenue

Edgar Leroy

③

④

rue des Carrières

chemin du barrage

②

①

chapel *(free admission; 9 AM to noon and 2 PM to 6 PM; Avenue Edgar Leroy).* A bust of the painter by the sculptor Zadkine, once stood along the path leading to the cloister, but was stolen the night of 29-30 June 1990.

The **Musée d'Archéologie (5)** *(adults 12 F, reduced rate 9 F; guided one-hour visits every hour; Apr to Jun and Sep and Oct, 10 AM, 11 AM and 2 PM to 5 PM; Nov, 10 AM, 11 AM and 2 PM to 4 PM; Dec, 10 AM, 11 AM, 3 PM and 4 PM; Jul and Aug, 10 AM, 11 AM and 2:30 PM to 6:30 PM; Place Favier, ☎ 90.92.13.07)* situated in the pretty 15th century Hôtel de Sade contains columns, architectural pieces and everyday objects from the ruins of Glanum.

The **Musée des Alpilles (6)** *(adults 12 F, reduced rate 9 F, children free admission; Apr to Jun, Sep and Oct, open everyday 10 AM to noon and 2 PM to 6 PM; Jul and Aug, open everyday 10 AM to noon and 3 PM to 8 PM; Nov and Dec, open everyday 10 AM to noon and 2 PM to 5 PM, closed Jan to Mar; Place Favier, ☎ 90.92.08.10)* of ethnology, archaeology and daily life (costumes, furniture, objects) in the region is housed in the 16th century Hotel Mistral de Montdragon which has just recently been restored (note the superb interior courtyard). There are interesting temporary exhibitions on the ground floor.

Another attractive 18th century residence in the centre of Saint-Rémy is the Hôtel Estrine, now home to the **Centre d'Art Presence Van Gogh (7)** *(adults 20 F; Sep to Jun, Tue to Sun 10 AM to noon and 2 PM to 6 PM; Jul and Aug, 10AM to noon and 3 PM to 7 PM; 8 Rue Estrine, ☎ 90.92.34.72).* It houses temporary exhibitions in beautifully-restored rooms linked themtically or historically to Vincent Van Gogh, as well as a permanent audio-visual exhibition about his work. This is not a Van Gogh gallery exposing the master's paintings. There is a well-stocked giftshop, selling books, post-cards, posters, etc.

The **centre of Saint-Rémy ★**, with its winding narrow streets, is easily visited in a half day. Alas, it is crowded with tourists during the summer, particularly during the day. Apart from fine 17th and 18th century mansions already mentioned, it is worth noting the Hôtel de Ville, or town hall in Place Pélissier, which is a former 17th century convent and the more recent Collégiale Saint-Martin church, opposite Place de la République, with a world famous organ entirely restored in 1985. Recitals are given as part of the "Oragana Festival" in summertime, enquire at the tourist office for details. At the corner of Rue Nostradamus and Rue Carnot is the mid-19th century Nostradamus Fountain, commemorating the writer Michel de Nostredame, known as Nostradamus. He was born nearby in a house on Rue Hoche in 1503, but lived in Salon-de-Provence (see page 127).

■ **Baux**

Baux is remarkably situated on top of a craggy plateau with amazing panoramic views. The entire village has been classified a historical monument, and has therefore received subsidies to restore its charming stone buildings. It is one of the most popular tourist sites in all of France, and therefore is terribly crowded. This, coupled with the incredible number of souvenir shops, may diminish the pleasure of the visit for some.

Baux was an important military centre in the Middle Ages until the early 15th century when the Baux seigneurs controlled much of present-day southern France. They considered themselves descendants of Balthazar, the Magi King. The village's fortunes faded when the Baux line died out, at the same time as Provence became part of France. Following this, the village was abandonded for a time. The aluminum-rich mineral bauxite was discovered in the quarries of Baux in 1822, hence the mineral's name.

The village can only be visited on foot and the entrance is by the Porte Mage at the north end. The road on the right (Place Louis Jou and Rue de la Calade) leads past the old ramparts, the Porte Eyguières and ends at the Place de l'Église containing 12th century Église Saint Vincent and Chapelle Pénitents Blancs. There is a terrific view of the valley from here towards Arles. Straight ahead from the Porte Mage, the Grand'Rue leads past the 16th century Hôtel de Manville (now the town hall and a contemporary art gallery) and tourist office, and winds up to the old city.

The medieval city known as the **Citadelle** ★ *(adults 32 F, reduced rate 22 F, children free; Mar to Nov, 8 AM to 7:30 PM; Jul and Aug, closes at 9 PM; Nov to Feb, 9 AM to 5:30 PM; ☎ 90.54.55.56)* is at the top of the Rue de Traencat. Beyond the ticket office is the well-presented village museum, exhibiting objects found during archaeological digs. The citadelle itself occupies three-quarters of the Baux plateau. You'll need an hour to explore the sights marked out. These include the restored Chapelle Saint-Blaise now housing a minor museum on the olive tree, the ruins of a feudal château destroyed by Louis XIII's

forces in 1631, castle-keep and a cemetery. The panoramic views are superb – especially overlooking the Val d'Enfer (Hell Valley).

■ The Alpilles

A pleasant day or two may be spent discovering the many small villages encircling the Alpilles chain. This is an area of contrasts - cherry orchards and fields of olive trees lead to pretty roads bordered by row upon row of tall plane trees, next to arid hills and the white, jagged limestone hills. The Alpilles are famous for olive oil. Two types of olives are cultivated here: the Picholine and the Salonenque. They are cultivated by hand, during the harvest months September to February.

Nowadays, three main co-operatives are the principal producers: Fontvieille, Maussane and Mouriès. For more details or information contact either Comité de Promotion des Produits Agricoles, 22 Avenue Henri Pontier, 13001 Aix-en-Provence, ☎ 42.23.06.11 or Comité Pour l'Expansion de l'Huile d'Olive, 68 Boulevard Lazer, 13010 Marseille, ☎ 91.25.40.71.

Our tour starts and ends at Saint-Rémy (adapt this circular tour to your own needs). Follow the scenic D 99 road with its canopy of plane trees for eight kilometres, then turn right on to the D 74. Pass the handsome 16th century Mas de la Brune mansion (private) and stop at **Eygalières** ★. The most interesting part is the old part of town, the **Vieux Village** ★, which is reached by leaving the Grand'Rue and climbing up the Rue de l'Église, past pretty stone houses. At the top, near the old village gate, turn onto a pathway leading to the ruins of a château, circular watch-tower and Église Saint-Laurent.

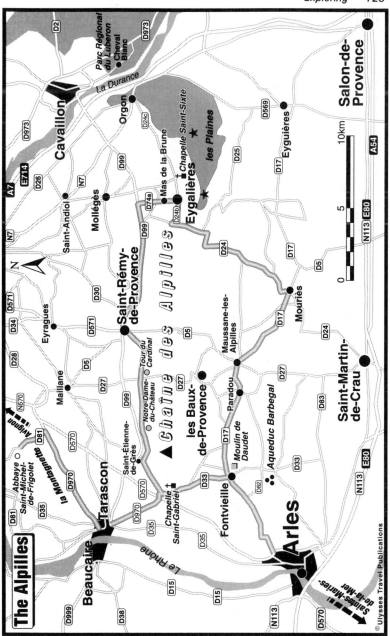

The Alpilles

The 17th century seigneurial Pénitents chapel contains the **Musée des Amis du Vieil Eygalières** *(free admission; Apr to Oct, Sun 3 PM to 6 PM;* ☎ *90.95.91.52)* a small museum with a collection of archaeological artifacts discovered in the Éygalières area – a reminder that the site has been inhabited since Neolithic times. The views are wonderful from here and along the pathway next to the buildings (marked "La Calade").

One kilometre east of Eygalières, along the D 24B (direction Orgon) is the 12th century **Chapelle Saint-Sixte** ★ *(interior often closed)*. It rests solemnly on a low hill, in the middle of a heat-scorched plain and is a simple, but moving example of Romanesque architecture.

Return to Éygalières and turn south on the D 24 for 12 kilometres to **Mouriès**. It is the region's most important olive oil producer, and visits of the co-operative mill are interesting, **Moulin à Huile Coopératif** *(Wed 2 PM tp 6 PM, Sat 8:30 AM to noon and 2 PM to 6 PM; Route D 17 just outside Mouriès village centre, direction Éyguières,* ☎ *90.47.50.01)*.

Next, take the D 17 west (past pretty fields of sunflowers in the summer) to **Maussane-les-Alpilles**. Activity in this lively village centres around the Place de l'Église, a typical Provençal square. There are a number of good restaurants and antique shops (see page 142 and page 146) and the place manages to be both animated and peaceful. Maussane's olive oil is famous throughout France for its high quality – you can buy it directly from the mill which dates from the 16th century, **Coopérative Oléicole de la Vallée des Baux** *(Mon to Sat 8 AM to noon and 2 PM to*

6 PM, closed holidays; Rue Charloun-Rieu, ☎ *90.54.32.37)*.

Follow the D 17 past Paradou to **Fontvieille** where the Provençal writer Alphonse Daudet spent much of his time. Daudet devotees will enjoy passing through the superb 19th century **Château de Montauban** *(joint ticket allowing entry to the Moulin de Daudet: adults 20 F, reduced rate 15 F; Apr to Sep, open everyday; Rue de Montauban,* ☎ *90.54.62.57)*. The writer visited his friends here many times, and the chateau is now a small museum recreating these sojourns. A short way along the picturesque D 33 sideroad is a mill which inspired Daudet's story *Lettres de Mon Moulin*. A small museum in the **Moulin de Daudet** exposes manuscripts and items related to the author *(adults 10 F, reduced rate 5 F; Oct to May, open everyday 9 AM to noon and 2 PM to 5 PM; Jun to Sep, closes at 7 PM; Jan, Sun 10 AM to noon and 2 PM to 5 PM;* ☎ *90 54 60 78)*. Fontvieille is the third in the triumvirate of great Alpilles olive oil towns - its mill can be visited, but attracts loads of people during peak periods, the **Moulin de Bédaride** *(Mon to Sat 8 AM to noon and 2 PM to 6 PM, Sun 2 PM to 6 PM)*.

Farther along the D 33, at the D 82 crossroads, are the ruins of the two **Barbegal aqueducts** which date from the 1st to 3rd centuries. Though crumbling, they have still provided historians with important insight into the Roman mechanical mind. One channelled water into an ingenous mill-like apparatus which ground wheat (access for the aqueducts is by a short pathway).

From Fontvieille, follow the D 33 north ten kilometres to the Romanesque **Chapelle Saint-Gabriel**, built around a Gallo-Roman site. Make your way back to Saint-Rémy, along the small sideroad west of **Saint-Étienne-du-Grès**, the hometown of the Provençal fabric manufacturer Olivades. Pass the **Notre-Dame du Château** chapel and later the **Tour du Cardinal** (Cardinal's Tower, a 16th century private residence). There a fine scenic views along the way.

■ **Salon-de-Provence**

Salon is centrally located east of the Alpilles and the Crau, north of the wetlands known as the Étang de Berre and west of the Trévaresse hill chain. The major highways A 7 - *Autoroute du Soleil*, N 113 and D 578 pass through Salon. Although there is a pretty centre with a few shaded streets and fountains, Salon is a bustling commercial town lacking the formidable history and charm of comparable places such as Arles and Aix-en-Provence. Salon's reputation is centred around the olive oil industry and the manufacture (along with Marseille) of the famous blocks of soap. An earthquake hit the region in 1909, damaging parts of Salon. A French Air Force training academy was created here in 1936. In the town centre, note the 17th century **Mairie** (Town Hall, Cours Victor Hugo) and the **Porte de l'Horloge** (Clock Gate, transformed into a bell tower) along the rampart wall. In front of the Porte de l'Horloge on the Place Crousillat is the 18th century **Fontaine Mousse** curious bulbous water fountain made from moss.

The old town is dominated by a hillrise, where the imposing **Château de l'Empéri** fortress with a crenellated watch-tower is found. This former residence for the archbishops of Arles has been heavily restored (12th, 13th and 16th centuries) and now houses a French military history museum. Af-

ficionados will appreciate the rich and comprehensive collection of costumed mannequins, weapons and cavalry standards, dating back to the time of Louis XIV at the **Château Musée de l'Empéri** *(adults 25 F, reduced rate 15 F, children free admission; Apr to Sep, open everyday 10 AM to noon and 2:30 PM to 6:30 PM; Oct to Mar, Wed to Mon closes 6 PM; Rue du Château, ☎ 90.56.22.36)*. Chamber music concerts are held in the château's Renaissance courtyard in early August *(details from the Théâtre Municipal Armand, 67 Boulevard Nostradamus, 13330 Salon-de-Provence, ☎ 90.56.00.82, ⇄ 90 56 69 30; tickets 100 F and 50 F)*.

The **Musée de Salon et de la Crau** *(adults 15 F, children free; Mon, Wed to Fri, 10 AM to noon and 2 PM to 6 PM, Sat and Sun, 2 PM to 6 PM; Avenue Roger Donnadieu, ☎ 90.56.28.37)* is a small museum housed in an elegant 19th century mansion, Le Pavillion. It examines the history, ethnology and popular traditions of the Crau plain and Salon-de-Provence region. A display on the first floor explains the history of the famous "Extra Pure 72% Oil" soap industry which blossomed during the late 19th century, and Provençal furniture, objects and paintings are shown.

The 16th century writer Michel de Nostradame, known as Nostradamus, lived and worked in Salon-de-Provence. Scenes from his life and writings about astrology, meteorology and medicine are on display in the home where he lived with his wife and children, the **Maison de Nostradamus** *(adults 25 F, reduced rate 20 F; mid-Jun to mid-Sep, 10 AM to noon and 3 PM to 8 PM; mid-Sep to mid-Jun, 10 AM to noon and 2 PM to 6 PM; 11 Rue Nostradamus, ☎ 90.56.64.31)*.

Nostradamus was acclaimed for his predictions published in *Centuries*, such as the death of King Henry II on a battle-field. His acclaim spread nation-wide and even Catherine de Médicis, Henry's widow, stopped in Salon in 1564 to speak with him. Nostradamus is buried in the XIVth century **Église Collégiale Saint-Laurent** (outside the old town on the Carré Jean XXIII), a sober example of the Provençal Gothic style.

■ Arles

Arles is often called the Rome of Gaul. It offers a number of world famous monuments within a very compact area bordered by old rampart walls. Evidence of human presence in the Arles area dates to 2,500 BC Greek traders moved here after their founding of Marseille, and a Ligurian tribe lived in the region from the 6th century BC

The Roman leader Marius linked Arles to the sea by digging a canal to the Mediterranean near the end of the 2nd century BC. Julius Caesar's lieutenant Tiberius Claudius Nero, along with the veterans of the Sixth Legion, founded the Roman colony of Arles on September 21, 46 BC It quickly became a major trading centre. Arles was not only connected to the sea but was strategically placed at the junction of the Rhône and the principal land route linking Italy and Spain. The Roman's developed a sophisticated urban centre during the next 200 years, which included a road network based on a grid pattern, arena, amphitheatre, baths, hygiene systems, gardens and promenades.

Following a quiet period, Arles experienced a period of great prosperity during the late 3rd century AD and early 4th century AD when Constantine temporarily made Arles his operations base. The town was an intellectual, military, political and religious centre of world-wide importance. It was a major ship-builder, weapons manufacturer and mint. Following the spread of Christianity in the 3rd century, Arles became a religious centre in 417 when it was designated primateship of Gaul by the Pope.

Nowadays, Arles is the business and supply centre for the vast agricultural territories of the Crau and the Camargue. Tourism is now an important source of economic activity. Take the time to discover the old, narrow streets and elegant mansions dating from the 17th and 18th centuries.

Roman Monuments ★★★

A museum pass costing 55 F includes one visit to each of the following monuments: Arènes, Théâtre Antique, Musée Réattu, Cloître Saint-Trophime, Alyscamps, Thermes de Constatine, Cryptoportiques du Forum, Musée Arlatan, Musée Réattu and the new Musée Archéologique. It may be purchased at any one of the sites or at the Tourism Office; otherwise the major Roman monuments, Musée Arlatan and Musée Réattu cost 15 F each, the Alyscamps, Théatre Antique, Thermes de Constantine and Cryptoportiques du Forum cost 12 F each and the Musée Archéologique costs 35 F. Visits for the Roman Monuments: Nov to Feb, 9 AM to 11:30 AM and 2 PM to 4:15 PM; Mar to Oct, 9 AM to 12:15 PM and 2 PM to 6 PM, though it is wise to check ahead for individual variations.

Perhaps the first reason why people make their way to Arles is to see the town's Roman monuments. A convenient group ticket for 55 F is available which allows admission to all the sites.

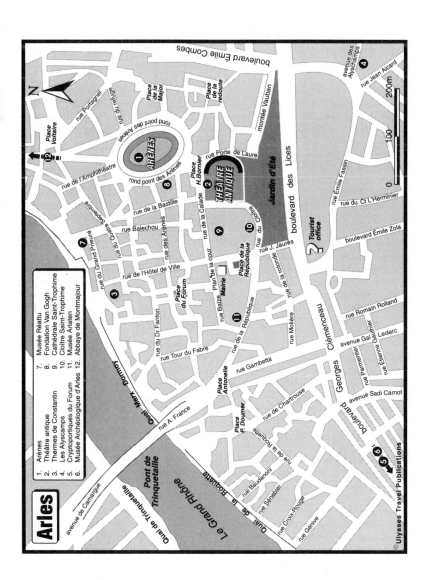

Arles

1. Arènes
2. Théâtre antique
3. Thermes de Constantin
4. Les Alyscamps
5. Cryptoportiques du Forum
6. Musée Archéologique d'Arles
7. Musée Réattu
8. Fondation Van Gogh
9. Cathédrale Saint-Trophime
10. Cloître Saint-Trophime
11. Musée Arlaten
12. Abbaye de Montmajour

© Ulysses Travel Publications

The **Arène (1)** *(Rond Point des Arènes)* or arena, is the best-preserved of the lot. This Roman amphitheatre was built at the end of the 1st century AD for gladiator events and spectacles. It measures 136 metres by 107 metres and is 21 metres high, with two levels of 60 arcades. The large oval shape originally had 34 rows of seats and today holds 1200 people. The monument was saved in the Middle Ages when it was transformed into a fortress, which included 200 houses, two chapels, and a church. Four watch towers where added which still remain. The arena was later restored in the 19th century by Charles X. Nowadays, it is used for Spanish *(corrida)* and local bull fighting (the non-violent course *à la cocarde*).

The **Théâtre Antique (2)** *(Place Henri Bornier)* or Roman theatre dates from the same period but little remains – two marble columns (out of 100 at the time), seating and the orchestra. Archaeologists surmise that it had 33 rows of seating and could accommodate 10,000 spectators.

The **Thermes de Constantine (3)** *(Rue du Grand Prieuré)*, the baths date from the 4th century AD, and despite heavy damage over the years, a large section of the hot baths, parts of the underground heating system and remains of the warm baths can be still seen.

The **Alyschamps ★ (4)** *(Avenue des Alyscamps)* is a pretty, tomb-lined promenade that once was the Roman cemetery in the 3rd century AD A tree-lined alley leads to the ruins of the necropolis, the Église Saint-Honoratus. It was used for this purpose up until the 12th century. In November 1888, Van Gogh painted the pleasant allies, and later, Gaughin did likewise. The more interesting decorated sarcophagi

from the Alyscamps are on display in the newly-opened (April 1995) archeological museum.

Access to the **Cryptoportiques du Forum ★ (5)** is through the former museum of Christian art, the Musée Lapidaire d'Art Chrétien *(Rue Balze)*. These are U-shaped underground galleries measuring 89 m-long and 59 m-wide which while acting as the foundations of the former Place du Forum, served as a granary and warehouse.

The **Musée Archéologique d'Arles (6)** *(35 F; call ahead for opening times; Avenue de la Première Division Française Libre, ☎ 90.96.92.00)* This new museum, created in 1995 in a new building designed by Peruvian architect Henri Ciriani on land where the Roman Circus once stood, houses the collections from the former Museum of Pagan Art and the Musée Lapidaire d'Art Chrétien (mosaics, statues, sarcophagi), plus a reference library, gift shop, seminar rooms and a cafeteria.

The **Muséon Arlaten ★★ (11)** *(adults 15 F, reduced rate 12 F; Nov to Mar 9 AM to noon and 2 PM to 5 PM; Apr, May, Sep and Oct, closes at 6 PM; Jun and Jul closes at 7:30 PM; Oct to Jun, closed Mon; Rue de la République, ☎ 90.96.08.23)* Dusty and old-fashioned for some people, this museum is an absolute must for visitors who are interested in the rich local folklore of the Arles region. Housed in a 16th century mansion, the Palais de Laval-Castellane, and founded in 1896 by the Provençal writer and Nobel Prize winner Frédéric Mistral, the Muséon Arlatan is a veritable treasure chest of discoveries. It is a major source of information on traditional life in Provence, with displays of furniture, costumes, ceramics and crafts – some of the descriptive tags are hand-written by Mistral himself. The recreated scenes of a large bedroom, women's sewing room, kitchen with hearth and generously-laden table are well-prepared. The female attendants wear the Arlésienne dress - dark and sober in the winter time and colourful in the summer.

The **Musée Réattu** ★ (7) *(adults 15 F, reduced rate 9 F; Nov to Feb, 10 AM to 12:15 PM and 2 PM to 5:15 PM; Mar closes at 5:45 PM; Apr to Sep, 9 AM to 12:15 PM and 2 PM to 6:45 PM; Oct, 10 AM to 12:15 PM and 2 PM to 6:15 PM; Rue du Grand Prieurié, ☎ 90.18.41.20)* houses a small selection of paintings and prints from the Provençal and European schools of the 18th and 19th century, plus tapestries, contemporary art and a small photography collection. Picasso donated 57 sketches to the museum – some of which are displayed. The beautiful 17th century building is the former priory of Saint Gilles, lived in by the Arles painter Jaques Réattu. His work is well-represented here.

The **Cathédrale Saint-Trophime** ★★ (9) *(Place de la République)* dates from the 12th century. After seven years of restoration, the outstanding beauty of the west door can now be fully appreciated. This celebrated door is a good reference point for the understanding of the Provençal Romanesque style. Inspiration is drawn from Roman architecture (notably triumphal arches): pediments supported by pilasters, Corinthian columns, the perfection of the size and manner of dress for the represented figures. Statuary reflect scenes from the Last Judgement, the Adoration of the Magis, the Massacre of the Innnocents and Jesus' life. The interior is also a fine representation of the Provençal Romanesque style – simple lay-out, single nave, exceptionally-high broken vaulted ceiling and rounded narrow windows.

Cloître Saint-Trophime ★★ (10) or cloister is reached by passing through the courtyard of the Palais de Archeveché (Archbishop's palace, now the municipal library) which is right beside the cathedral. Two of the cloister's galleries are Romanesque, dating from the 12th century. Building stopped, however, when the monks ran out of money halfway through the construction process. Almost two hundred years later, when sufficient funds were gathered, the style of the day had changed. Gothic was in vogue and so the two remaining galleries are in this style. Miraculously, there is a harmony of vision — no wonder some consider the Saint-Trophime Cloître one of the most refined in Western world. It should really be seen at different times during the day, when the sunlight gently falls on the sculptures adorning the columns and arches. The Roman gallery recounts scenes from the Old and New Testament, the Gothic gallery represents events in the life of Saint Trophime as well as the legend of Sainte Marthe of Tarascon and some mean-looking monsters.

Abbaye Montmajour ★★ (12) *(adults 27 F, reduced 18 F and 10 F; Oct to Mar, open everyday 9 AM to noon and 2 PM to 5 PM; Apr to Sep, open everyday 9 AM to 7 PM; 7 km from Arles, north along the N 570, then the D 17 in the direction of Fontvieille, ☎ 90.54.64.17)* A beautiful Benedictine abbey, originally built in the 10th century, though primarily of the Romanesque style and dating from the 12th century. It was closed down by Louis XVI following the French Revolution. The town of Arles and the state's historical monuments department have restored the 12th century cloister, the severe abbey with its formidable tower, plus the Notre-Dame church and crypt. If you have the strength to climb more than 100 steps, the panoramic view from the abbey tower is wonderful. Photographic exhibitions take place in the cloister every summer, as part of the *Rencontres Internationales de la Photographie.*

■ Tarascon

Tarascon lies on the banks of the Rhone River, facing the town of Beaucaire. Originally a trading port, Tarascon is now dependent on agriculture and industry for its livelihood. It is not crowded with visitors, and so a visit to the château, chuch and old town makes a pleasant half-day outing.

It is famous for the story of Sainte Marthe, the town's patron saint. According to legend, a diabolical land and sea monster known as the Tarasque lived in the Rhône under the present-day château, gobbled up women and children and caused havoc for river boats. He had a lion's head, dragon's body, spikey back and long serpent's tail. Sainte-Marthe came to Tarascon from Sainte-Maries-de-la-Mer in 48 AD to introduce Christianity to the pagan population. She converted the people by performing a miracle – with holy water and a cross, she tamed the horrible Tarasque. She threw her belt around the monster and showed it to the people of Tarascon who promptly pummelled it to death. Ever since the days of King René in the 15th century, the defeat of the beast is marked every June by a celebration the *Fête de la Tarasque*, (on the last Sunday in June), where a six-metre long effigy of the monster is paraded through the streets.

The **Château de Tarascon** *(adults 27 F, reduced rate 18 F and 10 F; Apr to Sep, open everyday 9 AM to 7 PM; Oct to Mar, 9 AM to noon and 2 PM to 5 PM; Boulevard du Roi René, ☎ 90.91.01.93)* is one of the best-preserved fortresses in France. Apart from a fine tapestry collection, the château is completely empty – its beauty is found in studying the magnificent stone structure itself. Built on the riverbank, it dates from the 13th century, but the present building was constructed by Louis II of Anjou and completed by his son, King René, Count of Provence, who lived here from 1471 until his death in 1480. It was a prison from the 1700s up until 1926, when it was restored by the historical monuments department.

The château is surrounded by a moat and tall defensive walls with imposing crenellated watch towers. Past the entrance gate, is a building once used as the castle's kitchen. Beyond the present-day gift boutique is a room housing the old apothecary of Tarascon's Saint Nicholas hospital. A remarkable collection of 205 earthenware pharmaceutical jars and pots line the wood shelves and date from 1742. Turning into the château's courtyard, the Cour d'Honneur, you'll find the vaulted Chapelle Basse and the Chapelle des Chantres. Upper floors include large reception rooms with huge stone fireplaces, the Queen's apartments and a council chamber. British marines, prisoners in the château, carved their names in the blond stone walls - their "graffiti" dating from 1757 and 1778 can be seen by the windows in the Salle des Fêtes. Exceptional **panoramic views ★★** can be had from the open roof terrace.

Église Sainte-Marthe ★ *(Boulevard du Roi René and Place de la Concorde)* was built following the supposed discovery of the relics of Sainte-Marthe in 1187. Part Romanesque, part Gothic this church holds a rich collection of 17th and 18th century religious paintings, primarily by Provençal artists including Mignard and Vien. Note the 3rd century crypt in the basement, with two sarcophagi – that of Sainte Marthe's dates from the late 4th century.

Abbaye Saint Michel de Frigolet *(regular free guided visits, usually Mon to Fri 2:30 PM, Sun and holidays 4 PM, enquire at the shop first; the churches are open to the public during the day; along the D 81, off the D 970, 12 km from Tarascon and 17 km south of Avignon,* ☎ *90.95.70.07)* Resting on the pretty hill range known as the **Montagnette** ★, Saint Michel de Frigolet is a working abbey of the Prémontré order of monks. Visitors may see the 12th century Notre-Dame du Bon-Remède chapel which was altered in the 17th century with Baroque decoration and gilded wood-panelling. The abbey includes a shop, hostel and restaurant.

■ **The Crau**

This vast plain area measuring 60,000 hectares southeast of Arles is the last natural steppe in Europe. The irrigated northern half is used for growing an excellent variety of hay, known as *foin de Crau*. The semi-arid terrain of the southern half, once the river bed of the Durance, is covered by millions of pebbles, and measures 11,500 hectares. The plain is principally used for raising sheep, who graze here during the cooler months, generally mid-October to mid-February.

Saint-Martin de Crau

Saint-Martin de Crau *(N 453 then N 213 east of Arles)* is the most important town of the area. Here you'll find the modest **Écomusée de la Crau** *(free admission, open everyday 9 AM to noon and 2 PM to 6 PM; Route N 113,* ☎ *90.47.02.01)* which explains the flora, fauna and history of the area. Next to the museum is a 14th century late-Romanesque church.

■ **The Camargue**

The Camargue wetlands delta are bound to surprise and fascinate first-time visitors to southern France. Leave behind the post-card image of charming Provençal villages perched on the sides of cliffs, with rolling fields of lavender and fruit orchards nearby. Here, 72,000 hectares of flat terrain, marshes, ponds and beaches, lie south of Arles wedged for the most part between the Petit Rhône and the Grand Rhône rivers and the Mediterranean Sea.

Much of the Camargue is a natural park and protected from development. As a result, large colonies of pink flamingoes (unique in Europe) and a variety of rare birds make this area an ornithologists paradise. The principal economic activity is agriculture and tourism.

The area is renowned for its black bull ranches, known as *manades*, and for the semi-wild Camargue horse. Traditionally used to help herders (*gardiens*) control their bulls and to grind wheat, the Camargue horses are now primarily bred for the tourists, who hire them to explore the region with a guide. Though pale-grey or white as an adult, ponies are born with dark, sometimes black, coats. They are relatively small,

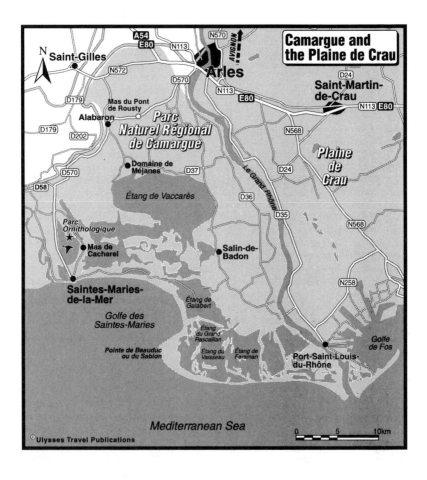

with large feet and hard hooves, particularly adapted for the soft earth.

Apart from horse-riding, bird-watching, visiting a *manade* to see a local rodeo (usually open to groups only) and visiting the seaside, there is not a lot to do in the Camargue. Some people spend days or a week enjoying the natural habitat. Others drive down from Arles or Avignon for just half a day, to get a taste of the region and say hello to the flamingoes (don't forget to bring along a pair of binoculars). Services like a gas station are difficult to find (there are none between Arles and Saintes-Maries-de-la-Mer), so fill your tank before setting out, and bring drinking water and insect repellent (mosquitoes and marshlands are the best of friends!)

To find out more about the area's unique history and flora and fauna, visit the **Musée Camarguais** *(adults 25 F, reduced rate 13 F, children free; Oct to Mar, Wed to Mon 10:15 AM to 4:45 PM; Apr to Sep, open everyday 9:15 AM to 5:45 PM; Jul and Aug closes at 6:45 PM; Mas du Pont de Rousty, 12 km south-west of Arles on the D 570,* ☎ *90.97.10.82).*

■ **Saintes-Maries-de-la-Mer**

A seaside tourist town, once a tranquil fishing port and now host to sun-loving vacationing families and teenagers. Legend tells us that in 40 AD, Mary Salome (mother of the apostles Jack the Major and John) and Mary Jacob (sister of the Virgin Mary), as well as Mary Magdelene, Martha, Lazarus and Maximus, were forced from Jerusalem by the Jews and landed by boat at this port, accompanied by their Ethiopian servent Sarah (patron saint of the *Tsiganes* or gypsies). Mary Salome and Mary Jacob remained in the Camargue (thus becoming the town's patron saints) with Sarah, while the others parted to spread Christianity to Provence. Pilgrimages every year celebrate the arrival of this trio of women, there is the very colourful gypsy festivals the *Fête des Gitans* on the 24th and 25th of May, and another in October (see p 145)

In the late 1980s, the Camargue's own Gypsy Kings popularized the latin guitar songs native to this region, some of which topped music charts around the world. The groups is no longer together, but one of its members, Chico, occasionally performs in the area. Some restaurants provide live gypsy music during the summer season (for example, La Manade in Sainte-Maries-de-la-Mer, see p 144).

Saintes-Maries de la Mer is touristy in the summer months. A visitor will be overwhelmed by street after street of seafood restaurants (with identical menus, some serving frozen fish) and the number of souvenir stands selling suntan lotion and ice-cream cones.

However, it is worthwhile noting the **Église Notre-Dame** ★★ *(Place de l'Église)* which dates from the 12th century, and was fortified in the 15th century against invasions by pirates and invaders. The upper chapel includes a shrine holding the relics of the two Sainte Maries found in 1448, while the **crypt** *(May to mid-Sep, 8 AM to noon and 2 PM to 7 PM; mid-Sep to Oct, Mar and Apr, 8 AM to 7 PM; Nov to Feb, 8 AM 6 PM)* holds an eerie statue of Sarah next to her altar. Near the machine selling chocolate bars inside the church door, are the stairs leading to the roof terrace *(11 F, closed between noon and 2:30 PM)* which has a superb **panoramic view** ★★ of the Camargue and seacoast.

Spring and autumn are the best times to see the greatest variety of birdlife in the Camargue, which includes all nine species of herons living in Europe. The **Parc Ornithologique du Pont de Gau** (*adults 28 F, reduced rate 15 F; open everyday 9 AM to sunset; Route D 570 just north of Saintes-Maries de la Mer,* ☎ *90.97.82.62)* is a 12 hectare outdoor bird sanctuary with explanatory panels that let you see the real thing up close with a museum describing the area's rich ornithological life.

Beaches

Beaches for sun-bathing and swimming are found in the Camargue along the seacoast. Long sandy beaches are best at Saintes-Maries-de-la-Mer (east and west of the village) and are popular during the summer months.

For followers of naturism, there is an authorized nudist beach 1 km east of the access road to the Plage d'Arles (Arles beach), located in the Camargue in the Salin de Giraud area. A second nudist beach created by the local municipality is located about 6 km east of Saintes-Maries-de-la-Mer, just before the Phare de la Gacholle lighthouse. It is reached only by walking along the Saintes-Maries-de-la-Mer beach.

Outdoor Activities

Hiking

One of the nicest trails is the GR 6 which crosses the Alpilles from west to east, passing by Les Baux-de-Provence. The path follows the ridge of the crag-gy hills and offers panoramic views as far as the Camargue, Mont Ventoux and the Luberon. Shorter, well-marked trails are found along the hilly area known as La Montagnette (starts at the Abbeye Saint-Michel-de-Frigolet north of Tarascon) and in the Alpilles starting from Saint-Etienne-du-Grès, Saint-Rémy-de-Provence, Les Baux-de-Provence and Éyguires. The Saint-Rémy tourist office publishes a free leaflet suggesting a number of walking trails of varying degrees of difficulty in the region. Note: outdoor activities are prohibited in wooded areas of the Alpilles during July and August due to the risk of forest fires. However, many fine walking trails are accessible around the villages and in the plains year-round.

Mountain Biking

Although the hilly Alpilles attract hardy mountain bikers, the scenic plains and pretty villages of this area are ideal for those wishing less taxing rides.

Bike Rental

Saint-Rémy-de-Provence
Florélia (35 Avenue de la Libération, ☎ 90.92.10.88)

Arles
Peugeot (15 Rue du Pont, ☎ 90.96.03.77)

Dall'Oppio (Rue Portagnel, Mar to Oct, ☎ 90.96.46.83)

Tarascon
Cycles Christophe (70 Boulevard Itam, ☎ 90.91.25.85)

MBK (1 Rue E. Pelletan, ☎ 90.91.42.32)

Saintes-Maries-de-la-Mer
Camargue Vélos (27 Rue Frédéric Mistral, ☎ 90.97.94.55)

Le Vélociste (1 Place des Rempaarts, ☎ 90.97.83.26)

Le Vélo Saintois (8 Route de Cacharel, ☎ 90.97.74.56)

 Horseback Riding

The following associations, farms and manades (ranches) propose guided tours of the region on horseback.

Saint-Rémy-de-Provence
Club Hippique des Antiques (Rue Etienne Astier, ☎ 90.92.30.55)

Tarascon
Ferme Equestre de Bernercac (Grand Domaine de Frigolet, ☎ 90.90.53.66)

Centre Equestre de Lansac (Mas Lansac, ☎ 90.91.42.87)

Arles and the Camargue
There is a plethora of manades in the Camargue and not all can be mentioned here, so enquire at your hotel or local tourist office for exact details. These four have good reputations:

Manade Jalabert (La Chassagne en Camargue, ☎ 90.97.00.54)
Domaine de Maguelonne (Saintes-Maries-de-la-Mer, ☎ 90.97.94.94) Next to the Étang de Ginès.
Domaine de Méjanes (Allbaron, ☎ 90.97.10.62) Large complex with a restaurant next to the Étang de Vaccares pond, rodeo shows, tourist train and tours on horseback.
Manade Jacques Bon (Le Sambuc, ☎ 90.97.20.62) Professional ranch with rodeos and tours on horseback;

managed by Jacques Bon, the charismatic host of the new luxury bed and breakfast Mas de Peint (see p 140).

 Golf

Les Baux
Golf des Baux de Provence (Domaine de Manville, 13520 Les Baux-de-Provence, ☎ 90.54.37.02) Proshop, restaurant, equipment rental, nine hole course.

Mouriès
Golf Club de Servannes (Château de Servannes, BP 6 13890 Mouriès, ☎ 90.47.59.95)
Proshop, restaurant, equipment rental, 18 hole course.

 Accommodation

■ **Saint-Rémy-de-Provence**

Auberge de la Reine Jeanne *(250-350 F, bkfst 30 F; pb, tv, ☎; closed Jan and Feb; 12 Boulevard Mirabeau, 13210 Saint-Rémy-de-Provence, ☎ 90.92.15.33, ⇄ 90.92.49.65)* Set back from Saint-Rémy's main street, this hotel offers 11 freshly-decorated rooms in a country-inn atmosphere. Shaded courtyard for summer meals (lunch and dinner) and rustic restaurant with large hearth for the cooler months.

Le Mas des Carassins *(400-500 F, bkfst 46 F; pb, ☎; closed mid-Nov to mid-Mar; 1 Chemin Gaulois, 13210 Saint-Rémy-de-Provence, ☎ 90.92.15.48)* Just south of the town centre off Avenue Van Gogh lies this quiet hotel nestled by a pretty garden with a variety of trees, shrubs and flowers. The rustic-style rooms are a bit dated but very clean and comfortable and the hosts are very hospitable.

Vallon de Vallrugues   *(980-1,480 F, bkfst 105 F; ℜ, bar, ≈, △, ☉, ≋, pb, mini-bar, tvc, ☎; Chemin Canto Cigalo 13210, Saint-Rémy-de-Provence, ☎ 90.92.04.40, ⇄ 90.92.44.01)* A four-star luxury resort, decorated with style, though lacking in local charm. Every need is taken care of, and the renowned gastronomic restaurant is excellent. Menus at 220 F (lunch only); 290 F, 380 F and 460 F *(menu dégustation)* make good use of fresh Provençal ingredients. All around professional, friendly service.

■ Les Baux

Auberge de la Benvengudo   *(495-650 F, bkfst 58 F; ℜ, ≈, pb, ☎, tv; closed end of Oct to Mar. 1; 13520 Les Baux-de-Provence, ☎ 90.54.32.54, ⇄ 90.54.42.58)* Tasteful rooms, pretty garden and inviting pool. True comfort in an exceptional site, though the Route d'Arles road rumbles quietly nearby.

La Burlande   *(340 F, no credit cards, bkfst 45 F; ≋, pb, tv; 13520 Le Paradou, ☎ 90.54.32.32)* Tranquil bed and breakfast, each of the three rooms and the one suite (2 rooms with communal bathroom for 540 F) has its own terrace. A cold lunch platter for the pool side and evening meal (125 F without wine) are available. Signposted from the D 78, south of Les Baux, near Le Paradou. Warm and considerate welcome.

■ Eygalières

L'Auberge Provençale   *(285-500 F, bkfst 38 F; ℜ, pb, ☎, tv; closed Nov and occ. in Feb; Place de la Pairie,*

13810 Égalières, ☎ 90.95.91.00) Comfortable rooms in an old 18th century roadside inn, next to the town hall. Restaurant (menu 185 F) with a very pleasant terrace in a landscaped inner courtyard.

Mas dou Pastré   *(300-450 F, bkfst 45 F; ≈, pb, ☎, tv, some rooms with mini-bar; Route d'Orgon, 13810 Égalières, ☎ 90.95.92.61, ⇄ 90.90.61.75)* In a stone farmhouse, 10 spacious, recently-decorated rooms in a cute, high-octane Provençal style. Well-equipped bathrooms and each room has a wicker basket with an extra towel for the swimming pool. Friendly hostess.

■ Mollégès

Le Mas de l'Ange   *(390 F, no credit cards, bkfst 40 F; pb; Petite Route de Saint-Rémy, 13940 Mollégès, ☎ 90.95.08.33, ⇄ 90.95.48.69)* Stylish bed and breakfast, with a designer country house look (two dogs and a stable with a horse add to the effect). Each of the four rooms has its own colour theme, and possesses quality bed-furnishings, cool stone floors and whimsical bric-a-brac. Salon and pleasant breakfast room with a wonderful buffet displaying old Provençal yellow and green *confit* pots. Hélène Lafforgue was a stylist for an interior-decorating magazine. Her husband Bruno goes out every morning to pick up fresh brioche and fougasse, served with apple, apricot or grape juice from the local manufacturer Jus de Fruits de Mollégès, and pots of steaming coffee. Large garden with a shaded terrace.

■ Maussane

L'Oustaloun   *(290-380 F, bkfst 34 F; ℜ, pb, ☎, tv; closed Jan 2 to Feb 10; Place de l'Église, 13520 Maussane,*

☎ *90.54.32.19)* A friendly, attentive welcome greets you in this attractively-decorated 10 room hotel, next to the shaded town square and church. The restaurant (closed Wednesdays) is recommended for its simple, Provençal cuisine – served in front of the town's fountain in good weather.

■ Salon-de-Provence

Hôtel Vendôme   *(250-270 F, bkfst 28 F; pb; 34 Rue Mal Joffre, 13300 Salon-de-Provence,* ☎ *90.56.01.96)* There's not much choice in this town where most hotels face noisy roads or lack charm. You can't go wrong with the Vendôme: 23 simple rooms (many face a quiet central courtyard with small basin) in a oldish building. Very clean, very friendly.

■ Arles

Auberge de Jeunesse   *(Avenue Maréchal Foch, 13200 Arles,* ☎ *90.96.18.25).* Restaurant, garden, tv room, 108 beds (dormitories and rooms). Closed December 16 to February 5.

Hôtel Le Cloître   *(270-295 F, bkfst 33 F; pb,* ☎*, tv in 17 rooms; closed Jan and Feb; 16 Rue du Cloitre, 13300 Arles,* ☎ *90.96.29.50,* ⇄ *90.96.02.88)* Arles lacks adequate inexpensive accommodation, but this one does the trick. 33 clean rooms, with small bathrooms. Large breakfast room with 13th century stone arch. Rooms 20 and 18, though tiny, have glorious views overlooking the Saint-Trophime cloister and church. A number of rooms suitable for three or four people (365 F and 415 F).

Hôtel d'Arlatan *(450-695 F, bkfst 58 F; bar, pb,* ≡ *in some rooms, mini-bar,* ☎*, tv; 26 Rue Sauvage, 13631 Arles,*

☎ *90.93.56.66,* ⇄ *90.49.68.45)* An utterly charming hotel in the elegant former residence of Roi René's intendant, the Count Jean d'Arlatan de Beaumont. 30 individually-decorated rooms (plus 11 apartments: 795-1350 F) with lovely Provençal furniture and antiques. Delicious breakfast with fresh croissants and pastries, jams and terrific coffee (served in the inner-courtyard next to a fountain during the summer). Friendly service and sincere smiles from the Desjardins family. Near the Place du Forum.

Le Grand Hôtel Nord-Pinus   *(760-900 F, bkfst 65 F; ℜ and bar, pb,* ≡*, mini-bar,* ☎*, tv; closed Feb; Place du Forum, 13200 Arles,* ☎ *90.93.44.44,* ⇄ *90.93.34.00)* Ideally-situated on the Place du Forum, this hotel has welcomed numerous toreadors and celebrities in its past. Anne Igou re-opened the hotel in 1989, and has kept the Nord-Pinus' charm, blending good taste with a touch of kitsch. Wrought iron beds and a fun mix of antiques and bric-a-brac items are found in each room; spacious, well-equipped bathrooms. Old photos and bull-fighting memorabilia fill the salon and bar (frequented by the fashion-designer and Arles native Christian Lacroix, among others). The sympathetic restaurant, Brasserie du Nord-Pinus, serves honest bistro meals, with a small selection of meat and fish dishes *(three-course menus at 120 F and 140 F, wine and coffee included).*

Hôtel Jules-César *(880-1,000 F, bkfst 65 F; ℜ, pb,* ≡*, mini-bar,* ☎*, tvc; Boulevard des Lices, 13631 Arles,* ☎ *90.93.43.20,* ⇄ *90.93.33.47)* Centrally-located, luxury hotel (part of the Relais & Châteaux chain) in a former 16th century convent. Well-equipped rooms, newly-decorated in an anonymous Provençal style. Interestingly there is a number of young Irish staff, serving six-month internships. Excellent dining room with good wine list; the superb breakfast *(and lunch menu at 98 F)* is served in the pretty, landscaped cloister. Professional welcome.

■ Tarascon

Auberge de Jeunesse *(45 F, bkfst 20 F, meals 45 F; 31 Boulevard Gambetta, 13150 Tarascon, ☎ 90.91.04.08).* Reception room, six dormitories (eight or 12 beds each), 65 places in total. Closed annually December 15 to March 1. Member of FUAJ (YHA).

Mas de Gratte Semelle *(400 F, no credit cards; ≈, pb, ℂ, ☎, tv; Route d'Avignon, 13150 Tarascon, ☎ 90.95.72.48, ⇄ 90.90.54.87)* In her old stone Provençal farmhouse, Thécla Fargepallet offers a large, split-level apartment with sitting room, two bedrooms, fully-equipped kitchen (including clothes and dish washer) and a large terrace with views of the rolling Montagnette hills. An evening meal *(table d'hôtes)* is available (130 F without wine), even for non-residents. Can be rented for weekends (Friday to Sunday nights, 1,200 F for four people) or by the week (3,000 F for four people). Close to all the Alpilles sites. Two more apartments are planned.

■ Crau

Château de Vergières *(800 F; pb; 13310 Saint Martin de Crau, ☎ 90.47.17.16, ⇄ 90.47.38.30)* A bed and breakfast in a late 18th-century château? Why not! Jean and Marie-Andrée Pincedé welcome you warmly, without ostentation, to their tasteful home which is set in a surprisingly verdant spot amidst the pebbly Crau plain. Six spacious bedrooms. Delicious, generous evening meal *(300 F, with wine and apéritifs)* taken with the hosts.

■ Camargue

Mas de Pioch *(230-250 F, bkfst 24 F; ≈, ps or pb, tv in some rooms; Route d'Arles, 13460 Saintes-Maries de la Mer, ☎ 90.97.50.06)* The Camargue has a surfeit of expensive, often mediocre, motel accommodations. This bungalow-style hotel with 12 basic, though clean rooms in a shaded park setting won't break your budget. Unfortunately-close to the highway (D 570 just south of the D 38).

Le Mas de Peint *(950-1500 F, bkfst 75 F; ℜ, ≈, ≡, pb, ☎, tvc, mini-bar; Le Sambuc, 13200 Arles, ☎ 90.97.20.62, ⇄ 90.97.22.20)* Brand new luxury accommodations in the middle of the Camargue: eight rooms, with mezzanine bathrooms, are superbly decorated with fine furnishings and materials. The tasty breakfast (not just good croissant and coffee but fresh fruit, cereal and yogurt) is served on a large wooden table in the lovely kitchen (lunch and dinner are available too, prepared by the resident cook). The charismatic Bon, a successful rice-farmer and *manade*-owner, and his architect wife Lucille, succeed in creating a warm and relaxed place with a low-key, refined atmosphere. Private tours of Bon's farm can be arranged. On the D 36 road between Arles and Salin de Giraud.

Lou Mas Dou Juge *(750-1,100 F half-board, no credit cards; pb, tv; Quartier Pin Fourcat, Route du Bac du Sauvage, 13460, Saintes-Maries de la Mer, ☎ 66.73.51.45, ⇄ 66.73.51.42)* This renovated farm house inn is renowned for jovial dinners, where

Renée Granier whips up a fine meal (usually fresh grilled fish) and husband Roger Granier entertains his guests with naughty tales, music and dancing — all helped with a running supply of his famous peach and pear *eau de vie* liqueurs. Though popular with corporate groups, individual guests are welcome to join in on the fun (though this is not a place for introverts!) Basic rooms, with tired furnishings. Dinner only... 350 F (wine included)! Horseback riding is arranged to discover the Camargue region. Route D 85, next to the Petite Rhône, below the D 58 road towards Saintes-Maries-de-la-Mer.

■ **Saintes-Maries-de-la-Mer**

Auberge de Jeunesse *(Piocht-Badet, Route de Cacharel, 13460 Saintes-Maries-de-la-Mer,* ☎ *90.97.51.72,* ⇄ *90.97.54.88).* Member of FUAJ (YHA); 76 beds, 10 km from Saintes-Maries-de-la-Mer.

Hôtel Mediterranée *(200-300 F, bkfst 26 F, pb in some rooms; 4 Boulevard Frédéric Mistral, 13460 Saintes-Maries de la Mer,* ☎ *90.97.82.09,* ⇄ *90.97.76.31)* 15 simply-decorated rooms in a hotel near the beach and port; pleasant garden courtyard. Jovial host.

Hôtel Mas de Rieges *(350-380 F, bkfst 40 F; ≈, pb, ☎, tv; Route de Cacharel, 13460 Saintes-Maries-de-la-Mer, closed October to March,* ☎ *90.97.85.07,* ⇄ *90.97.72.26)* Low-key, calm ranch resort with small but nicely-decorated rooms and an inviting pool. Possibility of snack meals at lunchtime, or drinks from the bar (dinner not available).

Hôtel le Boumian *(380-500 F, bkfst incl.; ℜ, ≈, pb, ☎, tv; Le Pont des Bannes, 13460 Saintes-Maries-de-la-Mer,* ☎ *90.97.81.15,* ⇄ *90.97.89.94)*

30 comfortable rooms, many bordering the swimming-pool. Good value dinner menu in the attractive dining room includes cheese, dessert and wine for 150 F. Friendly greeting. Horse-riding arranged. Along the D 570, just north of Saintes-Maries-de-la-Mer.

 Restaurants

■ **Saint-Rémy-de-Provence**

Lou Planet *($; 7 Place Favier,* ☎ *90.92.19.81)* Simple and attractive creperie, in pretty tranquil square opposite the restored façade of the Musée des Alpilles, where salads (40 F), crepes (12 F to 30 F) and galettes (20 F to 35 F) are tasty and won't hurt your pocketbook in a town with inflated prices. For lunch or dinner, but also open all afternoon for cool drinks, ice cream and coffee.

L'Assiette de Marie *($$; open everyday, dinner only; 1 Rue Jaume-Roux,* ☎ *90.92.32.14)* The young chef, Marie shows a confident hand in the kitchen, offering a set three-course menu at 160 F which might include grilled red peppers, chèvre and spinach canelloni, osso buco and delicious crème brulée. Meals are served in a charming room with blond stone walls, fresh flowers and wooden tables and chairs. Meals arrive on an eclectic selection of dinner plates — no two are alike! Friendly service.

Le Bistrot des Alpilles *($$; closed Sundays and Nov 15 to Dec 15; 15 Boulevard Mirabeau,* ☎ *90.92.09.17)* Large and jolly brasserie-restaurant in dark green and red, with provençal touches, serving pricey meals to the Saint-Rémy jet set. Starters are 65 F to

98 F, main courses 85 F to 130 F; the three-course menu is 150 F.

XA *($$; closed Wed and Dec to Mar; 24 Boulevard Mirabeau,* ☎ *90.92.41.23)* Comfortable restaurant with a welcome emphasis on fresh products. The 135 F menu (two courses, plus cheese or dessert) recently included Sicilian eggplant, marinated scallop, fresh grilled salmon, and rhubarb compote with raspberry sauce.

■ **Eygalières**

Sous Les Micocouliers *($$; closed Tue; Traverse Monfort,* ☎ *90.95.94.53)* Mediterranean emphasis in trendy casual restaurant behind the village centre, with, indeed, a wonderful terrace shaded by many *micocouliers* (nettle trees). Cooler months are pleasant inside where a large open hearth greets you, roasting lamb, perhaps over a wood fire. The menu changes daily, and recently included artichoke salad, ravioli in basil sauce, chicken with rosemary. Menus at 115 F (lunch) and 168 F (dinner), include two courses plus cheese or dessert.

■ **Maussane**

La Petite France *($$; closed Wed and Thu lunchtime and Jan; 15 Avenue de la Vallée des Baux,* ☎ *90.54.41.91)* The imaginative Provençal menu makes good use of this region's olive harvest (the 280 F menu includes four dishes incorporating oil from four different local olive presses). Good value three-course menus (150 F and 200 F) recently included green olive ravioli stuffed with ricotta cheese and sage, sea-breem with light broad-bean *coulis* and a number of excellent desserts. Extensive wine selection, with well-chosen local bottles.

Ou Ravi Provençau *($$; closed Tue, Nov 20 to Dec 20 and Jun 20 to 30; 34 Avenue de la Vallée des Baux,* ☎ *90.54.31.11)* A friendly restaurant, very popular with locals, serving Provençal specialties (beef *daube*, fresh cod with tomato *coulis*). Cheery, rustic decor with lampshades covered with Provençal fabrics and copper pans and bric-a-brac on the walls. Menus at 160 F (except Sunday lunch and holidays) and 230 F.

■ **Salon-de-Provence**

La Salle à Manger *($$; closed Sun PM and Mon; 6 Rue du Maréchal Joffre,* ☎ *90.56.28.01)* The Miege family moved south after owning a restaurant in Normandy, and opened this fabulous spot in 1993. Housed in an 18th century mansion and renovated by designer Gilles Dez, the Salle à Manger proposes a refined Provençal menu offering remarkably good value. Delicious grilled red mullet, mouth-watering roast lamb stuffed with *tapenade* (black olive paste). The 105 F menu includes two courses plus a selection from the extensive *Grand Mère* dessert menu. Pretty courtyard patio for summer dining.

■ **Arles**

Vitamine *($; closed Sun; 16 Rue du Docteur-Danton,* ☎ *90.93.77.36)* More than 30 types of salads (24 F to 48 F) and pasta dishes (32 F to 42 F), freshly prepared and delicious, in this light and pleasant eight-table cafe in the old part of town.

La Mule Blanche *($-$$; Mon to Sat; 8 Rue du Président Wilson,* ☎ *90.93.98.54)* Casual and friendly restaurant enjoyed by locals and serving a reasonably-priced Formule du Bistro (daily special, dessert and coffee) for 68 F. Otherwise, a selection of hearty salads (40 F to 58 F), pasta and meat dishes.

L'Affenage *($-$$; closed Tue and Wed PM in off-season and Sun year-round; 4 Rue Molière,* ☎ *90.96.07.67)* Good restaurant serving traditional dishes in the charming wood-beamed stable of a former 18th century inn. Reasonably-priced 90 F menu includes a "flavours of Provence" buffet offering a selection of *saucisson d'Arles* (sausage), fresh salads and terrines, followed by leg of lamb with thyme, duck confit or grilled fish, finished by home-made desserts (excellent lemon meringue pie, hazelnut tarte). Menu at 135 F. Efficient service, though locals appear to get preferential treatment.

L'Olivier *($$; Tue to Sat; 1 bis, Rue Réattu,* ☎ *90.49.64.88)* One of the better, refined tables in Arles where chef Jean-Louis Vidal's imagination turns fresh Provençal ingredients into inspired creations such as grilled mushrooms with a garlic and parsley cream sauce, poached haddock cakes with chèvre purée, roast lamb with rosemary and a steeming *pot au feu* with seafood rather than beef. Menus at 138 F, 178 F and 360 F (six courses, each served with a different glass of wine). Professional service.

Le Vaccarès *($$; closed Sun PM, Mon and Jan; Place du Forum, entrance: Rue Favorin,* ☎ *90.96.06.17)* Many locals consider this one of the best restaurants in Arles, and no wonder. Who can resist the temptation to eat good Provençal dishes (an emphasis on fish) with a charming view from the restaurants first floor balcony, during the warm summer months, of the Place du Forum and Mistral's monument? Menus at 175 F and 235 F.

■ **Tarascon**

Aux Mille Pâtes *($; closed Wed PM, and Sat, Sun lunch; 4 Rue Eugénie Pellatan,* ☎ *90.43.51.77)* This small, unpretentious cafe offers a large choice of freshly-made pasta dishes for 40 F to 50 F (with classic sauces or items such as seafood, scallops, Roquefort cheese or saffron) and salads (30 F to 35 F). The 55 F menu includes pasta and salad; a half-carafe of good local wine is 20 F. Wonderful in the summer, when a number of tables with umbrellas are set up on the terrace of the majestic Tarascon theatre, opposite the restaurant.

■ **Saint-Martin de Crau**

L'Oustau de Mamette *($$; closed Sun PM and Aug 15-30; 13 Avenue de la République,* ☎ *90.47.04.03)* Lovely restaurant on the ground floor of an old house on this quiet town's main street. Fresh provençal ingredients are cooked the way they should be — simply without fuss so that the natural flavours shine through. Recent items included eggplant in filo pastry with a tomato *coulis*; a light salad of chicken livers with raspberry vinaigrette; frogs legs with garlic and basil grilled sole. Delicious home-made fresh-fruit pies. Menus at 98 F and 130 F. Courteous service, shaded terrace.

■ **Saintes-Maries-de-la-Mer**

Lou Cardelino *($$; closed Wed, Feb and late Nov and Dec; 25 Rue Frédéric Mistral,* ☎ *90.97.96.23)* Pretty seafood restaurant with a blue interior and friendly management. Fresh grilled fish such as sole or catfish for 40 F/100 g.

Chante-Clair *($$, Easter to late-Nov, closed Tue except Jul and Aug; Place des Remparts,* ☎ *90.97.82.95)* Chante-

Clair serves some of the best seafood in Saintes-Maries. A variety of fresh fish (35-45 F/100 g) is weighed and grilled on the spot; *tellines*, tiny tasty shell-fish with garlic and parsley, are a good way to start the meal. *Boulliabaise Marseillais* for 180 F, menus at 67 F, 88 F, 119 F and 175 F. A few meat dishes for die-hard carnivores. Friendly, relaxed service.

La Manade *($$; closed Jan; 10 Rue Frédéric Mistral, ☎ 90.97.98.06)* For fresh fish and locally-raised beef. Menus at 79 F, 98 F, 130 F and 160 F. The shell-fish platter is 120 F, seafood platter is 210 F. Entertainment Friday and Saturday evenings with gypsy guitarists. Fresh pink and apricot interior.

 Entertainment

■ **Saint-Rémy-de-Provence**

La Forge
Avenue de la Libération
☎ 90.92.31.52
Discotheque.

La Haute Galine
Quartier de la Galine
☎ 90.92.00.03
Discotheque.

Café Latin
Rue Roger Salengro
Cafe with live music some evenings.

Organa Festival *(Association Organa,* ☎ *90.92.08.10)* Concerts for organ or newly-restored organ (one of the most important in France) at the Collégiale Saint-Martin church *(Boulevard Marceau, opposite place de la République),* plus classical concerts from July to September (call for a programme). Organ rehearsals in Saint-Martin every Saturday at 5:30 PM, July to September.

■ **Arles**

37°2
19 Place Honoré Clair
☎ 90 96 11 44
Piano bar.

Le Tropicana
7 Rue Molière
☎ 90 93 34 70
Piano bar, crêperie.

Le Café La Nuit *(11 Place du Forum,* ☎ *90.96.44.56)* Also known as the Café Van Gogh as this is the subject of a famous 1890 painting by the artist. For drinks and animated conversation in the heart of Arles — a popular meeting place.

Manades

Arles and the Camargue area are rich with tradition — many revolve around bulls and bull-fighting. Numerous *manades* (Black bull farms) dot the region, many with public rodeos once a week in the summer (times, prices, and quality vary, so check with the local tourist office for details). Bullfighting in the Arles region is done both Spanish style and a local non-violent variation where the animal is not injured, rather the goal is to deftly pluck a taught string from between the bull's horns.

■ **Saintes-Maries-de-la-Mer**

Flamenco - Bar Le Commerce
13 Rue Victor Hugo
☎ 90 97 84 11
Cafe with live entertainment, and yes, often flamenco shows.

■ **Traditional Festivals** ★★

There are dozens of traditional festivals in this region celebrating local customs, religious events and significant historic moments. The following are the most important *(complete lists of festivals are prepared by local tourist offices)*.

Saint-Rémy

One of the most unusual festivals in the area must be the **Fête de la Trans-humance** ★ festival held annually every Pentecost Monday (late May). Shepherds in traditional costume parade their 3,000 lambs through the town's streets, supposedly before taking them from the torrid Crau plain to the cool hill ground where they spend the summer. As well, a display of chèvres from local farms (with prizes for the best one), an all-day brocante fair with exhibitions.

Arles

The most colourful and interesting festival in Arles is the **Fête des Gardiens** ★ which occurs on May 1 every year. Costumed men on horses and pretty *Arlésiennes* (local women dressed in traditional long skirts, white blouses and carefully-draped shawls) parade through the streets, and special tauromachy and equestrian games take place.

Other annual events in Arles include:
La Feria Pascale, during the three-day Easter weekend, when toreadors and the herdsman run their bulls to the Roman arena);
La Pégoulado, in the first week of July, a torchlight procession, folkloric singing and dancing in the streets;
Les Rencontres Internationales de la Photographie, for one week in July, top-class photography festival attracting professionals and amateurs from around the world;
Les Prémices du Riz, in mid-September, the rice harvest festival with a parade with floats and entertainment.

Tarascon

Eight costumed young men parade a huge model of the fabled monster, the Tarasque, through Tarascon's streets during the **Fête de la Tarasque** *(last Sunday in June every year)*. Befitting the monster's grisly demeanor, the Tarasque menaces any on-lookers attempting to block its path!

Saintes-Maries-de-la-Mer

The popular **Fêtes des Gitans** in Saintes-Maries de la Mer *(May 24-25 every year)* sees a bejewelled statue of Sarah carried through the town's streets by *gitans*, followed by a procession of *Arlésiennes* (women in traditional Arles costume) and *gardiens* (horse and bull herders). Various entertainments are celebrated by the sea and through the streets, including games with the Camargue bulls. A similar event occurs on a Sunday around October 22.

 Shopping

■ **Saint-Rémy-de-Provence**

Confiserie des Alpilles *(Sun to Fri 8 AM to noon and 2 PM to 6 PM; 5 Avenue Albert-Schweitzer, ☎ 90.92.11.08)* For three generations the Lilamand family has been making their famous *Fruits confits* (candied fruits) using the finest local produce (apricots, melons, mirabelles, etc.).

■ **Maussane**

Bastide Saint-Bastien *(Tue to Sun 10 AM to 12:30 PM and 3 PM to 7 PM; 99 Avenue de la Vallée des Baux, ☎ 90.54.37.64)* Superb antique shop in a 19th century residence with pretty front garden. A large choice of Provençal furniture and objects, selected by François Calvia (press attaché for the French Ministry of the Interior until 1981) and Daniel Pourchez (descendent of a family of renowned jewellers).

■ **Arles**

Provençal Market ★ *(Sat AM, along the Boulevard des Lices)* Arles' Provençal market is particularly colourful and varied. In addition to the usual stands selling fresh regional vegetables, fruits, spices, herbs, flowers, soap and fabrics, you may find bric-a-brac dealers, plus harness-makers crafting bridles, saddles and stirrups for the horsemen of Camargue. It's also an opportunity to the see the *Arlésienne* women in traditional dress.

Pierre Milhau *(Tue to Sun 6:30 AM to 1 PM and 3 PM to 7:30 PM, closed Sun PM; 11 Rue Réattu, ☎ 90.96.16.05)* This *traiteur* (gourmet food shop) is famous for its own tasty Arles dried sausage *(saucisson d'Arles)* made from pork, beef and mild spices.

L'Arlésienne *(Mon to Sat 10 AM to noon and 2 PM to 7 PM; 12 Rue du Président Wilson, ☎ 90.93.28.05)* Traditional Provençal and Camarguais clothes, including the dresses and wide hair ribbons worn by woman for local festivals.

Librairie Actes Sud *(Wed to Sun 10 AM to 9 PM, Mon 2 PM to 9 PM, Thu 10 AM to 8 PM; Passage Méjan/47 Rue du Docteur-Fanton, ☎ 90.49.56.77)* Belgian publisher Hubert Nyssen created the Actes Sud publishing house in 1978. A year later his daughter Françoise took control of the Arles-based firm which now publishes about 10 titles a month, with an impressive roster of French and international authors (the American Paul Auster, the Russian Nina Berberova, plus Asian, Arab and Scandinavian writers). The Actes Sud bookjackets have won awards for their distinctive graphics; the entire collection is sold in this bookshop, along with a good selection of other publisher's work. Regular seminars and readings; art-house cinema and restaurant.

■ **Saint-Martin de Crau**

Chèvre Fermier Malbosc-Espique *(signposted 400 m east of the D 27, between Maussane and Saint-Martin de Crau, ☎ 90.47.05.95)* A wonderful variety of farm-house chèvre on sale direct from the manufacturer. The Malbosc's goats produce a rich milk due to careful breeding and their diet of select Crau hay.

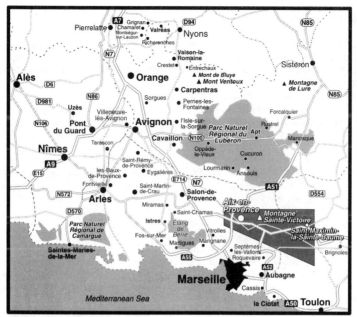

AIX-EN-PROVENCE ★★★

Aix-en-Provence is a beautiful Provençal city with tree-lined streets, elegant historic residences and numerous squares with almost 100 pretty fountains. The many interesting buildings and monuments along the pedestrian streets in the centre town must obviously be visited on foot. It is worth spending a few days in the Aix region. The Mont Sainte-Victoire hill range (painted so often by Cezanne) and the wooded Sainte-Baume Massif offer dramatic panoramic views and wonderful fragrant pathways. An added plus — this region is less frequented and equally pretty as the Luberon hillls to the north.

Aix became a Roman colony under Caesar and Augustus, and archaeological evidence suggests that an amphitheatre, as well as temples and ramparts existed in the area. But just as the ancient Entremont settlement was destroyed by the Romans, successive marauding over hundreds of years ruined these structures. Two invasions stand out - that by the Visigoths in 477 and by the Saracens in 731.

Aix became the capital of the Provence county in the 12th century. Rapid expansion started in the 13th century when the counts of Provence resided permanently here. They gathered cultural figures, poets, musicians and most notably the famous troubadours around them. Building projects advanced, principally of a religious nature, and a huge Palace was constructed. A university was started in 1409 by Louis II. Aix was hit by the Black Plague of 1348 when it struck the whole region.

The height of Aix's splendour occurred during the reign of King René, Count of Provence (1471-1480). He was a great patron of the arts, and possessed intelligence, enthusiasm and a common touch despite his aristocratic bearing. Civic building projects were undertaken, canvases by important Italian and Flemish painters were commissioned, and cultural events flourished. The *bon roi* René (good king René), as he was known by a beloved public, is even credited with introducing the muscat grape to France. By contrast, popular legend also indicates that the King didn't speak the Provençal language and only drank the Anjou wine from his ancestors' territory, thus shunning locally-produced varieties!

Along with the rest of Provence, Aix joined France in 1486. Following the installation of the Provence Parliament in 1501, the city experienced a second golden age. Parliament members brought new prosperity to the town and supported the cultural community. Just the same, the working class accused them of voting for more privileges for themselves and increasing taxes for the poor.

Aix was at the height of its splendour during the 17th and 18th century. Louis XIV visited the city and encouraged urban reconstruction. The aristocratic class built fabulous private residences called *hôtels particuliers* (notably along the Cours Mirabeau and neighbouring streets), made from blond limestone and featuring narrow terraces with pretty wrought-iron railings on the upper levels. Apparently, there are more than 160 *hôtels particuliers* in Aix. One of the most important builiding projects was undertaken in 1646 by Michel Mazarin (archbishop of Aix and brother to Cardinal Mazarin). An entire neighbourhood south of the Cours Mirabeau was constructed with elegant homes, squares and fountains - still known today as the Quartier Mazarin.

In the 1780s, Aix sent the prominent anti-monarchist Mirabeau to represent them as its elected member of the new *Tiers État* governing body in Paris which replaced the absolute monarchy. His memory lives on today, as Aix's principal avenue, the Cours Mirabeau with its four lovely rows of tall plane trees, is named after him.

Following the Revolution, Aix lost much of its prestige and power. No longer the Provençal capital, it became a sub-prefecture of the newly created French department Bouches-du-Rhône.

Aix today is made up of executives and workers employed by surrounding industry, magistrates from the important Court of Appeal, a large student population and an important influx of tourists. Summer months are lively - not the least due to the renowned summer music festival in August (unfortunately affected by budget difficulties and therefore presenting a reduced season since the early 1990s).

 Finding Your Way Around

■ **By plane**

Aix is a convenient 25 kilometres from the Marseille-Marignane airport (☎ 42.89.09.74). The **D 9** road links the airport and Aix-en-Provence. Avignon airport is 85 km away - take the **N 7** highway or the **A 7 Autoroute du Soleil** and bear left on the **A 8 La Provençal** highway, after

Salon-de-Provence and 17 km before Aix.

■ By train

Aix-en-Provence SNCF train station Rue G. Desplaces (at the base of Avenue Victor Hugo)
information: ☎ 91.08.50.50
reservations: ☎ 91.08.84.12

Aix is served by regional services (TER) of the SNCF French national train service. Overseas visitors arriving in Paris should take the TGV from either Charles-de-Gaulle Airport or Gare de Lyon and stop at Avignon or Marseille, then take one of numerous regional trains to Aix which run many times throughout the day. Overseas visitors flying to Lyon Satolas airport may pick up the TGV to Avignon or Marseille from the SNCF train station connected to the terminal.

SNCF information desks in all French train stations can organize the fastest, most efficient itinerary for you. The TGV ticket and journey to Aix by regional train may be purchased at the same time and from any station. Special "Joker" fares offer substantial discounts (50% or more) on train journeys for many destinations, if purchased two weeks or one month in advance.

■ By bus

Gare Routière
Avenue Camille Pelletan
☎ 42.27.17.91
Aix can be reached by bus from numerous destinations in Provence, notably Marseille, and Avignon.

? Practical Information

■ Tourist Offices

Aix-en-Provence
Place du Général-de-Gaulle
13100 Aix-en-Provence
☎ 42.16.11.61 ⇄ 42.16.11.62

Aix's large tourist office is professional, efficient and loaded with useful brochures about the city and events, and provides details about what to do in the surrounding countryside. The concise and extremely informative "Circuit Cézanne/In the Footsteps of Cézanne" leaflet (in French, English and Italian) offers a self-guided walking tour through the streets of Aix, past the buildings and sites which influenced the painter's life, plus a 40 km round trip circuit in the Mont Sainte-Victoire region. The tourist office also offers walking tours of the city *(mid-Jun to mid-Sep, everyday at 10 AM and 3 PM; mid-Sep to mid-Jun, Wed and Sat at 3 PM)* and excursions in the region. A small boutique sells books, T-shirts, local Coteaux d'Aix wine and souvenirs.

Saint-Maximin
Place de l'Hôtel de Ville
83470 Saint Maximin La Sainte Baume
☎ 94.59.84.59

■ Parking

Many of the streets in the centre of Aix are narrow or for pedestrians only, which makes sight-seeing enjoyable but also causes traffic problems. Avoid taking your car into the city-centre. Many well-lit, video-controlled underground parking lots are provided near-by (charged by the hour), just a few minutes walk from the centre.

They are indicated by signs upon entering Aix-en-Provence, and the tourist office at Place du Général de Gaulle publishes a map with these parking lots indicated.

■ **Car Rental**

Avis
11 Boulevard Gambetta
☎ 42.21.64.16

Budget
16 Avenue des Belges
☎ 42.38.37.36

Europcar
55 Boulevard de la République
☎ 42.27.83.00

Hertz
43 Avenue Victor Hugo
☎ 42.27.91.32

■ **Bicycle Rental**

Troc-Velo
62 Rue Beoulegon
☎ 42.21.37.40

Cycles Naddeo
Avenue de Lattre-de-Tassigny
☎ 42.21.06.93

 Exploring

■ **Aix-en-Provence**

Aix-en-Provence's principal street, the elegant **Cours Mirabeau** ★★ **(1)** divides the city in two. It was created in the mid-17th century and was lined with rows of tall plane trees and numerous mansions (built between 1650 and 1760 for the most part, and now banks and businesses). Cézanne's father founded a millinery business in 1825 at number 55. Three fountains are found along the road, the most unusual being the **Fontaine Moussue (2)** which is fed from a hot spring underneath and looks like a giant green mushroom. Farther east, the **Fontaine Roi René (3)** shows him holding a bunch of muscat grapes, which he introduced to Provence. Cafes, restaurants and shops line the right side of the Cours Mirabeau. Street musicians and performers entertain crowds here at night.

From the Fontaine de La Rotonde (*Place du Général de Gaulle*) heading towards Place Forbin, the calm **Quartier Mazarin** ★★ **(4)** neighbourhood is on the left of the Cours Mirabeau. The streets (designed in 1646 by the archbishop Michel Mazarin) follow a grid-pattern and reveal numerous *hôtels particuliers* from the period, antiques shops and museums.

Musée Granet ★★ **(5)** *(adults 15 F, reduced rate 8 F, children free; Sep to May, everyday except Tue and holidays 10 AM to noon and 2 PM to 6 PM; Jun to Oct, everyday, same hours; closed Christmas to late Jan; Place Saint-Jean-de-Malte,* ☎ *42.38.14.70)* Aix's fine arts museum contains a very good selection of oil paintings from the 16th to 19th centuries (Dutch, Flemish and Italian schools) and a number of rooms devoted to French masters which shouldn't be missed, notably works by Quentin de Latour, Nicolas de Largillière and Ingres. The elegant building, a former 19th century priory, also possesses important works by Provençal painters and sculptors (Mignard, Puget, the Le Nain brothers), a contemporary art department, Impressionist paintings and a small gallery devoted to the city's celebrated painter **Paul Cézanne** ★★. The base-

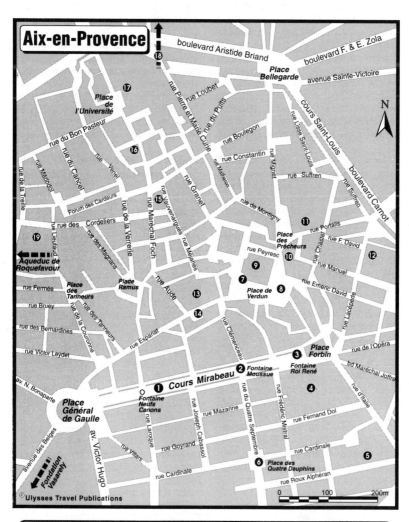

1. Cours Mirabeau
2. Fontaine Moussue
3. Fontaine du Roi René
4. Quartier Mazarin
5. Musée Granet
6. Fontaine des Quatre Dauphins
7. Quartier des Prêcheurs
8. Place de Verdun
9. Palais de Justice
10. Place des Prêcheurs
11. Église de la Madeleine
12. Collège des Jésuites
13. Musée d'Histoire Naturelle
14. Place d'Albertas
15. Hôtel de Ville
16. Musée du Vieil Aix
17. Cathédrale Saint-Sauveur
18. Atelier Cézanne
19. Pavillon de Vendôme

ment and ground floor of the Musée Granet are full of archaeological treasures, including the ruins found at the Entremont site (the Celto-Ligure settlement just north of Aix and dating from the 3rd century BC).

At the intersection of Rue des Quatre Dauphins and Rue Cardinale is the pretty **Fontaine des Quatre Dauphins (6)** (Four Dolphins Fountain) in the centre of the square of the same name.

The most lively areas of Aix are found to the left of the Cours Mirabeau. They are riddled with an astonishing number of clothes shops, cafes and restaurants (see our selection of Restaurants and Shopping). The **Quartier des Prêcheurs (7)** or preachers neighbourhood, includes **Place de Verdun (8)**, the **Palais de Justice (9)**, **Place des Prêcheurs (10)**, the **Église de la Madeleine (11)** (Cézanne was Christened here on February 22, 1839) and **Chapelle du Collège des Jésuites (12)**. The **Quartier Saint-Sauveur** is the oldest in Aix, and includes the cathedral and archbishop's residence.

Musée d'Histoire Naturelle / Hôtel Boyer d'Eguilles ★ (13) *(adults 15 F, reduced rate 9 F, children free; everyday 10 AM to noon and 2 PM to 6 PM, closed Sun AM; 6 Rue Espariat,* ☎ *42.26.23.67)* A striking late 17th-century mansion houses Aix's museum of paleontology, mineralogy, botany and prehistory. To be seen, if only for the elegant U-shaped building and its interior, including wrought-iron staircase and painted panelling.

Of all the many fountains and squares in Aix, the 18th century **Place d'Albertas ★★ (14)** must be one of the most elegant and simple. Three-sided, symmetrical façades with wrought-iron upper balconies face a central fountain

of the same name. Occasionally, evening classical music concerts take place here in the summer.

In the quartier Saint-Sauveur lies the animated Place de l'Hotel de Ville, with the 15th century **Tour de l'Horloge ★** or clock tower, and wrought-iron bell cage, the handsome **Hôtel de Ville ★ (15)** with its Baroque facade and **post office ★** containing the 17th century *halle aux grains* or seed exchange.

Musée du Vieil Aix ★★ (16) *(adults 15 F, reduced rate 10 F, children free; Oct to Mar Tue to Sun 10 AM to noon and 2 PM to 5 PM; Apr to Sep, 10 AM to noon and 2:30 PM to 6:30 PM, closed Oct; 17 Rue Gaston-de-Saporta,* ☎ *42.21.43.55)* is a marvellous 17th century baroque mansion containing a wonderful collection of decorative objects (mirrors, ceramics, dolls), and furniture. Plus, special rooms devoted to *santons* (clay figures for Christmas nativity scenes) and marionettes from the 19th century.

Cathédrale Saint-Sauveur (17) *(8 AM to noon and 2 PM to 6 PM; Rue Gaston de Saporta)* The cathedral offers a mix of styles, as seen in the austere Roman section (12th century), octagonal baptistry (5th century), Provençal Gothic nave (16th century) and Baroque nave (17th century). The pleasant arcaded **cloître ★★**, or cloister dates from the 12th century and was renovated in the 17th. Saint-Sauveur holds a beautiful triptych, the ***Buisson Ardent ★★*** (the burning bush) painted for King René by Nicolas Froment in the late 1400s. The centre panel represents the parable of the Virginity of Mary, positioned beside Moses and the flaming green bush; amongst the religious figure, King René appears on a side panel; his wife Jeanne on the other. The triptych is often closed, so ask the attendent on duty to open the panels.

Atelier Cézanne ★ (18) *(adults 14 F, reduced rate 8 F, children free; Oct to May, Wed to Mon closed holidays 10 AM to noon and 2 PM to 5 PM; Jun to Sep 10 AM to noon and 2:30 PM to 6 PM; 9 Avenue Paul Cézanne, ☎ 42.21.06.53)* Paul Cézanne (1839-1906) was born in Aix and studied law, then art, here. He spent most of his life painting this region, particularly the rugged limestone hills of the Mont Sainte-Victoire range with its ever-changing light and colours. He lived at this address for the last seven years of his life. The studio and garden where he worked is now a museum. Cézanne's furniture and personal objects haven't been moved since he died, making a visit here a solemn, moving experience for fans of the artist.

Pavillon de Vendôme ★ (19) *(adults 13 F, reduced rate 7 F; Mon to Sun 10 AM to noon and 2 PM to 5 PM; Jun to Sep, 10 AM to noon and 2 PM to 6 PM; 32, Rue Célony, ☎ 42.21.05.78)* Very pretty *hôtel particulier* set in its own landscaped park and French garden, dating from 1665. An entire upper level was added in the 18th century. The interior was meticulously renovated in 1992, and includes a number of fine paintings and period furniture. The facade includes an ensemble of Doric, Ionic and Corinthian columns, with two heroic Atlantes sculptures propping up an elegant balcony.

Roquefavour Aqueduct ★ (17 km due west of Aix along the D 64) Part of the Marseille Canal, this impressive arched aqueduct was built between 1842 and 1847 to carry water from the Rivière Durance across the Rivière Arc to the south.

■ **Montagne Sainte-Victoire ★★**

The Montagne Sainte-Victoire hill range extends for 20 km west of Aix-en-Provence. The site contains a number of quiet villages, excellent hiking trails and, hidden amongst the aromatic pine trees, vacation homes for wealthy *Aixois*. The north face is generally verdant and undulating, the south face is dramatic and craggy.

Forest fires devasted parts of Mont Sainte-Victoire in 1989 (thought to be the work of pyromaniacs during that particularly dry summer). Since then a number of precautions have been put in place - notably the installation of "anti-fire" mist-making machines and a surveillance team of 22 men and women on horseback (with uniforms inspired by the famous Royal Canadian Mounted Police). They control a territory of more than 700 hectares, give assistance to hikers and mountain bikers and evaluate the growth of vegetation in the area destroyed by fire.

Of course, Sainte-Victoire is known as the favourite subject matter of the artist Paul Cézanne. He is thought to have painted the mountain more than 60 times, capturing its varying geometric shapes and changing hues throughout the day and across the different seasons. In a letter to his son in 1906, Cézanne said "I spend every day in this landscape, with its beauuful shapes. Indeed, I cannot imagine a more pleasant way or place to pass my time."

A full day is necessary to explore this area, if a lunch or walking tour are planned. An easy circular circuit is suggested, starting and finishing at Aix-en-Provence. Take the D 17 eastward (past Le Tholonet and Puylobier) to Pourrières. Turn north on the D 23, then left, westward onto the D 223, which soon becomes the D 10, for the return journey to Aix (past Vauvenargues). Sites along the way include:

Le Tholonet is a pretty village nestled in park and woodlands, and a suitable spot to explore the countryside without venturing far from Aix. No doubt due to its proximity to Aix, it is crowded on weekends and in the summer. A pathway is indicated which leads to an arched dam (the barrage Zola), built by François Zola, father of the writer and Aix native Émile Zola. At the exit of Le Tholonet, in front of a mill, is an effigy to Cézanne. After passing the D 46 (leading to the peaceful hamlet of Beaurecueil) is the Roque-Hautes Park, and a walking path leading to the Refuge Cézanne resting point. From here, eastwards to **Saint Antonin-sur-Bayon**, the road becomes quite twisty and provides spectacluar views of the bald hill range up close.

From **Puyloubier**, take the D 57D (changing name to D 623 when crossing into the Var department) past sloping vineyards to **Pourrières**. Pass through the town, and head north through the Bois de Pourrières woodlands, climbing the D 223 for 7 km. Make a sharp left, westwards onto the D 223, just before the hamlet of **Puits-de-Rians**. The D 223 changes name to the D 10 upon re-entering the Bouches-d'Rhône department and passes through wooded spaces with a variety of wild-flowers in season. The *conseil général* (regional government) has placed information panels in this area (known as the Puits-d'Auzon) describing possible walking paths. Sheltered picnic tables are provided off the roadside.

Vauvenargues is a charming small village at the foot of the north side of Mont Sainte Victoire. The wonderful view from the village is dominated by the Château de Vauvenargues (not open to the public), a 17th century castle with two low, round towers and clay-tile roof. It was bought by the Spanish artist Pablo Picasso (1881-1973) in 1958, who painted the region in the years to follow.

Just west of Vauvenargues, a pathway is marked indicating the walking trail leading to the **Prieuré de Sainte-Victoire** and the **Croix de Provence** ★★★. (The walk takes a good hour, and requires proper footwear.) From the hilltop site of the 28-metre (92 foot) cross and base, are spectacular panoramic views as far as the Luberon hills, Sainte-Baume Massif and Alpilles range. From the D 10, Aix-en-Provence is 13 km westward.

■ **Saint-Maximin-la-Sainte-Baume**

Saint-Maximin-la-Sainte-Baume (42 km east of Aix-en-Provence along the N 7 highway) is famous throughout France for one thing — its splendid **Basilique** ★★. Experts consider it the most important Gothic structure in all of Provence. Construction started in 1295 under orders by Charles II (future Count of Provence) on the site of a 6th-century Merovingian church, but stopped in 1316 when only partially completed. Lack of funds meant work was delayed until the early 15th century, and then again in the early 16th century. Such stop-and-go construction methods remarkably did nothing to harm the harmony nor beauty of the finished structure.

Inside, the pure, luminous space is decorated with a magnificent wood pulpit by Louis Gudet and many paintings (unfortunately many need restoring) including a retable of the

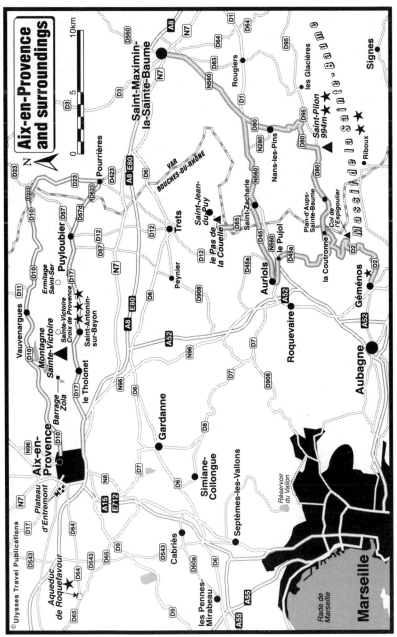

Aix-en-Provence and surroundings

Crucifixion by Françoise Ronzen. The organ dating from 1773 (one of the oldest still in use in France) was created by Jean-Esprit Isnard.

The **Couvent Royal ★** and verdant cloître *(adults 15 F, reduced rate 10 F, children free; Apr to Oct, Mon to Fri 10 AM to 11:45 AM and 2 PM to 5:45 PM, Sat, Sun and holidays 2 PM to 6:45 PM; Nov to Mar, Mon to Fri 10 AM to 11:45 AM and 2 PM to 4:45 PM, closed weekends; Place de l'Hôtel de Ville, ☎ 94.78.01.93)*. The former 17th century Dominican convent is administered by the *Collège d'Échanges Contemporains*, who organize temporary art exhibitions and classical music concerts of high standard. The **Hôtel de Ville ★** *(Place de l'Hotel de Ville)* is housed in the former hostel belonging to the convent.

■ Sainte-Baume Massif ★★

This hilly forest area offers dramatic views and excellent walking opportunities. The untouched beauty and remarkable variety of coniferous and deciduous trees make the Sainte-Baume Massif similar to that of the Vosges mountains in northeastern France. An easy circular tour, with stops for seeing the sites with access by foot only, will take at least half a day.

From Saint-Maximin-la-Sainte-Baume, take the N 560 to Saint-Zacharie (16 km). Turn right onto the D 85, where a very twisty road affords a number of remarkable southwesterly views, over the Montagne de Régagnas. Continue past the mountain pass called Pas de la Couelle, until you reach **Saint Jean-du-Puy**. On foot, past the private chapel, there are fine panoramic views of the entire region.

Return to Saint Zacharie and take the D 45 for 5 km, turning south onto the D 45A at the hamlet of le Pujol. At la Coutronne, turn south onto the D 2, another twisty road, and head towards the village of Gémenos.

This scenic stretch of road passes by the **Col de l'Espigoulier**, with the Pic de Bertagne and Roque Forcade mountain peaks on the east side. Following a series of hairpin turns, the tree-lined Saint-Pons valley appears upon descending the road. About 3 km before Gémonos is the **Parc de Saint-Pons**. Here, the ruins of the **Abbaye de Saint-Pons** are discovered by following a marked pathway on foot for a short distance. It was once a Cistercien convent for women, and visitors may discern the nuns' cloister, chapel and living quarters.

Gémenos ★ is a pretty village with a Hôtel de Ville dominating its central square. The building of the former town château was started in the Middle Ages but its main features date primarily from the 17th and 18th centuries. Next to it are the large Granges du Marquis d'Albertas, agricultural buildings dating from around 1750.

Return to la Coutronne by the same road (D 2) and turn right onto the D 80 (direction Saint-Maxilin-la-Sainte-Baume). Past the hamlet of Pland'Aups, is the Hôtellerie de la Sainte-Baume. This former Dominican convent is now a religious retreat.

Stop at the junction of the D 80 and D 95 (known as the Trois Chênes). According to legend, Mary Magdelene served penitence for 30 years in a cave here, the Grotte de la Baume *(30 minutes by foot, by following the indicated pathway and steps, wear proper footwear, everyday 8 AM to 6 PM)* Pilgrimages occur twice a year (Jul. 22, Dec. 24) to the cave, in which a natural spring and marble statue of Virgin Mary are found.

Spectacular panoramic views can be had from the peak, **Saint Pilon ★★** (994 m) south to the Mediterranean Sea, west to Marseille, and north to Montagne Sainte-Victoire. The steep pathway is marked from the Grotte (cave) and takes another half hour on foot. This circuit finishes back at Saint-Maximin-la-Sainte-Baume, after passing the village of Nans-les-Pins on the D 80, and picking up the N 560 northeast.

Outdoor Activities

Hiking

The Aix region is ideal hiking territory, as it offers a variety of easy to challenging trails, many with spectacular views. One of the most scenic paths is the GR 9, which starts from the D 10 road just west of Vauvenargues, leads to the Croix de Provence, continues along the Montagne Sainte-Victoire to the Pic des Mouches (1011 m) and descends to Puyloubier. A shorter path leads north from Vauvenargues (also marked GR 9) through gently sloping wooded landscape to the hamlet of Lambruise.

A third arm of the GR 9 heads south from Sainte-Victoire towards the Sainte-Baume Massif. Between Puyloubier and Trets (a village off the D 6 road), this path trails through vineyard territory and is relatively easy. The GR 9 continues on the south side of Trets - it becomes more rugged but the effort is worth it because it includes some amazing scenery. Here the GR 9 heads south of Trets, past the breath-taking Saint-Juan-du-Puy viewing point to Saint-Zacharie, trails the Huveaune river and reaches the Saint-Pilon peak (after crossing the D 80 and D 95 junction known at the Trois Chênes).

The Sainte-Baume Massif may be crossed using the steep GR 98 trail. This extensive route heads southwest in the direction of Gémenos, past the Parc de Saint Pons, and includes views over high cliffs. Many kilometres later it eventually ends at Mont de la Saoupe, the scenic fishing port of Cassis. This latter section of the GR 98 offers lovely views of the Mediterranean coastline.

Local tourist offices will put you on the right path, or buy one of the many fine maps and guidebooks in local bookshops. Please note that the major paths (Mont Sainte-Victoire and the Saint-Baume Massif) are closed during the summer (generally Jul. 1 to Sep. 15). This is to prevent forest fires which have recently destroyed many of these *grandes zones boisées* (large woodland areas).

Golf

The following 18 hole golf courses offer equipment hire and the services of a resident pro. Green fees and admission conditions vary, between 200 F and 300 F a day, so call ahead.

Golf Club Aix-Marseille
Domaine de Riquetti
13290 Les Milles
☎ 42.24.20.41

Golf International de Château l'Arc
Domaine de Chateau l'Arc
13710 Fuveau
☎ 42.53.28.38

Golf International Pont Royal Country Club
Route N 7
13370 Mallemort
☎ 90.57.40.79

 Horseback Riding

Club Hippique Aix-Marseille
Avenue du Club Hippique, Chemin des Cavaliers
13100 Aix-en-Provence
☎ 42.20.18.26

La Provence à Cheval
Quartier Saint Joseph
13950 Cadolive
☎ 42.04.66.76

La Galinière Provence Équitation
Route N 7, Châteauneuf-le-Rouge
13790 Rousset
☎ 42.53.32.55

 Bicycling

The following Aix-en-Provence companies rent bicycles for discovering the city, as well as sturdy mountain bikes for exploring the surrounding countryside.

Troc-Vélo
62 Rue Boulegon
☎ 42.21.37.40

Cycles Naddeo
Avenue de Lattre-de-Tassigny
☎ 42.21.06.93

Lubrano Location
37 Boulevard de la République
☎ 42.21.44.85
Lubrano also rents mopeds and motorbikes.

 Accommodation

■ **Aix-en-Provence**

Auberge de Jeunesse *(123 F first day, 112 F each following day; 3 Avenue Marcel-Pagnol, Quartier Jas-de-Bouffan, 13090 Aix-en-Provence, ☎ 42.20.15.99).* Well-equipped with tennis and volleyball courts, bar, library, laundromat, restaurant, tv room; 100 places in dormitories; 10 min from city centre. Full board 165 F, dropping to 153 F after the first day.

Hôtel le Prieuré *(298-400 F, bkfst 38 F; pb, ☎; Route de Sisteron, 13100 Aix-en-Provence, ☎ 42.21.05.23)* Comfortable, quiet hotel, just five minutes from the city-centre. Most rooms look out over the lovely 17th century Pavillon de L'Enfant park (no access however). Romantically decorated in lush reds, royal blues and pinks. Friendly. Off-street parking.

Hôtel des Quatre Dauphins *(320-400 F, bkfst 38 F; ps or pb, mini-bar, ☎, tv; 54 Rue Roux Alphéran, 13100 Aix-en-Provence, ☎ 42.38.16.39, ⇄ 42.38.60.19)* Located in the quiet, elegant Quartier Mazarin just a few steps from the Fontaine des Quatre Dauphins and the Cours Mirabeau, this charming hotel offers prettily-decorated bedrooms with Provençal fabrics and clay-tile floors. Modern bathrooms are small, but for location, comfort and price, who's complaining?

Hôtel Le Manoir *(245-485 F, bkfst 35 F; ps or pb, ☎, tv; 8 Rue d'Entrecasteaux, 13100 Aix-en-Provence, ☎ 42.26.27.20, ⇄ 42.27.17.97)* A 14th-centruy arched cloister is the stunning feature of this city-centre hotel which once was a monastery. Some of the 42 rooms have interesting features such as wood-beamed ceilings and antiques, but the furnishings and wall-paper are from another era and need refreshing.

Hôtel des Augustins *(600-1,200 F, bkfst 50 F; ≡, pb, ☎, tv; 3 Rue de la Masse, 13100 Aix-en-Provence, ☎ 42.27.28.59, ⇄ 42.26.74.87)* Sombre, elegant hotel in a former 15th century convent, fully-restored in 1984 with good-size, fully-equipped rooms. Excellent central location. Underground garage (50 F).

Villa Gallici *(800-1,550 F, bkfst 95 F; ≈, ℜ, pb, mini-bar, ☎, tvc; Avenue de la Violette / Impasse des Grands Pins, 13100 Aix-en-Provence, ☎ 42.23.29.23, ⇄ 42.96.30.45)* This exquisite grand villa set amongst fragrant pine trees is Aix's most charming and sophisticated hotel. The salons, dining room and 17 bedrooms have benefitted from the hand of interior decorator Gilles Dez, who mixes fabrics, textures and colours in perfect harmony. The pretty pool is surrounded by tall cypresses. Located in a tranquil haven a few minutes north of the city centre.

■ **Beaurecueil**

Relais Sainte-Victoire *(350-600 F, bkfst 60 F; ≈, ℜ, pb, tv, ☎; Route D 58 131000 Beaurecueil, ☎ 42.66.94.98)* This auberge is nestled in the wilderness, next to Mont Sainte-Victoire and so is perfect for a peaceful break. Nine spacious rooms (recently decorated yet in a dated style), with terraces facing the wooded grounds. It is Run with great care and attention by Gabrielle Jugy and René Bergès. Of course the excellent restaurant is just a few tempting steps away (see p 161) Delicious breakfast with home-baked croissants, fresh fruit and very good coffee.

■ **Gémenos**

Le Relais de la Magdeleine *(490-650 F, bkfst 68 F; pb, ☎, tv; 13420 Gémenos, ☎ 42.32.20.16, ⇄ 42.32.02.26)* A magnificent country inn with lovely parklands originally designed by royal landscape architect Le Nôtre. A total of 23 tastefully decorated rooms, dining room serving good Provençal classics and serene swimming pool set amidst the trees. Friendly, warm greeting. A good base from which to discover Aix and the Sainte-Baume Massif, or Marseille, Cassis and the Mediterranean coast.

 Restaurants

■ **Aix-en-Provence**

Les Rois Mages *($; Mon to Sat 7 AM to 7 PM; 67 Rue d'Italie, ☎ 42.21.42.91)* Casual cafe serving a variety of the fresh-brewed coffees, teas and pastries. Quotes about love by famous writers (everyone from Jean-Paul Sartre to Jean de la Bruyère) adorn the menus.

Pizzéria La Grange *($; 2 bis Rue Nazareth, ☎ 42.26.19.85)* Dependable and popular pizzeria, with typical red-check tablecloths and al fresco dining along this pedestrian-only street near the Cours Mirabeau. Pizza, salad and house wine for two will set you back 130 F.

Aux P'tits Soufflés *($; Tue to Sat; 9 Rue Félibre Gaut,* ☎ *42.26.02.79)* This is the spot to find a delicious array of sweet or savoury soufflés, reasonably priced between 28 F to 34 F each, served with cider or Provençal wine. The mid-day special includes soufflé and salad for 39 F.

Le Petit Verdot *($-$$; closed Sun and Mon PM; 7 Rue d'Entrecasteaux,* ☎ *42.27.30.12)* Charming wine bar serving terrines (40 F) and meat dishes (90 F to 95 F, including vegetables) to accompany the good selection of bottles. An Aix-en-Provence institution and worth stopping into for a glass or two.

Le Basilic Gourmand *($$; Mon to Sat; 6 Rue du Griffon,* ☎ *42.96.08.58)* A Ulysses favourite. A very pleasant place for lunch or dinner (especially on the front terrace) serving unfussy but delicious meals with a Provençal slant. Excellent value two-course menu at 60 F; three-course menu at 118 F. Located off Rue Paul Bert, away from the crowds.

Simple Simon *($$; Tue to Sat noon to 7 PM; 7 Rue Mignet,* ☎ *42.96.29.20)* Cosy English tea shop, with a peaceful garden serving lunches (eggplant tart, cheese and onion pie, Indian meat loaf, 55 F each) and afternoon snacks (fruit crumble, cheese cake, scones).

A La Cour de Rohan *($-$$, everyday 11 AM to 7 PM, Sat until 11:30 PM; May to Sep, everyday until 11:30 PM; 10 Rue Vauvenargues-Place Hôtel de Ville,* ☎ *42.96.18.15)* Large café with light lunches (eggplant purée on toast, 50 F; poached egg on a bed of spinach, 42 F), and numerous cakes (30 F to

35 F) and varieties of tea. The excellent location with a sunny terrace in front of the town hall makes this a popular afternoon spot, though 20 F for a cup of tea might put some people off.

Le Verdun *($$, Mon to Sat 6:30 AM to 9 PM; 20 Place de Verdun,* ☎ *42.27.03.24)* A comfortable and friendly local cafe serving breakfast, lunch and dinner. Recent items included roast pork with garden vegetables (55 F), a Saint-Marcellin and walnut salad (39 F) and rich chocolate cake (22 F). Those watching their waistline will fall for the *plats diététiques* (48 F to 55 F), which might be a fish, chicken or vegetable-based dish. Handy location opposite the Palais de Justice for the thrice-weekly outdoor flea market.

Jacquou le Croquant *($$; 2 Rue de l'Aumône Vieille, closed Sun, Mon and mid-Aug to mid-Sep;* ☎ *42.27.37.19)* A variety of tasty *tourtons* (whole-wheat crepes with different fillings) and salads are served by the bubbly, friendly female staff. Everything is fresh and appealingly presented — we enjoyed the *Salade Mistral* (chèvre, *tapenade*, herbs and olive oil). The midday menu at 57 F includes either salad or *tourton* followed by home-made dessert (caramelised apple pie, pear flan). Menus at 79 F and 95 F.

Le Bistro Latin *($$; 18 Rue de la Couronne,* ☎ *42.38.22.88)* Chef Bruno Ungaro offers superb contemporary Provençal cuisine made with the freshest local ingredients, such as profiteroles of sautéed snails and olive cream or baked chèvre tart followed by braised lamb with pistou or fried red mullet with spices. Menus at 119 F, 182 F and 250 F. Professional service and excellent wine list. Casually-sophisticated grey and pink decor; a good place for a refined dinner.

Côté Cour *($$; closed Sun evening and Mon; 19 Cours Mirabeau,* ☎ *42.26.32.39)* Fresh, luminous restaurant situated around a verdant inner courtyard of an elegant Cours Mirabeau *hôtel particulier*. The menu leans towards Provençal classics, updated with great verve. Menus at 180 F and 200 F. Stylish clientele.

■ **Beaurecueil**

Relais Sainte-Victoire *($$-$$$, closed Sun evening and Mon, first week of Jan, Feb and Easter school holidays; Route D 58 Beaurecueil,* ☎ *42.66.94.98)* René Bergès has established a reputation reaching far beyond this tiny hamlet near Aix for his refined Provençal cooking. Local suppliers provide the best ingredients, from vegetables and olive oil, to fish, lamb, rabbit and pigeon. Recent starters included mushroom stuffed zucchini, flower or lobster terrine with pistou and a white bean vinaigrette, followed by fresh red mullet with lavender butter or a lamb confit with ratatouille. The cheese trolley offers a particularly good selection of chèvre varieties. Desserts are sublime. Menus at 220 F (four courses including cheese and dessert), 295 F (five courses) and 410 F (six courses). Pleasant oak-panelled dining room or conservatory. Professional service. Worth the detour and best to book ahead as it is popular with local dignitaries and well-off *Aixois*.

■ **Vauvenargues**

Le Garde *($-$$, no credit cards; Mon to Wed PM only, Thu to Sat mid-day and PM, Sun mid-day and PM during the summer only; Route D 10 two km west of Vauvenargues,* ☎ *42.24.97.99)* Within viewing distance of the hill-top cross of the Prieuré de Sainte-Victoire, this friendly roadside restaurant serves up good grilled meats and fish, salads and home-made desserts. There's even a boules track next to the brightly-tiled patio bar.

Au Moulin de Provence *($-$$; open mid-Mar to Oct. 31; Avenue des Maquisards, 13126 Vauvenargues,* ☎ *42.66.02.22,* ⇄ *42.66.01.21)* Though the decor is nothing to write home about, the cuisine is: superb Provençal dishes cooked with care by Monsieur and Madame Yemenidjian which highlight the ingredients' natural flavours (eggplant terrine with a tomato-basil *coulis; daube à la provençale; nougat glacé)*. Reasonably priced menus at 90 F and 110 F. Friendly welcome. Simple rooms in the adjoining hotel are 250 F and, with a balcony overlooking the Sainte-Victoire hills, 280 F.

 Entertainment

■ **Aix-en-Provence**

Les 2 Garçons *(53 Cours Mirabeau,* ☎ *42.26.00.51)* An elegant cafe with large side-walk terrace which is perfect for watching the parade of people passing along the Cours Mirabeau while taking a coffee or a drink, night and day. Known as the "2 G", it was founded in 1792 and is an Aix insitution. Service can be rushed and aloof; eat somewhere else.

Bar Brigand *(17 Place Richelme at Rue Fauchier,* ☎ *42.26.11.57)* Better than average bar serving over 40 types of Belgian and European beers.

Hot Brass *(Route d'Eguilles, Celony, 1 3 0 9 0 A i x - e n - P r o v e n c e, ☎ 42.21.05.57)* Laid-back club with jazz music and frequent visiting musicians. Worth the trip from the city centre *(take route N 7, direction Eguilles/Avignon).* There is an entrance charge of 100 F (70 F for students) per person including one drink for major concerts.

IPN *(23 Cours Sextius, ☎ 42.26.25.17)* Popular nightclub with a young crowd dancing to the latest music.

■ **Festivals**

The Festival International d'Art Lyrique et de Musique d'Aix-en-Provence, commonly known as the Fesitval d'Aix, is an acclaimed annual music festival running since 1948. Musicians and singers of international renown perfom in recitals, concerts and excellent opera productions (in the Théâtre de l'Archevêqué), plus many impromptu events take place throughout the city. The festival generally runs between July 10 and 30. For a programme and guide contact the Festival d'Aix office *(Palais de l'Ancien Archevêché, 13100 Aix-en-Provence, ☎ 42.17.34.20, ⇄ 42.96.12.61)* or the city's tourist office.

 Shopping

■ **Aix-en-Provence**

Léonard Parli *(8 AM to noon and 2 PM to 7 PM, closed Sun and Mon; 33 Avenue Victor Hugo ☎ 91.26.05.71)* Manufacturers of the famous *Calissons*

d'Aix since 1874. Delicious oblong candies made from almond paste, syrup and preserved melon, the *calissons* reportedly were first served for the wedding banquet of good king René and his second wife, Queen Jeanne.

Sienne *(Tue to Sat 9 AM to 1 PM and 3 PM to 7 PM; 9 Rue Rifle Rafle ☎ 42.21.42.20)* A fine selection of tasteful gifts (decorative objects, household linens and furniture) and no Provençal fabrics in sight! Promise.

Librairie de Provence *(Mon to Sat 9:15 AM to 7:15 PM; 31 Cours Mirabeau, ☎ 42.26.07.23)* Large bookshop with a good choice of regional titles (travel, literature, cuisine, etc.), including Ulysses travel guides!

Makaire *(Mon to Sat 9 AM to noon and 2 PM to 7 PM; Rue Thiers/Place du Palais, ☎ 42.38.19.63)* Quality bookshop with the latest fiction and non-fiction releases (strong on Provençal titles), rare books, plus a large section devoted to paper supplies and writing instruments. Professional service.

Riederer *(Mon to Sat 7:45 AM to 7:30 PM Sun 1 PM to 3 PM; 6 Rue Thiers)* Long-established (five generations) pastry shop for morning croissants and a large selection of cakes, including the house specialty, *tarte aux pommes* (apple pie). Continental breakfast, light lunches and afternoon cake are served in a pleasant tearoom.

Richart *(Tue to Sat 10 AM to 1 PM and 2:15 PM to 7 PM, Mon 2:15 PM to 7PM; 8 Rue de Thiers, ☎ 42.38.16.19)* Superb chocolates from this contemporary shop, plus delicious chocolate cones filled with a variety of refreshing fruit-flavoured sorbets. Dark chocolate is Richart's speciality.

Rue d'Italie A visit to the shops along this street *(south of Place Forbin at the east end of Cours Mirabeau)* to prepare a picnic is recommended before heading out for a day-trip to the Montagne Sainte-Victoire or Sainte-Baume Massif areas. There are a couple of fruit and vegetable sellers, a cheese shop, **La Baratte** *(21 Rue d'Italie)*, a wine shop, **Bacchus** *(25 Rue d'Italie)* and two bakeries for fresh bread, **La Paneria** *(45 Rue d'Italie)* sells a mesmerizing selection of whole wheat varieties. *(These shops are generally open 8 AM to 12:30 PM and 4 PM to 7:30 PM)*.

■ **Markets**

Flea Market
Tuesday, Thursday and Saturday morning: Place Palais de Justice

Fruit and Vegetable Market
Tuesday, Thursday and Saturday morning: Place de la Madeleine
Every morning: Place Richelme

Flower Market
Tuesday, Thursday and Saturday morning: Place de la Mairie
Sunday morning: Place de la Madeleine

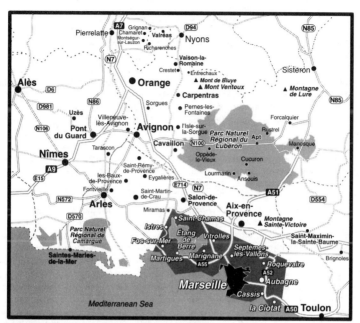

MARSEILLE AND THE MEDITERRANEAN COAST ★★

Marseille has an image problem. France's oldest city is frequently misunderstood, due to negative press reports and public misconceptions formulated from afar. Let's clear things up.

Marseille is a great place to visit. The spectacular white cliffs (Les Calanques) which rise above the turquoise sea are unique in southern Europe. The small fishing port of Vallon des Auffes remains untouched by modern property developers yet is part of the city-centre. Ages-old neighbourhoods whose shops and market-stalls are reminiscent of the streets of a Greek village or Arab souk entice passersby. Not far away, boutiques sell the finest fashion and luxury goods. Cathedrals charged with history, prized art collections and a dizzying variety of museums provide an endless fix for even the most demanding culture junkie. Countless eating possibilities exist, ranging from an incredible number of pizza spots to restaurants offering the best bouillabaise and fresh seafood that France has to offer.

So Marseille provides a variety of sight-seeing possibilities whether your interest is the great outdoors, cultural, culinary or more blatantly materialistic. What doesn't it offer? It is not for those searching out a quaint little corner of Provence like something out of an old French film. These spots exist in the Vaucluse and Bouches-du-Rhône departments and are described in the preceding chapters.

Neither is it an upscale place with beautiful, harmonious architecture in the city-centre like Bordeaux or Paris. Years of neglect and the lack of a cohesive urban development policy (until recently that is) have denied it that. Marseille has grown in fits and starts, building projects seem to have been erected willy-nilly and events such as World War II (the occupying German forces destroyed much of the Vieux Port) have left their mark. Instead, Marseille has isolated sites and individual buildings of architectural importance, at times plunked down in undistinguished areas. The 19th century Hôtel de Ville on the Quai du Port is squeezed between banal low-rise apartment blocks, the elegant opera house rests in an area frequented by *femmes de charme* (call girls) and the brilliantly-restored Vieille Charité museum is in the heart of the colourful working class neighbourhood known as Le Panier.

Indeed, Marseille is more accurately termed picturesque than beautiful. Apart from the extraordinary Calanques which extend eastwards from Marseille all the way to the port of Cassis, the city offers a couple of vantage points from which to enjoy amazing panoramic views. From the Notre Dame de la Garde cathedral, visitors get a 360° view of Marseille — it is best at sunset when the multi-coloured sky reflects on the sea and places Château d'If (the island fortress immortalized in Alexandre Dumas' *The Count of Monte Cristo*) in silhouette. Otherwise, the lovely views looking back over the entire Vieux Port from the gardens of Napoléon III's Palais du Pharo are picture postcard beautiful.

The city has been a trading centre since day one, which in Marseille's case was around about 600 BC when Greek merchants from Phoenecia landed on the coast. Protis, the Greek leader, was chosen by Gyptis, daughter of the local Celto-Ligurian chief, to marry her. Thus started a tradition of mixed-marriages in the city. Marseille has been proudly multi-cultural ever since.

The Greeks called the spot Massalia, and they competed with the Etruscans and the Carthaginians for trade routes throughout the Mediterranean region. The Marseillais even pushed north by sea towards the British Isles and Scandinavia, and south towards Senegal in search of new markets. Outposts along the coastline, notably at present-day Antibes, Nice and Hyères, were established. The community had its ups and downs as a trading centre — 6 BC and 4 BC were prosperous periods, 5 BC was particularly difficult.

Squirmishes were frequent between the Greek settlers and the Celto-Ligurian tribes. The *Marseillais* twice called upon the Romans to help them defend their trading colony, in 181 BC and 154 BC. Thus started a Roman presence in the region, which grew following 125 BC. The Roman consul Sextius Calvinus took hold of the Celto-Ligurian settlement at Entremont in 124 BC and created a base nearby, called Aquae Sextiae (present-day Aix-en-Provence). Roughly 6,000 people lived in the Marseille area.

So from 118 BC to 472 AD, a permanent Roman colony known as Provincia Romana, dominated the area today called Provence (soon after called Narbonne). Strategically, Provence gave the Romans control of the all-important land route between Italy and Spain.

Arles became its prinicipal city - both on land and by sea (a canal was dug linking it to the Mediterranean). Because of Arles importance, Marseille forturnes floundered somewhat during the Roman occupation, although the city continued to develop trade. Christianity grew, especially after a bishop was installed in the city in the early 5th century AD, and with creation of the Saint-Victor monastery at the same time.

Relative stability came to the region in the 10th and 11th centuries following the establishment of political and geographic boundaries, administered by the Counts of Provence. Marseille profitted economically by the increased trade passing through its port. Spices, silk, precious wood and food-stuffs came from newly-established trading posts in north Africa and the Orient. Though ruled by the Counts of Provence, Marseille was an independent force with its own city council made up of trade leaders and craftsmen.

A series of political crises elsewhere, along with the plague of 1348 and competition from Italian trading ports brought economic difficulties in the 14th century which took over one hundred years to resolve. Following the arrival of King René in 1470, and then the union with France in 1481, Marseille developed its trade routes over the next century and a half. Cotton, carpets, leather, wheat, fish and coral were added to the list of imported goods. These were exchanged notably for cloth, refined sugar and soap - three growing Marseillais industries.

The city controlled its own affairs for most of the 16th and 17th century, though the situation was anything but calm. A consulat, based at the Aix Parliament and made up of the aristo-

cracy was often criticized for looking out for its own interests which led to popular uprisings in Marseille. The plague struck again in 1649. Throughout France, Louis XIV replaced the consulats in 1669 with local municipal councils headed by a *viguier*, a handpicked royal representative.

Perhaps the greatest economic period passed during the late 17th century and throughout the 18th century. Local industries flourished, abetted by successful foreign trade. Raw goods were made into manufactured goods and exported; new contracts with the French state ensured steady work. Overseen by a newly formed Chamber of Commerce, Marseille controlled trade to the East and exported cloth, soap and sugar. The plague of 1721 struck Marseille particularly badly, half of its 80,000 population died.

Marseille was anti-monarchist and supported the revolutionary activities with vigour following the storming of the Bastille prison in Paris in 1789. France was declared a Republic by the country's ruling Assembly, known as the *Convention*, and controlled by the *Girondist* party. In 1793 Louis XVI was guillotined, yet France was far from being the idealic democratic nation wished for by the children of the Revolution. She lacked consolidation and order. The country lead a war against Austria and Prussia and was invaded by a coalition of European powers which included England, Holland and Spain. At home, the Paris-based political group known as *Jacobins* struggled for political control against the *Girondins*. *Girondin* deputies were sent to the scaffold as traitors in the 1790s. Later, in Marseille and other southern communities the *Girondins* rebelled and imprisoned *Jacobin* supporters during a period known as the *terreur blanche*, (the white terror). At one point, in June 1795, *Jacobin* prisoners in Marseille' Fort Saint Jean were massacred.

The arrival from Corsica of the brilliant General Bonaparte in the 1790s (later crowned head of state and known as Emperor Napoléon), settled many of France's domestic and foreign affairs. England, with her mighty sea power, resisted Napoléon's forces and in retaliation the Emperor forbid trade with the British Isles. The traders in Marseille suffered greatly as a result of these politically-motivated economic sanctions. It was only following the downfall of Napoléon in 1815 and the return of the monarchy during the period known as the Restoration, that Marseille could recover its financial losses.

Indeed, the city returned to the world market-place with renewed vigour. Old markets were revitalised and new territories exploited. Marseille was at the height of its economic power during entire 19th century. It was a major world business centre during the so-called Second Empire in the 1850s (under Napoléon III), followed by the *Troisiéme République* (third republic). Trading activity was centred around the Joliette docks due north of the old port. The agglomoration included a series of docks running perpendicular to the quay, huge warehouses and a maritime train station linking a new coastal railroad. French colonization in the East and in Africa introduced new trade routes. The population hit the 300,000 mark in 1869, nearly doubling in 30 years.

The local economy has suffered greatly during the 20th century, although rapid industrialization has brought some respite. Marseille was hit hard by the world-wide depression of the 30s. The city was isolated from Paris and northern France during the World War II, and was itself occupied by German forces (November 11 1942 to August 29 1944). They destroyed parts of the city and most of the Vieux Port. Postwar political events, namely the Indochina war in the 50s and French de-colonization in Africa (particularly the loss of Algeria in 1962), have meant a reduction of markets.

Marseille has been an attractive refuge for immigrants fleeing political troubles. Greeks arrived in the 1820s and Italians in the 1870s and 1880s. During this century, immigrants have included Armenians (1915), Greeks and Armenians fleeing Turkey (1920s), Italian anti-Fascists (1930s), north-African Arabs from Morocco, Algeria and Tunisia (since the end of World War II, including an influx of Algerians following their country's independence in 1962). They settled in the city-centre, principally in two neighbourhoods — Besunce (east of the Vieux Port) and Le Panier (north of the Vieux Port). Both merit a visit today.

Until recently, the former ship-building docks known as Les Arcenaux (just south of the Vieux Port below the Quai de Rive Neuve) housed a hideous 60s above-ground concrete parking lot. It was torn down and replaced by a harbour-side site with restaurants and a few shops. Centred around Place Thiers and Cours d'Esteinne d'Orves, it is now particularly animated at night.

One of the most important projects is the cleaning up of the grand Boulevard Le Canebière, which leads right to the Quai des Belges and the Vieux Port. Built by Haussman under orders by Napoléon III in the 1850s, it once housed elegant residences and smart shops, but over the years has been banalized by offices, fast food outlets and down-market shops. The city is currently revitalising the Canebière. Already it has restored the Bourse, created a fashion museum in a smart building the Musée de la Mode, renovated a Place du Général de Gaulle and pedestrianized near-by streets, Rue Saint Ferréol for example.

This intoxicating cocktail of commerce, industry, politics and a multi-cultural population is nothing new to Marseille. Such a dynamic concoction spills over at times - hence the stories of violence, racial tension, drug hauls, football hooliganism and political corruption. Marseille is France's second most populus city (after Paris) and third largest in terms of area (after Paris and Lyon). The city is shrinking however, in 1982 there were 878,689 people, and in 1990 just 807,726.

Visitors are safer here than in most international capitals. Simply follow the usual precautions: keep a close eye on your wallet, stick to well-lit areas at night, don't keep valuables in your car. The Marseillais are friendly and helpful to tourists. Visitors who take the time to discover this city agree, in everything it does, Marseille is different. So much so that you might feel you're in a completely different country.

Finding Your Way Around

■ By plane

The Vieux Port of Marseille is a convenient 25 kilometres from the Marseille-Marignane airport:
information ☎ 42 89 09 74, reservations ☎ 91 91 90 90

The A 55 highway links the airport and Marseille. Numerous daily flights link Paris' Orly airport and Marseille-Marignane airport (the major carrier is Air Inter, 20 La Canebière, 1300 Marseille, ☎ 91.39.36.36). Special shuttle buses (navettes) connect the airport to the central Saint Charles SNCF train station. They leave every twenty minutes from the airport (from 6:20 AM to 10:50 PM) and from the train starion (from 5:30 AM to 9:50 PM). For information ☎ 42.78.24.17.

■ By train

Gare SNCF Marseille Saint Charles
Avenue Pierre Semard (Place des Marseillais)
information: ☎ 91.08.50.50
reservations: ☎ 91.08.84.12
Recorded message: late arrivals and departures: ☎ 91.50.00.00

Overseas visitors arriving in Paris may pick up the TGV from either Airport Charles-de-Gaulle or Gare d'Austerlitz travelling to Marseille Saint-Charles train station. Eleven Paris-Marseille TGV trains make this journey daily (not all are direct); it takes 4 hours and 15 minutes; the distance is 813 km. Overseas visitors flying to Lyon Satolas airport from abroad may pick up the TGV to Marseille from the SNCF train station connected to the terminal. Take a taxi or the efficient Marseille underground transit system, the métro, from the train station to your accommodation or city centre. There is a tourist office (opening times below) in the train station.

Marseille is conveniently close to a number of important destinations in Provence. The TER regional train service links Marseille to coastal ports including Cassis and La Ciotat, to larger centres including Cannes and Nice, and to inland towns including Aubagne and Aix-en-Provence. For example, 19 TER trains travel to Aix every day; the journey is 30 minutes. The Information desk on the ground floor of Saint Charles station provides local train schedules and will answer travel questions. Special "Joker" fares offer substantial discounts (50% or more) on train journeys for many destinations (including Paris-Marseille), if purchased two weeks or one month in advance.

■ By bus

Gare Routière (bus station)
Place Victor Hugo
☎ 91.08.16.40

The Gare Routier bus station is next to the principal Marseille-Saint-Charles SNCF train station, making connections from the Paris-Marseille TGV to a local bus easy. Local buses (*autocars régionaux*) run regularly to destinations throughout Provence and the Côte d'Azur. Visitors making day-trips to nearby places like Aubagne and Cassis might prefer the convenience of the local bus (for example, Cassis' Gare Routier/bus station is centrally-located, yet its SNCF train station is three kilometres from the port).

 **Practical Information**

■ Tourist Offices

Marseille
4 La Canebière
13001 Marseille
☎ 91.13.89.00 ⇄ 91.13.89.20

SNCF Gare Saint Charles (in the train station)
13003 Marseille

Ville d'Art et d'Histoire *(reservations are necessary for some tours; start at 2 PM; 40 F, 50 F, 90 F or 130 F depending on the tour chosen)* 36 different guided walking tours organized by the tourist office and conducted by professional guides in a choice of seven languages, several tours examine parts of Marseille unknown to most tourists in addition to more classic circuits: the 18th century mansions of *Marseillais* notables; the Estaque hills favoured by Braque, Cézanne, Dufy and where Cubism was born; the old docks and warehouses in the Joliette area.

Independent-minded tourists may follow a painted red line on the sidewalk which passes in front of the major sites and conduct their own self-led city tour (it starts at the tourist office, where people may pick up a free map explaining the route).

Taxi Tourisme Marseille (Tourist Taxis) is a new scheme organised by the tourist office in which visitors are given a guided tour of Marseille in a designated taxi (drivers are rigourously selected) equipped with professionally-made taped commentary of the sites. Four circuits are offered in French, English or German. Tickets are sold at the tourist office five minutes in advance *(duration 1h30 to 4 hours; 140 F to 500 F)*.

Bon Week-End is the name of a valuable nation-wide operation, which is strongly followed in Marseille. More than 40 hotels in all price categories offer two nights accommodation for the price of one, provided you arrive either Friday or Saturday. Contact the tourist office in advance to receive its *Bon Week-End à Marseille* brochure, which includes reduction coupons for the city's museums and car rental.

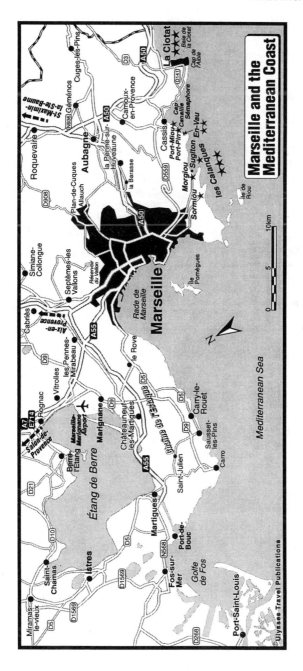

Marseille and the Mediterranean Coast

Cassis
Place Baragnon
13260 Cassis
☎ 42.01.71.17 ⇌ 42.01.28.31

Aubagne
Esplanade Charles de Gaulle
13400 Aubagne
☎ 42.03.49.98

La Ciotat
Boulevard Anatole France
13600 La Ciotat
☎ 42.08.61.32 ⇌ 42.08.17.88

■ Post Office

Hôtel des Postes
Place de l'Hôtel des Postes, 13101
Open Monday to Friday 8 AM to 7 PM,
Saturdays 8 AM to noon

■ Currency Exchange

Branches of the leading French banks
with foreign exchange counters are
found throughout Marseille. They close
at 4 PM.

Foreign exchange offices with longer
opening hours include:

Comptoir de Change Méditerranéen
Gare Saint Charles
☎ 91.84.68.88
Everyday 8 AM to 6 PM

Change de la Bourse
3 Place du Général de Gaulle, 13101
☎ 91.13.09.00
Open Monday to Friday 8.30 AM to
6.30 PM and Saturday 9 AM to
12.30 PM and 2 PM to 5 PM, closed
Sunday.

Transportation

■ Métro

An efficient, inexpensive and safe way
to quickly get around Marseille is to
take its subway, a rapid transit underground system called the métro. A
single ticket for the two-line system
costs 8 F. A set of six tickets, known
as a carnet, costs 36 F (reduced rate
29 F). All métro stations and the tourist
office can provide you with a map,
otherwise contact Info RTM *(6 Rue des
Fabres, 13001, Marseille,
☎ 91.91.92.10)*. Métro service runs
from 5 AM to 9 PM, although métro
ticket offices are open from 6.30 AM
to 7.30 PM.

■ Car Rental

Avis
SNCF Gare Saint Charles,
13101,
☎ 91.64.71.00

267 Boulevard National,
13103,
☎ 91.50.70.11

92 Boulevard Rabatau,
13108,
☎ 91.80.12.00

Hertz
27 Boulevard Rabatau,
13108,
☎ 91.79.22.06

16 Boulevard Nédelec,
13101,
☎ 91.14.04.24

**Emergency Travel Help / (SOS Voya-
geurs)**
☎ 91.62.12.80

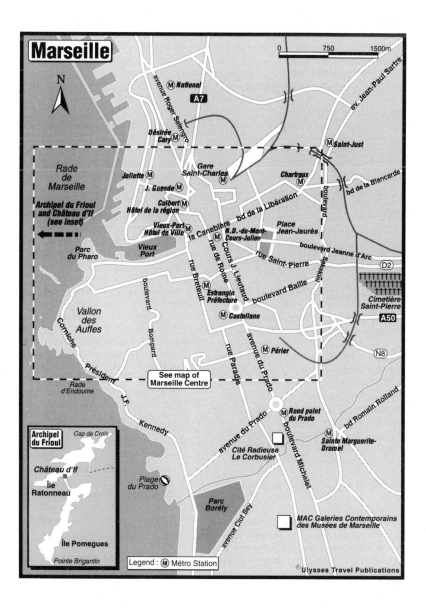

Marseille

■ **Taxis**

Some Marseille taxi drivers have a bad reputation. For example many don't like to make the journey from the Saint-Charles train station to the city-centre (presumably they feel it's not worth the effort because of horrible traffic and the short distance). Note the denomination of the bank note you give the driver, so that you are sure you receive the correct change in return.

Local taxi companies:
Marseille Taxis ☎ 91.02.20.20
Taxis France ☎ 91.49.91.00
Taxis Tupp ☎ 91.05.80.80
Taxis Plus ☎ 91.03.60.03
Eurotaxi ☎ 91.97.12.12 (multi-lingual drivers)

 Exploring

■ **Marseille**

All the museums in Marseille, except the Musée de l'Histoire, the Musée de la Mode and the Galerie des Transports, are open everyday from 10 AM to 5 PM (October to May) and 11 AM to 6 PM (June to September). Entrance is free on Sunday mornings and for children under 10, the over-65s, handicapped and unemployed. Tickets are half price for students, children between 10 and 16 and teachers. The museums are closed Monday.

Centre de la Vieille Charité ★★★ (1) *(2 Rue de la Charité, métro Joliette, ☎ 91.56.28.38, ⇄ 91.90.63.07)* The 17th century hospice with its pretty pink arcades facing a **central chapel ★★★** built by Pierre Puget is now an exciting arts complex, including the **Musée d'Archéologie Méditerranéen-**

ne ★ *(adults 10 F)*, with an t Egyptology collection, plus artifacts from Mediterranean civilisations, tracing customs and daily life; the **Musée des Arts Afrcains, Océaniens, Amérindiens** *(adults 10 F)*, a fresh insight into the art and culture of different ethnic groups, particularly West African; opened in 1992; a very good book shop and small cafe Good temporary exhibitions *(adults 10 F, children free)*.

Musée des Docks Romains (2) *(adults 10 F; Place de Vivaux, métro Vieux-Port, ☎ 91.91.24.62)* A unique museum in that it sits on the actual site of the subject examined. It deals with commercial life in the Marseille port during the Roman times. Housed in the former Roman warehouse on the south quay, ruins and artifacts examine an important moment in Marseille history when it controlled Mediterranean trade routes.

Musée du Vieux Marseille ★★ (3) *(adults 10 F; Maison Diamantée, Rue de la Prison, métro Vieux Port, ☎ 91.55.10.19)* This 16th century residence has a façade made of stone cut in diamond shapes (hence its name, Maison Diamantée) and now houses a charming museum devoted to furniture, Provençal costumes and folklore from the time when Marseille was at the height of its power and influence during the 18th and 19th centuries.

Hôtel de Ville (4) Proudly facing the old port on the Quai du Port, the three-story 17th-century building was not damaged during the bombing by German forces during World War II (though much of the surrounding quayside was).

The **Vieux Port (5)** Surrounded on three-sides by the Quai du Port, the

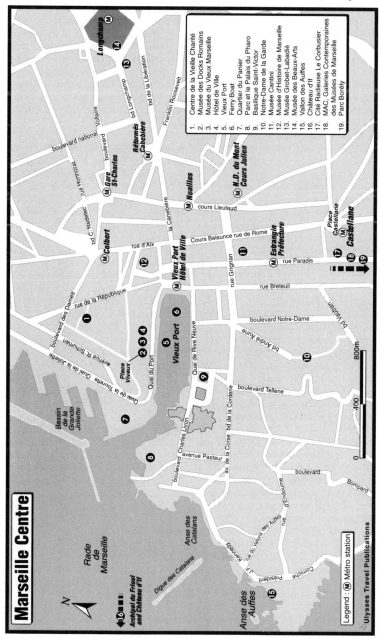

Marseille Centre

N

◄ 16 ■ ■ ■
Archipel du Frioul
and Château d'If

Rade
de
Marseille

Anse des
Catalans

Digue des Catalans

Anse des
Auffes

1. Centre de la Vieille Charité
2. Musée des Docks Romains
3. Musée du Vieux Marseille
4. Hôtel de Ville
5. Vieux Port
6. Ferry Boat
7. Quartier du Panier
8. Parc et le Palais du Pharo
9. Basilique Saint-Victor
10. Notre-Dame de la Garde
11. Musée Cantini
12. Musée d'Histoire de Marseille
13. Musée Grobet-Labadié
14. Musée des Beaux-Arts
15. Vallon des Auffes
16. Château d'If
17. Cité Radieuse Le Corbusier
18. MAC, Galeries Contemporaines
    des Musées de Marseille
19. Parc Borély

Legend : (M) Métro station

© Ulysses Travel Publications

Longchamp

bd de la Libération
bd Longchamp
Franklin Roosevelt
Voltaire
boulevard

Réformés
Canebière

Gare
St-Charles

rue Honnorat
boulevard national

bd C. Nédélec

Colbert
rue d'Aix

Noailles

N.D. du Mont
Cours Julien

cours Lieutaud

la Canebière

Cours Belsunce rue de Rome
rue de Rome

Estrangin
Préfecture

rue Paradis

Place
Castellane

Castellane

Château d'If

Vieux Port
Hôtel de Ville

rue de la République

boulevard des Dames

avenue R. Schuman

Quai de la Tourette

Bassin
de la
Grande
Joliette

Place
Vivaux

Quai du Port

Vieux Port

Quai de Rive Neuve

rue Grignan

rue Breteuil

boulevard Notre-Dame

bd André Aune

bd Vauban

boulevard Tellene

bd de la Corderie

boulevard Charles Livon

avenue Pasteur

av. de la Corse

boulevard

Bompard

Corniche

Président

rue Kennedy

rue d'Endoume

rue du Vallon des Auffes

800m

400

0

Quai des Belges and the Quai du Rive Neuve, the old port is the symbolic centre of Marseille. Fishermen still display their morning catch along the Quai des Belges (at the base of La Canebière). Avoid eating in any of the fish and seafood restaurants situated directly on the quais and supposedly serving the *vrai bouillabaise* (authentique bouillabaise). They are touristy and not all reliable (see Restaurants for our choice).

Le Ferry Boat (6) *(5 F; between the Hôtel de Ville on the Quai du Port and the Place Aux Huiles on the Quai du Rive Neuve)* A quick way to cross from one side of the old port to the other is to hop on this water bus just like the *Marseillais*, who call it Le Ferry *Bo-At*. It's been operating since 1880.

Quartier du Panier (7) *(south of the Quai du Port)* This is Marseille's oldest area and source of many colourful tales of rough living and prostitution from days gone by. Today it is a colourful working class neighbourhood whose buildings and narrow streets are slowly being restored. It is still home to fishermen, small businesses and artisans and has kept its authentic character.

Parc and Palais du Pharo (8) *(enter via Boulevard Charles Livon)* Though the imposing Palace built by Napoléon III is not open to the public (it is being restored and will be used for receptions and seminars), the surrounding gardens are pleasant and provide one of the best **view points** ★★ from which to see the sailboats and buildings surrounding the old port, plus the 17th-century Fort Saint Nicholas opposite.

Basilique Saint Victor ★★ **(9)** *(8 AM to noon and 2 PM to 6 PM, except Sunday mornings; Place Saint Victor* ☎ *91.54.23.37)* Founded in the 5th

century by the monk Saint John Cassian, this basilica is one of the oldest in France. Much was destroyed during raids by the Saracens in the 8th century, leading to reconstruction in the 11th century. Be sure to descend the stone stairs to visit the crypts, one of which dates from the original 5th century structure.

Notre-Dame de la Garde (10) *(basilica and crypt, Oct to May, 7:30 AM to 5.30 PM; Jun to Sep 7 AM to 7.30 PM, steep walk or take bus 30 from the Vieux Port)* The Romanesque-Byzantine Basilique Notre-Dame de la Garde dominates Marseille and has become the city's symbol much like the Eiffel Tower in Paris or Statue of Liberty in New York. Like those two monuments, there are spectacular panoramic views from the terraces surrounding the basilica. (It's best to come at sunset for splendid views of the old port and of the Mediterranean.) Though swamped with tourists, the 19th century structure is a place of worship. It's patron saint is Mary Magdelene, and the rows of model fishing boats hanging by chains above the nave remind us that this is the fisherman's basilica.

Musée Cantini ★ **(11)** *(adults 10 F; 19 Rue Grignan, métro Estrangin-Préfecture,* ☎ *91.54.77.75,* ⇄ *91.55.03.61)* The contemporary canvases have been transferred to the new MAC gallery, and so the Musée Cantini now specializes in the modern period dating from 1900 to 1960. This intimate museum is worth a visit just for its good Fauve and Cubist selection. Housed in the impressive 18th century Hôtel de Mongrand mansion. Excellent temporary exhibitions (see tourist office or the local press for details).

Musée d'Histoire de Marseille ★★ **(12)** *(adults 10 F; same hours as other mu-*

seums except closed Sun and Mon; Centre Bourse-Square Belsunce, métro Vieux-Port, ☎ 91.90.42.22) Starting with the Phoceaen occupation of the city in 600 BC, Marseille's history museum displays a number the city's archaeological treasures including items found in the under-water sea cave known as the Grotte Cosque and a 3rd century Roman trading ship (found on this spot while building around the new stock exchange in 1974). Greek and Roman artifacts dating from the 1st to 4th century are also on view in the **Jardin des Vestiges** garden.

Musée Grobet-Labadié ★★ (13) *(adults 10 F; 140 Boulevard Longchamp, métro Longchamp Cinq-Avenues, ☎ 91.62.21.82)* The elegant *hôtel particulier* built in 1873 for the industrialist and art collector Alexandre Labadié holds a marvellous collection of furniture, paintings (16th-18th century French), Middle Ages and Renaissance sculpture, Moustiers ceramics and Flemish tapestries. An absolute must for amateurs of painting and decorative arts.

Musée des Beaux-Arts ★ (14) *(adults 10 F; Palais Longchamp, métro Longchamp-Cinq-Avenues, ☎ 91.62.21.17, ⇄ 91.84.73.72)* Fine arts museum situated in the grand rooms of the left-wing of the marvellous Palais Longchamp. The ground floor includes 16th and 17th century masters and sculpture including that of local hero Pierre Puget, while the first floor displays 18th and 19th-century French artists, as well as works by Provençal painters. Behind the museum is a very pretty garden with tree-lined paths and a waterfall, which is popular with locals and little-known by tourists.

Vallon des Auffes ★★ (15) *(Corniche Président John Kennedy, immediately*

south of the Monument au Morts d'O-rients, under the bridge) an authentic fishing port, untouched by modern development and imperceptable from the Corniche and cliff-side above. Colourful fishing boats, rows of *cabanons* (fishermen's huts) and three popular restaurants.

Chateau d'If ★★ (16) *(adults 10 F; open everyday except Monday during school periods, 9 AM to 5PM, ☎ 91.59.02.30)* Visitors may take a short boat-ride to this small island and visit its château, immortalized by the writer Alexandre Dumas in his book *The Count of Monte-Cristo*. The three hectare area of white rocks was untouched by man up until the 16th century. On a visit to Marseille in 1516, François I realised the island's strategic position and gave orders to build a fortress there. The heavy triple-towered structure was completed in 1531. However, it quickly became a prison and following 1689 had a particularly grisly history when many Protestants perished there under horrible conditions. It has been open to the public since 1890. Visitors can see the famous dungeons and the escape hole dug by Dumas' famous Count, Edmond Dantès, plus the courtyards and prisoners cells. The panoramic view is spectacular. *(Boats for the island leave regularly from the Quai des Belges, ☎ 91.55.50.09).*

Cité Radieuse Le Corbusier (17) *(280 Boulevard Michelet, south of the Rond Point du Prado)* All-in-one high-rise building, created by avant-garde architect Le Corbusier in 1954 and controversial in its day, includes apartments, shops, a school, sports facilities and a hotel.

MAC, Galeries Contemporains des Musées de Marseille ★ (18) *(adults*

15 F, 69 Avenue d'Haïfa, bus 23 and 45, ☎ 91.25.01.07, ⇄ 91.72.17.27) New in 1994, this museum of contemporary art holds a particularly rich collection (one of the best in France outside of Paris) of works created post-1960. Also on the premises: a cinema, contemporary art bookshop and restaurant "Au Macaroni".

Parc Borély ★★ (19) (free, Avenue du Parc Borély, south of Avenue du Prado, ☎ 91.73.21.60) Beautiful botanic garden includes rosary, pretty pathways and a lake. The elegant Château Borély dates from the 18th century (closed for renovations).

■ Calanques ★★★

The Calanques are a series of fjords or inlets along the coastline between Marseille and Cassis. The wonderful white cliffs are loved by rock-climbers, the clear turquoise waters favoured by swimmers and small pleasure craft. **Sorgiou ★**, **Morgiou ★** and **Sugiton ★** are closest to Marseille and may be visited by car (Oct to May only) or by boat (trips start from Quai des Belges, details about prices and times from the tourist office).

The most beautiful calanques lie just west of Cassis: **Port-Miou ★**, **Port-Pin ★★** and the most glorious **En-Vau ★★**. Small, sandy beaches lie hidden at the end of Port-Pin and En-Vau. Boat trips lasting about one hour (45 F, numerous boats depart between 9 AM and 6 PM) leave the port of Cassis and visit all three. Unfortunately, because of their natural beauty, the calanques are crowded on weekend summer days and one wonders if those petrol emmissions from pleasure boats are helping the already polluted Mediterranean coast. Port-Min and En-Vau are not accessible by road, but there are well-marked trails leading to each of them. A hiking visit to En-Vau will take complete day; wear sturdy footwear and carry appropriate supplies (notably drinking water). Fires devastated trees and vegetation in this area in the early 1990s, so as with the Sainte-Victoire hill range near Aix-en-Provence, some walking trails are prohibited to hikers during summer months. Enquire before setting out.

■ Cassis

Situated at the foot of Cap Canaille, the highest maritime cliff in Europe (416 m), Cassis is a charming fishing port loved by artists such as Matisse and Dufy at the turn of the century. It is famous for the nearby calanques (one-hour visits by boat with commentary, 45 F; departures from the Cassis port from 9 AM to 6 PM by a number of different boats), the fresh, fruity white wine produced nearby, a couple of beaches but most of all for its fishing community. Coral and sea-urchins are its specialty. Cassis is crowded in the summer-time so try to visit the port in the morning or off-season. Be sure to see the **port ★★** with its tall, narrow houses and cafes, as well as the 17th century Hôtel de Ville near the pretty Place de l'Église. Above the tourist office is the **Musée des Arts et Traditions Populaires** (free admission; Wed to Sat 4 PM to 7 PM; Rue Xavier d'Authier/Place Baragnon, ☎ 42.01.88.66) devoted to archaeological ruins found inthe nearby Baie de l'Arène, local history and a small number of Provençal paintings.

■ La Ciotat

The spectacular **coastal road linking Cassis to La Ciotat ★★★**, known as Route des Crêtes (D 141) passes along the sheer cliff-sides of **Cap Canaille** and

Sémaphore. This coastal city lacks the charm of the smaller ports along the Mediterranean, perhaps due to it shipyards and post-World War II urbanization. However, it does shelter the **Chapelle des Pénitents**, a pretty chapel dating from 1626, and a local history and folklore museum in the old town hall, the **Musée Ciotaden** *(free admission; Mon, Wed, Fri and Sat 4 PM to 7 PM, Sun 10 AM to noon, closed Tue and Thu)*. La Ciotat was home to the first movie theatre (Cinéma Eden, still open) in the world, created by the Lumière brothers.

Beaches

Plage du Prophète *(Corniche John F. Kennedy, take bus 83 from the Vieux Port)* Large sandy beach with lots of activities including sailing, windsurfing, canoeing, volleyball. Services include showers, toilets, a first-aid post and refreshment stand.

Sometimes called the Plages Gaston Defferre, the **Prado Beach** south of the city-centre actually is a series of beaches: **Plage du Roucas Blanc** sand and pebble, includes volleyball court, a playground, raft and diving boards; **Plage du David** pebble; **Plage Borely** pebble, good for windsurfing; **Plage Bonneveine** pebble, includes restaurants, swimming pool, scooter and waterski hire; **Plage de la Vieille Chapelle** pebble, children's games and skateboard track and finally, one which is not accessible by bus 83, **Plage de la Pointe Rouge** sand, restaurant, good for windsurfing.

Frioul Islands *(20 min shuttle boat service throughout the day from the Quai des Belges, Vieux Port, contact*

Groupement des Armateurs Cotiers de Marseille, ☎ *91.55.50.09)* A series of rocky islands next to Château d'If (see p 177), with a number of beaches (pebble except for the sand beach Plage de la Maison des Pilotes) and a few restaurants in the village Port Frioul. An idyllic spot to relax.

Outdoor Activities

Marseille's location on the rugged Mediterranean coast means water sports and hiking are favourite activities for locals and visitors alike. The tourist office publishes a free comprehensive guide called Marseille By The Sea (in French, English, and German) with full details about what to do in the great outdoors. Here are some ideas:

Scuba Diving

The Mediterranean coastline offers unparalleled opportunities for scuba divers to discover plant and marine life and even the shipwrecks. An important archaeological find was made in July 1991 by the professional diver Henri Cosquer, who discovered an underwater prehistoric cave with rock paintings at the Morgiou Calanque near Marseille. A number of scuba clubs provide supervised half-day initiation courses, weekend packages or longer excursions, plus equipment hire. Among the many interesting possibilities are:

Espace Loisirs *(17 Rue Phocéens,* ☎ *91.56.66.17)* Weekend or weeklong training, with the possibility of food and accommodation (hotel or boat) all-inclusive packages; year-round training for all levels.

ASPTT (Port de la Pointe Rouge, ☎ 91.73.14.03) Special Friday afternoon to Sunday training sessions, plus five day courses.

Label Bleu Vidéo (19 Rue Michel Gachet, ☎ 91.59.25.23) From its base of operation in the old port on Frioul Island, this group offers beginners' courses on weekends (including a video cassette of the first dive to mark the occasion).

Club du Vieux Plongeur (116 Cours Lieutaud, ☎ 91.48.79.48) Another club based on Frioul Island, this one offers short and long-term courses, plus dives looking at wrecks, archaeological discoveries and trips for underwater photographers. All-inclusive packages including accommodation (boats, hotels, studio apartments) are arranged.

 Windsurfing

The Prado Beach area offers excellent facilities for windsurfers. Equipment is hired out by two groups operating there, at the Port de la Pointe Rouge beach:
Pacific Palissades (☎ 91.73.54.37) and **Sideral's Time Club** (☎ 91.25.00.90).

 Deep-Sea Fishing

Société Mare Nostrum *(165 Rue Saint Jean du Désert,* ☎ *91.73.05.08 or 91.72.01.72)* offers one-day excursions called *Découverte du Large* (Discovery of the open sea), an introduction to competition fishing (including tuna, swordfish, shark and smaller friends such as mackeral and bonito). Otherwise, **Espace Loisirs** *(17 Rue des Phocéens,* ☎ *91.56.66.17)* will guide tourists about local fishing possibilities.

 Sailing

A couple of groups at the Port de la Pointe Rouge beach rent small sail boats and catamarans by the hour: **Pacific Palissades** (☎ 91.73.54.37) or by the day: **Sideral's Time Club** (☎ 91.25.00.90).

 Hiking

Apart from hiking through the Calanques area, there is a wonderful inland walking trail starting north of Cassis. The GR 98 trail starts south of Cassis, turns inland past the Mont de la Saoupe and rises sharply in the direction of the Sainte-Baume Massif (see p 156). Looking back, there are superb views of the Provençal coastline.

■ Calanques by the sea and by foot

A visit to Marseille is not complete without seeing the spectacular white limestone cliffs rising from the clear turquoise Mediterranean. The series of inlets or fjords known as the Calanques stretch for 20 km between Marseille and Cassis. Though a few may be reached by road from October to May, the Calanques are primarily accessible by sea or by foot, see p 178.

The Calanques are favourite spots for scuba divers and rock-climbers. Most satisfying, if you have the time and are physically-fit, are the numerous walking trails in the area. Only one main trail, the GR 98, is open during the summer months (others are are closed from mid-June to mid-September due to forest fire threat). The Marseille tourist office publishes a free brochure on the Calanques, with a detailed map of walking trails.

The following hiking clubs offer walks through the Calanque trails, with experienced guides: **Le Club Alpin Français** *(12 Rue Fort Note Dame, ☎ 91.54.36.94)*, **La Société des Excursions Marseillais** *(16 Rue de la Rotonde, ☎ 91.84.75.52)*, **Touring Provence Méditerranée** *(11 Place Général de Gaulle, ☎ 91.33.40.99)*.

 Rock-climbing

The sheer cliffs of the Calanques are perfect for dedicated rock-climbers (non-professionals should not attempt to climb them). Contact the local chapter of the *Fédération Française de la Montagne et de l'Escalade* for guide books and names of local groups:

Comité Départemental 13 de la FME
Daniel Gorgeon
5 Impasse du Figuier
13114 Puylobier
☎ 42.66.35.05

 Mountain Biking

Mountainbike rental, plus excursion packages, are offered by: **SERAC** (25 Rue Kruger, ☎ 91.08.96.08) and **Green Bike** (135 Avenue Clot Bey, ☎ 91.25.36.26).

 Accommodation

■ **Marseille**

Few of Marseille's many hotels are worth recommending. A great many, in each price category, show their wear and tear and need serious renovation.

There are a few good accommodation possibilities however.

Auberge de Jeunesse Bois Luzy *(42 F, bkfst 17 F, Allée des Primevères, 13012 Marseille, ☎ 91.49.06.18)* Sitated in the east of Marselles in a quiet suburb surrounded by greenery and with a view over the harbour. Rooms with four and six beds, plus individual rooms; 90 places in total. Open all year.

Auberge de Jeunesse Bonneveine *(85-120 F, meals 46 F; 47 Avenue Joseph Vidal, 13008 Marseille, ☎ 91.73.21.81)*. Near the Prado beaches, open from mid-January to mid-December. Shaded terrace, 150 places in dormitories and single rooms; cafeteria; handicapped welcome.

Hôtel Saint-Louis *(210-250 F, bkfst 25 F; ps or pb, tv, ☎; 2 Rue des Récolletes, 13001 Marseillle, ☎ 91.54.02.74, ⇄ 91.33.78.59)* Unbeatable for the price and friendly welcome by the young owner and his staff, this hotel offers simple, clean rooms in the heart of Marseille, near the Canebière and old port.

Hôtel Phocea *(250 F, bkfst 35 F; pb, tv, ☎; 6 Rue Beauveau, 13001 Marseille, ☎ 91.33.02.33, ⇄ 91.33.21.34)* Another good budget hotel, with 45 basic, modern rooms. Centrally-located off the Canebière, near the tourist office and Quai des Belges.

St Férréol's Hôtel *(330-390 F, bkfst 38 F, pb, tvc, ☎; 19 Rue Pisançon, 13001 Marseille, ☎ 91.33.12.21, ⇄ 91.54.29.97)* Marseille's best hotel for comfort, value and location. Rooms are named after famous painters and each is decorated with appropriate prints and furnishings; smallish bathrooms are in marble. Breakfast includes better-than-average croissant and coffee, plus freshly-squeezed orange juice. The owners, Bernard Brulas and his wife, are friendly and helpful. On the corner of Rue St Férréol, an animated pedestrian shopping street during the day.

Hôtel Concorde Palm Beach *(655 F, bkfst 63 F; ≈, ℜ, tv, ☎; 2 Promenade de la Plage, 13008 Marseille, ☎ 91.16.19.00, ⇄ 91.16.19.39)* A large resort-style hotel on the seafront south of the city-centre. Supremely comfortable modern rooms have small balconies overlooking the Mediterranean, meals are served on an outside terrace during fine weather. Not far from Parc Borély and the Prado beach. Professionally managed by the Marseille-based Del Prête group, who also own the city's Hôtel Concorde Prado.

Grand Hôtel Beauvau *(750-950 F, bkfst 65 F; pb, tv, ☎; 4 Rue Beauvau, 13001 Marseille, ☎ 91.54.91.00, ⇄ 91.54.15.76)* European-style hotel in operation since 1816 (fully renovated in 1987) and facing the old port on the Quai des Belges. The 72 rooms offer sober Provençal furnishings and a number of 19th century antiques. Resist the temptation to take a room overlooking the port (they are terribly noisy night and day) and opt for one facing Rue Beauvau. The copious buffet breakfast includes whole-grain bread, yogurt and fruit for the health-conscious. Since 1982, it is part of the Pullman hotel chain. For 1950 F, you may stay in the Chopin Suite, where the composer and authoress George Sand sojourned in 1839.

■ **Cassis**

Le Clos des Arômes *(290-450 F, bkfst 45 F; ℜ, pb, ☎; 10 Rue Paul Mouton, 13260 Cassis, ☎ 42.01.71.84,* ⇄ *42.01.31.76)* In the centre of Cassis, not far from the port lies this charming homey inn with eight nicely-decorated rooms (the most pleasant face the garden). Breakfast is served on the garden terrace in good weather, and the very good dinner menu incudes freshly-prepared Provençal classics.

Les Roches Blanches *(842-1062 F, bkfst 70 F, closed Nov to late Jan; ≈, ℜ, pb, tvc, ☎; Route des Calanques, 13714 Cassis, ☎ 42.01.09.30, ⇄ 42.01.94.23)* For those in need of pampering by the seaside, this restored 19th century residence is the place. There's a swimming pool facing the sea and a small private beach, while the hotel itself is nestled in sweet-scented pine groves. Though some rooms are compact, all are comfortable and tastefully decorated. Not surprisingly, considering its location, the restaurant specialises in seafood.

 Restaurants

■ **Marseille**

L'Art et Les Thés *($; 10 AM to 6 PM; Centre de la Vieille Charité, 2 Rue de la Charité, ☎ 91.56.01.39)* Light meals are served at lunch-time, while cakes and drinks are at other times in this small cafe within the Vieille Charité museum complex. Inventive offerings include spinach and mussel gratin (45 F), chicken curry pie (49 F) and tagliatelle with salmon (55 F). Cakes (25 F) are home-made.

Espace Mode Méditerranée *($, Tue to Sun noon to 7 PM; 11 La Canebière, ☎ 91.14.92.20)* Sleek and stylish little cafe inside the fashion museum serving a selection of sandwiches on whole-wheat bread (25 F to 35 F), light lunches (30 F to 48 F) plus a number of different teas, coffees and cakes.

Chez Jeannot *($-$$, closed Mon, and from Oct to May Sun evening, 129 Vallon des Auffes,* ☎ *91.52.11.28)* Chez Jeannot is a real Marseille institution, a place to eat good pizzas and salads right in front of the tiny Vallon des Auffes fishing port in the city's 7e arrondissement. Popular during hot weather when the large terrace is open.

Chez Etienne *($-$$; closed Sun; 43 Rue de Lorette)* Etienne Cassaro's restaurant and his pizza and home-made pasta dishes are famous throughout Marseille. The place is bustling, the food terrific and you're likely to strike up a conversation with your neighbour while waiting for a table (don't try reserving — there's no telephone!) Situated in the colourful Quartier Le Panier north of the old port.

Le Bar de la Marine *($-$$, no credit cards; 7.30 AM to 2 AM, meals served at lunchtime, closed Sun; 15 Quai de Rive Neuve,* ☎ *91.54.95.42)* Wonderful bar overlooking the old port with a lively mix of local residents, fishermen, students and business people. Typical bistro fare (salads, meat and fish dishes) is served. The best is the 50 F *assiette gourmande*, a mix of paté, cold meats, shrimp and salad.

Le Bistrot à Vin *($-$$; closed Sun; 17 Rue Sainte,* ☎ *91.52.02.20)* A small though bustling wine bar attracting a youngish clientele, which offers a large selection of wines by the glass (15 F to 28 F) and tasty bistro dishes such as a charcuterie plate (49 F), the famous tripes dish *pieds et paquets Marseillais* (69 F), plus salads, meat dishes and cheeses. Tasting menu includes small portions of a number of dishes and a glass of wine for 150 F.

Les Menus Plaisirs *($$, no credit cards; closed Sat and Sun and every evening; 1 Rue Haxo,* ☎ *91.54.94.38)* A tiny café serving simple but good lunchtime meals (roast pork with rosemary, braised lamb) to an appreciative local clientele. The rich home-made chocolate cake is out of this world. Reservations advised.

Il Caneletto *($$; closed Sunday; 8 cours Jean Ballard,* ☎ *91.33.90.12)* Many locals agree, the best Italian food in Marseille is found here in this charming tratorria next to the Arsenaux complex and old port. The fresh home-made pasta and carpaccio of tuna are excellent; be sure to leave room for the heavenly tiramisu. No set-price menu, count on 220 F to 280 F for two people.

La Côte de Boeuf *($$, closed Sunday, 35 cours d'Estienne d'Orves,* ☎ *91.54.89.08)* This long-established restaurant serves up succulent roasted meats (rib of beef 240 F for two people; beef fillet 99 F,) in a refined rustic atmosphere, with dark wood beams and a hearth at the back. Reputed for the quality of its meat, as well as for the impressive (and heavy!) wine list.

L'Ambassade des Vignobles *($$; closed Sat PM and Sun; 42 Place Aux Huiles,* ☎ *91.33.00.25)* With the same ownership as the Côte de Boeuf next-door (see above), this popular spot proposes four menus where each dish is accompanied by a different glass of wine. (Two courses 140 F, three courses 180 F and 230 F, four courses 280 F).

Le Bistro Gambas *($$; closed Sat PM and Sun; 29 Place Aux Huiles,*

☎ *91.33.26.44)* This simple yet refined restaurant serves a variety of *gambas* (crustaceans) in a number of inventive ways: grilled, on salads, with fragrant Asian flavours. A number of affordable local white wines are proposed. Lunchtime menu 89 F, evening 115 F.

Le Carré d'Honoré *($$; closed Sat PM and Sun; 34 Place Aux Huiles,* ☎ *91.33.16.80)* Amongst a fresh yellow and blue neo-Provençal decor, the Rutano family serves a menu inspired by the region's offerings, namely fish. The 95 F menu might include shrimp or calamari to start, then sea breem grilled with dill, followed by dessert. A more elaborate 145 F menu (three courses plus cheese) recently included a very good cod with olives and grilled sole as the main dishes.

Le Miramar *($$-$$$; closed Sun and first three weeks of Aug; 12 Quai du Port,* ☎ *91.91.10.40)* Marseillais love to debate over which seafood restaurant serves the best bouillabaise. The name Le Miramar comes up time and time again. The decor is 60s kitsch, but what's important is that the fish here is delivered fresh every day. Patrons don't leave disappointed. Such goodness has a price, count on 500 F for two people with wine (there are no set-price menus).

Patalain *($$-$$$; closed Sat PM and Sun; 49 Rue Sainte,* ☎ *91.55.02.78)* The talented chef Suzanne Quaglia has created a name for herself with this casually-sophisticated restaurant loved by Marseille professionals. Her cuisine is best-described as modern Provençal where fresh ingredients are enlivened by matching flavours and textures, such as red mullet with eggplant or cod and sea breem with cognac and a delicate raspberry cream sauce. Menus

at 160 F (lunch), 190 F, 220 F and 280 F. Professional service.

■ **Cassis**

La Marine *($; closed Nov 15 to Jan 2; 5 Quai des Baux,* ☎ *42.01.76.09)* Typical bar/cafe with lots of rustic character facing the Cassis port, it started in the 1930s and has been a meeting place for locals ever since. Marcel Pagnol filmed scenes for a number of his movies here.

 Entertainment

Pick up the free weekly newspaper *TakTik* (available in the tourist office, bookshops, cafes and bars) for an up-to-date guide to what's on in Marseille and the region. The following list though far from complete, indicates a wealth of things to do in Marseille.

■ **Theatre, Dance, Music:**

Opéra Municipal *(1 Place Reyer,* ☎ *91.55.00.70)* Call ahead or pick up a programme in order to catch one of the in-house or travelling opera and dance productions, performed in this grand Art Deco masterpiece.

La Cité de la Musique *(4 Rue Bernard du Bois,* ☎ *91.39.28.28)* Classical and contemporary music concerts are performed regularly in the **Auditorium** of this arts complex, while some excellent jazz masters groove in the **Cave à Jazz**, playing standards and contemporary selections.

La Criée/Théâtre National de Marseille *(30 Quai de Rive Neuve,* ☎ *91.54.70.54)* Excellent home-grown productions plus pieces created elsewhere (often major works from Paris) are performed here. Other theatres to look out for are: **Théatre du Gymnase** *(4 Rue du Théâtre Francais,* ☎ *91 24 35 24)* and the **Théâtre Gyptis** *(136 Rue Loubon,* ☎ *91 11 00 91)* plus countless smaller venues, including cabarets and café-theatres.

La Passerelle *(noon to midnight; 26 Rue des Trois Mages,* ☎ *91.48.77.24)* A dynamic arts centre attracting lots of local young people, incorporates **La Planete Livres** *(for "BDs" comic books for all ages),* **Gégé le Chinois** *(used books, open 3 PM to 8 PM),* **Voyages Pour Tous** *(travel agency, open 10 AM to 10 PM, closed at meal-times),* **Marseille Café** *(lunch menu 45 F, dinner menu 60 F)* and a small cinema showing experimental films.

■ **Bars and Clubs**

The area known as La Plaine (Place Jean Jaurès leading to the nearby Cours Julien) and the Arsenaux area (Cours d'Estienne d'Orves, Place Aux Huiles) are two lively places at night-time, with loads of restaurants, bars and nightclubs. Take your pick, according to your taste.

Le Pelle-Mêle *(5 PM to 2 AM; 45 Place Aux Huiles,* ☎ *91.54.85.26)* Piano bar with established jazz groups.

Quai 9 *(closed Sun and Mon; 9 Quai de Rive Neuve,* ☎ *91.33.34.20)* Nightclub/discotheque for Marseillais youth, particularly students, with the latest music (top 40 to house).

The New Cancan *(Wed to Sun, 11 PM onwards; 3-5 Rue Sénac,* ☎ *91.48.59.76)* Near Métro Noallies, the largest gay male disco in the area. Live entertainment Thursdays and Sundays.

Enigme Bar *(daily from 5 PM to 2 AM; 22 Rue Beauvau,* ☎ *91.33.79.20)* Centrally-located male gay bar, near Métro Vieux-Port.

Le Bar de la Marine *(7.30 AM to 2 AM, meals served at lunchtime, closed Sun; 15 Quai de Rive Neuve,* ☎ *91.54.95.42)* This renovated bar with its tiled floor and zinc counter was first created in 1936 and is still a great place to relax and observe the Marseillais. Tapas snacks are available in the evening.

■ **Festivals**

Marseille

Le Chandeleur *(Feb 2)* Procession of the Vierge Noir (the Black Virgin) to the Saint Victor basilica;
Festival de Musique *(early Apr)* recitals in the Saint Victor basilica;
Festival de Création de Musique du XXe Siecle *(early May)* Contemporary music festival;
Nuits Blanches Pour La Musique Noir *(Jun-Jul)* Celebration of Black music;
Festival Marseille Méditerranée *(Jul)* Dance, theatre, music;
Festival du Film Féminin *(Jul)* Fesitval of women's films;
Festival de Musique Sacrée *(autumn)* held at Saint-Victor;
La Fiesta des Suds *(Oct)* Music, dance, concerts, bodegas;
Pastorales *(mid-Nov to mid-Jan)* Live enactment of Nativity with spoken text and sometimes Provençal songs at Théâtre du Lacydon *(1 Montée du Saint Esprit, 13002,* ☎ *91.90.96.70)*
Théâtre Mazenod *(88 Rue d'Aubagne, 13001)*
Théâtre de l'Odéon *(162 La Canebière, 13002,* ☎ *91.42.90.90)*
Théâtre Nau *(9 Rue Nau, 13006,* ☎ *91.92.36.97)*

Crêches *(Dec and Jan)* Christmas nativity scenes with coloured Provençal clay figurines, some a large as 60 square metres (645 square feet), in local churches. *santons* are sold throughout the region in *foires aux santons* (santon fairs). Check local papers or tourist offices for details;
Festival of Children's Film *(Dec)*.

Aubagne

Festival International de l'Humour et des Rires *(Jun and Jul)* Comedy festival;
Crêche *(Dec)* Christmas Nativity scene with santons, held in the tourist office; at the same time the clay figurines are sold at the **Foire Aux Santons** held along the Cours du Maréchal-Foch;
Biennale de l'Art Santonnier *(mid-Jul to late Aug, Dec)* Aubagne is the centre for the manufacture of *santons*, therefore it is only natural that its artisans show off their stuff (exhibition/display on the Cours du Maréchal-Foch);
Pastorale *(Dec)* Live enactment of the Christmas Nativity *(Théâtre le Comoédia, ☎ 42.71.19.88)*.

Cassis

Fête des Pêcheurs (Fishermen's Festival) last Sunday in June;
Fêtes des Vins *(early Sep)* Wine tastings from the reputable Cassis vineyards, plus Provençal dancing;
Pastorale *(Jan)* Live enactement of the Christmas Nativity story *(Centre Cultural, ☎ 42.01.77.73)*.

La Ciotat

Lumières du Jazz *(last two weeks of July)* Jazz music festival.

 Shopping

Four des Navettes *(everyday 7 AM to 7.30 PM; 136 Rue Sainte, ☎ 91.33.32.12)* The oldest bakery in town (founded in 1782) is famous for its *navettes*, small boat-shaped sweet biscuits which supposedly symbolise the arrival by sea to Provence by the Saintes-Maries. The recipe is secret. Every February 2 during the Fête de la Chandeleur (Candlemas celebration), the wooden statue of the Vierge Noir (Black Virgin) is taken from the crypt of the nearby Saint-Victor abbey. According to tradition, the *four des navettes*, the oven and its production is blessed, whereupon the participants buy a green-coloured candle and a freshly-blessed biscuit following the service. The two items will protect the owner's household for the rest of the year.

Dromel Aîné *(Mon 2:30 PM to 7 PM, Tue to Sat 9 PM to 7 PM, closed Sun; 6 Rue de Rome, ☎ 91.54.01.91)* Specialist candy manufacturer since 1760, with excellent *marrons glacés* (preserved candied chestnuts), plus teas and coffees. Dromel Aîné sells three types of navettes which are tastier and softer than its rival Le Four des Navettes (see above).

La Chocolaterie *(4 Place des Treize Cantons, ☎ 91.91.67.66)* Michèle Le Ray has recreated her father's artisanal chocolate-making business with great success. Her specialties are bars with nuts or perfumed with orange or passion fruit. The white chocolate galette, perfumed with real lavender, is sublime. Le Ray doesn't keep fixed hours, so just knock on her door if there doesn't appear to be anyone around.

Georges Bataille *(Mon to Sat 8 AM to 12:30 PM and 3:30 PM to 8 PM; 16-18 Rue Fontange,* ☎ *91.47.06.23)* A marvellous gourmet food shop selling bread, a vast selection of cheese (including a delicious house camembert), wine, prepared meats, fresh meat, prepared foods, *oreillettes* (sugar coated deep-fried dough shaped like ears), smoked salmon and house foie gras. A veritable feast for the eyes and stomach.

Eupalinos *(Mon to Sat 9:30 AM to 12:30 PM and 2 PM to 7 PM; 72 Cours Julien,* ☎ *91.48.74.44)* Comprehensive selection of books on architecture, photography, music, cinema and art.

L'Invitation Au Voyage *(Mon to Sat; 132 Rue Paradis,* ☎ *91.81.60.33)* This new bookshop specializes in foreign language editions (including English) and has a comprehensive travel section.

Librairie Maurel *(95 Rue de Lodi,* ☎ *91.42.63.44)* English-language bookshop.

Les Arcenaulx *(Mon to Sat; 25 Cours d'Estienne d'Orves,* ☎ *91.54.39.37)* Two Marseillais women, the Lafitte sisters, renovated a warehouse in the Arsenaux area and created a bookshop *(10 AM to midnight, Mondays until 7 PM)* and a housewares shop called **Arts de la Table** *(10 AM to 8.30 PM)* and restaurant serving Provençal specialities.

■ **Markets**

Monthly Second-Hand and Rare Book Market - Cours Julien, second Saturday of the month, all year:
Fish Market - every morning: Quai des Belges (Vieux Port);
Flea Market (Marché Aux Puces) - Friday, Saturday and Sunday: Cours Julien;
Brocante Market - second Sunday of the month: Cours Julien;
Fruit and Vegetables - everyday except Sunday: Cours Pierre-Puget, Cours Julien, Boulevard Michelet; everyday: Place des Capucins;
Flower Market - Monday morning: Place Félix-Baret and Cours Pierre-Puget; Tuesday and Saturday morning: Allées de Meilhan; Thursday morning: Boulevard Michelet.

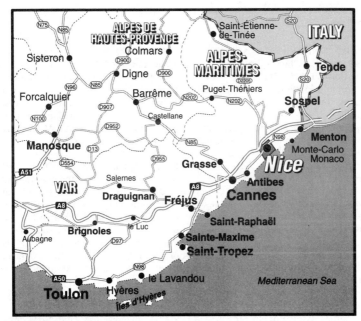

NICE ★★★

The capital of the Côte d'Azur, Nice (pop. 342,000), is blessed with the kind of climate that sun-lovers dream of. It also has the advantage of being exceptionally well located, on one of Europe's most beautiful bays. The Baie des Anges is surrounded by hills that offer a sort of natural protection, and essentially explain why Nice was so popular even in Prehistoric times. The Terra Amata encampment and Lazaret cave, which date back 400,000 years, are a living testimony.

Nice itself has a very favourable micro-climate, with pleasant temperatures in the winter (around 11°C), and temperate warmth from mid-June to September (around 24°C). The weather in September is especially pleasant. As early as 1850, the English and Russian upper-classes were already spending winters here to escape their own colder climates. Thanks to the development of a major tourist infrastructure, Nice has since become a leading international tourist centre, drawing visitors year-round.

Despite its status, Nice remains a friendly city and a pleasant place to explore on foot. It offers all the advantages of a much larger city, in an urban environment that has retained a human dimension. In the summer, Nice is overrun with tourists, as is the entire Côte d'Azur. But what saves Nice is its abundance of delightful neighbourhoods, which have benefited from careful urban planning.

True to their reputation, the locals are as friendly as one would expect of the so-called "Southerners" of any country in the northern hemisphere. Furthermore, these French "Southerners" have been greatly influenced by their Mediterranean neighbours.

Nice has a turbulent history, especially because its geographical location places it unavoidably on the route between Italy and France. Around 600 BC, the Greeks established a trading post here. Nikaïa, a town of modest size, served mainly as a military base and was easily defended from a castle atop a hill. The castle was later razed during the reign of Louis XIV.

In the first century BC, the Romans built the Via Julia, a high road which follows the coastline. Cemenelum, on the Cimiez Hill, became the administrative capital of the Roman province of Alpes-Maritimes. The reign of Cemenelum ended with the fall of all of the Roman Empire in the fifth century, and the Roman town disappeared after it was pillaged by Barbarians. Fortunately today, the Cimiez hill has regained some of its former glory, thanks to its museums and attractive parks. Cimiez is also a lovely residential area, very popular with the *Niçois*.

Comté de Nice, or the county of Nice, belonged to Provence until 1388, when it was annexed to the house of Savoy. In those days, Europe was made up of various duchies, counties and kingdoms. France was a kingdom whose borders changed according to the outcomes of the constant wars that were fought between these entities.

It was not until 1860 that France was able to reclaim the county of Nice once and for all by virtue of the treaty signed on March 24, 1860, by Napoleon III and the King of Piémont-Sardinia. Following this treaty a plebiscite was held

in April of the same year, the results of which indicated that 84 per cent of the *Niçois* were in favour of the county of Nice joining France. Of course, between 1388 and 1860, there were times when Nice did belong to France, for example under Louis XIV, or during the post-Revolution years.

Nice's population of 50,000 in 1860 grew within a century to approximately 400,000 (450,000 including the suburbs), making Nice the fifth-largest city in France after Paris, Marseille, Lyon and Lille. The *Niçois* and inhabitants of the surrounding area take a certain pride in their region; they consider themselves *Niçois* first and French second.

Nice enjoys an enviable world-class status. Indeed, the city hosts many national and international conferences, and benefits from the large industries established in the area. Furthermore, Nice offers an abundance of cultural activities. There are lots of theatres, as well as many museums, most of which are free.

L'École de Nice

At the end of the World War II, international artist Yves Klein started a major artistic wave in Nice which would come to be known as the *École de Nice*, or the Nice School. He became famous worldwide for creating a colour: a deep blue, which he often juxtaposed with gold in his paintings and sculptures. In the '50s, he organised "art-happenings", featuring young, beautiful, naked women coated with fresh paint, who danced and slithered on canvasses. Later Klein, together with now well-known Arman and Raysse, created *Nouveau Réalisme*.

Today, artists Ben and César are key figures of the third generation of the École de Nice. Ben, himself an enthusiast of happenings, is mostly famous for his work with graffiti art. César is known for his work in bronze, and his sculptures made from compressed objects. He is the superstar of this school, and there is a small gallery honouring his work in Marseille.

L'École de Nice is strongly represented at both the **Museé d'Art Moderne** and the **Musée d'Art Contemporain**. This is quite exceptional in itself, since compared to other countries such as the United States, Germany or Italy, contemporary art is currently under represented in the museums in France.

 Finding Your Way Around

To help you discover Nice, we suggest five walking tours: **Vieux-Nice** ★★★ (see p 193), **Nice-Cimiez** ★★★ (see p 194), **Promenade des Anglais** ★★ (see p 196), **Quartier du Paillon** ★★ (see p 198) and **Quartier du Port** ★ (see p 199).

■ **By Car**

You can reach Nice via the **A 8** highway, which follows an east-west axis. This autoroute allows you to cross the region, and connects Aix-en-Provence in the west, to Menton, on the Italian border to the east. This is the fastest way to get to Nice. Nice is only 200 km from Aix-en-Provence, and Menton is only 40 km away. The autoroutes charge tolls which are on the expensive side, as is fuel, for that matter. But you can also get there by the *routes nationales* **N 7**, **N 98**, and **N 202** (from the north) and Route

Napoléon (coming from Grasse, in the north-west). The N 7 and N 98 are very busy in July and August. Traffic is often at a standstill and it can take hours to travel just a few kilometres.

■ **Car Rentals**

There are several car rental agencies at the airport and at the SNCF station. Rental rates at the station are usually better because of the packages they offer.

■ **By Plane**

Nice Côte d'Azur International Airport
☎ 93.21.30.30

Air Inter
☎ 93.31.55.55

Helicopters: Héli Air Monaco
☎ 93.21.34.95

■ **By Boat**

SNCM *Ferryterranée* car ferry (regular service to/from Corsica)
Gare Maritime, Quai du Commerce
☎ 93.13.66.66, ⇄ 93.13.66.81

■ **By Train**

The TGV links Paris to Nice in seven hours, with two departures every day (three, from June to September). Many daily connections from large cities within France, and regular connections from outside of France.

Gare SNCF
Av. Thiers
☎ 93.87.50.50, ⇄ 93.88.68.88

Circuit Digne-Nice
Chemins de fer de Provence
4 bis, Rue Alfred Binet
☎ 93.88.28.56 or 93.82.10.17

■ By Bus

National and international connections:
Gare routière de Nice
Promenade du Paillon
☎ 93.80.08.70

■ Public transportation

Bus transit maps and schedules are available at the tourist office. You can purchase a tourist pass which entitles you to unlimited access to bus transportation for one, five or seven days.

Bus Masséna
Parc Autos Place Masséna
Mon to Fri 7:15 AM to 7 PM
Sat 8 AM to 6 PM
☎ 93.16.52.10

■ Taxis

Station Centrale
☎ 93.80.70.70

Main stations: Esplanade Masséna, Promenade des Anglais, Place Garibaldi, Gare SNCF and Acropolis.

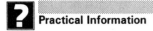

Practical Information

■ Tourist Offices

To obtain information before you leave, write to the **Office de Tourisme de Nice** (service du courrier, B.P. 79, 06302 NICE CEDEX 4). Include return postage in stamps or international reply coupons.

Gare SNCF
Av. Thiers
☎ 93.87.07.07

5 Av. Gustave V
☎ 93.87.60.60

Nice Ferber (near the airport)
Promenade des Anglais
☎ 93.83.32.64

Comité Régional du Tourisme
5 Promenade des Anglais
☎ 93.44.50.59, ⇄ 93.86.01.06

■ Emergencies

Police
☎ 17

S.O.S. Médecins (for medical emergency 24 hours)
☎ 93.85.01.01

S.O.S. Dentaire (for dental emergency)
☎ 93.80.38.40

Night Pharmacy
7 Rue Masséna
☎ 93.87.78.94

Lost and Found
Municipal Police, Cours Saleya
☎ 93.80.65.50

■ Banks

Banks are usually open from 8:30 AM to noon, and from 1:30 to 4:30 PM, from Monday to Friday. Most have automatic teller machines.

In case of credit card loss or theft:
American Express: ☎ 47.77.72.00
Visa: ☎ 42.77.11.90
Mastercard: ☎ 45.67.84.84

■ **Currency Exchange**

American Express
11 Promenade des Anglais
Nov to Apr, Mon to Fri 9 AM to noon
and 2 PM to 6 PM; May to Oct, Mon to
Fri 9 AM to 6 PM, Sat 9 AM to noon.
☎ 93.97.29.82

B.P.C.A. Nice Côte d'Azur Airport:
8:30 AM to 7 PM, open until 8:45 PM
in the summer
☎ 93.21.39.50

Change Or Charrière
10 Rue de France
8 AM to 8 PM, open 24 hours in the
summer
☎ 93.82.16.55

 Exploring

You will need at least two to three
days to really see Nice. There are a lot
of museums and interesting neighbourhoods to be explored.

■ **Vieux-Nice ★★★**

Vieux-Nice, the old town, is best visited
by foot. If you have a car, leave it in
one of the four parking lots in the area,
where you pay at the end of the day.
Street parking is extremely difficult to
find in Nice, and costs money. There
are parking meters everywhere, so you
will have to fill the meter all day.

*The tour begins at the western limit of
the Cours Saleya, which is near the
seashore.*

Le Cours Saleya (1) ★★ is a long public
square where merchants sell flowers
and vegetables. On Mondays, the area
becomes an enormous flea market for
second-hand goods. On Wednesday
and Saturday evenings, the square is
taken over by artists and artisans selling their work. You can also stop at
one of many bars and restaurants in
the area to really get a feel for the
action, and there is plenty of it. Of
course high prices, but not necessarily
quality, are part of the deal, with the
possible exception of "La Criée" (see
p 202) which offers a reasonably-
priced menu.

Also located in the square, the **Palais
de la Préfecture (2)** is the former residence of the Savoy dynasty rulers and
of the kings of Sardinia in the 17th
century. The palace's current appearance dates back to 1907, when the
main façade was redone. The interior
decoration is a tribute to the *belle
époque.*

At the corner of Place Pierre Gautier
you will find the **Chapelle de la
Miséricordia (3)**, the work of an 18th-
century Piedmontese architect. The
arrangement of curves and use of
space in the lavishly decorated interior
produce a rather spectacular effect.

L'Église de l'Annonciation (4) or Ste-
Rita, one of the oldest churches in
Nice, is located at the far east end of
the Cours Saleya. Originally, around
AD 900, it was the site of a Benedictine priory; in the 17th century, under
the authority of *L'Ordre des Carmes*
(the White Friars) it became a Baroque-
style church.

Leave the Cours Saleya.

Here Vieux-Nice's picturesque alleys
abound with artisans' booths, fragrant
produce stalls, little restaurants,
sweetshops, churches, and art galleries.

Sooner or later you will end up at the **Place Rossetti (5)** where you will find the **Cathédrale Ste-Réparate (6)**, a Baroque-style building, originally built in 1650. Its current appearance is the result of several centuries of construction (the bell-tower was completed only in 1757 and the façade was finished in the 19th century). The cathedral was also restored in 1980.

After visiting the square, an ice cream at Fenocchio's is a must! Their old-fashioned ice cream and sherbets are home-made and are among the best in Nice, if not the best in the world.

Leave the square by rue Rossetti.

Turn left on Rue Droite, and the **Palais Lascaris (7)** is only a few metres away. This aristocratic house has undergone several transformations over the years. The City of Nice purchased it in 1942 and recreated a noble household, exhibiting rooms with painted ceilings. There is even a recreation of an 18th-century apothecary shop on the main floor.

A few metres further, you will find the **Palais Communal (8)** in the Place Saint-François. Today, this square is famous for its fish market.

The **colline du château ★★ (9)**, the chateau's hill is at the far east end of Vieux-Nice. As you go up the hill, you will pass the **Couvent de la Visitation du Vieux Nice (10)** and the **Galerie Renoir (11)**. Go along the edge of the cemetery and take one of the little lanes to get to the waterfall, the castle ruins and finally to the Frédéric-Nietzche terrace at the top. Here there is a **magnificent view ★★★** of the city and surrounding area.

To go back down, there is an elevator on the waterfront side. At the bottom, you will see the **Tour Bellanda (12)**, a historical monument which houses the **Musée Naval (13)** (*free admission; in summer 10 AM to 12 AM and 2 PM to 7 PM; in winter until 5 PM closed Nov. 15 to Dec. 15*). A little further, on the Quai des États-Unis (the boulevard along the sea), you will find two art galleries. The **Galerie des Ponchettes (14)** houses the **Musée Raoul Dufy (15)** a tribute to the famous French painter who immortalized Nice at the beginning of the century.

Further along this street you will find the **Opéra de Nice**. The main entrance is in the rear, on Rue St-François-de-Paule. Drop in at the **Pâtisserie Auer (16)**, just beside the opera. This family bakery, decorated in the rococo style (extremely ornamental baroque style), has been around since 1820. A bit further along the street, be sure not to miss the **Magasin Alziari (17)**, a store specializing in olive products. It offers a wide array of different olives and olive oils, including the small Nice olive.

■ Nice-Cimiez ★★★

To get to Cimiez, take Boulevard Caracel, which becomes Boulevard de Cimiez further along. In any case, up is the only way to go since Cimiez is on a hill. Once you reach the top you will soon see signs for the **Musée National Marc Chagall (18)** (*adults 26 F; in summer Wed to Mon 10 AM to 7 PM; off-season 10 AM to 12:30 PM and 2 PM to 5 PM; ☎ 93.81.75.75*), located on avenue du Docteur Ménard. This museum was built at the heart of a small park filled with flowers where there is a charming cafe open during tourist season. The permanent collec-

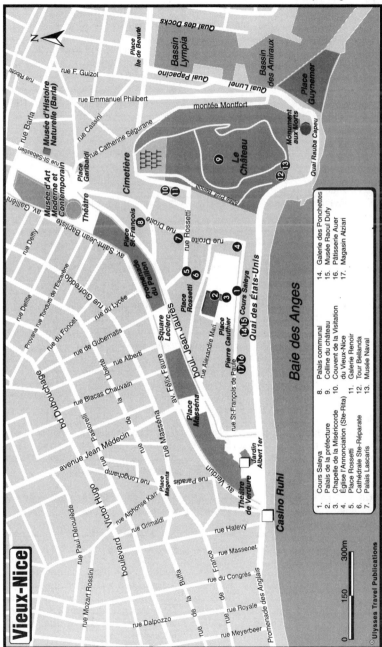

Vieux-Nice

N

rue Ribotti

rue F. Guizol

Place Ile de Beauté

Quai des Docks

Bassin Lympia

Quai Papacino

Quai Lunel

Bassin des Amiraux

rue Emmanuel Philibert

Place Guynemer

rue Barla

rue Cassini

montée Montfort

Musée d'Histoire Naturelle (Barla)

rue Catherine Ségurane

Monument aux Morts

rue St-Sébastien

Place Garibaldi

Cimetière

Le Château

Quai Rauba Capeu

av. Galliéni

Musée d'Art Moderne et Contemporain

Théâtre

Place St-François

Allée Prof. Benott

rue Droite

rue Droite

rue Rossetti

rue Delfly

Promenade du Paillon

Le Château

rue du Lycée

av. Saint-Jean Baptiste

rue Giofredo

Place Rossetti

Quai des États-Unis

Provana rue Tonduti de l'escarène

rue du Foncet

Square Leclerc

bout. Jean Jaurès

rue de Gubernatis

rue Alexandre Mari

Place Pierre Gauthier

Baie des Anges

rue Alberti

bd Dubouchage

rue Blacas Chauvain

la

Liberté

av. Félix Faure

Place Masséna

rue St-François de Paule

avenue Jean Médecin

de

Pastorelli

rue Masséna

rue Longchamp

rue Alphonse Karr

rue Paradis

Place Magenta

Jardin Albert 1er

Victor Hugo

rue Grimaldi

Théâtre de Verdure

Casino Ruhl

boulevard

rue Halevy

rue Paul Déroulède

rue Mozart Rossini

Buffa

rue Massenet

de

la

rue du Congrès

France

rue Royale

rue Dalpozzo

rue Meyerbeer

Promenade des Anglais

1.	Cours Saleya	8.	Palais communal	14.	Galerie des Ponchettes
2.	Palais de la préfecture	9.	Colline du château	15.	Musée Raoul Dufy
3.	Chapelle de la Miséricorde	10.	Couvent de la Visitation	16.	Pâtisserie Auer
4.	Église l'Annonciation (Ste-Rita)		du Vieux-Nice	17.	Magasin Alziari
5.	Place Rossetti	11.	Galerie Renoir		
6.	Cathédrale Ste-Réparate	12.	Tour Bellanda		
7.	Palais Lascaris	13.	Musée Naval		

0   150   300m

© Ulysses Travel Publications

tion includes the 17 large paintings of the *Message Biblique* by Chagall. There are also many sketches, gouaches, etchings, and lithographs that were donated to the museum after the artist's death in 1985.

Continuing further along Boulevard de Cimiez, you will come to the former Roman site of **Cemenelum (19)**, where the ruins of the public baths and arenas stand. *(Buses number 15, 17, 20 and 22, "Arènes" stop.)* Beside the **Arènes**, on Avenue Monte Croce, is the **Musée d'Archéologie (20)** *(free admission to the museum, admission charge for the site; in summer Tue to Sun 10 AM to noon and 2 PM to 6 PM; off-season until 5 PM; closed Sun mornings and Nov; ☎ 93.81.59.57).* This museum, inaugurated in 1989, recalls the life and history of the people who lived at Cemenelum and in the Roman province of Alpes-Maritimes. A collection of objects of all kinds is displayed, including ceramics, glass, and money, in a recreation of the atmosphere in which they were used. These articles date as far back as 1100 BC.

The **Musée Matisse (21)** *(25 F; Apr to Sep, Wed to Mon 11 AM to 7 PM; ☎ 93.81.08.08)* stands a few steps from the Roman site. During the 1992 renovation of the original pink, 17th-century Genoese villa, a new, modern-style concrete wing was added — a highly criticised architectural accomplishment. The museum contains Matisse's personal collection of works. The painter lived in Nice from 1917 until his death in 1954. You will see works from every period of the painter's life, from his first works painted in the 1890s to his last, painted in the '50s. Finally, there are several drawings and etchings as well as the entire collection of books illustrated by Matisse.

■ **Promenade des Anglais** ★★

The **Promenade des Anglais (22)** is the place *par excellence* to take long walks while admiring the magnificent sea, with its sweeping colours ranging from deep blue to emerald green. This is where Nice's beaches are. The public beaches have no admission charge and no sand, only small flat pebbles called *galets* "shingles." Privately-owned beaches, often belonging to hotels offer lounge chairs or beach mats for rent for about 50 F per day. In all, there are 6 km of beaches, of which 4 km are public. The water is surprisingly clean, considering the crowds of bathers.

The area bordering the Promenade des Anglais has an abundance of stores and restaurants. Many of the streets allow only pedestrian access.

The tour begins at Place Masséna and heads west.

Place Masséna (23) is one of Nice's busiest spots. There's lots of traffic, and the fountain attracts crowds of tourists who come to cool off. The public square is bordered on the north by handsome buildings painted in warm *Niçois* colours. The major French department store, **Les Galeries Lafayette (24)**, is here.

Leave the square and take Rue Masséna.

Rue Masséna is Nice's largest pedestrian street, with many shops and restaurants. The restaurants have large patios and offer pleasant meals at reasonable prices, although the quality of the meals is not always outstanding. Once you get to Place Magenta, there are several places that offer delicious ice cream.

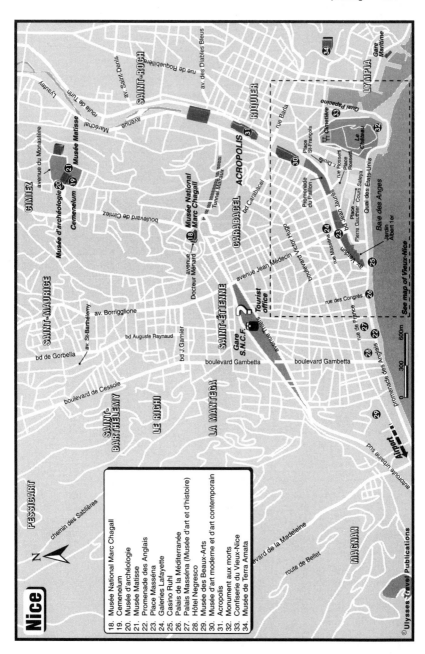

Nice

PESSICART

N

18. Musée National Marc Chagall
19. Cemenelum
20. Musée d'archéologie
21. Musée Matisse
22. Promenade des Anglais
23. Place Masséna
24. Galeries Lafayette
25. Casino Ruhl
26. Palais de la Méditerranée
27. Palais Masséna (Musée d'art et d'histoire)
28. Hôtel Negresco
29. Musée des Beaux-Arts
30. Musée d'art moderne et d'art contemporain
31. Acropolis
32. Monument aux morts
33. Confiserie du Vieux-Nice
34. Musée de Terra Amata

© Ulysses Travel Publications

Leave Place Magenta and return to Avenue de Verdun towards the seashore.

You will come across the Jardins Albert Ier gardens and their spectacular foliage. A few steps away is the Promenade des Anglais and the departure point of a little tourist train. If you continue west along the promenade, you will pass by the **Casino Ruhl (25)**. It is located in a building featuring very ordinary modern architecture that hasn't aged well. A sad sight made even sadder when one sees the **Palais de la Méditerranée (26)**, a bit further along the promenade, at the corner of Rue des Congrès. Built in 1929, only the exterior walls remain of this Art Deco building, which used to hold an extravagant casino with a monumental staircase. The Palais has been closed since 1977, but since it is designated as a historical monument, it will soon be restored as a conference and recreation centre.

A few museums can also be found in this part of the city. The **Palais Masséna** is farther along the Promenade at number 35. (It can also be reached from behind, via Rue France). Here you will find the **Musée d'Art et d'Histoire (27)** (*in summer Tue to Sun 10 AM to noon and 3 PM to 6 PM; off-season 10 AM to noon and 2 PM to 5 PM; closed Nov;* ☎ *93.88.11.34*). This museum is devoted to regional history and houses a library containing over 10,000 rare books and manuscripts on the ground floor.

Next door is the famous **Hôtel Negresco ★★ (28)**, which was constructed in 1913 and is now designated a historical monument. The salons and boutiques inside the palace have to be seen. The *Salon Royal* is in the shape of an ellipse and features a Baccarat crystal chandelier. The Negresco is the most luxurious hotel in Nice, and receives celebrities from all over the world, particularly those in show business.

Continue west.

The **Musée des Beaux-Arts (29)** (*free admission; in summer Tue to Sun 10 AM to noon and 3 PM to 6 PM; off-season 10 AM to noon and 2 PM to 5 PM;* ☎ *93.44.50.72*) is on a street just north of the Centre Universitaire Meditérranéen at 33 Avenue des Baumettes. This museum, also known as Musée Chéret, is located in an unusual house that was built in 1876. Its vast European collection includes works from the 17th to the 20th century. The museum offers an overview of the *École Française* of the 19th-century, from neo-classicism to impressionism and everything in between with Academicism being particularly well-represented. Sculptures by Rodin and Carpeaux are also part of the collection.

■ Quartier du Paillon ★★

The Rivière Paillon used to flow into the sea exactly where the Jardins Albert Ier now stand. The banks at the mouth of the river, where the water level was low, were filled in and developed. The parts close to the sea were set up as green spaces, ideal for taking a walk. To get to the Masséna area from the Jardins Albert Ier, cross Place Masséna. The fountains here are a very popular place to cool off in the summer.

You will reach the end of Promenade du Paillon, where a row of cultural complexes begins. The first, built of grey Carrare marble, houses the new theatre and the **Musée d'Art Moderne**

et d'Art Contemporain ★ (30) *(free admission; Tue to Sun 11 AM to 6 PM, Fri until 10 PM; closed on holidays;* ☎ *93.62.61.62)*. The artistic movements of the '60s and '70s, such as neorealism, pop art, American abstraction, minimalism and, of course, the *École de Nice* are especially well-represented in this museum's collection. There is even one very beautiful room entirely devoted to Yves Klein. Before leaving the museum, go up to the terraces at the very top, where you can catch a breathtaking view of Nice. The theatre holds 1,100, and the very red interior is the work of designer Jacqueline Morabito. To finish off, you might enjoy a cocktail at the bar between the theatre and the museum.

Across from this complex, on the Boulevard Jean-Jaurès side, you will come to Place Garibaldi.

A bit further along the same boulevard stands the **Acropolis (31)**, a monster of a building that was constructed in 1983. It contains a bowling alley, shops, the Cinémathèque, a large exhibition room and an auditorium with 2,500 seats and a stage measuring 1,200 m².

Finally, the **Palais des Congrès**, with a capacity of 20,000 people, is the last building constructed on the Paillon. The river continues on behind it.

■ **Quartier du Port ★**

There are two ways to get to the port. You can take the road along the seashore that follows the castle hill where you will find the **Monument aux Morts (32)**. The other way is via Place Garibaldi to the north, on the other side of the hill. The port hardly has any tourist attractions, with the possible exception of the flea market at Place Guynemer.

As you leave place Guynemer, heading towards the central area of the port, you will pass by the **Confiserie du Vieux-Nice (33)**, at 14 Quai Papacino. This sweetshop sells handmade candies flavoured with local fruits and flowers (violets, mimosa and vervain), chocolates and jam, at factory prices. Further along, in the main port area, Place Île-de-Beauté awaits, surrounded by a few beautiful buildings and a church.

In general, be wary of restaurants at the port. The quality leaves a lot to be desired.

At the eastern end of the port, a piece of land juts out into the sea. Ferry boats destined for Corsica, a French island in the Mediterranean, dock at the end of this point (see p 191).

For lovers of things Prehistoric, the **Musée de Terra Amata (34)** *(free admission; Tue to Sun 9 AM to noon and 2 PM to 6 PM; closed first two weeks of Sep;* ☎ *93.55.59.93)*, is located at 25 Boulevard Carnot, about 500 m from the port. There you can see, among other things, a recreation of an elephant-hunters' camp in Nice as it may have looked 400,000 years ago.

 Outdoor Activities

Nice is a popular spot for water sports, although perhaps a bit too popular. Along the Promenade des Anglais private beaches offer food and refreshment, and rental of equipment such as catamarans, pedal boats, sailboards, waterskis and parasails.

The Promenade des Anglais is also a popular place for taking a stroll or going for a run. However, the public park on the colline du Château is still the nicest place to take a walk. The view is magnificent and the shade it offers is appreciated on hot summer days.

Accommodation

Nice is a major tourist city, and consequently also has a multitude of hotels to choose from, in a wide range of categories. Unfortunately, the heavy traffic and very limited number of pedestrian streets make it quite difficult to find a truly peaceful hotel. Of course, this is not a problem in exclusive hotels, since they usually have double- or triple-glazed windows as well as air conditioning. We have nevertheless managed to find a few hotels that are sheltered from the noise of the traffic.

Suggestion: Reserving well in advance is strongly recommended, especially during high season, since Nice hosts several international conferences and receives many tourist groups. By booking in advance, you're one step ahead.

Relais International de la Jeunesse Clairvallon *(70 F per person, bkfst incl., 105 F half-board; Avenue Scudéri,* ☎ *93.81.27.63)*. The prices are reasonable here. This hotel is located at Cimiez in a park with a swimming pool. To get there, take bus number 15 or 22 from the station or Place Masséna and get off at the "Scudéri" stop.

Les Collinettes *(95 F per person; open only in summer; 3 Av. Robert Schumann;* ☎ *93.97.06.64)*. Conveni-

ently located in a nice area, this place is better than a youth hostel since there are individual rooms with sinks.

■ Hotels

Vieux Nice

Beside the old opera and a few steps from the sea: the **Hôtel Cresp** *(250 F, 350-400 F for three or four people; pb, ≡ in some rooms, C, tv; 8 Rue Saint-François-de-Paule,* ☎ *93.85.91.76)*. This hotel is our favourite in the "one-star" category. It offers a family *pension* atmosphere. A large hallway leads to a terrace overlooking the sea. Very good value. Note: credit cards are not accepted.

If luxury is what you're looking for, the **Hôtel la Pérouse** *(775-1,180 F, 1,970 F for a suite; pb, ≡, R, tvc, ≈, ℜ, △, ☺, tv; 11 Quai Rauba-Capeu;* ☎ *93.62.34.63,* ⇄ *93.62.59.41)* is for you. Although it's just steps from Vieux-Nice, you might not even notice it. The front of the building facing the street is quite small, but the back of the building extends to the hill that overlooks the Baie des Anges. A sublime spot, this is a modern hotel with rustic decor and a truly charming appeal. There's a large rooftop terrace nestled against the hill, which provides a spectacular panoramic view. There is also a small meeting room that can accommodate 20 people.

Nice-Cimiez

Former residence of Sacha Guitry, **Le Petit Palais** *(480-720 F; pb or ps; 10 Av. Bieckert,* ☎ *93.62.19.11,* ⇄ *92.62.53.60)* has the advantage of a superb location with a magnificent view of the sea and a garden. As part of the *Relais du Silence* chain, tranquillity has a special place here. You'll hardly realize you are in a big city. With a welcoming atmosphere, this hotel is very comfortable and even offers parking which is a rarity in Nice.

La Promenade des Anglais

Le Magenta *(200 F; pb or ps, C, tv; 10 Rue Paradis, ☎ 93.87.72.27)*. A few steps from the sea, this little hotel is located on a pedestrian street. Simple studio style. We highly recommend this hotel because of its proximity to Vieux-Nice, and because it offers very good value. The young owner is very friendly.

Close to the very beautiful Hôtel Windsor, **Les Cigales** *(210-250 F, 245-350 F for three or four people; pb or ps, ≡ in some rooms, tv; 16 Rue Dalpozzo, ☎ 93.88.33.75)* is a few minutes from the sea in modern Nice's pedestrian zone. This is a small, simple, respectable, owner-run hotel. Ask for a room at the back. Note: credit cards are not accepted.

If you prefer a modern hotel with all the modern comforts, choose the **Alfa I** hotel *(300-460 F, extra bed 100 F; pb, ≡, tv; 30 Rue Masséna, ☎ 93.87.88.63 ⇄ 93.88.17.30)*. Located on a commercial pedestrian street close to the sea, this hotel offers very good value. There are four rooms on the top floor which share a large terrace.

The **Alfa II** *(430-580 F, extra bed 100 F; pb, ≡, R, ℜ, tvc; 2 Rue Maccarani, ☎ 93.87.26.20, ⇄ 93.87.71.11)* is a few steps away from the Alfa I. Part of the same chain, this is a three-star hotel, and therefore somewhat more luxurious. Like the Alfa I, the Alfa II is close to many of the city's tourist attractions and to the sea.

For traditional style, we strongly recommend the **Windsor** *(415-670 F, extra bed 100 F; pb, ≡, R, ≈, ℜ, ☉, tv; 11 Rue Dalpozzo, ☎ 93.88.59.35, ⇄ 93.88.94.57)*. The hotel is less than 10 minutes from the sea, and close to pedestrian streets filled with antiques shops and art galleries. There's lots of ambience, beautiful Chinese furniture and several *objets d'art*. Some of the rooms were decorated by local artists, and the results are often spectacular. What gives this hotel its charm is the garden. With a pool, terrace and the sounds of birds singing, it is a small paradise. Very good value. Try to get a room on the garden side. There is pay parking close by.

And of course we can't forget the famous and illustrious **Negresco** *(1,550 F-2,250 F, 3,750 F for a suite, extra bed 500 F; pb, ≡, R, tvc, ℜ; 37 Promenade des Anglais, B.P. 379, ☎ 93.88.39.51, ⇄ 93.88.00.58)*, the favourite hotel of international celebrities. Sometimes you can see people lining up at the entrance to the hotel, hoping to get an autograph from their favourite star. The hotel, with its pink turret and roof and little yellow lights, is the most beautiful address on the Promenade des Anglais. Even if you don't stay there, it is at least worth seeing the interior of this unusual building (see detailed description on p 198).

Quartier du Paillon

Close to the SNCF station: the **Hôtel Durante** *(350-410 F; pb, C, tvc; 16 Rue Durante, ☎ 93.88.84.40, ⇄ 93.87.77.76)*. There are many hotels around the station, but they are often noisy. We've found a very nice one, in a quiet little courtyard, removed from the noise. The rooms look out over the small garden where breakfast is served during tourist season. This hotel is close to the main commercial streets of modern Nice and is only 10 minutes from the sea and Vieux Nice.

In a completely different category, you will find the very well-maintained **Hôtel Vendôme** *(450-550 F, 620 F triple occupancy, 750 F for a studio with mezzanine; pb, ≡, ℝ, tv; 26 Rue Pastorelli, ☎ 93.62.00.77, ⇄ 93.13.40.78).* It is five minutes from Nice's modern city centre and 15 minutes from the sea. This hotel, an old private villa dating back to the end of the 19th century, has just recently been renovated. There is a beautiful central staircase and a lounge with period furnishings. The pastel decor and the owner's warm reception combine to create a friendly and welcoming atmosphere. **If you show her this guide, she will even offer you a free breakfast during your stay!** This old-fashioned hotel has rooms with large terraces on the fifth floor, and a small parking lot. The owner can also recommend some little restaurants nearby which offer a free cocktail with the meal. How's that for service!

 Restaurants

■ **Vieux Nice**

Lou Pistou *($; closed Sat and Sun; 4 Rue de la Terrasse, ☎ 93.62.21.82)* offers *Niçois* specialities such as *beignets de fleurs de courgettes, pâtes au pistou, farcis,* tripe and *andouillettes.* Isabelle and Michel welcome you in this rustic family setting.

Also small and very nice, **La Merenda** *($; 8 Rue de la Terrasse)* serves stuffed sardines, beef tripe, and lentils. Their daily menu is written by hand on a blackboard. This restaurant is well-known and much sought after by the *Niçois.* You will have to go there directly to get a table, since they don't accept reservations by telephone.

One of the finest Italian restaurants in Nice, **La Villa de Sienne** *($; 10 Rue Saint Vincent, ☎ 93.80.12.45)* is located on a little side-street, behind the Cours Saleya, close to the Palais de Justice. You can sit outside on the little terrace, or inside in a simple, rustic atmosphere. The servings are generous. The menu is basic but shows a masterful balance of flavours. Try the *raviolis à la niçoise,* the osso bucco, the rabbit *porchetta,* or one of their many pasta dishes. Fast service.

La Criée *($-$$; 22 Cours Saleya, ☎ 93.85.49.99)* is one of the best choices of restaurants in the Cours Saleya, especially because it offers good value. For 109 F, you can enjoy the *menu navigateur,* complete with appetiser, entrée and dessert. If you're not quite so hungry, the 85 F selection allows you to choose between the appetiser and dessert. You'll be spoiled with seafood, oysters and shellfish platters. Finally, the service is skilfully orchestrated by the friendly and efficient manager.

The **Don Camillo** *($$; 5 Rue des Ponchettes, ☎ 93.85.67.95),* falls into a higher category in every respect, including price. Their excellent meals are served in a traditional upper-class ritzy decor. House specialities include rabbit *porchetta,* squab with *jus de foie,* and fig tarts. The *tarte tatin* is prepared with apricots. In short, everything is special here. Considering the quality, the prices are not so unreasonable. Located in the east end of Vieux-Nice, this restaurant is a favourite with many *Niçois.*

■ La Promenade des Anglais

If you can't afford to stay at the "modest" hotel Negresco, at least go and eat there. **Le Chantecler** *($ $; 37 Promenade des Anglais, ☎ 93.88.39.51)* offers good cuisine at a relatively reasonable price in a very unique setting. In the *"menu plaisir" (250 F wine and coffee included)* the chef combines colours and fresh produce from the Provençal market to create a work of art: *gratin de fruits de mer á la crème langoustine* as an appetiser, *feuilleté de pigeon* with fried vegetables for the main dish, and for desert, *gratin de fruits rouges*. It's a change from regular tourist fare.

Entertainment

For an overview of cultural activities, sporting events and nightlife, buy *l'Officiel des Loisirs* or *La semaine des spectacles*, available at all newsstands.

■ Bars

Bar à Tapas Los Gringos *(from 8 PM except Mon; 8 Reine Jeanne, close to the railway bridge on avenue Jean Médecin, ☎ 93.88.67.56).* Video screen, live music, beer, cocktails, tapas, tacos and tequila.

Au Pizzaïolo *(4 Bis Rue du Pont-Vieux, ☎ 93.62.34.70).* Dinner theatre, Provençal cuisine. Ambience, shows, dancing. 170 F.

Mark's Place *(from 10 PM; 2 Rue Desboutins, close to Place Masséna, ☎ 93.62.06.62).* The place where art and film writers meet. Cocktails. Piano bar.

Le Trap's *(from 2 PM, closed Sun; 26 Bd. Risso, ☎ 93.56.88.77).* A swinging pub with a very casual atmosphere.

Le Fourquet *(7:30 PM to midnight; 21 Rue Auguste-Gal, 200 m from the Acropolis, ☎ 93.56.96.48).* Billiards, games and the best Belgian beers.

Le Blue Boy *(11 PM to 5 AM; closed Mon and Tue from Oct to May; 9 Rue Spinetta, ☎ 93.44.68.24).* Two bars on two floors. Gay clientele.

L'Ascenseur *(6 PM to 3 AM; 18 bis, Rue Emmanuel Philibert; ☎ 93.26.35.30).* Gay night club. No cover charge. Ring to get in.

■ Casinos

Casino Ruhl *(1 Promenade des Anglais, ☎ 93.87.95.87).* Gaming room: blackjack, *punto banco*, French and English roulette *(8 PM to 4 AM Fri and Sat 5 PM to 5 AM, Sun 5 PM to 4 AM).* Slot-machine room *(Sun to Thu 10 AM to 4 PM, Fri and Sat 10 AM to 5 AM).*

■ Festivals

Festival de l'École au Théâtre first half of April; Théâtre Lino Ventura; information: ☎ 93.27.37.37.

Festival de Musique Sacrée June; Cathédrale Sainte-Réparate and other venues; information ☎ 93.13.20.52.

Carnaval de Nice Each year, during the second half of February, Nice is transformed. Stands are erected in Place Masséna and along the sea, so people can watch the parades of allegorical floats, cheerful masquerades and cavalcades. Of all of France's carnivals, Nice's stands out for its extravagant costumes and parades.

This tradition dates back to the 13th century. Of course, the Church tried many times, most often in vain, to control this flood of excitement. Beginning in 1539, in the middle of the Renaissance, city officials charged designated *abbés des fous* with organising and managing the event. In the 18th century, the Carnaval was celebrated in accordance with very specific rules. There were four celebration locations, for four classes: the nobles (the Dukes of Savoy sometimes joined in with this crowd), the merchants, the artisans, and the fishermen. Later, beginning in 1873, a Festival Committee was set up to give this traditional celebration a new orientation. There was a break between the two world wars, but festivities resumed in 1946 with even greater splendour. Soon Nice will be celebrating the 50th anniversary of this renewal.

 Shopping

■ Gifts

A dream shop in the land of fragrances: **Aux Parfums de Grasse** *(10 Rue Saint-Gaëtan, ☎ 93.85.60.77)*. A tiny little shop where the air is filled with the scent of 84 perfumes. The miniature bottles at 14 F make ideal gifts. For 15 F, you can buy large soaps, and as for lavender, well, it comes by the litre...

If you have a passion for old bronze jewellery, take a peek at **Bijoux et Sculptures Rémy** *(32 Rue Droite, in Vieux-Nice, ☎ 93.80.62.60)*. The jewellery is made using age-old techniques,

with only a few produced of each. A bracelet costs about 280 F, a necklace, 380 F.

■ Antique and Second-Hand Shops

Every Monday *(8 AM to 5 PM, except the day before holidays)*, you will marvel at the variety of things for sale in the kiosks of the Cours Saleya in Vieux-Nice. There is a bit of everything, and at a range of prices. Unfortunately, quality is becoming more expensive and harder to find. You have to bargain.

The **Promenade des Antiquaires** *(7 Promenade des Anglais)* houses no less than 22 shops. You can spend hours rummaging through the Provençal objects that are sold there.

Le Village Ségurane *(Rue Antoine Gauthier)*, at the port, is another area for second-hand shops. You will find no less than 80 shops of various sizes and quality.

To find practically anything you want, visit the **Loft Galerie** *(2 Rue Saint-Suaire, at the end of Cours Saleya, ☎ 93.85.51.20)*. In an unexpected way, this shop combines everything ranging from classic second-hand goods to contemporary art.

You can't leave Nice without buying a bottle of extra-virgin olive oil at **Alziari** *(14 Rue St-François-de-Paule, ☎ 93.85.76.92)*. Not only can you choose from a variety of the best olives in the world, but you can also buy honey in this store, where a welcoming atmosphere is the order of the day.

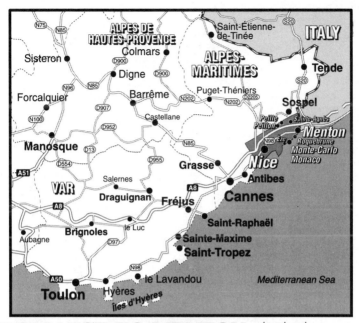

FROM NICE TO MENTON ★★★

 Finding Your Way Around

This region stretches from the eastern part of the Côte d'Azur to the Italian border. The Italian influence is clearly present here, in the inhabitants' names, their appearance and in the local dishes. This is not at all surprising since throughout its history, the region actually belonged more often to Italy than to France.

This part of the Côte d'Azur has to be seen, above all for its landscape. It is traversed by three mountain roads called *corniches*, which follow the coastline at different elevations. They are called La Basse, La Moyenne and La Grande.

Since each *corniche* offers a different panorama, having your own car is almost the only way to capture all of the beauty of the various landscapes. Other modes of transportation don't allow the flexibility of changing from one road to the next.

The villages and towns that border the sea are all accessible by train and bus. However, those located inland can only be reached by bus, which limits access considerably. For example, there are a few daily connections from Menton to Ste-Agnès, Gorbio and Castellar (inland villages in the Menton area).

We strongly recommend renting a car at one of the rental agencies in Nice for this part of your trip.

To get to the three *corniches* from Nice, leave the city from the east end near the port.

The *Basse Corniche* is to be avoided absolutely in July and August. The road follows the coastline and is jammed with traffic, especially in the late afternoon and early evening when everyone is coming back from the beach. This is an experience that you can afford to miss! In any case, there are many smaller roads that connect the *corniches*, which allow you to go from one to the other.

■ By Air

Menton and all the towns east of Nice are less than 30 km from the airport in Nice.

Aéroport International de Nice
☎ 93.21.30.12

■ By Train

There are a number of daily trains serving the region between Nice and Menton every day. They run to almost all the towns on the Côte d'Azur, and a few go as far as Vintimille in Italy.

Enquire at the SNCF stations:
Menton: ☎ 93.87.50.50
Èze (village): ☎ 93.01.53.45
Beaulieu: ☎ 93.80.50.50
Villefranche: ☎ 93.01.71.67

■ By Bus

Menton-Nice: every half-hour with Rapides Côte-d'Azur; ☎ 93.55.24.00

Menton serves nearby inland villages (Gorbio, Ste-Agnès and Castellar) with a relatively regular schedule.

Bus Station
Route de Sospel, (near the SNCF station), ☎ 93.35.93.60, or enquire at Autocars Breuleux: ☎ 93.35.73.51.

■ By Car

Three *corniches* link Nice to Menton:
- The **Grande Corniche** or **D 2565**
- The **Moyenne Corniche** or **N 7**
- The **Basse Corniche** or **N 559**, which is the coast road. It provides access to all the seaside resorts between Nice and Menton.

The quickest route from Nice to Menton is the **A 8**.

？ Practical Information

■ Villefranche-sur-Mer

Tourist Office
Jardin François Binon
☎ 93.01.73.68, ⇄ 93.76.63.65

■ Èze-Village

Tourist Office
Place du Général De Gaulle
☎ 93.41.26.00, ⇄ 93.41.04.80

■ La Turbie

Tourist Office
Office du Tourisme à la Mairie
☎ 93.41.10.10

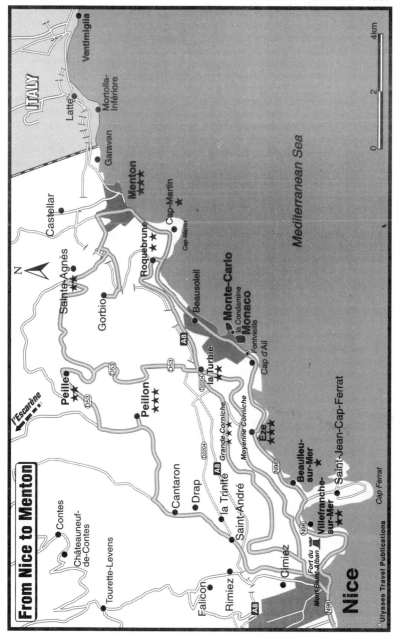

From Nice to Menton

ITALY

Ventimiglia
Latte
Mortolla-Inférieure
Garavan

Menton ★★★

Castellar

Cap-Martin ★
Cap Martin

Sainte-Agnès ★★
Roquebrune ★★

Gorbio

Beausoleil
Monte-Carlo ★★
la Condamine
Monaco
Fontvieille
Cap d'Ail

Peille ★★

l'Escarène

Peillon ★★★

la Turbie ★★

A8
D53
D53

Cantaron
Drap
la Trinité
A8
Saint-André

Grande Corniche
Moyenne Corniche

Éze ★★★

Beaulieu-sur-Mer
Saint-Jean-Cap-Ferrat

Contes
Châteauneuf-de-Contes
Tourette-Levens

Falicon
Rimiez
Cimiez

Fort du
Mont Saint-Alban

Villefranche-sur-Mer ★★

Nice

N98
A8
N98

Cap Ferrat

Mediterranean Sea

N

4km
0   2

© Ulysses Travel Publications

■ **Peille**

Tourist Office
Syndicat d'Initiative à la Mairie
☎ 93.79.90.32

■ **Roquebrune Cap-Martin**

Tourist Office
☎ 93.35.62.87

■ **Menton**

Tourist Office
8 Av. Boyer, BP 239
☎ 93.57.57.00

Service du Patrimoine
5 Rue Ciapetta
☎ 92.10.33.66

Hôpital La Palmosa
Rue A. Péglion
☎ 93.28.77.77
(Emergencies) ☎ 93.28.72.41

Currency Exchange
Office de Change St-Michel
5 Rue St-Michel
☎ 93.57.18.31

Taxis
at the station, ☎ 93.35.72.37, and at
the casino, ☎ 93.35.73.75

Car Rental
Avis: 9 Rue Victor Hugo
☎ 93.35.50.98
Europcar: 9 Av. Thiers
☎ 93.28.21.80

Exploring

Leaving Nice, take La Moyenne Corniche.

The road passes by the **Fort du Mont Alban**, one of the most beautiful examples of Renaissance military architecture. Transformed into a fortress in the 18th century, this fort was an important military installation until World War II. It offers a magnificent view of the coast. Nearby Mont Boron, closer to the sea, is a nice place for a hike.

Whichever road you choose, make sure to stop in Villefranche-sur-Mer.

■ **Villefranche-sur-Mer ★★**

This is the first town east of Nice. This seaside village was founded in the 13th century on the site of Olivula, an old Roman port and commercial centre. The village has a network of charming pedestrian side-streets. One of these lanes, **Rue Obscure ★**, has remained unchanged since the 13th century, when it served as shelter during unstable times. It is completely covered, (a little like a tunnel), and is very dark, hence the name.

In the village stands **La Citadelle St-Elme**, a restored 16th-century building. The citadel was built by Emmanuel Philibert, Duke of Savoy, in reaction to the siege of Nice by François I in 1543. Later the citadel became an important defence complex, after the occupation of the port by a Muslim fleet. Today, it is still a port-of-call for some of NATO's military units and for cruise ships.

At the port, make sure you visit the tiny **Chapelle St-Pierre** ★★*(admission charge, Tue-Sun; ☎ 93.76.90.70)*, built in the 14th century. In 1957, Jean Cocteau decorated the inside of the chapel with paintings honouring "his friends the fishermen." The **Galerie Jean Cocteau** *(Sep to Jun, 10 AM to 7 PM; Jul and Aug, 10 AM to 11 PM; ☎ 93.01.73.92)* is on the first floor.

Across the street from the church, there are lovely terraces where visitors can stop for a drink. Tourists might not want to stay overnight in Villefranche. There is only a tiny beach and very few hotels.

Continue on the seaside road.

■ **St-Jean-Cap-Ferrat** ★★★

This cape extending out into the sea is famous for the great wealth of its residents. Yet, before the turn of the century, it was nothing more than a fishermen's hamlet, a still untamed place without any buildings to speak of. Everything changed when Béatrice de Rothschild had the **Villa Ephrussi-Rothschild** ★ *(entrance fee; Apr to Oct everyday 10 AM to 6 PM, Jul and Aug until 7 PM; Nov to Mar. 15 Sat and Sun only; ☎ 93.01.33.09)* built here at the beginning of this century. If you like formal splendour, you will love this. This home stands in testimony to the grandeur of the wealthy families of the *belle époque*. It contains a collection of paintings, furniture, rare objects, porcelain pieces, tapestries and sculptures. The grounds are also worth seeing as they include seven gardens in various themes (Spanish, Japanese, Provençal, Oriental, Exotic and, of course, French) complete with ornamental ponds, waterfalls, benches for visitors to rest on, and even a Temple of Love!

Finally, visitors can stop at the tea-room located in a lovely glassed-in rotunda that looks out onto the garden.

The cape can be toured on foot, by bicycle or by car. Hikers might want to set off on the 11 km trail that follows the coastline all the way around the cape. Along the path, visitors will catch an occasional glimpse of the grounds of the magnificent villas hidden behind the pine trees.

This excursion begins near Plage de Passable, not far from Villa Ephrussi-Rothschild and the **Zoo** *(everyday 9:30 AM to 5:30 PM, in summer until 7 PM; ☎ 93.76.04.98)*, which has a wide collection of animals in the unique setting of tropical and mediterranean vegetation. There is a lighthouse at the tip of the cape. Beyond it lies the **Hôtel Bel-Air**, a very luxurious palace built at the turn of the century. This building is a member of the *Relais et Châteaux* chain and has its own private beach.

On the other side of the cape, the path continues towards the peninsula which retains a rugged look. Near the eastern point, your walk will take you up towards the pretty little **Chapelle Ste-Hospice**. This site offers a lovely view of the surrounding area. A little further, on the north side, there is the charming La Paloma Beach where you can get a bite to eat and rent water-sports equipment. A little further is the port, with its many shops and variety of restaurants.

Leave the cape and go back to the seaside road.

■ **Beaulieu-sur-Mer** ★

You can also go on foot via Promenade Maurice-Rouvier from the cape. It makes for a most pleasant walk. The path follows the coast and has several benches where you can rest in the shade of pine trees and admire the magnificent view.

A visit to the **Villa Kerylos** ★ *(entrance fee; summer, Tue to Sun 10 AM to 7 PM; Oct to mid-Mar 1:30 PM to 5:30 PM; mid-Mar to end of June 10 AM to noon and 2 PM to 6 PM;* ☎ *93.01.01.44)* is a must. When it was built at the beginning of the century, the owner intended it as a tribute to life in ancient Greece, but with all the modern comforts of the 20th century. Designated a historical monument in 1967, this seaside residence features an exceptional wealth of materials and a highly luxurious decor: walls, floors and ceilings made of white, yellow or lavender Italian marble, frosted glass, alabaster, ivory and bronze.

Leave Beaulieu, still following the seaside road.

■ **Èze**

Èze is made up of three communities: **Èze-Bord-de Mer** on the *Basse Corniche*, **Èze-Village** ★★★, higher up on the *Moyenne Corniche*, and finally **Le Col d'Èze** ★★ even higher up on the *Grande Corniche*.

Èze-Bord-de-Mer has two public beaches that are still undeveloped, one private beach and a sailing club near the train station. Make a short stop at **Chapelle St-Laurent**, built in the 12th century.

From there you can reach Èze-Village by car. The more athletic will want to hike up via the Chemin Nietzsche. This trail offers magnificent vantage points over the sea and takes around one hour to complete. The incline is, however, quite steep!

You should stop in at the tourist office *(Place Général de Gaulle,* ☎ *93.41.26.00)* as soon as you arrive at Èze-village. They have an excellent brochure about Èze called *Èze Guide Pratique*, as well as a pamphlet for hikers about various trails in the area.

Èze-Village is located on a rocky peak at an altitude of 429 m. In the Middle Ages, people settled here for the protection the terrain offered. Today, it is a perfect place for relaxing, except maybe in July and August. You can enter the village by the **Paterne** — two guard-towers, now designated historical monuments, which were built in the 14th century to guard the only entrance to the village. Beyond them is the church, which was built around 1772. Its sober façade, pierced by a single bull's-eye window, contrasts sharply with the very rich Baroque-style interior.

Next comes the trek up through charming, narrow streets. Near the top, two luxurious hotels offer excellent service in a virtual paradise. The **Jardin Exotique** *(admission 12 F; summer 9 AM to 8 PM; off-season 9 AM to noon and 2 PM to 7 PM;* ☎ *93.41.10.30)* is at the top of the village. This garden contains numerous species of cacti, most of which are native to South America. The garden is laid out on several levels, and the top level features a large terrace offering a spectacular panorama that spans from Cap Ferrat to l'Estérel. On a clear winter day you can even see Corsica.

From Èze-Village, head up towards the **Grande Corniche** ★★★, a road built under the orders of Napoleon I. It offers even more spectacular panoramas stretching as far as Hyères to the west, and Italy to the east. At the top, there is a wilderness park covering 60 ha from Mont Vinaigre to the Mont Bataille promontory. You can learn about the park at the Maison de la Nature, where there is also a parking lot. At the Révère, an old military building, there is a viewing table indicating to find to the region's various capes, bays, seaside towns and alpine peaks.

Next to the Hôtel Hermitage (see p 218), a walking trail invites hikers of all ages on a short excursion (1.4 km). There is also a small playground for children, and picnic tables shaded by oak trees.

Head east out of Éze, regardless of whether you are taking the Moyenne or Grande Corniche.

■ La Turbie ★★

If you've planned a different itinerary than that proposed, La Turbie can also be reached via A 8. In fact, this is the fastest way to get there as there is an exit specifically for the town.

Already populated during Prehistoric times, La Turbie was at its height during the Gallo-Roman era. It was located on Via Julia Augusta, a strategic road at the time. In Emperor Augustus' days, the Roman senate decided to erect a monument, Le Trophée, to commemorate Augustus' victories over the rebels he conquered.

In the early '30s, this monument was partially restored to its original architecture thanks to the generous donations of a wealthy American art patron. There is even a museum devoted to retracing the evolution of the monument throughout the years.

The sovereigns of Genoa, Savoy and France had always fought over La Turbie, because of its location on the borders of these kingdoms. In 1713, Monaco gave the village back to France once and for all.

The town and surrounding area is truly spectacular. Don't miss visiting the **Église Saint-Michel**, built in 1777. This beautiful pink and grey Baroque church contains two magnificent paintings: a Bréa original and a work said to be by Veronese in the Chapelle de la Piétà.

HINT: This spot on the *corniche* offers a very beautiful view of Monaco and is generally off the tourist track in summer. It is cooler than right by the sea, and the restaurant and hotel prices are much more reasonable.

Leave La Turbie by D 53 for a short excursion inland.

Here is a short tour which will allow you to discover Monaco's interior via Peille and Peillon. This side-trip can be done by car or even by bike if you wish. This road allows you to discover some splendid landscapes. It is best, however, not to undertake this adventure during the summer vacation period, when car traffic is heavier, as the road is rather narrow.

■ Peille ★★

In the Middle Ages, Peille was a consular city. The town is worth visiting mostly for its unusual location, almost hidden below the road. Visitors can park their cars in a roadside parking lot and walk down to the town below. Peille has some very lovely squares, including one near a gorgeous Gothic fountain. This square is home to the tiny Musée des Arts et Traditions Populaires, which is worth visiting. The village also contains the Chapelle Saint-Martin de Peille, a uniquely designed chapel built in the '50s.

The Peille area offers many possibilities for excursions and walks in the nearby forests. Hikers can set out for 20 minutes or 3 hours. Some of the walking trails even go all the way to Monaco.

The road winding out of Peille, D 53, leads past the Vicat cement quarry, which is a bit of a blemish on the landscape. The white Turbie stone that was used to build the cathedral and the ocean museum in Monaco came from this quarry.

If you head down and south, you will soon arrive at Peillon.

■ Peillon ★★★

Perched way up high is one of the most beautiful towns on the Côte d'Azur. Many artists have immortalized the view over the village. There are two reasons why you absolutely must stop here: first to stroll through the narrow streets, stairways and vaulted passages that climb to the church at the top; and second, to eat or even spend the night at the **Auberge de la Madone** (see p 220).

There's not much to see in the village, save the **Chapelle des Pénitents Blancs**, decorated with gorgeous frescos. However, you will find tranquillity and a haven from the tourist frenzy. This village has fortunately not been invaded by the many businesses which often undermine the charm of some other very beautiful towns on the Côte d'Azur, Saint-Paul-de-Vence for example.

Continue on D 53 to D 2204, which leads to the highway to Roquebrune.

■ Roquebrune Cap-Martin ★★

Superbly situated between Menton and Monaco, this community offers great diversity. Its climate (annual average 17° C) is said to be the best in Europe, and is characterised by dazzling skies and an absence of fog. The lush fauna comes as no surprise.

This town's past is marked by the history of its castle, which dominates the picturesque medieval village of **Roquebrune ★★★**. The castle was built in AD 970 and is one of France's only Carolingian castles, precursor of those erected two centuries later, which mark the height of the feudal era. Over the centuries, it belonged to the Counts of Vintimille, then the Counts of Provence, and finally to the Grimaldis. The castle was designated a historical monument in 1927.

You can enter the **castle ★** by a stone bridge which has replaced the ancient 16th-century drawbridge. The ground floor, carved out of rock for the most part, holds a guard's room which has also served as a prison, and the water cistern, fed by rain water. The first floor once contained the great hall but is now an open courtyard. It was used for banquets and ceremonies. The second floor housed the men charged with defending the castle itself. The third floor housed the seigneurial apartments: two vaulted rooms and a kitchen. In the 10th century, one of the two bedrooms doubled as a dining room. The parapet walk on this floor allowed guards to survey the surrounding area. It offers a beautiful view of the landscape. Finally, on the top floor were the lodgings for the guards on duty.

Take the time to explore the stairways and vaulted passages and charming little squares. Rue Pié has a large number of support arches very close together.

Cap Martin ★ is a magnificent rocky overhang scattered with villas and gardens hidden among the pine trees and the secular olive trees. Nature lovers will be delighted by its walking trail, the **Promenade Le Corbusier ★★**, which follows the wild and steep contours of the coastline.

Cap-Martin shelters luxurious villas set in magnificent gardens, which can be explored on foot. No cars are allowed. This site has attracted many famous people: royalty, writers, artists, stage and screen stars, including Empress Sissi of Austria, the great architect Le Corbusier and Coco Chanel.

■ Menton ★★★

Because of Menton's proximity to the Italian border, it has long been influenced by that country's culture. The colours of the houses attest to this. In fact, Menton only really became French in the 19th century, under Napoleon III.

The city enjoys an exceptional climate because of its advantageous location between the sea and the mountains. The result is an average temperature of 17°C in January. Furthermore, this microclimate has allowed Menton to cultivate citrus trees and tropical plants. It is known as the "lemon capital of the world", and for good reason. Its climate attracted many visitors near the end of the 19th century, including wealthy Northern-Europeans hoping to be cured of tuberculosis.

Menton has a lot of green spaces, which is why the city has adopted the slogan: *"Ma ville est un jardin"* (My city is a garden).

The City Centre

The best place to begin your tour is the square in front of l'Église Saint-Michel, in the heart of the old city. Guided tours organised by the *Service du Patrimoine* start in front of this church *(30 F; ask at the tourist office for schedule information).*

The **Parvis St-Michel (1)** is an important place in Menton. This square, situated between two beautiful baroque churches, is a mosaic of black and white cobblestone. There has been a chamber music festival held here since 1949. An excursion up the Rue du Vieux-Château, reveals quaint houses painted in warm colours interspersed with splashes of green vegetation. At the top of the street lies the cemetery, which was founded on the site of the old castle.

Take one of the winding side streets to go back down to the square. Head towards Rue St-Michel, a commercial pedestrian street.

There are many stores and restaurants along Rue St-Michel. It's the perfect place to stop for a coffee or a light lunch.

Head towards the water, in the direction of the port and the bastion.

The bastion was built in the 17th century for the purpose of defending the city. Today it houses the **Musée Jean Cocteau (2)** *(free admission; Wed to Mon 10 AM to noon and 2 PM to 6 PM; ☎ 93.57.72.30).* The only museum in the world dedicated to this artist, it holds a permanent exhibition of his works including drawings, tapestries, water-colours, pastels, ceramics and writings.

Walk west, towards the tourist office.

The market is directly across from the tourist office. Here, regional specialities such as *la pichade, la socca,* and *la fougasse* to name but a few await sampling. This is a must-see. Continuing west is the Promenade du Soleil and the casino, this is a popular place for a stroll.

Behind the Casino lie the **Jardins Biovès (3)** where the 10-day long **Fête du Citron** (lemon festival) takes place every year. The **Palais de l'Europe (4)** stands on the avenue bordering the gardens to the east. Site of the old casino, this building is now home to the tourist office and the municipal library. Various shows and cultural events are held there as well.

Go back east by Rue Parouneaux.

You will soon reach Rue de la République. At number 17 is the **Salle des Mariages (5)** *(admission 5 F; Mon to Fri 8:30 AM to 12:30 PM and 1:30 PM to 5 PM;* ☎ *93.57.87.87),* decorated by Jean Cocteau with frescos in 1957 and 1958.

Continue to Rue Lorendan Larchey.

At the end of the long esplanade, is the **Musée de la Préhistoire Régionale (6)** *(free admission; Wed to Mon 10 AM to noon and 2 PM to 6 PM, in summer until 7 PM;* ☎ *93.35.49.71).* It displays a collection of regional Prehistoric specimens which were collected over the last one hundred years or so, including the "Menton man" skeleton which dates back to 25,000 BC. In the basement there is a section devoted to the traditional arts and customs of Menton.

Garavan

This area is on the Italian border at the far east end of the town. A garden-lover's paradise, Garavan is overflowing with parks and gardens. Start with the **Jardin Botanique Exotique Val Rahmeh ★ (7)** *(admission 20 F, children 10 F; everyday 10 AM to noon and 2 PM to 5 PM, in summer until 6 PM; Av. St-Jacques,* ☎ *93.35.86.72).* The gardens at this designated historical site are stunning, and the staff is friendly. You can stroll along the little footpaths that feature more than 650 plant species native to five continents. This wide diversity is possible because of the area's sunny climate (216 days of sun per year on average).

Just beside, is the **Parc du Pian (8)**, a thousand-year-old olive grove. Three hectares of olive trees growing on the terraced hillside overlooking the sea can be visited.

A bit further to the east lie the gardens of **Villa Fontana Rosa (9)** (*Av. Blasco Ibanez),* designed by the dramatist and writer Ibanez. The Valencia-style garden features benches, pergolas and ornamental ponds. The gardens are only open to the public on the third Saturday of the month at 10 AM *(Contact the Service du Patrimoine* ☎ *92.10.33.66).*

A bit further to the north is the **Domaine des Colombrières (10)** *(admission 20 F; everyday 10 AM to noon and 2 PM to 6 PM; Route des Colombrières,* ☎ *93.35.71.90).* A tour of the garden is like a trip around the Mediterranean. Most of the trees are olive and cypress and there is a superb view of the old town and Baie de Garavan.

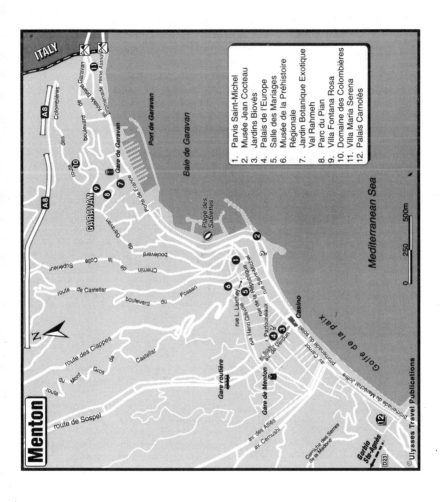

Menton

1. Parvis Saint-Michel
2. Musée Jean Cocteau
3. Jardins Biovès
4. Palais de l'Europe
5. Salle des Mariages
6. Musée de la Préhistoire Régionale
7. Jardin Botanique Exotique Val Rahmeh
8. Parc du Pian
9. Villa Fontana Rosa
10. Domaine des Colombières
11. Villa Maria Serena
12. Palais Carnolès

ITALY

© Ulysses Travel Publications

Finally, just beside the border, is the **Villa Maria Serena (11)** *(admission 30 F; Promenade Reine Astrid)*, built in 1880 by Charles Garnier (Opéra de Paris). The gardens include a large collection of subtropical and exotic plants. They are open on Tuesdays at 10 AM. *(For information, call the Service du Patrimoine ☎ 92.10.33.66).*

Go back downtown to the Promenade du Soleil.

The **Palais Carnolès (12)** *(free admission; Wed to Mon, 10 AM to noon and 2 PM to 6 PM, in summer until 7 PM; ☎ 93.35.49.71)* is located at the very end of the Promenade du Soleil, at the far west end of the town. It houses the Musée des Beaux-Arts. Here the contemporary collections acquired at the biennial festivals of Menton are on display. This old palace was built in 1717 as a summer residence for the Prince of Monaco. The park in which the building stands is the oldest garden in Menton. It contains the largest collection of citrus fruit trees in Europe, including over 400 trees of 50 different species.

Leave Menton by D 22 towards Ste-Agnès.

■ Ste-Agnès ★★

This old Saracen town perched on the mountain is the highest town along the European coast. Here, the proud beauty of the rugged landscape embraces the coast. The town is charming, and hikers will find it a nice place to stop. In fact, the surrounding area offers many possibilities for hiking, whether you prefer a short or long, easy or difficult trail. One possibility is a hike to Gorbio or Roquebrune-village from here.

Outdoor Activities

Between Nice and Menton, the beaches are generally small and often privately owned (by a hotel or chain of vacation resorts). The largest beaches (public and private) are at Menton and Èze.

This area offers many beautiful hiking trails along or close to the water.

■ St-Jean-Cap-Ferrat

The walk around the cape makes a wonderful excursion for the young and not so young alike. Start at Pointe de Passable (at the northwest end of the peninsula, close to the zoo), where there is a small sandy public beach and a restaurant (on a private beach). The path follows the sea as far as the lighthouse (southern point) and then continues on the Chemin de la Carrière, which leads you to the new port. Duration of the tour: 90 minutes. For more information, ask for a map at the tourist office.

■ Èze

Around Èze there are many beautiful walking trails that are easy, even where there are inclines. From here you can hike from Èze Bord de Mer to Èze-Village *(Moyenne Corniche)* to Saint-Laurent d'Èze and to Col d'Èze *(Grande Corniche)*. Ask for the *Les Chemins d'Èze* map at the tourist office.

■ Roquebrune Cap-Martin

A beautiful and picturesque walking trail leads around the cape. The avenues on the privately-owned area in the interior of the peninsula are wide and peaceful, with magnificent villas along the way.

■ **Menton**

Menton, with its many botanical and exotic gardens, is perfect for those who enjoy a casual stroll. (See "Exploring" section). The city has a *Service du Patrimoine*, which tends the numerous gardens. Some of the gardens may only be seen with the permission of this administrative service.

 Accommodation

There are two options — to be close to the sea, and all the action (including the nightlife), or to get away from the hustle and bustle and enjoy the tranquillity of the countryside. Of course, hotel prices are higher by the sea. However, as you head up hill, you will still enjoy panoramic views of the water.

■ **Villefranche-sur-Mer**

There is really only one hotel in this town that is worth mentionning: the **Hôtel Provençal** *(330-400 F; ps, ℜ, tv; in the centre of the village,* ☎ *93.01.71.42,* ⇄ *93.76.96.00)*. From June to September, the accommodation is half-board *(440 F for one person, 400 F per person for two or more)*. The hotel, which was built in the 30s, has been restored and offers a spectacular view of the sea and the public garden behind. The rooms are pretty, bright and modern, and some also have a terrace. The hotel's restaurant has a glassed-in terrace overlooking a garden where you can eat during the summer.

If you're planning to **stay for one week or longer**, we recommend the **Résidence Pierre & Vacances** *(3,010-*

5,880 F for a studio-cabin and 3,185-5,640 F per week for a two-room apartment; pb, C, ℜ, tv extra; ☎ *93.76.40.00)*. Built on terraces facing the sea and overlooking the bay, the residence opens up to a lovely park, a beautiful pool and tennis courts. The beach is only 300 m away. Note: minimum stay is one week, beginning on a Saturday.

■ **St-Jean-Cap-Ferrat**

Here's a place we strongly recommend if you want to spend a few pleasant days on the coast. The cape has plenty of magnificent villas and lots of greenery.

There is a charming little hotel here, hidden in the middle of a lush garden. A stop at the **Résidence Bagatelle** *(280-430 F, 400-500 F for 3 people; ps, tv; Av Honoré Sauvan,* ☎ *93.01.32.86,* ⇄ *93.01.41.00)* is a must. The owner offers her guests a warm welcome and her *joie de vivre* is contagious. The hotel is near the Ephrussi-Rothschild villa (see p 209).

Hôtel Brise Marine *(625-700 F; extra bed 150 F; pb, ps, ≡ in some rooms; 58 Av. Jean Mermoz,* ☎ *93.76.04.36,* ⇄ *93.76.11.49)* Ulysses guide travellers, beware! "Penelope would have died alone... if Ulysses had made a stop here." This hotel is particularly attractive, offering tranquillity in a pleasant setting with magnificent views. Close to **Paloma Beach,** with all the facilities and services that a beach should offer.

■ **Beaulieu-sur-Mer**

Beaulieu is a sailing harbour and therefore has many hotels.

If you're on a limited budget, here's a good address: **Le Select** *(140-250 F, 280-380 F for 3 or 4 people; ps; Place Générale de Gaulle,* ☎ *93.01.05.42,* ⇄ *93.01.34.30).* In the very heart of the village, this modest hotel is located in a quaint old building that has been restored. There is a Crédit Lyonnais branch on the main floor. It is in a pleasant square but, because the road passes just beside the hotel, it can be a bit noisy especially in the summer. If this hotel is full, you can try the **Hôtel Riviera** *(220-280 F;   6 Rue   Paul Doumer;* ☎ *93.01.04.92),* which is closer to the sea, or the **Hôtel Flora** *(180-280 F;   11 Av.   Edith   Cavell;* ☎ *93.01.02.01),* which has a garden and parking.

If you prefer a more personalized welcome, try the **Hôtel de France** *(240-340 F and 430-540 F for 3 or 4 people; ps;   1 Montée   des   Orangers,* ☎ *93.01.00.92).* This is a family-run boarding-style hotel with an old-fashioned atmosphere. It's like your grandmother's house, but this grandmother is young! In the sittinng room there's a grand piano, books and all kinds of games to entertain children of all ages. There are some very charming rooms with wooden floors that creak just slightly. How's that for ambience! This hotel is a very good value and the owner is very pleasant.

Looking for luxury? Head to the **Réserve de Beaulieu** *(2,700-4,000 F, 5,400 F for a suite; luxury furnishings,* ℜ*;* ☎ *93.01.00.01,* ⇄ *93.01.28.99).* This turn-of-the-century style hotel was completely renovated in 1994. There are enormous, tastefully decorated rooms that look out onto the sea. This little palace has a small beach with rocky cliffs and a pier from which you can dive into the sea. Pleasure boats can also dock here. If you're not in a

hurry, relax beside the big beautiful pool. As for value, it's expensive, but it is the height of luxury, after all!

■ Èze-Village

The "queen" of the *corniches*, and with a view please!

Camping   Les   Romains *(Grande Corniche, Èze;* ☎ *93.01.81.64)* is in a totally different category. To get there: take D 2564 *(Grande Corniche).* If you're coming from the water, go up by D 45. This campground, on Italy's doorstep, offers a magnificent panoramic view of the Alps, the sea, and Cap-Ferrat. Sunshine, tranquillity and comfort, hot showers and a snack-bar can be found here as well as beaches, sports and recreation. The campground is 10 minutes from Nice and 15 minutes from Monaco.

Around 3 km from the village, in the direction of Col d'Èze, the **Auberge des 2 Corniches** *(320 F, extra bed 40 F, half-board 600 F for 2 people; ps, tv,* ℜ*;   15 Bd   Maréchal   Leclerc,* ☎ *93.41.19.54),* will appeal to travellers seeking a comfortable and reasonably-priced hotel. It is about three kilometres from the village, towards Col d'Èze. Monsieur and Madame Maume, the friendly owners, offer you a quiet spot away from the tourist scene. You'll feel like you're out in the country! Ask for the corner room in the front. It has two windows and a nice view. Very good value.

The **Hôtel Hermitage** *(400-490 F, 640 F for 3 people, extra bed 30 F; half-board. mandatory in Jul/Aug; pb, tv,* ℜ*,* ≈*; Èze Grande Corniche,* ☎ *93.41.00.68)* is another good address. A member of the *Logis de France*, this establishment is 5 kilometres from Èze-Village, and still relatively close to Nice and Monaco. It is located at the entrance to a departmental park with several walking trails. Sure to satisfy anyone with a taste for the back-country. Reserve the room with the extra-big bathroom. This hotel also has a pool.

For an unforgettable night in a dream hotel, choose one of these two luxury hotels located in the very heart of the old medieval village:

Le Château de la Chève-d'Or *(1,300-3,300 F; every comfort, luxurious, ℜ, ≈, Èze-Village;* ☎ *93.41.12.12,* ⇄ *93.41.12.24).*

Le Château Eza *(2,000-3,500 F; every comfort, luxurious, ℜ; Éze-Village,* ☎ *93.41.12.24,* ⇄ *93.41.16.64).*

These two hotels offer essentially the same services and have the same advantages. The atmosphere is most refined and there are pretty gardens and terraces overlooking the sea. The food is very also good. The restaurant at Château Eza is more spectacular because the terrace literally looks down over the sea. Both of these places are out of this world, simply extraordinary. Guests staying at the Château Eza can use the pool at the other hotel without charge and, in exchange, guests of the Chèvre d'Or may park at the Château Eza.

■ **Cap d'Ail**

If you want to avoid the tinsel of Monaco/Monte Carlo, here are two good places to stay in this small adjacent village.

At Monaco's door, 15 km from Nice and near the main road, the **Hôtel Normandie** *(360 F, half-board 720 F; pb, ℜ; 6 Allée des Orangers,* ☎ *93.78.77.77)* has all you need for a short stay in the pleasant atmosphere of a well-run *pension*. Meals are served on the terrace and the pretty little beach is easily accessible. Very good value.

If you're planning to stay for a week or more, the **Résidence Pierre & Vacances** *(studio 2,660-5,285 F per week, 2 rooms 2,870-5,635 F per week; pb, C, R, ≈, tv extra;* ☎ *93.41.73.00)* is a must! This impressive building made of glass and stone was designed by Jean Nouvel, a well-known French architect. Perched way up high over the sea, the hotel was built on terraces at various levels to offer a spectacular view. The swimming pool is absolutely fabulous. Note: although it's only 800 metres from the village, it is still off the beaten path — and a most vertical path it is! Generally the best way to get there is by car or taxi. There is pay parking. **There is a minimum one-week stay, starting on a Saturday.** The two-room apartments are ideal for families, since there is a separate room for the children. Good value!

■ **La Turbie**

The **Hôtel la Turbie** *(300-400 F, half-board, 560 F; pb, tv, ℜ; 7 Av. de la Victoire,* ☎ *93.41.00.54,* ⇄ *93.41.28.93)* is located in the centre of the village, facing the town hall. This establishment combines modern comfort with traditional architecture. Ask for a room at the back where it is more peaceful.

■ **Peille**

If you're on a budget, the **Hôtel Belvédère** *(180-220 F; two rooms with a shower; half-board 230 F; ℜ; 1 Place Jean Miol,* ☎ *93.79.90.45)* will fit the bill. The view looks out over Nice and the hills of Monaco. Unfortunately, it also looks out over a huge rock quarry. This hotel offers a rustic atmosphere and a large dining room with an open terrace. Ask for room No. 1! Member of *Logis de France.*

■ Peillon-Village

Let yourself dream a bit, and enjoy life at the **Auberge de la Madone** *(400-610 F, 550-650 F for 3 people; pb, tv, ☎; ☎ 93.79.91.17, ⇄ 93.79.99.36).* Located at the entrance of a most beautiful medieval village, this hotel is furnished with lovely period pieces. The modern, spacious rooms overlook the village. There is also an excellent restaurant on the premises (see p 222). This hotel exudes elegance, and benefits from the owner's very fine taste. All of this makes it worth seeing!

For travellers on a smaller budget, the owner has added an annex below the hotel. The **Auberge du Portail** *(from 250 F; ps)* opened only recently.

■ Roquebrune Cap-Martin

The **Hôtel Europe Village** *(250-330 F and 400 F for three people; half-board extra 160 F; ps, tv, ℜ; Av. Virginie Hériot, ☎ 93.35.62.45, ⇄ 93.57.72.59)* is nestled in the heart of Cap-Martin, three kilometres from both Monaco and Menton. You will be impressed, if not seduced, by the beauty and tranquillity of the garden surrounding the hotel. It is an oasis of nature between these two cities. The rooms are comfortable and some have a terrace overlooking the garden. It is located at the starting point of a superb walking trail that leads around the cape. The hotel also offers a reasonably-priced restaurant.

■ Menton

Camping Fleurs de Mai *(67 Val de Gorbio, Menton, ☎ 93.57.22.36).* To get there: from Autoroute A 8 take the Menton exit and go towards D 23. This campground offers a peaceful, green setting and is within 1.5 kilometres of the beaches. Pool, tennis, supermarket, stores, etc.

Auberge de Jeunesse *(67 F, bkfst incl.; Plateau Saint-Michel, ☎ 93.35.93.14).* A minibus goes to the youth hostel from the bus station. Note: reservations made by telephone are not guaranteed.

The hotel **Le Mondial** *(230 F, extra bed 70 F; ps, tv, ℜ cafeteria-style; 12 Rue Partouneaux, ☎ 92.10.20.66, ⇄ 92.10.20.70)* is five minutes from the sea, across from the chic Hôtel des Ambassadeurs. Le Mondial offers everything and then some of what you would expect from a simple, inexpensive hotel. The decor is nice and old-fashioned, with a turn-of-the-century look that is quite inviting. The hotel offers small but very clean rooms. The cafeteria-style restaurant serves breakfast and a variety of simple meals that you can take into the hotel's garden, which seats up to 80 people. This hotel is an excellent value and very popular! With only 10 rooms, it can be full even in January, so reserve in advance.

The **Narev's Hôtel** *(350-450 F; pb, ≡, tv; 12 bis, Rue Lorédan Larchey, ☎ 93.35.21.31, ⇄ 93.35.21.20)* is another great place. In a higher category than Le Mondial, Narev's is a newly-built hotel surrounded by 19th century buildings. It is a family business run by father and sons who are all very nice. The very pleasant rooms (some with terrace) are furnished with all the comforts of a modern hotel. Well-located, it is 5 minutes from the sea and faces the Musée de Préhistoire Régionale. The hotel also has a conference room and is open year-round.

The **Hôtel Paris-Rome** *(340-450 F; pb, ≡, tv, ℜ; 79 Porte de France, ☎ 93.35.73.45, ⇄ 93.35.29.30)* faces the sea near the sailing harbour. It is a quaint little hotel, with a tiny garden where you can relax over breakfast. A few of the rooms look out over the sea, and also over the busy road in the summertime. This can be noisy, but second-floor rooms (which are the most expensive) have double-glaze windows. The decor is rustic and the restaurant features a fireplace. Member of *Logis de France*. Good service. If you spend a week here, you can take advantage of a package deal *(1,840 F)* which includes free guided tours of the city.

The **St-Michel** *(380 F, extra bed 80 F; pb, tv, ℜ; 1684 Promenade du Soleil, ☎ 93.57.46.33)* is another hotel facing the sea. Run by a charming Italian gentleman and his wife, this hotel is just at the entrance of the old city. There are a few quiet rooms in the back, as well as rooms with a view of the sea. This hotel is a very good value. There is also a restaurants, see p 223.

For luxury in the heart of the city centre, choose the **Hôtel des Ambassadeurs** *(680 to 1,100 F, 1,400 to 1,900 F for a suite; pb, ≡, ℝ, tvc, ℜ; 3 Rue Partouneaux, ☎ 93.28.75.75, ⇄ 93.35.62.32)*. This late 19th century-style hotel has just been completely restored and is quite an impressive sight with its pink exterior. The entrance is extravagant, and the hotel's lounges are decorated with Art Deco furniture. The rooms are bright and offer the modern comforts of a world-class luxury hotel. Bathrobes are

even provided. Finally, the hotel has a very chic piano-bar and a conference room that can hold 150 people. All in all, this hotel is a good value. There is also a restaurant, see p 223.

 **Restaurants**

■ Villefranche-sur-Mer

La Grignotière *($$; 3 Rue du Poilu, ☎ 93.76.79.83)* is an exceptional value. Located in one of the narrow streets in the old village, this restaurant has been serving fine cuisine for 10 years. The fish soup with its *rouille* comes in a generous portion and is pure delight. House specialities are meat and salmon pastries. The 149 F menu, which includes two appetizers, a main dish, cheese and dessert is recommended. Servings are very generous. To manage to eat it all would be quite a feat. The young manager is friendly, and the service is efficient.

At the port, there are several restaurants with terraces overlooking the sea. Beware, however, because you will pay for this luxury. Locals prefer **La Mère Germaine** *($$)*. Although the setting is delightful, the 195 F menu offers only one choice of appetizer.

■ St-Jean-Cap-Ferrat

Three restaurants captured our attention at the port on the peninsula. Simple restaurants that serve simple fare.

La Goélette *($)*: pizza, pasta, salads and fish make up the menu. Pretty terrace. Children's menu. Locals eat here.

Le Capitaine Cook (*$; 11 Av. Jean-Mermoz; ☎ 93.76.02.66)*: this restaurant features mainly fish specialities.

Le Cala-Blu (*$; ☎ 93.76.01.66*): like the other restaurants, there is a picturesque terrace. It is very popular with the locals.

■ **Èze-Village**

For a light meal, **La Fenice** (*$; closed Tue*) is a *crêperie* in the heart of the medieval town.

If you prefer a terrace with a view, stop at the very top of the village, near the entrance to the exotic garden. Perfect place for a cocktail!

Le Troubadour (*$ table d'hôte; closed Sun and Mon AM; ☎ 93.41.19.03*) is a "classic" restaurant at the entrance to the village. The local people highly recommend it. The atmosphere is drenched in old-fashioned charm, and the value is good.

If money is no object, try one of the two château restaurants (see p 219). We did, however, prefer the **Château Eza** (*$$$ table d'hôte*) because its marvellously situated terrace gives a wide-open view over the sea. Both châteaux offer equally fine cuisine at similar prices.

■ **Cap d'Ail**

If you enjoy grilled fish, don't miss **La Pinède** (*set menu 200 F and 280 F, 90 F for children; 10 Bd de la Mer, ☎ 93.78.37.10*). The large terrace where you can eat literally hangs over the sea, and is completely covered when the weather is poor. You can also eat inside in a rustic, warm setting. There is even a tree that is integrated into the architecture of the building!

The friendly owner, Monsieur Guglielmi, makes sure that everything is perfect, from the reception to the service to the food. This is an address to remember!

■ **La Turbie**

About seven km from La Turbie, on the road to Peille, make a stop at the **Ferme de l'Agora**. Prince Albert of Monaco is said to dine there occasionally.

■ **Peille**

On the road joining La Turbie and Peille, is the **Relais Saint-Martin** (*$-$$-$$$; ☎ 93.41.16.03*). Take in the panoramic view of Monaco's inland hills while dining. The huge fireplace gives this restaurant a rustic atmosphere. There is also a terrace and a banquet hall. An ideal place to enjoy the local cuisine and savour the taste of food grilled over a fire.

■ **Peillon-Village**

L'Auberge de la Madone (*$-$$*) promises hearty, gourmet, traditional Provençal cuisine. You can eat outside on the pretty terrace or in the lovely dining room (see p 220).

■ **Roquebrune-Village**

There are many restaurants in this old medieval village. It's hard to know which ones are the best, but these three seem to be quite good.

Le Grand Inquisiteur (*$$; Rue du Château, ☎ 93.35.05.37*) is a restaurant with a special setting. It is located in a medieval cave, which, in years gone by, was a shelter for livestock. The restaurant is listed in several restaurant guides.

L'Idée fixe (*$*) is a small restaurant perched at the top of a staircase. It offers an intimate atmosphere and there are small temporary art exhibitions held here. Gnocchi lovers must stop here if only for the selection of sauces.

Le Piccolo Mondo (*$; 15 Rue Grimaldi)* serves typical Italian cuisine in a convivial atmosphere decorated with antique porcelain. It's a nice little place located at the entrance of the old town.

Finally, at the entrance of the town, at the Place des Deux Frères, there are two other restaurants with outdoor dining. If you prefer a quieter atmosphere, it might be better to look elsewhere because this square is quite busy, especially during tourist season.

■ **Cap-Martin**

Beside the Hôtel Europe Village, there is a cute little restaurant called **le Jardin du Cap** (*$; closed Tue; Av. Virginie Hériot,* ☎ *93.57.26.71).* Diners savour simple regional dishes in a peaceful garden setting.

■ **Menton**

The restaurant of the Hôtel St-Michel, (see p 221) called **le Grand Bleu** (*set menu 95 F),* is famous for its delicious fish dishes. You can enjoy your meal right on the seashore.

The **Hôtel des Ambassadeurs** (see p 221) has a highly esteemed restaurant that offers a *table d'hôte* for 220 F called *"Les Ambassadeurs."* The dining room has many windows and is very comfortable. For a description of the hotel

Au Pistou (*$; 2 Rue du Fossan,* ☎ *93.57.45.89)* is a simple and pleasant restaurant. The house speciality is fresh pasta. It is located in the city centre.

For fish and Italian cuisine, try **Don Cicco** (*$; 11 Rue St-Michel,* ☎ 93.57.92.92). You won't be disappointed!

La Nautique (*$; 27 Quai de Monléon,* ☎ *93.35.78.74)* is also recommended for fish-lovers.

In a higher category, **La Mamounia** (*$$; 51 Porte de France,* ☎ *93.57.95.39)* offers you regional and Moroccan specialities.

L'Olivier (*$$; 21 Place du Cap,* ☎ *93.35.45.65)* was recommended to us by local connoisseurs.

■ **Ste-Agnès**

If you'd like a change from the city, take a breath of fresh air at **La Vieille Auberge** (*$; closed Tue;* ☎ *93.35.92.02)* in Ste-Agnés. The village is magnificently situated. You can enjoy simple, typical country fare in a modest setting and you can also spend the night at the hotel, run by the Revel family.

 Entertainment

Enquire at the tourist office in each town and village for their *Info-Animations*. Here are a few suggestions:

■ **Beaulieu-sur-Mer**

Grand Casino de Jeux
7 PM to 4 AM Mon to Thu, 6 PM on
weekends and 5 PM in summer
Av. Blundell Maple,
☎ 93.76.48.00.

Piano Bar

La Réserve de Beaulieu
5 Bd Maréchal Leclerc
☎ 93.01.00.01

■ **Menton**

Menton holds a number a fairs and
festivals each year, including:

**La Grande Foire d'antiquité brocante-
troc** (antiques and collectibles) end of
Jan;
La Fête du citron (lemon festival) Feb;
La Foire commerciale, Sablettes beach
Apr;
La Bourse numismatique et philatélique
(coin and stamp exchange) one Sun in
May;
La Festival de musique de chambre
Parvis de l'Église St-Michel (Chamber
Music Festival) Aug;
La Festival des oiseaux (bird festival)
mid-Nov;
Le Salon de l'artisanat d'art (arts and
crafts fair) mid-Dec.

Casino de Menton
slot machines 11 AM to 3 AM, gamb-
ling room (roulette, blackjack, punto
banco) 8 PM to 3 AM, 5 PM to 4 AM
on weekends;
Av. Félix Faure,
☎ 92.10.16.16.

Parc de loisirs de la Madona - Koaland
10 AM to noon and 2 PM to 6 PM,
10 AM to 1 AM in summer
5 Av. de la Madone.

■ **Bars**

Brasserie de l'Europe *(1 Rue
Partouneaux;* ☎ *93.35.82.93)* is a pub
open in the evenings.

La Namouna (*Quai Gordon Bennet;*
☎ *93.28.28.00)* has live bands on
weekends.

Le Brummell (*cover charge 90 F one
drink included; open till dawn on weekends;* ☎ *92.10.16.16*) is the Menton
Casino's discotheque.

La Case du Chef
Av. R. Schumann
☎ 93.35.91.43

Le Queenie Club
1 Av. Pasteur
☎ 93.57.58.46

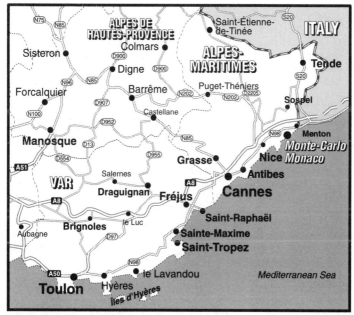

MONACO ★★

A fter the Vatican, the *Principauté de Monaco* is the world's smallest sovereign state. It is only 195 ha in area, but with its population of approximately 30,000, it has the greatest population density per square metre in the world.

Monaco's unique status in the world is attributed to its size, its great wealth and its somewhat incredible history. The marriage of Prince Rainier III to the stunning and famous American actress Grace Kelly in 1956 was a historical event that enchanted millions all over the world. It was a modern fairy tale that ended tragically in 1982 when Princess Grace was killed in a car accident on one of the area's winding roads. Since then, the royal family seems to have had its share of misfortunes, at least according to the tab-

loids, which track the family's every move.

Monaco's real history goes back much further. It begins at the end of the 13th century, at a time when the Genoese nobility fought over control of the territory. They were divided in two camps: the *Guelfes*, who were papal supporters; and the *Gibelins*, who were partisans of the German empire. In 1297, Rainier Grimaldi, of the *Guelfes* nobility, took control of the rocky land that is Monaco. In 1342, this dynasty today 700 years old, expanded its territory by taking over Roquebrune and Menton.

In the 16th century, Monaco became a Spanish protectorate and remained so until 1641, when France took over. It only regained a semi-sovereign status in 1815, after the Vienna Conference. This agreement reinstated all the European monarchies in their territories as they had existed before the French Revolution. Monaco was therefore placed under the protectorate of the King of Sardinia.

The 50-year period that followed was somewhat difficult economically, especially because of the loss of Menton and Roquebrune, which were sold to France. Monaco only began to regain its former glory in 1863 with the creation of the *Société des Bains de Mer* and the construction of a casino. Monaco's rapid development continued when the principality was linked to Nice by rail in 1869. Shortly afterwards, Charles Garnier, architect of the Opéra de Paris, was commissioned to add a theatre to the luxurious casino. Finally, in 1910, Prince Albert I, who was an oceanographer, decided to add to the city's wealth by having an ocean museum and an exotic garden built.

Monaco launched into a new chapter of its history in 1949 with Prince Rainier III's ascension to the throne. An era of great economic growth had begun. From then on, the adoption of favourable laws attracted many investors and real-estate speculators. They have provided Monaco with luxurious earthquake-proof buildings, and have built new museums and theatres as well as a huge sports stadium. Monaco has become the real-life dream world of an exclusive and privileged society.

Today, the principality hosts several sporting and cultural events that have brought it international acclaim. The *Festival du Printemps des Arts*, a spring arts festival, under the patronage of the Prince, welcomes many of the big names of music and dance each year. And don't forget the world-famous

Monaco Grand Prix. Moreover, Monaco has its own orchestra, *L'Orchestre Philarmonique de Monte-Carlo*, as well as a dance troupe, *Les Ballets de Monte-Carlo*. Much emphasis is placed on the cultural life in Monaco. Indeed, patronage is widely practised and Monaco allocates 5% of its national budget to culture. Finally, Monaco's climate and exceptional site make it an ideal place for many international seminars and conventions (often of a scientific nature).

Monaco's special statutes are mostly what set it apart from other States. Indeed, the Prince retains absolute legislative, executive and judiciary power. The customs union between Monaco and France has been in place since 1865, but following a treaty signed between the two states in 1919, the Prince of Monaco must conjugate his sovereign rights with France's political, military, naval and economic interests. Nevertheless, Monaco's status as a fiscal paradise remains its most lucrative trademark.

Two things are striking about Monaco: the impressive body of security forces and the cleanliness. There are police officers everywhere, and numerous cameras watch over and protect all the billionaires, millionaires and even the everyday tourists that stroll through its streets.

Finding Your Way Around

■ By Train

During the summer, because the roads are so congested with traffic, the train is your best bet for a day trip to Monaco. The *Métrazur*, which links

Saint-Raphaël to Vintimille, stops in Monaco about every half-hour.

All the international trains stop at the Monaco/Monte-Carlo station on Avenue Prince Pierre.

Information: ☎ 93.25.54.54

■ By Air

Monaco is about 22 km from the Nice Côte d'Azur international airport. From there you have the choice of helicopter transport *(Héli Air Monaco,* ☎ *93.21.34.95)*, coach or taxi. Many daily connections are available.

■ By Car

Monaco is accessible by the **A 8** road from the east or the west. If you are coming from Nice, you may want to choose a more scenic route via one of the three departmental roads, the *Basse*, *Moyenne* and *Grande Corniche*. Of course, this way takes more time, especially in summer. Once in Monaco, you can park your car in one of the many covered parking lots. There are 6,000 pay parking spaces available in the city.

■ By Bus

Also, a coach service offers connections between the Nice airport and Monaco 90 minutes from 9 AM to 7:30 PM daily. The coach takes the highway and makes the trip in 45 minutes. Once in Monaco, the coach stops in several places.

The *Compagnie des Autobus de Monaco* has six urban bus lines that serve the main corridors of the territory. During the week, the buses generally run every 11 minutes, between 7 AM and 9 PM.

3 av. du Prés. J.-F. Kennedy
☎ 93.50.62.41

■ By Sea

Pleasure boats of all sizes may dock at the various ports with landing facilities: the Monaco-Condamine port in the Baie d'Hercule or one of the two ports in Fontvieille, one of which is located at the foot of the Monaco rock cliff, and the other in Cap d'Ail, in France.

For more information, enquire at:
Services de la Marine - Direction des Ports
7 Av. du Prés. J.-F. Kennedy
B.P. 468
MC 98012 Monaco Cedex
☎ 93.15.86.78

■ Taxis

There is a central telephone number for taxis: ☎ 93.50.56.28

? Practical Information

Since Monaco is built on ridges, public elevators are available to facilitate access to various locations. There is also a tourist train, the *Azur Express (20 F; Jul and Aug, 8:30 PM to midnight; tour commentary in English and French, departure/arrival: Stade Nautique Rainier III, Quai Albert I,* ☎ *92.05.64.38)* which offers two routes within the principality, by day or by night.

Monaco's beaches are all located east of Monte-Carlo and can be reached via Avenue Princesse Grace. Bus service to the beaches is also available.

■ Tourist office

Direction du Tourisme et des Congrès
de la Principauté de Monaco
2a Bd des Moulins
Monte-Carlo
MC 98030 Monaco Cedex
Administration:
☎ 92.16.61.16, ⇄ 92.16.60.00
Information: ☎ 92.16.61.66

■ Hospital

Centre Hospitalier Princesse Grace
Av. Pasteur
☎ 93.25.99.00
Emergencies: ☎ 93.25.98.69

■ Car Rental

Budget
9 Av. J.-F. Kennedy
☎ 92.16.00.70

Hertz
27 Bd Albert I
☎ 93.50.79.60

 Exploring

To make exploring easier, the principality can be divided into four tours: **Monaco-Ville ★★★** (Le Rocher, which encompasses the cathedral, the royal palace and several museums), **Monte-Carlo ★★** (with the Casino and the Musée National), **Quartier du Jardin Exotique ★★**, and **Quartiers Portuaires ★** (Condamine and Fontvieille, located on either side of the Rocher of Monaco-Ville).

■ Monaco-Ville ★★★

Since cars from other countries are not allowed in this part of the city, there are only two ways to explore the area known as the Rocher de Monaco: on foot or on board the tourist train *Azur Express (15 F, Feb to Oct 10 AM to noon and 2 PM to 6 PM; tour commentary in French, English, Italian and German, departure/arrival: Musée Océanographique, Av. St-Martin, ☎ 92.05.64.38).* This tour passes alongside the main monuments of the Rocher and can help you decide which sites are worth a closer look.

To get to the Rocher take either the Rampe Major, a wide stairway that leads to Place du Palais, or the elevator that leads to the Musée Océanographique which is located in the covered parking lot at the end of Avenue de la Quarantaine. On this street stands Fort Antoine, an early 18th-century fortress that was transformed into a summer theatre.

If you are arriving by elevator, you can learn about the history of the Lords and Princes of Monaco through a multivision presentation called the **Monte-Carlo Story** *(adults 36 F, children 16 F; Mar to Oct, everyday 11 AM to 5 PM; Jul to Aug, until 6 PM; in winter, 2 PM to 5 PM; ☎ 93.25.32.33).* The elevator brings you to the **Musée Océanographique** and its **Aquarium (1)** *(60 F adults, 30 F children; Mar to Oct, 9 AM to 7 PM; Jun to Aug 20, in winter 10 AM to 6 PM; av. St-Martin, ☎ 93.15.36.00).* It took 11 years to build this museum; its impressive façade overlooking the sea is of white stone from La Turbie. Prince Albert I, oceanographer and lover of the sea, inaugurated it in 1910. The museum contains remarkable collections of marine fauna presented on two floors of huge open rooms. The aquarium, at the basement level, exhibits several rare species in some 90 tanks fed directly from the

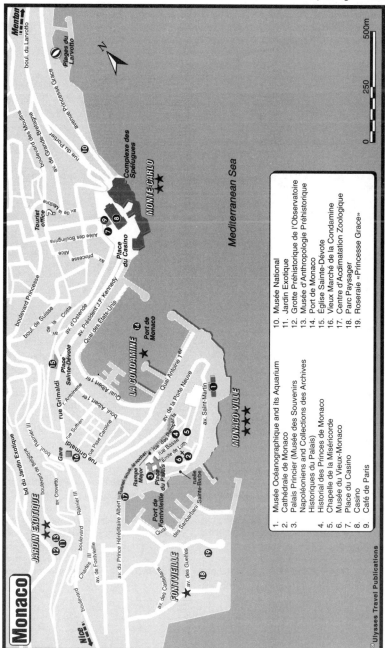

Monaco

1. Musée Océanographique and its Aquarium
2. Cathédrale de Monaco
3. Palais Princier (Musée des Souvenirs Napoléoniens and Collections des Archives Historiques du Palais)
4. Historial des Princes de Monaco
5. Chapelle de la Miséricorde
6. Musée du Vieux-Monaco
7. Place du Casino
8. Casino
9. Café de Paris
10. Musée National
11. Jardin Exotique
12. Grotte Préhistorique de l'Observatoire
13. Musée d'Anthropologie Préhistorique
14. Port de Monaco
15. Église Sainte-Dévote
16. Vieux Marché de la Condamine
17. Centre d'Acclimatation Zoologique
18. Parc Paysager
19. Roseraie «Princesse Grace»

© Ulysses Travel Publications

sea. In addition, Jacques Cousteau's films are shown all day long in the conference room. Finally, the terrace offers a very beautiful panorama over the sea and the coast, from Italy to l'Estérel.

Leave the museum and head towards the gardens known as the Jardins de St-Martin, facing the open sea.

Here is a wonderful opportunity to take a pleasant stroll through gardens that stretch out along the coastline. Your walk will take you to Ruelle Ste-Barbe, which opens up onto Place du Palais. A little before you get to Ruelle Ste-Barbe, there is a wonderful view of the **Cathédrale de Monaco (2)**, where Monaco's former princes are buried. The cathedral, built out of white stone from La Turbie, also contains a reredos by Bréa that dates back to 1500.

Head towards Ruelle Ste-Barbe.

Ruelle Ste-Barbe opens up onto Place du Palais. Visitors can watch the changing of the guard everyday at 11:55 AM, in front of the main gate of the royal palace. The *Garde des Carabiniers* are an impressive sight in their black winter uniforms or their white summer ones.

The **Palais Princier (3)** *(adults 25 F, children 12 F; Jun to Oct, 9:30 AM to 6:30 PM;* ☎ *93.25.18.31)* stands on the site of a fortress built by the Genoese in 1215. Visitors can see the Grand Appartements, which include the Salon Louis XV decorated in blue and gold, the Salon Mazarin, the Throne Room, where Prince Rainier and Grace Kelly were married, the Chapelle Pala- tine, built in the 17th century and, finally, the Tour Ste-Marie, from the top of which the royal colours are flown when the Prince is in residence.

In the south wing of the Palace, you can visit the **Musée des Souvenirs Napoléoniens et Collections des Archives Historiques du Palais** *(adults 15 F, children 7 F; in summer and Oct, everyday 9:30 AM to 6:30 PM; Dec to May, Tue to Sun 10:30 AM to 12:30 PM and 2 PM to 5 PM; closed in Nov;* ☎ *93.25.18.31)*. This museum contains a collection of objects and documents from the First Empire and its emperor, Napoléon I, as well as various items that recall the history of the principality.

Leave the square via Rue Basse.

You are now in the very heart of the Vieux-Monaco of medieval times, on one of the most picturesque streets of the Rocher. At 27 Rue Basse, the **Historial des Princes de Monaco (4)** *(adults 24 F, children 12 F; Feb to Oct, everyday 9:30 AM to 7 PM; Nov to Jan, 10:30 AM to 5 PM;* ☎ *93.30.39.05)* recalls the historical events of the Grimaldi dynasty, from the end of the 13th century to the present, with life-sized wax statues. The street opens up onto Place de la Mairie, where the **Chapelle de la Miséricorde (5)** stands. Built in 1639, it was the seat of the *Confrérie des Pénitents Noirs*.

Leave this square and head back towards the palace via Rue Émilie de Loth.

This street is where you will find the **Musée du Vieux-Monaco (6)** *(free admission, in summer, Wed to Fri 2:30 PM to 5 PM; Wed only in winter;* ☎ *93.50.57.28)*, where stories from the past about life at the Rocher are presented.

You can end your visit to the Rocher with a walk around the streets of the old city.

■ Monte-Carlo ★★

The main attraction of this part of Monaco is unquestionably the **Place du Casino (7)**. The **Casino (8)** *(admission to European rooms 50 F, private rooms 100 F; everyday from noon; restricted to ages 21 and over;* ☎ *92.16.21.21)* attracts many wealthy people, as you can tell by the number of limousines and luxury cars that parade on the circular drive in front. Around here, wealth prevails: from the Hôtel de Paris, at the east end of the square, to the storefronts of the luxury boutiques in the nearby streets. Of course showing off one's wealth is not always tasteful, and you'll see the gaudy as well as the glamorous! The terrace at the **Café de Paris (9)**, a *belle époque*-style brasserie on the west side of the square is definitely the best place from which to watch the display.

The Casino was built in 1878 by Charles Garnier, the architect who designed the Opéra de Paris. The Casino contains the Salle Garnier, decorated in red and gold, where opera performances are held. For more than a century, Salle Garnier has been the venue of international lyrical performances, prestigious concerts and famous ballets. Caruso, among others, sang here.

Most popular are the games rooms. Here you can play all the European and American games, and for an additional charge, you can have access to the private rooms.

Across from the Casino, spectacular gardens slope gently upwards. The manicured lawn is complemented with magnificent flowers, ornamental ponds and numerous sculptures by famous artists including César and Botéro. In fact, the **Balade des Soixante-Seize Sculptures**, a 76-statue walking tour leads you through Monaco with commentary on the sculptures that decorate its many parks and gardens. The itinerary is outlined in a free brochure called *La Découverte de l'Art à Monaco*, which you can pick up at the tourist office. Finally, behind the Casino you can stroll on the huge sun-drenched terraces that offer a splendid view of the sea.

Before leaving the square, be sure to make one final foray into flamboyant luxury by visiting the lobby of the Hôtel de Paris, or the Hôtel Hermitage behind it, just off of the square.

Another must-see is the square at night when it is brilliantly illuminated and becomes a completely different place.

Head east, towards the sea.

Avenue Princesse Grace leads to the beaches of Larvotto. Just before you reach the beach, you will pass by the **Musée National (10)** *(adults 26 F, children 15 F; Apr to Oct, everyday 10 AM to 6:30 PM; Nov to Mar, 10 AM to 12:15 PM and 2:45 PM to 6:30 PM; 17 Av. Princesse Grace,* ☎ *93.30.91.26)*. This museum displays a collection of dolls and old mechanical toys in a magnificent 19th-century villa built by Charles Garnier.

■ Quartier du Jardin Exotique ★★

This is Monaco's most prominent neighbourhood. Its **Jardin Exotique (11)** *(adults 34 F, children 17 F; open year-round, 9 AM to 6 PM; May to Aug, 7 PM; Bd du Jardin Exotique,* ☎ *93.30.33.65)*, or exotic garden, graces the slope of the *Moyenne Corniche* and offers a breathtaking view over the sea. Inaugurated in 1933, this extraordinary labyrinth clinging to the rock face features a collection of some 7,000 varieties of cactii and succulents. Monaco's exceptional microclimate ensures the survival of this rock garden, the largest of its kind in the world.

On site you can also visit a prehistoric cave with stalactites and stalagmites, in the **Grotte Préhistorique de l'Observatoire (12)**, 60 m below the gardens. It seems that the very first Monocans lived here up to 300,000 years ago.

Near the garden you will see a modern building which holds the **Musée d'Anthropologie Préhistorique (13)**. This museum is home to the remains of ancient tombs collected from the area surrounding the principality, indicators of the most important milestones in the history of humanity.

■ **Quartiers Portuaires** ★

There are two port districts: La Condamine, separating the Rocher and Monte-Carlo, where you will find the Port de Monaco; and Fontvieille, to the west of the Rocher.

The **Port de Monaco (14)**, also known as the Port d'Hercule, harbours some of the most beautiful yachts in the world. The Stade Nautique Rainier III stands in the centre of the port. It is the departure point for the *Azur Express* tourist train, which offers a night ride between the port and the Rocher. During the day, it provides a shuttle service between the port and the beaches of Larvotto, at the far east end of the principality.

You can take a walk along the docks at the port, or spend the day at sea on the **Yacht Winnaretta Singer** *(480 F and 240 F per child, in summer Tue to Thu, Sat and Sun; departure at 10 AM, return at 5 PM; ☎ 93.25.36.33)*. Enjoy a relaxing day at sea in comfortably decorated lounges. There are several stops scheduled for swimming at Menton, Beaulieu and Villefranche. There are also evening cruises on Fridays and during the International Fireworks Festival in the summer.

If you prefer, you can explore the depths of the Mediterranean Sea in the submarine **Le Seabus** *(295 F and 150 per child; everyday on the hour, several descents lasting 45 minutes; Quai des États-Unis, ☎ 93.30.64.15)*. Its transparent hull, which allows a panoramic view of the sea floor, makes for a unique ride.

The seashore can also be explored on board the **Catamaran Le Monte-Carlo** *(70 F, 55 F per child; Apr to Aug, everyday, several trips lasting 55 minutes; Quai des États-Unis, ☎ 92.16.15.15)*.

Although you may have imagined that the biggest yacht would belong to the Royal Family, this is not the case. It is privately owned by an extremely wealthy Greek.

Leave the port and head towards Place Sainte-Dévote, at the far east end.

Named after the principality's and the royal family's patron saint, the **Église Sainte-Dévote (15)** was built in the 11th century, and was expanded and restored in 1870. This church is particularly important to the Monegasques because, each year on January 27, Sainte-Dévote is celebrated with a candlelight procession followed by a mass and the benediction. At the end of the day, a small boat is set on fire in the port.

Rue Grimaldi begins at this church and leads to the train station. The street is a blaze of orange, from the fruits in the trees that line the road to the building façades painted this colour. In front of the station you'll find the **Vieux Marché de la Condamine (16)**, the old covered market that was built in the early 1900s and restored in 1993. It is a meeting place for the servants of some of the oldest families in Monaco, who have always lived in the La Condamine area.

A little to the west of the station, towards Fontvieille, is the **Centre d'Acclimatation Zoologique (17)** *(adults 20 F, children 10 F; in summer, every-day 9 AM to noon and 2 PM to 7 PM; Oct to May, 10 AM to noon and 2 PM to 5 PM; Place du Canton, ☎ 93.25.18.31)*. Founded by Prince Rainier in 1954, this park is perfect for various species of tropical and African animals because of its geographic location. Located on the south face of the Rocher, it is protected from the wind coming in from the sea and as a result benefits from a particularly mild climate.

You are now at the last stage of your visit to Monaco: **Fontvieille**. This part of Monaco lies to the west of the Rocher. Its port faces the Place du Palais on the Rocher. You can take a leisurely stroll along the docks, of course, but the main point of interest of Fontvieille is its **Parc Paysager** or landscaped park **(18)** and the **Roseraie "Princesse Grace" (19)**, reached via Avenue des Papalins. This magnificent park, where several bronze sculptures by famous artists are exhibited, covers almost 4 ha. This is a wonderful place to take

a stroll! The shaded park has a small ornamental pond, where ducks and swans swim peacefully. The fragrant air in the rose garden is thanks to over 3,500 rosebushes contained within it.

 ## Accommodation

Although we can recommend a few hotels in Monaco, we strongly suggest that you choose a hotel in the outskirts of the city. There are some marvellous villages or towns in the area, such as Cap-d'Ail or Menton, that are higher up on the *corniches* or closer to the sea. You'll find these places less expensive and less put-on than Monaco.

We especially recommend the **Cosmopolite** *(275-330 F, 360 F for 3 people; pb or ps, ℜ; 19 Bd Général Leclerc, 06240 Beausoleil, ☎ 93.78.36.00, ⇄ 93,41.84.22)*. This early 1900s hotel has been completely restored and all the rooms are equipped with modest, modern bathrooms. The hotel is only 300 m from the Casino, a little higher up on the mountain, on a quieter street. The hotel offers an American all-you-can-eat buffet breakfast for 28 F. And the reception is very friendly.

If you're nostalgic for the days when traditions were still respected and everything still had "real" value, then stay at the **Balmoral** *(550-850 F, 1200-1500 F for an apartment; pb, ≡, tv, ℝ, ℜ; 12 Av. de la Costa, Monte-Carlo, ☎ 93.50.62.37, ⇄ 93.15.08.69)*. This Victorian hotel near the sea and the Casino offers a beautiful view of the port. The tasteful decor includes an abundance of antiques from various periods. The reception is very good; you'll feel like an important guest. The price is fairly reasonable, but you can take advantage of group rates if you are holding a meeting in their conference room.

If you want to experience the splendour of the late 1800s, when Prince Albert transformed Monaco into an island of luxury, then stay at the sumptuous **Hôtel Hermitage** *(1,400-2,700 F, 2,500-3,000 F for a suite, every luxury; Square Beaumarchais,* ☎ *93.92.16.40,* ⇄ *93.50.47.12)*. This first-class hotel with magnificent bathrooms is very close to the Casino. It is divided into two wings and looks out over the port and La Condamine at one end. The hotel and its restaurant are so grandiose that you could easily imagine that you are a personal guest of the Grimaldis. In addition, the hotel has recently added a thalassotherapy centre. In short, luxury fit for a king, impeccable and discreet service. You'll feel transformed into a Prince or Princess overnight.

 Restaurants

Location, location, location... that is the name of the game in Monaco, and higher prices are the result.

We have found a cute little restaurant on Monte-Carlo's only old street: **Le Périgordin** *($; closed for two weeks in August, Sat noon and Sun evening; 5 Rue des Oliviers,* ☎ *93.30.06.02)*. It offers specialties from the Southwest of France: *magrets et confits de canard* (duck cutlets and preserves), foie gras, cassoulet, etc. The friendly owners will greet you in a decor that seems like it's a world away from the glitter of Monaco. Portions are generous and the service is friendly and personal. This restaurant is a pleasant spot to enjoy a lovely evening at a reasonable price.

There is a multitude of restaurants in Monaco that can be qualified as tourist traps. Some have charming decors, others profess to sophistication. **Le Café de Paris** *($$; Place du Casino,* ☎ *92.16.20.20.)*, located on Place du Casino in Monte-Carlo, offers the most beautiful and elegant *belle époque* decor. If you want to be where the action is, have a cocktail or dessert on its large terrace. However, we have our doubts as to the value this restaurant offers, and the service does leave something to be desired.

If you hit the jackpot at the Casino and you want to blow it all in a very luxurious setting, treat yourself to an evening at the **Louis XV**, Hotel de Paris *($ $ $; Place du Casino,* ☎ *92.16.36.36)*. The decor is princely and very ornate. The chef, Alain Ducasse, is internationally famous. This is one of the finest restaurants of the Côte d'Azur.

 Entertainment

Casino de Monte-Carlo
Place du Casino
☎ 92.16.23.00 or 92.16.24.29
European and English roulette, chemin de fer, black jack, craps from 3 PM.

The Casino also houses the **Opéra de Monte-Carlo** and a cabaret club where musicals are performed.

■ Bars

JIMMY'S
Monte-Carlo Sporting Club
Av. Princess Grace
☎ 93.16.22.77

Piano-Bar The Living Room *(7 Av. des Spélugues)*. Refined decor with cosy atmosphere. To make your evening last into the night...

■ Festivals and Events

The **Festival du Printemps des Arts** begins in April. It presents a multitude of musical events featuring famous as well as new artists.

Le **Grand Prix de Monaco** also takes place in April each year. It is a most prestigious race that counts for the Formula I World Cup.

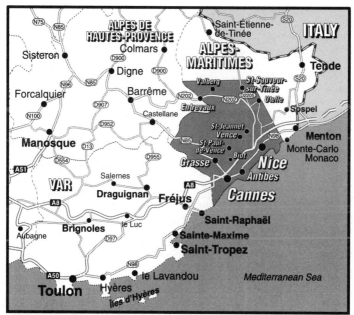

BETWEEN NICE AND CANNES ★★★

This part of the Côte d'Azur evokes not only splendour and opulence but also landscapes whose natural beauty inspire great spirituality. However, this region is famous mostly for its great artistic and cultural strength. Above and beyond the fashionable myth, fed by grandiose events — namely the Cannes Film Festival — this area remains an exceptional site where the soul may wander freely between waves of nostalgia and heavenly visions. This is why many artists settled here, leaving behind a rich artistic and cultural heritage.

Unfortunately, there are two sides to every coin. This region, still undeveloped at the turn of the century, experienced rapid urban growth and an enormous wave of construction, and the resulting heavy flow of traffic has become difficult to manage. To meet the need for more roads, the region, department and urban communities had to sacrifice much of their wilderness areas.

New roads have been built, but some of them are congested to the point of being unusable at certain hours in July and August. A prime example is the N 98, which is the main link between Nice and Cannes. It is so crowded that bumper-to-bumper traffic inches along for hours under the hot sun.

So don't make a mistake you'll regret. Avoid travelling on the main roads to the beaches during rush hours, which are usually between 10 AM and 1 PM, and between 5 PM and 8 PM.

This magnificent region abounds in beautiful natural and cultural attractions. The food is excellent. Côte d'Azur remains a place of great charm and grace with many interesting places to see. Although superficially quite accessible, the "real" Côte d'Azur, only reveals itself to life's true pleasure-seekers, according to the *Comité Régional du Tourisme* in Nice (*55 Promenade des Anglais, 93.37.78.78, ⇄ 93.86.01.06*).

You may wish to see architectural treasures, take the time to examine the ancient stones, and tour through all the museums and discover the many artists on whom this region has left its indelible mark. But the simpler pleasures are also within reach, such as a stopping in a quaint inland village where the contacts with people are more free and real, and where nature holds a place of honour.

 Finding Your Way Around

■ By Air

See Between Nice and Menton chapter, p. 206. It contains all the information you need. From the airport, a vast transportation network provides access to the city or town of your choice.

■ By Car

The highways are nearby. Roads lead from Nice to Cannes via Cagnes-sur-Mer, Antibes and Juan-les-Pins. There are also exits to the near interior (Cagnes, Vence, Mougins, Grasse, etc.) from these roads.

■ By Train

There are many daily connections to the seashore between Nice and Cannes, via St-Laurent-du-Var, Cagnes-sur-Mer and Antibes. During the summer, the train runs frequently, ensuring a link between the many seaside resorts. These train stations are also departure points for the network of buses that provide transportation to the interior. For information on train schedules and bus services available from the stations, enquire at the Information Service at the SNCF stations:

Cagnes
☎ 93.22.46.47

Antibes
Av. Robert-Soleau *(Antibes exit towards Nice, behind Port Vauban)*
☎ 93.33.63.51

Cannes
Rue Jean-Jaurès, ☎ 93.99.19.77 *(in summer, everyday 9 AM to 8 PM; in winter, Mon to Sat 9:30 AM to 12:30 PM and 2 PM to 6:30 PM)*
Information: ☎ 93.99.50.50
Reservations: ☎ 93.99.50.51

■ By Bus

A vast network of bus and coach services provides many connections. Enquire at the bus station or tourism office in each city or town. Phone numbers are listed below.

Antibes
Rue de la République, near Place du Général-de-Gaulle
Note that buses for Nice, Cannes, Juan-les-Pins and Cagnes leave from Place du Général-de-Gaulle.

Cannes

Next to the S.N.C.F Station:
☎ 93.39.31.37 for buses to Grasse, Mougins, Golfe-Juan and Vallauris.

Place de l'Hôtel de Ville:
☎ 93.39.11.39 to get to Juan-les-Pins, Antibes, Nice, Saint-Raphaël and Vallauris.
City bus: Société des Transports Urbains (city bus service)
Place de l'Hôtel de Ville, ☎ 93.39.11.39
There are 11 city bus lines.

■ By Boat

Shuttle from Cannes to the Îles de Lérins
At the port, next to the Palais des Festivals
☎ 93.39.11.82

 Practical Information

■ Cagnes

Motorcycle and Bicycle Rental
3 Rue du Logis, ☎ 93.22.55.85

■ Vence

Tourist Office
Place du Grand-Jardin, ☎ 93.58.06.38

■ St-Paul-de-Vence

Tourist Office
2 Rue Grande, ☎ 93.32.86.95
(Thu to Tue 10 AM to noon and 2 PM to 6 PM)

■ Antibes

Tourist Office
11 Place du Général-de-Gaulle
☎ 92.90.53.00, ⇄ 92.90.53.01 *(Mon to Fri 9 AM to noon and 2 PM to 6 PM and Sat morning; in summer, every day from 9 AM to 8 PM except Sat morning)*

■ Juan-les-Pins

Tourist Office
51 Bd Guillaumont, ☎ 93.61.04.98

■ Cannes

Tourist Office
Palais des Festivals, Esplanade du Président-Georges-Pompidou
☎ 93.39.01.01 *(9 AM to 6:30 PM, in summer until 7:30 PM)*

Car Rental
Avis (SNCF Station)
☎ 93. 39.26.38, ⇄ 93.21.44.53

Europcar
59 la Croisette
☎ 93.94.20.00, ⇄ 93.43.74.89

Main Post Office
22 Rue du Bivouac-Napoléon
☎ 93.39.13.16

Bicycle Rental
5 Rue Allieis (near the SNCF Station)
☎ 93.39.46.15

■ Grasse

Tourist Office
3 Place de la Foux, ☎ 93.36.03.56

■ **Valberg**

Tourist Office
☎ 93.02.52.77 or 93.02.52.54 *(9 AM to noon and 2 PM to 6 PM)*. Information on skiing conditions in winter.

■ **Isola 2000**

Tourist Office
☎ 93.23.15.15

 Exploring

It takes at least a week to properly explore the beautiful natural areas of this region as well as its many cultural points of interest, especially if you wish to take full advantage of the many magnificent hiking opportunities in the interior in summer. In winter and early spring, there is skiing at Isola 2000, Valberg or Auron. All of this is only 90 minutes from Nice.

Organizing a schedule is no easy task, since there are so many towns and magnificent places to see, each with their own cultural and historical richness. It all depends on where you decide to stay. Because distances are so short, you could opt to stay in just one place. Accommodations on the Côte d'Azur are very different from those available inland. It all depends on your tastes and personal interests.

To help you organize your trip in this region, and to more adequately address your preferences, we propose two itineraries. These tours can start from either Nice or Cannes, and concentrate essentially on places offering a particular interest. The best way to do these tours is by car.

■ **Tour A: For nature-lovers**

From Nice: one day, about 130 km

Saint-Jeannet *(take N 98, exit at Saint-Laurent-du-Var, then take D 118)*, Vence *(D 2210)*, Coursegoules *(D 2)*, Gréolières *(D 2)*, Gourdon *(D 3)*, Bar-sur-Loup *(D 2210)*, Tourrettes-sur-Loup, Vence, Saint-Paul-de-Vence *(D 2)*, La Colle-sur-Loup, Cagnes-sur-Mer, Nice.

From Cannes: one day, about 130 km

Mougins *(via N 285)*, Grasse *(N 85)*, Châteauneuf-de-Grasse *(D 2085)*, Gourdon *(D 3)*, Coursegoules *(D 2)*, Vence *(D 2)*, Saint-Paul-de-Vence *(D 2)*, La Colle-sur-Loup, Cagnes *(Haut-de-Cagnes can be added)*, and then highway A 8 to Cannes.

■ **Tour B: For art and history lovers**

From Nice: one day, about 60 km

Haut-de-Cagnes *(take N 98, then A 8 to the Vence exit, continue towards Vence for about 7 km and then take D 36)*, Vence *(D 36)*, Saint-Paul-de-Vence *(D 2)*, La Colle-sur-Loup *(D 2)*, Biot *(via A 8)*, Antibes *(N 98)*, Vallauris *(N 7)* and back to Nice by A 8.

From Cannes: one day, about 100 km

Mouans-Sartoux and Grasse *(N 285)*, Gourdon *(via Châteauneuf-de-Grasse D 2085 and D 3)*, Tourrettes-sur-Loup *(D 6)*, Vence, Saint-Paul-de-Vence *(D 2)*, La Colle-sur-Loup *(D 2)*, add Haut-de-Cagnes by back-tracking towards Vence, then taking D 36 towards Cagnes and highway A 8 to Cannes.

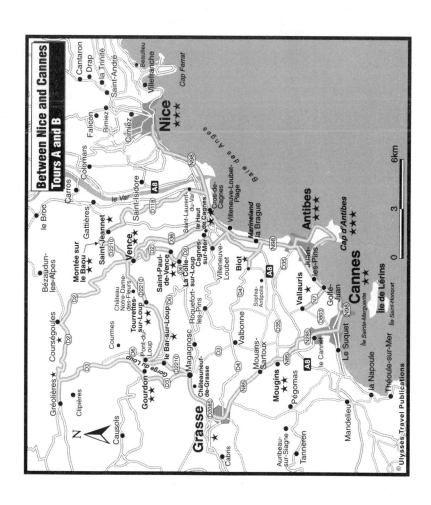

■ Cagnes

The urban area of Cagnes is divided into three parts: **Le Cros-de-Cagnes**, an old fishing village that has become a tourist town and seaside resort with a water sport centre and an international-ly-famous racetrack; **Cagnes-centre**, a new town with no points of interest for tourists and **Haut-de-Cagnes** ★, the old town on the hill, dominated by its castle. Cagnes was densely populated in the early Middle Ages. In the 6th century, monks from Lérins founded a monastery here. Haut-de-Cagnes was built as protection against the Sara-cens, and later became a castle-fortress under the protection of one of the Grimaldis. It was later destroyed during Charles Quint's rule.

In 1625, Jean-Henri Grimaldi built a beautiful residence out of the castle, blending Renaissance and Baroque styles.

Today, the castle houses the **Musée de l'Olivier** and the **Musée d'Art Moderne Méditérranéen** ★ *(admission charge; in summer, Wed to Mon 10 AM to noon and 2:30 PM to 7 PM; in winter, 10 AM to noon and 2 PM to 5 PM;* ☎ *93.20.85.57)*. The most spectacular area within the castle is without a doubt the indoor courtyard, overlooked by three floors connected by a monu-mental staircase. A beautiful ceiling with frescos painted in 16th-century post-Raphaelesque style graces the audience hall. The old boudoir is devoted to portraits of the famous singer Suzy Solidor. There are also works from the '30s to the '60s by many of Jean-Henri Grimaldi's artist friends, among them Dufy, Cocteau, Kisling and Picabia. This stunning col-lection features many different styles of painting. As well, an international art festival is held here every year in July,

August and September, with prizes awarded under the sponsorship of UNESCO.

The **Musée de l'Olivier** occupies the ground floor and basement. It contains a collection of ancient tools used in the production of olive oil.

Place du Château has several restaur-ants, and is a pleasant spot for cock-tails or a light meal. It also houses the **Maison des Artistes**, which holds paint-ing exhibitions featuring various artisitc styles and tastes.

Cagnes is also home to the **Domaine Renoir** ★ *(Wed to Mon 10 AM to noon and 2 PM to 5 PM; in summer until 6 PM; closed mid-Oct to mid-Nov;* ☎ *93.20.61.07)*, bought in 1907 by the famous impressionist painter. This is where Renoir spent the last years of his life, after having spent time in Magagnosc, Le Cannet, Villefranche, Cap-d'Ail, Vence, La Turbie, Biot, Antibes and Nice. The spirit of the artist still haunts this enchanting gar-den where ancient olive and orange trees grow. Inside hang about ten of his paintings, and his studio is open to visitors. *Les Grandes Baigneuses* which the master considered the highest point of his art was painted here.

Finally, there are many lovely places to walk near Cagnes, for example to Hautes Colettes.

■ Vence ★

Vence is a medieval city where art and tradition are sovereign. It is the essence of Provence.

Vence's origins go back to the Roman Empire; "Vintium" was then the heart of a region where pastoral cultures prospered. In the Middle Ages, however, Grasse surpassed Vence because of its superior location. Nevertheless, Vence remained a bishopric until the French Revolution. Alexandre Farnèse, who was later to become the future Pope Paul III, was its bishop for many years.

This city has retained a special charm. Situated on a plateau at an elevation of 325 m, the ancient city's narrow streets with its countless shops and bistros, the portals of its medieval fortifications and its fountains make Vence a most attractive place indeed. Gide, Valéry, Soutine, Dufy, Céline, Cocteau, Matisse, Chagall, Carzou, Dubuffet and many more have stayed here. Today, the city enjoys a rich artistic life with its many art galleries, exhibitions and concerts.

A bird's eye view of the city reveals an oval shape inside its medieval walls. Its charming rooftops give the city a special character.

If you are travelling by car, it may be difficult to find parking, especially during peak season. The city can be accessed by one of three doors at the east, south and west. Any of the narrow streets will inevitably lead to Place Clémenceau, where the city hall and the **Cathédrale ★** stand. The nave and aisles of this 11th century building betray its Romanesque origins. The façade is late 19th century. The cathedral contains a superb mosaic by Chagall entitled *Moïse sauvé des eaux* (Moses saved from the waters).

At the west entrance to the old city, at Place du Frêne, the **Château de Villeneuve/Fondation Hughes ★** *(admission charge; in summer, Tue to Sun 10 AM to noon and 3 PM to 7 PM; in winter 10 AM to noon and 2 PM to 6 PM; ☎ 93.24.24.26)* is open to visi-

tors. This entirely renovated museum was formerly the home of the *Seigneurs de Villeneuve*. Its bright spaces are used for temporary exhibitions. Part of the museum is dedicated to works by artists such as Matisse, Dufy, Chagall, Dubuffet and many others, created during their visits to Vence.

■ Outskirts of Vence

On the road to St-Jeannet, the **Chapelle du Rosaire**, also called the **Matisse Chapel ★** *(admission charge; Tue to Thu 10 AM to 11:30 PM and 2:30 pm. to 5:30 PM; closed beginning of Nov to mid-Dec)* includes an artistic collection which Matisse considered his "masterpiece despite all its imperfections." Completed in 1951, this chapel was a gift from Matisse to the Dominican Sisters who had nursed him back to health during a period of exhaustion. The chapel is designed in a profoundly simple style: "The inner soul is moved all the more by simple colours" (Matisse). The play of light is most fascinating. The cactus motif, symbolizing the tree of life, is repeated throughout the stained-glass windows. Ceramic tiles are brush-painted with ink and then enamelled. The stations of the Cross, which the artist rendered in all their drama and torment is represented on the white ceramic walls.

On the road to Grasse, follow the signs to **Château-Notre-Dame-des-Fleurs ★**. This magnificent castle recently became a foundation under the patronage of the owners of the Galerie Beaubourg in Paris. On the way to the castle, visitors walk through a garden of sculptures created, for the most part, by artists from the *École de Nice* (Klein, Arman, César, Ben, etc.), and by other illustrious sculptors, such as Niki de Saint-Phalle, Stellas, Spoerri and many more. Inside, the huge spaces contain exhibits of a multitude of works by artist friends and protegés of the owners over the past 25 years. In addition to works by the artists represented in the garden, there are works by Vol, Boisrond, Combas, Villeglé, Dado and more. The old Romanesque chapel contains a mechanical sculpture by Jean Tinguely, who died in 1992. The stained-glass windows are by Jean-Pierre Raynaud.

Saint-Jeannet ★

Saint-Jeannet, only 7 km from Vence (or 20 km from Nice), makes for a nice change of scenery. Here you can stroll through a superb ancient town perched upon a famous rock peak, the Baou de Saint-Jeannet. There are no cars allowed in this village. Visitors leave their vehicles in the parking lot (with security guards on duty at night) and continue on foot. The little square at the entrance to the town, across from the Auberge de Saint-Jeannet (see p 259), is often bustling with the conversations of the village's old-timers, who gather here. The point of greatest interest is **Place sur le Four**. It can be reached via a narrow passageway from a small street behind the church. This square is truly charming and offers a panoramic view encompassing Nice and the sea.

Before leaving the village, make sure you stop at the Roatta bakery, surely one of the best in the region. You can even buy the ingredients for a picnic lunch at the peak of the Baou.

The peak of the Baou ★ *(elevation 400 m; duration about three hours, return)* can be reached by a path from the village. The Provençal word *Baou*, often used in the region to designate rocky peaks, comes from a word mean-ing "precipice". The summit is a desert-like area at an elevation of 800 m. It offers a magnificent view of the town, the Baou de la Gaude and the sea. It's a bit of a shame that the surrounding hills have undergone so much development over the past few years. The view is nonetheless spectacular, and extends to the hills behind Nice, and even as far as Cap d'Antibes.

Saint-Paul-de-Vence ★

It's hard to believe that a town like Saint-Paul was once as quiet and "normal" as Saint-Jeannet. Its remarkable beauty makes it a popular stopover for tourists visiting the region. Of course, fame does come at a cost. The best way to appreciate the natural charm of this village at its best is to go in the early morning before the tour coaches arrive, or at the end of the day to admire the sunset.

Despite its "tourist attraction" side, this village has indeed earned its fame. Located on a slightly rocky plateau, its harmonious beauty conquers the heart, especially when seen from the road coming from La Colle-sur-Loup. This is undoubtedly one of the most beautiful villages in the world.

The oldest mention of the town's name dates back to 1016, when the "community" became free of serfdom and feudal taxes. In 1536, François I ordered the construction of ramparts to surround the town. This made it an imposing fortress capable of rivaling Nice, which was becoming more and more powerful. Later, when the town no longer had a strategic role to play, Saint-Paul shifted to a more pastoral lifestyle, like other medieval cities. *Art de vivre* reigned above all else. Local customs, celebrations, and the

Provençal language were guarded like treasures.

From 1925 onwards, some of the most illustrious painters, poets and writers visited or settled here, no doubt entranced by the area's natural beauty.

After the war came the stars of the silver screen, who would stop at the Colombe d'Or, at the entrance to the town. They included Simone Signoret and Yves Montand (Montand would play pétanque in the main square at the entrance), Marcel Carné and Prévert, to name only a few. Tobiasse and Blais also came here to paint.

The town wasn't completely taken over by artists and tourists. Today, farmers still represent almost a third of the active population, which no doubt contributes to Saint-Paul's charm.

The tour begins at the main square

Rue Grande crosses from one end of town to the other. This strictly pedestrian street is lined with stone buildings dating back to the 16th and 17th century, magnificent reminders of the town's former prosperity. Souvenir shops, artisans' workshops and art galleries can be found on the street level.

The street goes through several small squares. One of these contains the magnificent **Grande Fontaine** ★, which has been photographed thousands of times. The noble **Collégiale** ★ (description below), the **Campanelle**, the ancient **Donjon Seigneurial**, which now houses the city hall, the **Chapelle des Pénitents** and the **Tour des Remparts** are also along this street. The cemetery where Chagall is laid to rest is at the other end of town. The tour ends with a stroll along the ramparts, featuring

breathtaking views over the hills and sea.

La Collégiale de la Conversion-de-Saint-Paul ★ was built in the 12th century, but has since undergone many transformations. The Romanesque choir is the oldest part of the building. The bell tower was built in 1740. Chapelle Saint-Clément, with its rich blue and white decor, is worth seeing as well. The portrait *Sainte-Catherine d'Alexandrie*, attributed to Tintoret, hangs to the left as you enter.

The **Trésor de l'Église** ★, among the richest and the most beautiful of the Alpes-Maritimes, has a remarkable *ciborium*.

Several trails begin at the entrance to the town, providing an opportunity for a pleasant stroll over the hills north of the Poste. One of these trails heads west to the wooded estate of the Fondation Maeght.

The **Fondation Maeght** ★ *(adults 40 F, 10 F for cameras otherwise they must be checked; in summer 10 AM to 7 PM; in winter 10 AM to 12:30 PM and 2:30 PM to 6 PM; closed Nov. 15 to Dec. 15)* is without a doubt one of the world's most beautiful museums. It is a perfect union of nature, architecture and art. Created in 1964 by art dealers Marguerite and Aimé Maeght, it was inaugurated by André Malraux, the illustrious Minister of Cultural Affaires during the De Gaulle administration. The Maeghts worked closely with Catalonian architect Joseph Lluis Sert and their artist friends, who included Miro, Braque, Calder and Chagall.

To reach the museum, visitors must first go through a small park where pine trees and sculptures stand side by side. The large windows allow the exhibition rooms to come together in harmony with the gardens and terraces outside. Domed skylights let in a profusion of natural light.

The gardens contain a collection of statues by Giacometti (not always on exhibit), a labyrinth of sculptures and ceramics designed by Miro, "moving" sculptures by Calder, a Chagall mosaic and stained-glass by Braque, who was the subject of a retrospective in 1994. Finally, a small, modest chapel and several ornamental ponds add a freshness and spiritual dimension to this heavenly place.

Major exhibitions are held here every year. Catalogues, posters and etchings are sold in the pretty little bookstore, recalling the tributes paid in past years to artists such as Dubuffet, Max Ernst, Fernand Léger, Nicolas de Staël and many more. The permanent collection contains works by Bonnard, Kandinsky, Matisse, Hartung, and Klee. Among the more recent works are those by Tapiès, Paul Bury, Tal-Coat and Québec artist Jean-Paul Riopelle.

This museum hosts various artistic and musical events. Contemporary art enthusiasts and experts can also consult the films, books, magazines and catalogues at the documentation centre. Finally, a small bar-restaurant serves refreshments during the summer.

Tourrettes-sur-Loup ★

After having survived invasions by the Franks, the Huns, the Visigoths and the Lombards, ramparts were finally built around this ancient town during the Middle Ages. All that remains of them now are two doors that open onto the church square, and the 13th-century dungeon, which now houses the city hall.

It is said that, over the last century, the shade of the Tourrettes olive trees has provided a perfect climate for the violets to grow. These flowers are used in decoration, distillation in the perfume factories in Grasse and in the manufacture of sweets (candied violets). Tourrettes boasts of being the "city of violets" because of their abundance here.

This town is a wonderful place for a leisurely stroll. Go in one door, to the square, and out the other — the Grand'Rue forms a loop between the two. Discover the beautiful romantic houses, pleasant restaurants and many artisan shops, many of which belong to the artisans themselves. Built outside of the ramparts, the **early 15th century church** ★ contains, among other things, paintings from the School of Bréa. If you like naïve frescos, stop for a moment at the **Chapelle St-Jean**, just outside of the village.

Gourdon ★

Gourdon and its hamlet, Pont-du-Loup, form a picturesque village with only 242 inhabitants. The imposing 13th-century **château** *(admission charge; guided tours, Wed to Mon, closed Tue)*, rebuilt in the 17th century, is sure to capture your attention. Constructed in pure Provençal style, it surrounds a square courtyard flanked by two towers and a dungeon which was destroyed during the French Revolution. It contains a collection of antique weapons, a torture table in the old prison, beautiful old paintings (French, Flemish, Dutch and Rhenish) and, in the chapel, a statue of Saint-Sebastien attributed to El Greco. The first floor houses a museum of naïve painting.

This castle has had a succession of owners during the 20th century. It was last restored in 1972-73.

Place Victoria ★ offers a breathtaking panoramic view of astonishing depth and scope over the entire Côte d'Azur, with colours that change according to the time of day and the season. From left to right the view encompasses Cap-Ferret, Nice, the mouth of the Var, Cagnes, Antibes and it cape, Juan-les-Pins, the Îles de Lérins, Cannes, and even Mont-Chevalier, Napoule, l'Estérel and the Maures. In the foreground you will see the huge green valley, the Fleuve Loup, fields, olive, orange and cypress trees. In the distance you can just make out Mougins.

Gourdon has lots to offer shoppers, including several establishments that sell regional products, such as pâté, Provençal herbs, *tapenade*, goat's cheese, jams and honey.

■ From Cagnes to Cannes

Biot ★

Biot has always been famous for its pottery. Already in Roman times, Biot pottery was of particular importance. "Bizoto", as Biot was called in the 11th century, had many dark periods in its history, with a succession of wars and dominations, as well as a plague that ravaged the town in the 14th century. At the end of the 15th century, when the town was almost deserted, King René encouraged its repopulation by welcoming Italian families from Impéria, in Italy. Agriculture and the potter's art were revived. But Biot's trials continued and the town was again ravaged by two wars in the 18th century. Since then Biot has flourished and the population is still growing.

Pottery is an age-old tradition in Biot that has carried on because the area is rich in clay, sand and stones. Up until the early 20th century, Biot's reputation spread far and wide with the exportation of its beautiful earthenware jars. Biot dishes are characterized by their pale yellow enamel marbled with green and brown. But it seems that the most beautiful pieces ever made in Biot remain the apartment fountains. They stand in testimony to the skill of the artisans of the 18th and 19th century. It was during this time that pottery art in Biot was at its height. The fountains speak of a tradition that is not completely lost, even today.

Great blown-glass artists, painters, potters, basket makers, ceramists, and silver and goldsmiths settled in this town. Their works can be admired in the **Musée d'Histoire Locale et de Céramique Biotoise ★** *(5 F; Thu to Sat and Sun 2:30 PM to 6:30 PM; Place de la Chapelle, ☎ 93.65.11.79).*

If you are interested in glassware, the **Verrerie de Biot ★** *(8 AM to 7 PM; Chemin des Combes, ☎ 93.65.03.00),* at the bottom of the village, is open to visitors. This factory employs about 80 people.

Absolutely worth visiting is the **Musée Fernand-Léger ★** *(adults 30 F, students 20 F; 10 AM to noon and 2 PM to 5 PM, in summer until 6 PM; ☎ 93.65.63.61).* It is well-indicated before the town, and is 3 km from the seashore. This lovely museum is dedicated to the great French painter Fernand Léger (1881-1955). It was built by his widow in a beautiful park and was expanded in 1989. The museum was architecturally designed to harmonize with the incredible multicoloured ceramic that dominates the facade. Fifty-thousand enamel tiles, covering an area of 500 m² are mounted at different angles to better reflect the sunlight.

Two floors of the gallery house the painter's works showing the evolution of his art, from his purely impressionist *Portrait de l'Oncle*, to his powerful, characteristic cubist style, and finally the painting he was working on when he died. The collection includes *Les Constructeurs* (1950), his greatest work. This painting is an excellent example of the "social realism" style that characterizes his work. Moved by the drama of the two world wars, Léger wanted to express the causes of the people, whom he felt were his equals in a universe of technological advancement.

Antibes ★

Even though Antibes has traces of civilization that are 3,000 years old, its true history begins with the Greeks. Around the 4th century BC, the Greeks founded Antipolis — meaning "city in front of" — on this site which served as a supply port between Corsica and Massalie (Marseille). In 43 BC, it became a Roman city and was chosen as the site of great Roman constructions including an arch of triumph, theatre, amphitheatre, forum, aqueducts and thermal baths. Christianity arrived later, with the first bishop settling here in AD 442. Eight centuries of religious administration followed. The city's name was changed to Antiboul and it became an episcopal centre. But the repeated invasions by barbaric peoples and the murderous pillages by the Saracens during this period forced the population to abandon the city in the 9th century. They fled into the interior, only to return one hundred years later.

With the departure of the bishop to Grasse in 1236, Antibes lost much of its status and shifted to a new, more democratic administration. Under the rule of Henri III near the end of the 16th century, Antibes regained some status when the impressive **Fort Carré ★**, fortification wall and bastions were built. The fort, which can be seen on the way from Nice, was restored in 1967. Henry IV later bought the city from the Grimaldis in 1608 and made of it a royal city and powerful stronghold, taking advantage of its strategic location. Unfortunately, the fortifications were destroyed in 1894.

After 1920, the city began to grow, and many artists, writers and actors came to stay in this spectacular area of the Côte d'Azur. They included Guy de Maupassant, Georges Sand, Mistinguett, Rudolf Valentino, Max Ernst, Picasso, Prévert, Sydney Bechet, Nicolas de Staël, Hans Hartung, Scott Fitzgerald and Julien Greene.

Antibes and Juan-les-Pins have grown together, encompassing Golfe Juan, to form a single urban community called Antibes-les-Pins with a population of 80,000. While Antibes is "alive" all year round, Juan-les-Pins is rather deserted during the winter.

Many cultural events are held here in the spring. Antibes hosts a large antique show. During the first two weeks of July, the **Chantier naval Opéra ★** invites opera enthusiasts for the *Musique au coeur* festival, where Wilhamina Fernandez, among others, often performs. And of course the *Festival International de Jazz*, is held here in mid-July.

A tour of Antibes usually begins with a stroll in the old yachting port, where wealthy boat owners show off their luxurious crafts. Follow the ramparts (Quai Rambaud) to the small bay and pretty sandy beach. Nearby is the *Marine* door leading to the old city, which is divided in two. The high part is the site of the ancient Ligurians, Greek and Roman cities. The lower city is where the market is held. The streets leading towards the sea take you back to the ramparts. A magnificent view of Cap d'Antibes and the seashore extends to Nice, with the Mercantour appearing behind it on the horizon. Only a few steps away sits the "Château Grimaldi", an old episcopal residence which now houses the **Musée Picasso ★** *(20 F; Wed to Mon 10 AM to noon and 3 PM to 7 PM; in winter, 2 PM to 6 PM; closed on public holidays; ☎ 93.34.91.91)*. This museum owes its existence to a fortunate coincidence by which Picasso met the castle's curator in 1946. He suggested that Picasso set up his studio in the building. The painter spent several months here creating a multitude of works. These, along with others that were either bought or donated are now on exhibit.

The works can be grouped into three main themes: mythology, nudes in cubic style, and the every day life of fishermen, fish, etc.

Other rooms in the museum display works of Fernand Léger, Modigliani, Picabia, Magnelli, Ernst and Hartung. The most spectacular room is the one dedicated to Nicolas de Staël. It contains, among others, his enormous painting entitled *Le Grand Concert*, de Staël's final work prior to taking his own life in Antibes in the mid-'50s.

The terrace facing the sea features sculptures by Calder, Miro, Arman, and Patrick and Anne Poirier, who created a sculpture incorporating tons of white marble and Roman remnants.

Finally, ceramic lovers can admire 150 ceramic works created by Vallauris potters between 1947 and 1949.

Next to the museum stands the **Cathédrale ★**, which contains pieces representing very different periods and styles. The choir and the transept date back to 1125, but the recently restored façade was built in 1751.

A market is held every morning near the Cours Masséna. Vegetables, fruit and fish rival each other in flavour and freshness. The nearby streets are the lower city.

The picturesque Rue du Bas and Rue du Haut-Castelet both lead to Placette du Safranier. This small square is a special place. It is the heart of a tiny, almost independent community whose city hall is located in a little restaurant.

Near Square Albert I, Bastion Saint-André houses the **Musée d'Archéologie ★** *(6 F; Wed to Mon 9 AM to noon and 2 PM and 7 PM; in winter until 6 PM, closed Nov; ☎ 93.34.50.91)*. It contains artifacts from ancient Antipolis.

Walk along the beaches to the cape's entrance.

Around Antibes

Marineland *(adults 78 F, children 52 F; from 11 AM, two or three shows from 2:30 PM, Jul and Aug evening shows at 9:30 PM; ☎ 93.33.49.49)* is around 4 km from Antibes, towards Cagnes-sur-mer (near Biot). The aquarium and shows featuring dolphins, sea lions and seals will delight children young and old.

The area around Marineland is like a huge theme park because, next to it, there are several activities for children. **Adventure Golf** *(in summer Wed to Sat and Sun 2 PM to midnight)* is an enchanting spot for miniature golf enthusiasts because of its exotic setting. **Aquasplash** *(mid-Jun to mid-Sep 10 AM to 7 PM; ☎ 93.33.49.49)*, is a refreshing spot with its water slides and a wave pool. **La Jungle des papillons** *(10 AM to sunset; ☎ 93.33.55.77)* is a unique place where hundreds of butterflies fly freely. **La Petite ferme** *(10 AM to 6 PM)*, with its farm animals is always fun for children.

Cap d'Antibes ★

Although Cap d'Antibes is really only the southern tip of the peninsula, the name is often used to refer to the entire area, whose highest elevation is 73 m. You can go all the way around it by following the beach, or walk through narrow streets to reach the tip. Famous for its sumptuous estates, the cape is also the site of the Hôtel du Cap Eden Roc, considered one of the most luxurious establishments in the world. All along the cape, there are numerous inlets with little ports and velvet beaches. The beaches of the Garoupe are very popular. Beyond these beaches the landscape becomes more wild. The rocks provide excellent opportunities for fishing and scuba-diving. A walk along the **Sentier Tripoli ★**, a pretty trail, is a wonderful way to enjoy all this wild beauty.

The top of **Phare de la Garoupe** *(in summer 2:30 PM to 6 PM; in winter 3 PM to 5 PM; ☎ 93.61.57.63)* offers a wonderful vantage point from which to admire the view of the seashore spanning from l'Estérel to the Italian Alps. On a clear day, you can even see Corsica in the distance. Next to the lighthouse stands a small chapel from which Notre-Dame de Bon-Port watches over sailors.

Cap d'Antibes owes its fame mostly to the many celebrities from all spheres who have lived or visited the area. They include wealthy shipping tycoons, royalty, politicians and writers, not to mention those who have stayed at the Hôtel du Cap Eden Roc. This hotel is very popular with film stars during the Cannes Film Festival.

The cape also has a botanical garden, the **Jardin Thuret** *(free admission; Mon to Fri 8 AM to 5:30 PM, in June until 6 PM; 62 Bd du Cap, ☎ 93.67.88.66)*. It covers an area of 7 ha and contains a vast number of plant species.

Finally, if you're curious to see what's hidden inside some of the Cap d'Antibes sumptuous estates, stop in at the **Villa Eilen-Roc** *(Wed 1:30 PM to 5:30 PM; Bd du Cap, ☎ 92.90.50.00)*. This villa, with its palatial facade, was built by Charles Garnier, architect of the Opéra de Paris. Among other things, it contains a bathroom featuring a green marble bath.

Juan-les-Pins

Although it's hard to imagine, Juan-les-Pins was covered by a huge pine forest before 1880.

Unfortunately, those days are in the past. The history of Juan-les-Pins is best summed up as a series of miscalculated real estate speculations, but you can be the judge.

Today, the **Festival International de Jazz à Antibes-Juan-les-Pins** *(Pinède Gould, ☎ 92.90.53.00)* remains Juan's main point of interest. Each year since 1960, the stars of the jazz world have been coming here to perform during the second half of July. For several years now, the Festival's most famous performer has been Keith Jarrett.

Unfortunately Juan has little to offer tourists besides the festival. There is a spirited nightlife during the summer months, but in the winter the scene is quite dead.

Vallauris ★

Situated between the sea and mountains, Vallauris-Golfe-Juan is actually made up of two communities, with a total population of 25,000. Vallauris is a pottery town, Golfe-Juan, a seaside resort.

Vallauris' past is similar to that of Biot. Devastated by the plague and one war after another, the village was repopulated by Italian families from Genoa, who brought with them their pottery skills. Even today, pottery is the primary craft and commercial activity in Vallauris. The town's streets are lined with pottery shops which, unfortunately, are not always in the best taste.

Between 1946 and 1955, Picasso took up residence in Vallauris. In 1952, upon the community's request, he created an enormous fresco entitled *Guerre et paix*, which can be admired in the **Musée National Picasso ★** *(8 F; Wed to Mon 10 AM to noon and 2 PM to 6 PM, off-season until 5 PM; closed on public holidays; Place de la Libération,* ☎ *93.64.18.05)*. This museum has found a home in a Renaissance-style castle, whose 12th-century **Chapelle Sainte-Anne** houses the Picasso fresco. Otherwise, the museum is dedicated mostly to pottery, including some produced by the great master himself. Every two years, the museum hosts the *Biennale Internationale de céramique d'art*.

Cannes ★

Cannes, world famous for its *Festival International du Film*, devotes all of its energy to being the second largest tourist, commercial, conference and trade show city in France. Over 400 events are held here each year. Top television, cinema, recording, real estate and computer professionals from all over the world come to meet.

Cannes' real history began when the Roman colony "Canoïs" was established in AD 154. A succession of invasions and wars followed, testimony to the attractiveness of this splendid site. The territory was coveted in turn by the Saracens, the German Empire under Charles Quint, the Spanish, the Duke of Savoy Victor-Amédée II and once again by the German imperial troops in the 18th century.

The tides turned for Cannes in 1834 with the arrival of an English aristocrat, Lord Brougham. He commissioned the construction of a sumptuous winter residence, a move which was later imitated by the international aristocracy. There was a proliferation of homes and luxury villas in Cannes around this time. But it wasn't until after 1853 that Cannes really took off, with the arrival of the railroad, followed by the construction of a yachting harbour, hotels and creation of the illustrious Croisette. Cannes had already established itself as *the* place to go in winter. And so, rich Northern-Europeans, especially the English, French and Russians, came each winter to take advantage of the healthy, mild climate.

Cannes' economy has been based mainly on tourism since the 1930's, when the city also became a summer tourist spot. Since the end of World

War II, Cannes has been transformed by real estate developers who have built thousands of apartment buildings, all for the benefit of those who come seeking a calm and pleasant place to stay. Fortunately, many luxurious residences, often of rather extraordinary design, have resisted the assault of time, thus keeping alive a certain nostalgia in this part of the Côte d'Azur. Every year since 1939, this nostalgia is perpetuated with the *Festival de Cannes*, where the stars and starlets create a commotion by their appearance or absence thereof on the famous Croisette.

It is extremely difficult to find a place to park on the street. The underground parking lot of the **Palais des festivals (1)**, located at one end of the Croisette, offers a convenient alternative. This building, whose architecture in no way resembles the palaces of old, has sparked many comments (usually negative) since its inauguration in 1982. In any case, it is very practical and well-equipped to accommodate the conferences and many events that are held there.

West of the Palais, the old port harbours many pleasure yachts. The boat service to the Îles de Lérins leaves from here. Across the street, among the ancient plane trees, lie the **Allées de la Liberté (2)**, the site of the Hôtel de Ville. The old part of the city can be reached from here by going up Rue de Montchevalier.

The old city, the cradle of Cannes, with its medieval buildings overshadowing the old port, is also known as **Suquet**. The square at the top of the hill is surrounded by the ruins of the old 14th-century castle and its ramparts. **Église Notre-Dame-d'Espérance (3)**, a

church built in 1627, is an example of late Gothic Provençal architecture.

The square offers a captivating panoramic view of the city, the port, l'Estérel and the Îles de Lérins. The **Nuits Musicales de Suquet** *(programme and reservations:* ☎ *92.98.62.77)* is held here every year in July, featuring many concerts and classical music recitals.

Inside the castle, the **Musée de la Castre (4)** *(10 F; Wed to Mon 10 AM to noon and 2 PM to 5 PM, in summer 3 PM to 7 PM; closed Jan;* ☎ *93.38.55.26)* offers ethnological and archaeological collections from five continents. Paintings from Cannes and Provence are also represented, with 19th-century works on exhibit. The **Tour du Suquet (5)**, towers 22 m above the yard, and the entire area. Construction of the tower began in 1070 and was completed in 1385. There is a terrace at the top of the tower and viewpoint indicator that points to some of the region's interesting sites.

To go back downtown, take Rue Saint-Antoine. This picturesque street is lined with flowery old houses and little restaurants. The old city streets often carry the names of families who lived in the area, or recall the trades that were practised there long ago.

At the foot of Suquet, behind the old port, is the Forville market, where vegetables, fruits and fresh fish are sold. The commercial area begins a little further along, where the street is lined with a multitude of shops of all kinds. Some of these are pedestrian streets, such as the **Rue Meynadier ★ (6)**. This narrow street has a special ambience and an intimate atmosphere despite the bustling crowds. There are many narrow streets and vaulted passages to

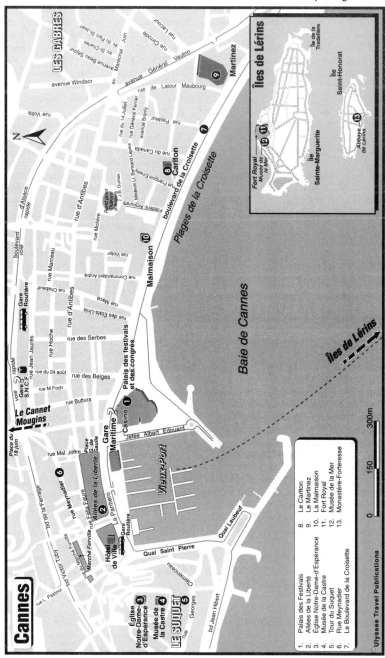

Cannes

Île de Lérins

1. Palais des Festivals
2. Allées de la Liberté
3. Église Notre-Dame-d'Espérance
4. Musée de la Castre
5. Tour du Suquet
6. Rue Meynadier
7. Le Boulevard de la Croisette
8. Le Carlton
9. Le Martinez
10. La Malmaison
11. Fort Royal
12. Musée de la Mer
13. Monastère-Forteresse

© Ulysses Travel Publications

discover. Well-renowned specialty shops offer all the delicacies needed to put together an exquisite picnic lunch. For shopping of any kind, Rue d'Antibes is a must because it has the most shops.

Boulevard de la Croisette ★ (7) professes to be the quintessence of luxury with its exorbitantly-priced hotels and boutiques. People parade along the Promenade on the beach, often in a great show of prestige. The name Croisette comes from a small monument on the site where the Casino Palm Beach has stood since 1929. It carries a cross placed at the end of the bay. With the construction of the boulevard in the second half of the 19th century, Cannes officially entered in competition with Nice, which already had its beautiful Promenade des Anglais.

La Croisette houses several palaces that date back to the end of the last century or the beginning of the 20th century. They include the **Carlton (8)**, with its *belle époque* architecture, and the **Martinez (9)**, with its Art Deco interior. At Number 47, **La Malmaison (10)** was formerly a pavilion of the Grand Hôtel, a colossus built in 1864. Repurchased by the city, it hosts large exhibitions each year. dedicated to modern and contemporary painters and sculptors.

Les Îles de Lérins ★

Buy tickets at the Gare Maritime (on the west side of the Palais des Festivals) to go to the two magnificent islands that you see when you stroll along the Baie de Cannes. In summer, there are departures almost every hour and sometimes even more often depending on the flow of tourists *(return fare 40 F for Sainte-Marguerite, 45 F for Saint-Honorat and 60 F for both islands, keep your tickets! ☎ 93.39.11.82, ⇄ 92.98.80.32; for a tour of the ocean bottom, ☎ 93.38.66.33)*. On the islands you can visit historic sites, stroll through the Alep pine and eucalyptus forest, and swim and dive from the top of the rocks.

The Îles de Lérins were already well known to navigators in Antiquity, as confirmed by archaeological evidence. Today these islands continue to attract pleasure craft, many of which drop anchor here.

Sainte-Marguerite

The island was originally called Lero. The Ligurians, the Greeks and the Romans each occupied it in turn, as the artifacts on exhibit in **Fort Royal (11)** *(Wed to Mon 10 AM to noon and 2 PM to 5 PM; ☎ 93.20.61.64)* show. The fort, built under Richelieu, was used as a prison from 1685 until the early 20th century. Its most illustrious occupant was without a doubt the "Masque de Fer", who was imprisoned here in 1687. The search for his identity has given rise to all sorts of theories, including one claiming that he was Louis XIV's eldest brother. The mystery has yet to be resolved. Visitors can see the cell where he was held. Other cells are decorated with mural frescos painted by French artist Jean Le Gac in the early '90s. The painter created the collection after being inspired by the site.

Now restored and reorganized, the fort houses a diving centre, a centre for dance and artistic expression for children and the **Musée de la Mer (12)**, which occupies the oldest part of the building. This museum contains artifacts, collected on archaeological digs on the island, and objects recuperated from ships sunken off the island's shores. Interesting note: some of these collections are presented in the ancient Roman cisterns that used to hold the island's drinking water.

A tour of the island could not be complete without a long stroll on its walking paths. The area is protected and there is a wide variety of plant species to discover.

Saint-Honorat

This island is smaller than Sainte-Marguerite, and belongs to the *Congrégation Cistercienne de Sénaque*, a community of monks who have maintained a very active monastery here since 1869. They strictly observe the 72 monastic rules established by Saint-Benoît, which dictate that spiritual and physical life must be balanced. Accordingly, the monks devote a certain amount of time to meditation, but also cultivate lavender and grapes, harvest honey and produce a liqueur made from aromatic Provençal plants. The liqueur is known as *Lérina*, which comes from the name of the island in Antiquity.

An important Christian landmark, Saint-Honorat's monastery has a history that reaches far into the past. The monastery, where many theologians, bishops and even several saints were trained, had an unparalleled reputation as early as the 6th century.

Despite all the piety on the island, the monastery wasn't spared from the pillages by the Saracens and the wars waged during the Middle Ages. Shortly after the French Revolution, the monastery was closed with the secularization of the area by the pope. Monastic life resumed only after the second half of the 19th century.

The **monastère-fortresse (13)**, which was built in 1073, is open to visitors during tourist season. On the first floor, the cloister opens up to two levels of galleries with Gothic vaults. The cistern in the centre dates back to Roman times. The upper gallery provides access to Chapelle Sainte-Croix. Its original vault contains relics of Saint-Honorat.

Finally, there is a shaded trail that leads all the way around the island. It is a beautiful place for a walk, and along the way you can discover the seven chapels scattered across the island. The most interesting is Chapelle de la Trinité. It has three vaults forming a trefoil, reminiscent of Byzantine art.

Mougins ★

This lovely town is located seven kilometres from Cannes, at an elevation of 260 m. It is a wonderful place to take a walk. And since walking works up an appetite, Mougins is the right place to be, with its many gourmet restaurants of long-standing reputation. You can't go through Mougins without stopping to eat here. The hard part is choosing a restaurant, since there are so many good ones. See p 263.

Mougins is almost a thousand years old. It is built around the old church at the top of the hill, according to the typical layout of Provençal villages in the Middle Ages. The Romanesque church dates back to the 11th century, and has since undergone several modifications.

Take the time to stroll about in the lanes of the old town. The soft light and welcoming ambience of the Place de la Mairie are positively charming on summer evenings.

For those interested in photography, the **Musée de la Photographie** *(5 F; Jul to Aug, 2 PM to 11 PM; Sep and Oct, Wed to Sun 1 PM to 7 PM; closed Nov to Jun; Porte Sarrazine,* ☎ *93.75.85.67)* is located at the Place de l'Église. The first floor features temporary exhibitions. The second floor displays the permanent collection, which formerly belonged to Picasso. It includes photographs by Doisneau, Lartigue, Clergue, Colomb, Quinn, Duncan and others.

Grasse ★

Located 16 km from Cannes and 35 km from Nice, Grasse is known internationally for its perfumes. Signs along the roads to Grasse point out how closely the history of the town and the perfume industry are intertwined.

Parking spots are hard to find, so we suggest leaving your car in a public parking lot.

Place aux Aires is the site of a flower market every morning. From this square, the winding streets lead into the old medieval town surrounding Puy, the peak that used to protect the city against attacks. Many beautiful homes line these streets. Three major 13th-century buildings dominate the medieval town: These are the **Donjon**, the **Palais de l'Évêque ★**, which is now the Hôtel de Ville, and the **Cathédrale ★**, a modest church built of limestone, which houses works by Rubens and Fragonard as well as a Ludovic Bréa reredo.

The lower part of the town has three museums. The **Musée International de la Parfumerie ★** *(in summer 10 AM to 7 PM; Place du Cours,* ☎ *93.36.80.20)* is the most interesting. It is dedicated to the history and evolution of perfume production techniques. The entire process of creating a perfume is revealed, from combining raw plant, animal or synthetic materials to actually producing the perfume (*enfleurage*, distilling and extraction). This journey into the land of fragrances leads into a room where a remarkable collection of flasks, some dating back to Antiquity, are displayed in glass cabinets. The tour ends on the roof, in the museum's greenhouse where fragrant plants such as jasmin, vetiver, *rose de mai* and vanilla are cultivated.

The **Musée d'Art et d'Histoire de la Provence** *(in summer, 10 AM to 1 PM and 2 PM to 7 PM; off-season, 10 AM to noon and 2 PM to 5 PM; Rue Mirabeau,* ☎ *93.36.01.61)*, located in Grasse's most elegant residence, evokes scenes of daily life. Complete with furniture, paintings and accessories, the museum illustrates a true Provençal *art de vivre*.

At the entrance to the town, coming from Cannes, there are many signs indicating the **Villa-Musée Fragonard** *(in summer, 10 AM to 1 PM and 2 PM to 7 PM; off-season, 10 AM to noon and 2 PM to 6 PM; 23 Bd Fragonard,* ☎ *93.40.32.64)*. A native of Grasse, famous 18th-century painter Jean-Honoré Fragonard made a gift of four paintings representing the stages of a suitor's conquest — *Le Rendez-Vous, La Poursuite, Les Lettres,* and *L'Amant Couronné* — to the Comtesse du Barry, mistress of Louis XV. Magnificent replicas of these paintings adorn the rooms of the Villa.

Outdoor Activities

This area is perfect for all kinds of sports, including winter sports from December to April. Tennis courts are in great abundance, and the tourism office can direct you to the closest one.

 Beaches and Water Sports

Every kind of beach can be found along this coast. There are sandy beaches, rocky beaches and near Nice, there are pebble beaches. They tend to get sandier as you approach Cannes. Cap d'Antibes has a few pleasant little beaches; some of them charge admission but do offer certain facilities. Beaches on the Cape are mostly rocky but become sandy again towards Juan-les-Pins. At Cannes, the beaches offer many facilities. There is an admission charge to most of these beaches since they belong to the hotels on the Croisette. Lounge chairs and parasols can be rented by the day or half-day, with prices ranging from 30 to 60 F. These beaches usually offer water sports equipment rental at reasonable prices.

For **windsurfing**, Antibes (at the entrance to the Cape) or Cannes (near the Palm Beach Hôtel, at the far end of the Croisette) are the best places to go. Rental costs about 60 F per hour.

Boats and sailboats can also be rented. Enquire at the tourism offices at the beach resorts for more information.

 Golf

The biggest and most beautiful course is between **Opio** and **Valbonne**, 16 km from Cannes and 35 km from Nice (*Château de la Bégude; Route de Roquefort-les-Pins,* ☎ *93.12.00.08,* ⇄ *93.12.26.00).* This golf course was established in a beautiful nature park by Club Med, whose vacation "village" is in Opio.

 Hiking

From Antibes

The Cours de la Brague *(elevations between 100 and 120 m; duration: 3 hours 30 minutes).* Go to Biot (by N 98 and D 4) and park in the village. Take Chemin de l'Ibac. An *Office national des Forêts* sign indicates the way to the river. Go to the sign indicating the Pont des Tamarins and continue to Point de la Verrière. Double back along the same route.

Gorges de la Cagne *(starting elevation: 425 m, highest point: 730 m; duration: six hours).* Begin at **Vence**. Take D 2 towards Coursegoules for one kilometre, then turn right on Chemin du Riou. Follow this road for three kilometres and leave the car at the little parking lot. Cross over the footbridge and follow the red markers. The trail climbs up along the Cagne River. Take a dip along the way in one of the little ponds. At the fallen bridge of the abandoned mine, go back along the same trail. You could also continue on one of the trails indicated on the sign, either the GR 51 or the Cap S.S.E, which is the marked trail connecting Baou des Blancs in the west to Baou des Noirs in the east. Go back to the sign and go down the hill. Head towards the Chemin du Riou and walk two kilometres to the parking lot.

Baou de St-Jeannet ou de la Gaude *(starting elevation: 400 m, highest* *point: 800 m and 750 m respectively; duration: three or four hours there and back).* Go to St-Jeannet (see "Tour A: For nature-lovers" in the "Exploring" section, p 240). Leave your car at the parking lot. Climb up to the village and turn right after the Auberge St-Jeannet. Climb up and follow the signs. The huge peak on the left is the Baou de St-Jeannet; the smaller peak on the right is the Baou de La Gaude. A pretty little oak forest stands at its peak. The Summit of Baou de St-Jeannet offers a fabulous panoramic view over St-Jeannet, the neighbouring hills and the Côte d'Azur.

  Downhill and Cross-Country Skiing

The climate and skiing conditions in the Alpes-Maritimes vary considerably from year to year. Call for information before heading out (see the "Practical Information" section on p 239 for the telephone numbers). The best months for skiing are January, February and March. Trails and runs usually have enough, even a lot of snow at this time. Equipment rental is available on-site at reasonable prices.

Valberg

This pretty winter resort has a multitude of mountain chalets. To reserve a hotel or rent an apartment, refer to the "Practical Information" section, p 240.

A bus service connects Valberg to Nice *(from the bus terminal, Promenade du Paillon, ☎ 93.85.61.81)* and the airport. Information: Tourist Office, ☎ 93.23.02.66. Note: Reservations required.

By car, take N 202 from the Nice airport towards Digne-Les-Bains for about 50 km, then take D 28 towards Beuil.

The road crosses the Gorges du Cians. Valberg is just 6 km from Beuil.

Isola 2000 ★

This modern resort was built in the '70s in a completely remote area. Concrete must have been a bargain when this town was built, with its succession of chairlifts, restaurants, hotels, shops, cinemas etc. All is very functional, but you won't find romantic ambience here!

To get to Isola from Nice by car, take N 202 towards Digne for about 30 km, then take D 2205 towards St-Sauver-de-Tinée. D 97 rises 17 km up to Isola.

 Accommodation

■ Cagnes

Hôtel **Le Cagnard** *(650-900 F, app. 1,400 F; pb, ≡, ℝ, ℜ; Rue Pontis-Long, ☎ 93.20.73.21, ⇄ 93.22.06.39)* is at the heart of the old town and is a member of the *Relais et Châteaux*. All the rooms have modern bathrooms. Most of the apartments have large terraces with a panoramic view of the sea and the hills. The area is very romantic and the prices are reasonable considering the remarkable location. Getting there is a bit complicated, but a valet service is available to take care of your car. The hotel is three kilometres from the Nice Airport. Horseback riding, tennis, golf and a pool aren't far away. The restaurant *($$$-$$$$)*, known for its very fine, traditional cuisine, has a terrace with a wide-open view of the Côte d'Azur.

■ **Vence**

L'Hôtel de Provence *(200-350 F, 400 F for three people; ps or pb; closed mid-Jan to mid-Feb; 9 Av. Marcellin Maurel, ☎ 93.58.04.21)* is a pretty little hotel in a quiet courtyard, located near the south entrance to the old town. Ask for room 6 *(350 F)* which has a large rooftop terrace, or rooms 1 and 2 *(320 F)* each with smaller terraces.

On the other side of Vence, at the beginning of Route du Col de Vence, **La Roseraie** *(370 F, 550 F for three people; pb or ps, tv, R, ≈; closed Nov. 15 to end of Feb; Av. Henri Giraud, ☎ 93.58.02.20, ⇄ 93.58.99.31)* offers good value. Surrounded by a most beautiful garden, this hotel has a pool and a lovely view over the old medieval town. La Roseraie is not pretentious and makes you feel at home. The staff is very friendly.

■ **Saint-Jeannet**

L'Auberge de Saint-Jeannet *(300 F; ps, tv; closed mid-Jan to mid-Feb; ☎ 93.24.90.06, ⇄ 93.24.70.60)* is located at the entrance to the old town. Register at the restaurant first, since the rooms are in a separate building. The hotel is simple, very clean and very quiet. The main floor has a little salon for guests on the main floor. It feels good to escape to the silence of this old town after having spent a day in the hustle and bustle of the Côte d'Azur.

■ **Gattières**

Le Beau Site *(220-240 F, extra bed 60 F; ps, tv lounge, full-board 80 F; Route de Vence, ☎ 93.08.60.06)* is located at the town's entrance, coming from Vence. This charming hotel is a lovely place to relax at a very reasonable price. The rooms are very clean, and the ones at the back overlook a beautiful garden. The dining room is big and bright, and there is also a garden where you can eat when the weather permits. We strongly recommend this hotel. It is very close to Nice, but offers a country atmosphere in a quiet, beautiful setting. The owners are very friendly and serve excellent food.

■ **Saint-Paul-de-Vence**

The **Hostellerie de la Fontaine** *(350 F; ps, ℜ; centre of town; ☎ 93.32.80.29 or 93.32.74.12)* offers the charm of days gone by. For those who like old-fashioned, modest style, this hotel offers rooms with a rustic appeal. The floors are tiled with *tomettes*, traditional Provençal ceramic. The family atmosphere is strong here. This hotel is a romantic island, and only a door separates it from the heart of the city. The food *($)* is also simple, but hearty and delicious. Enjoy a piece of home-made pie on the terrace overlooking the town's beautiful fountain.

Le Hameau *(390-650 F, extra bed 70 F; pb or ps, ≈, tv in some rooms, R, ≈; closed mid-Nov to mid-Feb except Christmas and New Year's; Route de La Colle, ☎ 93.32.80.24, ⇄ 93.32.55.75)* is one of the best places to stay in terms of value. It is just one kilometre from the town, close to the Fondation Maeght. The large garden and lovely pool offer a splendid view of Saint-Paul. The hotel was built in modern Provençal style with special attention paid to detail. The garden is a bit wild, just enough to give it a charming and romantic natural appeal. This is a paradise of beautiful flowers and green foliage. Families or groups of friends can take advantage of a special arrangement: two rooms sharing a living room that opens directly onto the garden are available for 720 F.

La Colombe d'Or *(1,150-1,350 F, half-board 1,550-1,750 F; pb,* ℝ *≈;* ☎ *93.32.80.02,* ⇄ *93.32.77.78)* is among the most prestigious hotels in the area. Formerly a post house, and later a modest inn run under the name of Robinson, this hotel was transformed into a hotel-restaurant by the son of the innkeeper. Over the years, a number of famous or soon-to-be-famous artists have stayed here. The owner, an art-lover, has created a living museum here. Sleep and dine in a sumptuous setting among paintings by the great masters, including Picasso, Matisse, Léger and many more. The rooms and dining areas are as rustic as they are elegant. Here, art and space are one. The pool in the indoor courtyard is highlighted by a large moving sculpture by Calder. In the summer, guests can enjoy breakfast or lunch in a very beautiful, shaded garden. But this sought-after little place is fairly expensive. They do not offer a *table d'hôte*, and a basic but fine gourmet meal costs about 300 F per person. Yves Montand and Simone Signoret adored staying here, so much that at one time, they actually became co-owners.

Le Mas d'Artigny *(885-1,425 F; app. 2,440 F-2,680 F, extra bed 180 F; pb,* ≡*,* ℝ *≈; Route de la Colle,* ☎ *93.32.84.54,* ⇄ *93.32.95.36).* In a huge 9 ha park perched high in the *Niçois* interior, this place offers a splendid view of the sea and the neighbouring hills. The hotel is a member of the privately-owned chain of *Grandes Étapes Françaises*, and it more than merits its membership. The hotel has a large pool measuring 11 by 25 m right in the park, and guests in the apartments enjoy exclusive use of their own smaller pool in absolute privacy. The hotel has a few boutiques and offers cultural excursions. They have prepared a brochure on this subject. Finally, the hotel is very well run. The reception is friendly, and the efficient staff are always available to help you. Guests are guaranteed a pleasant stay. This is a perfect place for a conference or celebration. There is also a restaurant, see p 264.

■ **Tourrettes-sur-Loup**

L'Auberge Belles Terrasses *(290 F, 390 F for three people; half-board 450 F, 600 F for three people; ps, pb,* ℜ*;* ☎ *93.59.30.03)* makes quite an impression. This Provençal establishment, in a lush, natural setting, is on Route de Grasse, one kilometre from Tourrettes-sur-Loup, and only 10 minutes from the sea. The rooms have terraces overlooking either the Côte d'Azur or the garden. There is also a television room for guests. The hotel is kept by a couple whose first priority is quality and comfort of the guests. Simplicity and a good atmosphere prevail. The hotel offers good value. See p 264 for a description of the restaurant.

A more comfortable, more exclusive and very quiet place to stay is the **Résidence des Chevaliers** *(420-680 F; pb, tv,* ≈*; Route du Caire,* ☎ *93.59.31.97).* This modern, Provençal-style hotel resembles an enormous villa. Perched on a hillside above the village, the hotel offers a lovely panoramic view of the sea. It is run by a very discrete couple. The rooms have a terrace and beautiful bathrooms. The two rooms in the southeast and southwest corners are especially charming. The beautiful garden and the lovely pool make this hotel a fair value.

■ **Antibes**

Hotels are abundant in this very beautiful coastal city. Here are a few establishments that are well-known for the charming and quiet atmosphere they offer their guests:

Le Ponteil *(half-board 480-640 F, mandatory during high season; ps, ℜ; closed end of Nov to end of Dec; 11 Impasse Jean Mensier, ☎ 93.34.67.92, ⇄ 93.34.49.47)* is located at the gates of Cap D'Antibes. We loved this place! The hotel is in the heart of an oasis of flowers and greenery, sheltered from the noise, yet still close to the sea. A warm family ambience makes you feel welcome right away. The rooms are small but nice. The owners themselves do the cooking, and during the summer you can eat on the tree-shaded terrace. In short, a carefully-tended country inn right in the heart of the city.

If you're on a budget and are looking for good value, go to **La Jabotte** *(240-340 F with shower on the landing or ps; half-board 500-590 F; closed Nov; 13 Av. Max Maurey, Cap d'Antibes, ☎ 93.61.45.89)*. To find this quaint little hotel, head towards the Cap along Boulevard Maréchal Leclerc and then Boulevard James Wyllie. At La Salis beach, turn right and go up the very narrow Rue Max Maurey. The hotel is only 50 m from the sea, yet is a quiet spot. It is run by a very nice young couple and offers comfort above its class. The owner serves typical French cuisine, and the sunny garden has a barbecue. It's the perfect place for the young at heart!

For a more comfortable place to stay, we suggest the **Petit Castel** *(460-490 F; ps or pb, ≡, tv; closed mid-Feb to beginning of Mar; 22 Chemin des Sables, ☎ 93.61.59.37, ⇄ 93.67.51.28)*. This charming '30s-style villa sits at the edge of Cap d'Antibes, in a residential area close to the beach, Casino and convention centre. The hotel has a rooftop solarium with a view of the sea and the mountains. It offers all the modern comforts but lacks a restaurant. However, breakfast is served on a beautiful veranda decorated with flowers.

■ **Juan-Les-Pins**

Bed and breakfast hotel **Juan Beach** *(240-370 F; ps or pb, tv room; closed Nov to Feb; 5 Rue de l'Oratoire, ☎ 93.61.02.89)* is near the Pinède Gould, 100 m from the beaches. It is close to the convention centre and the casino. The owners guarantee you a relaxing and enjoyable holiday. Although the rooms are rather small, they are clean and well-kept. A few rooms have terraces. Meals are alfresco, and breakfast is served in the garden shaded by lime and orange trees. The owner prepares regional specialities.

Close to Antibes and away from the main thoroughfares, we strongly recommend **Le Pré Catelan** *(half-board 860-890 F; ps or pb, ℜ; 22 Av. des Lauriers, ☎ 93.61.05.11, ⇄ 93.67.83.11)*. This '30s-style hotel is surrounded by trees, and the only sound to be heard is that of birds singing. Surprisingly, it is only 200 m from the beach and the casino. The hotel has a warm, country-inn atmosphere. The interior is tastefully decorated with beautiful antiques. The bathrooms are original, but very well maintained. A separate pavilion overlooking the large garden could accommodate four to six people. The restaurant has a nice fireplace and the kitchen is run by the friendly owner's son.

■ Cannes

The **Touring Hôtel** *(350-400 F; ps, tv, ℝ; 11 Rue Hoche, ☎ 93.38.34.40, ⇄ 93.38.73.34)* appealed to us because of its old 19th-century façade. It is located in the centre of the city on a semi-pedestrian street. The huge French doors open onto balconies, which makes the old-fashioned rooms very bright. The interior decoration is quaint and there is an elevator.

The **Beverly Hôtel** *(320-350 F; ps, tv; 14 Rue Hoche, ☎ 93.39.10.66, ⇄ 92.98.65.63)* is on the same pedestrian street. This family-run hotel has a more modern style and guarantees a pleasant stay. The rooms are slightly outdated but clean and comfortable nevertheless. The lobby is modest and a bit "American." There is an elevator.

In a higher category, we strongly suggest the **Hôtel Splendid** *(700-970 F; pb, ≡, C, tvc; 4 Rue Félix-Faure, ☎ 93.99.53.11, ⇄ 93.99.55.02)*. This huge hotel *(two top-floor suites with sloping ceilings and 62 rooms, 42 with C)* is marvellously situated in the centre of a huge public garden. The hotel is in the heart of Cannes and faces the sea and the Vieux Port. It is also close to the casino and the Palais des Festivals, and only a few steps from the sandy beaches. You will be delighted with the comfort and excellent service of this late 19th century-style hotel. Beautiful antique furniture graces the lounges as well as the rooms. Most of the rooms have a balcony or a terrace overlooking the sea. The comfort is irreproachable, and the bathrooms are very modern. Bathrobes are provided. This hotel offers very good value.

■ Mougins (old town)

If you're looking for a hotel with unbelievable charm and style, go to **Les Muscadins** *(750-950 F, 1,200 F for the suite; half-board 300 F extra; pb, ≡, tv, ℝ, ℜ; closed Feb and for two weeks before Christmas; 18 Bd Courteline, ☎ 93.90.00.43, ⇄ 92.92.88.23)*. There are eight rooms, the two most expensive of which look out over the sea. Every room is comfortable, and each is different, decorated with *objets d'art*, old paintings and specially selected pieces of furniture. The bathrooms are spacious and very modern. The main floor has a British pub and a restaurant that opens onto the terrace. The house, tucked away at the bottom of the old town exudes a modest sort of beauty. The reception is excellent. The value is good, and even better when you opt for half-board, since the food is amazing (see p. 266).

■ Mougins

Le Moulin de Mougins *(Chemin du Moulin, ☎ 93.75.78.24, ⇄ 93.90.18.55)* is not only a very fine restaurant, (see p 266) but also a wonderful place to stay. It offers three rooms *(800 and 900 F; pb, ≡, tv)* and two apartments *(1,300 F; pb, ≡, lounge, tv)* in a separate building. You will enjoy the magnificent fairy-tale surroundings, which abound with trees and flowers.

 Camping

■ La Colle-sur-Loup

La Vallon Rouge *(bungalow and trailer rental; stores, s, ℝ, ≈; Route de Grólières, ☎ 93.32.86.12)*. To get here from La Colle, take D 6 towards Gréolières. Alongside the river, on a flat, shaded area, you will enjoy the charming Niçois countryside, just 10 minutes from the sea. Lawn bowling, animation, sports, videos and evening activities are offered.

Le Castellas *(trailer and bungalow rental; s, R; Route de Roquefort,* ☎ *93.32.97.05).* To get here from La Colle, follow D 7 towards Roquefort for 5 km. This campground is 6 km from the sea, in a shaded area beside a river. Facilities are clean. Animation, games, fishing, swimming.

■ **Tourrettes-sur-Loup**

La Camassade *(trailer and studio rental; stores, s, R, ≈; 523 Route de Pie Lombard,* ☎ *93.59.31.54).* To get here, follow the signs around Tourrettes. This campground lies between the sea and the mountain, at an elevation of 400 m. It is most peaceful here in the shade of century-old oaks and olive trees.

■ **Antibes**

Le Rossignol *(tent and trailer rental; stores, s, R, ≈; 2074 Av. Jules Grec,* ☎ *93.33.56.98).* From Nice take N 7 towards Antibes. About 2 km before Fort Carré turn right on Chemin des 4 Chemins, and then turn right on the fourth street. The lush green setting is perfect for relaxation. The beaches are one kilometre away. Reserve by mail.

 Restaurants

■ **Vence**

L'Oranger *($; 3 Place de la Rouette,* ☎ *93.58.75.91)* is located in a quiet corner of Vieux-Vence, east of the church, near a Vietnamese restaurant in a sort of cul-de-sac. The owner herself will greet you and ensure the best service. Her husband prepares the dishes with special talent. The atmosphere is warm, with lots of ambience, perhaps because of the artistic personality of the owner. He will suggest a variety of dishes, and also offer you a complete fish and seafood menu. Try the *gratin de crabe* as an appetiser. For the main course, the meat dishes are all very tender. One stands out in particular: the exquisitely prepared *veau aux cinq parfums*. Note: this restaurant is not open for lunch and does not accept credit cards.

■ **Saint-Jeannet**

Au Vieux Four *($; closed Mon, Tue and Sat noon; 23 Rue du Château,* ☎ *93.24.97.41)* offers you excellent pizza cooked in a wood-burning oven. But pizza is not all you will find here, since Pascal, the young chef, also prepares quality fish and meat dishes. The atmosphere is warm and convivial.

We strongly suggest lunch or dinner at the **Auberge de Saint-Jeannet** *($; at the entrance to the old village;* ☎ *93.24.90.06).* This restaurant is one of the places that makes the French countryside so charming. The setting is rustic, and in the summertime the windows are wide open. You can also enjoy your meal on the little terrace. Jackie and her team ensure wonderful service and offer excellent menus at reasonable prices. We suggest the *farcis* or the *raviolis frais niçois* as an appetiser, and the catch of the day as a main course.

■ **Saint-Paul-de-Vence**

See the "Accommodations" section for the restaurants at the Hostellerie de la Fontaine (p 259) and of the Colombe d'Or (p 260).

The restaurant of the **Mas d'Artigny** *($$; Route de La Colle,* ☎ *93.32.84.54,* ⇄ *93.32.95.36)* offers excellent, beautifully presented, gourmet cuisine. If you like fish and shellfish, you've come to the right place. The desserts are pure delight. The quality is so impeccable that the prices are justified. Service is excellent and the wine waiter offers very good suggestions. See p 260 for a description of the hotel.

There are several quaint little restaurants along the ramparts at the west end of the town. We especially recommend **La Sierra** *($$)*. The Texan-style decoration is a little surprising to see in this part of the country. Provençal cuisine is served here. Make a reservation or arrive early to get a table on the little terrace from which you can enjoy the magnificent view.

■ **Tourrettes-sur-Loup**

Le Mediéval *($; closed Thu; 6 Grand'Rue,* ☎ *93.59.31.63)* is on the little street that goes around the old town close to the main square. In a medieval-Provençal setting, you will enjoy excellent service, provided by the very friendly owner himself. Provençal cuisine is served at a very reasonable price.

The restaurant at the **Auberge Belles Terrasses** *($;* ☎ *93.59.30.03)* offers three standard menus. Their specialities are *cuisses de grenouilles provençales* (frogs legs), *canard à l'orange* (duck) and *lapin à la moutarde* (rabbit). Game is also served in the fall. See p 260 for a description of the inn.

■ **Antibes**

La Taverne du Safranier *($; closed Mon and Tue at noon; Place du Safranier,* ☎ *93.34.80.50)* looks out over a pleasant, calm square where the many lanes and streets of Vieux Antibes begin. The restaurant is removed from the crowds since it is off the beaten tourist path of Antibes. This square is most charming, and so very Provence. You can enjoy your meal outdoors beneath the awning or beneath the stars. Provençal specialities and mussels are served. For dessert, we suggest their excellent home-made pie.

The **Restaurant de la Gravette** *($; closed Tue; 48 Bd d'Aguillon;* ☎ *93.34.18.60)*, offers seafood specialities including bouillabaisse, grilled fish, scampi and fried seafood. This restaurant has a huge terrace looking out onto a pedestrian street. It is just behind the big wall on the right side just past the entrance to Vieil-Antibes. They offer a lunch menu which includes appetiser, main course and dessert for 58 F.

Le Caméo *($; closed Nov and Dec; Place nationale,* ☎ *93.34.24.17)* is a combination of hotel, bed and breakfast and bar. Their specialities are paella and *marmite des pêcheurs* (fish stew). Other dishes are more ordinary. The value is very good, and you can eat outdoors under the plane trees of the Place National, in the heart of Vieil-Antibes.

L'Auberge provençale *($$; closed Mon and Tue noon; Place nationale,* ☎ *93.34.13.24)* is also in the square in the heart of the city. Inside, there is a very attractive summer garden. The setting is rustic and spacious. The menu consists of fish, seafood and shellfish, and house specialities are bouillabaisse and *paupiettes de saumon.*

■ **Juan-les-Pins**

For a meal that is truly a seafood feast, go to **L'Oasis** *($$; closed in the evenings during winter; Bd Charles Guilaumont,* ☎ *93.61.45.15).* This popular restaurant is right on the beach. Guests may park in the large lot across the boulevard, just behind the railroad tracks. During the summer you can eat outside, on the beach. Otherwise, the dining room has large bay windows, which are all that separate you from the sea. The view extends from Cap d'Antibes to yhe Îles Lérins. This family-run restaurant has established a reputation for their fish and seafood specialities. You can enjoy a walk on the beach after dinner. The value and service are both excellent. On weekends during the summer, or on request, the restaurant organises dancing evenings.

■ **Cannes**

If you'd like to take a break for coffee and dessert, stop at **Brasserie d'Gigi** *($; 5 Rue Meynadier,* ☎ *92.98.81.88).* Enjoy a piece of *tarte tatin* along this lively pedestrian street.

À la table d'Oscar *($; closed Sun evening and Mon; 26 Rue Jean Jaurès,* ☎ *93.38.42.46)* offers you a *table d'hôte* for 65 F. Oscar's speciality: *la choucroûte alsacienne.*

On a pedestrian street between the sea and the station, the **North Beach cafe** *($; closed Sun; 8 Rue du 24 août,* ☎ *93.38.40.51)* offers a *table d'hôte* at 67 F. House specialities are pasta, crepes and salads. It's an "in" spot, decorated all in white and very bright. Highly recommended.

Don't worry, you'll be comfortable at **Au mal assis** *($$; closed Nov to Christmas; 15 Quai Saint-Pierre,* ☎ *93.39.13.38).* This pleasant restaurant at the Vieux-Port offers a fixed menu for 120 F. You can sit outside on the terrace and enjoy the house specialities, which the local fish and bouillabaisse.

Also in the Vieux-Port is another restaurant recommended to us by the locals. The **Gaston Gastounette** *($$; closed for two or three weeks in Jan; 7 Quai Saint-Pierre,* ☎ *93.39.47.92)* specialises in fish dishes and bouillabaisse, which are served on the air-conditioned terrace.

If you prefer Italian cuisine, go to **Vesuvio** *($$; 68 La Croisette,* ☎ *93.94.08.28).* Excellent pizza and fresh pasta can be enjoyed at the bar or on the terrace. A meal will cost about 150 F to 200 F.

A restaurant for connoisseurs: **Astoux & Brun** *($$; 27 Rue Félix Faure,* ☎ *93.39.21.87, telephone reservations are not accepted)* has a very good reputation. House specialities include fish and shellfish served on the air-conditioned terrace. Not to be confused with "Chez Astoux."

Very fine cuisine comes at a price, but **Royal Gray** *($$$; closed Sun, Mon and Feb; Hôtel Gray d'Albion, 6 Rue des États-Unis,* ☎ *93.99.79.60)* offers nothing but the best. The air-conditioned terrace, neighbouring garden and background music guarantee a most pleasant atmosphere. The *table d'hôte* is expensive at 550 F, but the quality fully justifies the price.

■ **Mougins (old town)**

Mougins is a beautiful town to see, and also a good place for a gastronomic adventure or two.

Muscadins *($$; closed Feb and Dec until Christmas and Tue between Oct and Easter; 18 Bd Courteline, ☎ 93.90.00.43)* is one restaurant you must try. The young cook, Noël Mantel, uses only quality ingredients. With his Provençal-Italian flavours, he convinced us of his talent. Indulge your taste buds with huge poached lobster *ravioles* in a clear shellfish broth. But then you'd have to do without the Italian *risotto* with *fleurs de courgettes* or the *rougets* fried in olive oil with purple artichokes and fresh herbs. Of course there is the *magret de canard sur la peau* in pepper sauce sweetened with honey. In other words, you will eat well here. The atmosphere is equally pleasant in winter when the beautiful dining room is warmed by the fireplace, and in summer when the terrace, decorated in blue and white where flowers and sparkling silverware come to life.

But Mougins also has another very good restaurant called the **Relais à Mougins** *($$; closed Mon and Tue at noon; Place de la Mairie, ☎ 93.90.03.47)*. The chef, André Surmain holds the title "*maître cuisinier de France*." In his younger days, in 1961, he established the famous Lutèce restaurant in New York. Still today, this master chef has but one ambition: to create dishes inspired by products that are in season. The chef loves to make suggestions. Let him guide your choice and you won't be disappointed. You can eat well for 200 F or for 400 F. Maître Surmain tends to his guests in a Provençal-style dining room, or in a rustic setting on the terrace (covered in winter), which opens up onto a beautiful square that invites you to linger in the summertime. It is obvious that Maître Surmain lives for his profession. In short, fine dining is guaranteed.

■ **Mougins**

Another great master of French cuisine is Roger Vergé, who runs **Le Moulin de Mougins** *($$ at noon, $$$ in the evening; closed Mon, Thu noon and Feb and Mar; Chemin du Moulin, ☎ 93.75.78.24)*. This restaurant is set in a marvellous 16th-century mill, in the Notre-Dame de Vie district, on the old road that used to lead up to the old town. It is surrounded by a lush garden. Every dish prepared in this kitchen is a culinary masterpiece. The presentation is beautiful, and sophisticated ingredients are often used. The service is invisible, impeccable and always attentive. In the dining rooms, much attention has been paid to the decor, where the modest setting is complemented with period furniture and works of art from the *École de Nice*. You can enjoy your meal in one of the mill's lounges, or in the beautiful room with windows overlooking the garden. There are two set menus, one at 585 F and the other at 700 F. Expensive...yes...but worth every *sou*. A business lunch in served at noon for 245 F. Here is a wonderful opportunity to discover this prestigious Mougins restaurant and meet a master chef.

If you'd like an introduction to Vergé's techniques, his cooking school offers an enlightening and amusing course *(Moulin de Mougins; ☎ 93.75.35.70)*.

A small boutique also sells home-made products. And finally, *La lettre de mon Moulin*, published on an irregular basis, provides all sorts of information about Monsieur Vergé's establishment.

 Entertainment

To find out about all the events in the area, consult the *L'Officiel des Loisirs* or *La Semaine des Spectacles*, sold at newsstands.

During July and August, there are little music and theatre festivals in almost all the towns along the Côte d'Azur. Check with the tourism bureau in each town for dates and programmes.

■ Cagnes

Le Diamant *(1 Chemin du Lautin, RN 7 Pont de la Cagne, ☎ 93.73.48.22).*

■ Biot

Musical Recitals in Biot
End of May to end of Jun; Église de Biot; ☎ 93.65.05.85.

■ Antibes

Le Sucrier *(Wed to Sat evening; 6 Rue des Bains, ☎ 93.34.22.00).* In the heart of Vieil Antibes. You can enjoy imaginative cuisine, painting exhibitions and evening musical or theatre performances, all under one roof.

Casino La Siesta *(May to Oct; Route du bord de Mer, ☎ 93.33.31.31).* Slot machines, French and English roulette, blackjack.

Antibes Music Festival
Beginning of Jul; Chantier Naval Opéra, Port Vauban, ☎ 92.90.54.60.

■ Juan-les-Pins

Antibes Juan-les-Pins International Jazz Festival End of Jul; Pinède Gould, ☎ 92.90.53.00.

EDEN Casino *(8 PM to 5 AM; Bd Baudoin, across from the Pinède, ☎ 92.93.71.71).* Roulette, black jack and slot machines.

■ Cannes

El Flamenco *(10 Bd Jean Hibert, on the seashore, 150 m from Sofitel, ☎ 93.39.00.16).* Enjoy traditional Spanish cuisine and a flamenco dancing show in an Andalusian atmosphere.

Le Galion *(3 Rue Félix Faure, in Place de l'Hôtel de Ville, ☎ 93.39.74.00).* This restaurant, with its elegant decor, is open 24 hours.

Lobby Bar *(Royal Hôtel Casino, 605 Av. du Général-de-Gaulle, ☎ 92.07.70.00).* Relaxing, comfortable, convivial atmosphere. Dance floor.

Carlton Casino Club *(70 F; 7:30 PM to 4 AM; 58 La Croisette, ☎ 93.68.00.33).* English and French roulette, black-jack, punto banco.

Casino Croisette *(11 AM to 3 AM, until 4 AM on weekends, until 5 AM Jul-Aug; Palais des Festivals, ☎ 93.38.12.11).* Two rooms with 290 slot machines; English and French roulette, black-jack, chemin-de-fer, punto banco.

Festivals

Cannes Musique Passion End of Apr; Palais des Festivals, ☎ 92.99.31.08.

International Film Festival Mid-May; Palais des Festivals, ☎ 93.39.01.01.

Nuits musicales du Suquet (Music Festival) End Jul; Parvis de l'Église Notre-Dame d'Espérance, ☎ 92.98.62.77.

International Dance Festival Last week of Nov; Palais des Festivals; information: ☎ 92.99.31.08, ⇄ 92.98.98.76.

 Shopping

■ **Around Vence**

La Confiserie des Gorges du Loup *(9 AM to noon and 2 PM to 6 PM; 12 km from Grasse, on Route de Vence)* offers traditionally prepared jams and candied fruit. Entirely decorated with 18th and 19th-century Provençal furniture, the store features beautiful armoires, buffets, bread boxes, tables and benches. They also have a store in the port district of Nice.

■ **Mougins (old town)**

La boutique du Moulin et la cave du Moulin *(at the entrance to the village, going up towards the main square, ☎ 93.90.19.18 or 92.92.06.88)* is one of Roger Vergé's sidelines. He is the head chef at the Moulin de Mougins. This store sells the *Produits du Soleil* line, which includes seasonings, jams and jellies, mixed spices as well as a selection of teas and books by Roger Vergé. There are also quality wines, including some selected by Vergé. Exquisitely gift-wrapped bottles of cognac, eau-de-vie or champagne can be sent abroad as gifts.

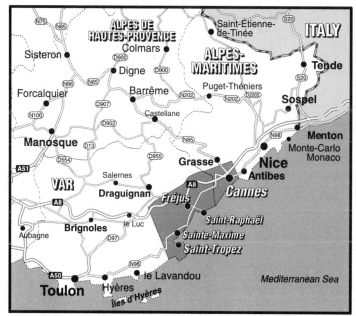

FROM CANNES TO SAINT-TROPEZ ★★★

Fanatics of the sea, the beach, and beautiful landscapes of rolling hills perfect for hiking will find exactly that in the magnificent region stretching from Cannes to Saint-Tropez. A multitude of seaside resorts are spread out along the coast, and behind them, the countryside awaits exploration — by car, by bicycle or by foot. Beyond the Massif de l'Estérel, which extends to Fréjus, are the Maures, a vast hilly area stretching to Hyères. Its highest peaks reaching altitudes from 550 to 650 metres.

Unfortunately, the Côte d'Azur is becoming very developed. The hot-spot of the area is unquestionably Saint-Tropez and its peninsula. Saint-Tropez is incredibly charming, but its charm is best appreciated outside of the peak summer season. Don't miss visiting the peninsula, where one superb beach follows the next, and two lovely villages await: Ramatuelle and Gassin.

Finally, to complete your visit of this region, a picturesque tour through the Massif des Maures is suggested.

 Finding Your Way Around

For those planning to spend most of their vacation in the region of the Massif des Maures or around the Îles d'Hyères, it would be better to land at the Toulon/Hyères airport rather than at Nice. However, there are coach connections to Fréjus/Saint-Raphaël and Saint-Tropez from the Nice airport.

■ By Car

The easiest way to see this beautiful corner of the world is by car. However, remember to avoid driving in rush hour between noon and 1 PM, or in the early evening during the peak season. The outskirts of Saint-Tropez between 5 PM and 8 PM are to be especially avoided, unless you want to waist precious time in your car.

There are two ways to get to Fréjus from Cannes: by Route **N 98**, which follows the sea, or **N 7**, which goes through the magnificent Massif de l'Estérel. Both are very scenic roads and offer dazzling vistas. Of course, by doing a loop from Cannes you could see both the mountains and the sea in the same day. Hikers and walkers can and should stop while crossing l'Estérel by car for a quick stroll or a major hike.

From Fréjus, there is only one way to get to Saint-Tropez. Follow the coastline road **N 98** that passes through Sainte-Maxime and Port Grimaud. In fact, once past Fréjus, the other road, the **N 7**, swings north and follows the highway.

If you want to cut down your travelling time between Cannes and Saint-Tropez, take the **A 8 - E 80**. Exit at **D 25** (12 km past Fréjus) which will take you to Saint-Maxime and Saint-Tropez.

■ By Train

The train is another good option if you limit your visit to the seaside resorts between Cannes and Fréjus, as the rail line follows the coastline beside the **N 98**. However, from Fréjus, the train goes all the way north of the Massif des Maures and follows the highway (**A 8**) to Toulon. The portion between Fréjus, Saint-Tropez and Le Lavandou cannot be reached by train, despite certain efforts that were made at the end of the last century. Of course, these cities are accessible by bus from Fréjus.

■ By Bus

Several coach and bus services are available between the villages and towns of this region but these can prove to be long trips. On the other hand, there is a shuttle every hour between Cannes, Saint-Raphaël and Fréjus. Enquire about schedules with the tourist offices, which you will find listed in the following section.

 Practical Information

■ Fréjus

Tourist Office:
Office municipal du tourisme
325 Rue Jean Jaurès
☎ 94.17.19.19

Tourist Office:
Gare SNCF
123 Rue W.-Rousseau
☎ 94.82.16.88

■ Grimaud

Tourist Office
1 Bd des Aliziers
☎ 94.43.26.98

■ Saint-Tropez (83990)

Tourist Offices
Quai Jean Jaurès
☎ 94.97.45.21

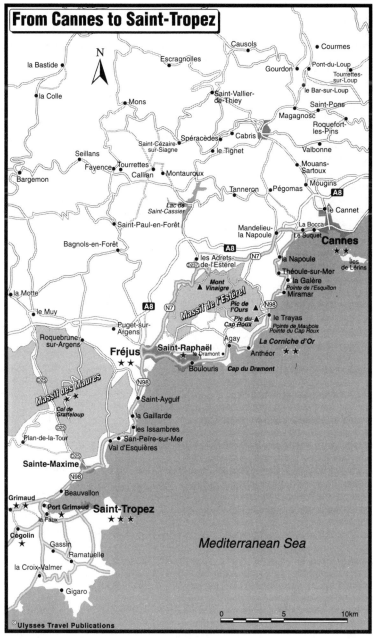

From Cannes to Saint-Tropez

N

Causols

• Courmes

la Bastide •

Escragnolles

Gourdon •

Pont-du-Loup
Tourrettes-
sur-Loup

• la Colle

• Mons

Saint-Vallier-
de-Thiey

le Bar-sur-Loup

Saint-Pons

Magagnosc

Roquefort-
les-Pins

Spéracèdes   • Cabris

Saint-Cézaire-
sur-Siagne

le Tignet

Valbonne

Seillans

Fayence• Tourrettes
Callian   • Montauroux

Mouans-
Sartoux

• Mougins

Bargemon

Tanneron   • Pégomas

A8

Lac de
Saint-Cassier

• le Cannet

Saint-Paul-en-Forêt

Mandelieu-
la Napoule

La Bocca
Le Suquet

Bagnols-en-Forêt

A8

les Adrets-
D237 de-l'Estérel

N7

• la Napoule

Cannes
★ ★

îles
de Lérins

Théoule-sur-Mer

• la Galère

la Motte •

Mont
Vinaigre

Pointe de l'Esquillon
Miramar

le Muy •

Massif de l'Estérel

Pic de
l'Ours

A8   N7

N98

Puget-sur-
Argens

Pic du
Cap Roux

• le Trayas

Pointe de Maubois
Pointe du Cap Roux

Roquebrune-
sur-Argens

Fréjus
★ ★

Saint-Raphaël
le Dramont •

Agay

La Corniche d'Or

Anthéor   ★ ★

Boulouris   *Cap du Dramont*

N98

Massif des Maures

Col de
Gratteloup

D25

D25

Saint-Aygulf

• la Gaillarde

Plan-de-la-Tour •

• les Issambres

• San-Peïre-sur-Mer
Val d'Esquières

D25

Sainte-Maxime

N98

• Beauvallon

Grimaud
• ★ ★

• Port Grimaud

Saint-Tropez
★ ★ ★

le Faux

Cogolin
★

Gassin

Ramatuelle

la Croix-Valmer

Mediterranean Sea

• Gigaro

0   5   10km

© Ulysses Travel Publications

Bus Station
Av. Général Leclerc
☎ 94.65.21.00 or 94.97.41.21
Summer coach schedules for connections to Toulon-Hyères Airport:
☎ 94.97.45.21

Location Deux Roues (bicycles, mountain bike, and scooter rental)
3 and 5 Rue Quaranta (near Place du XVe Corps)
☎ 94.97.00.60

Hospital
☎ 94.97.47.30

Duty Pharmacy
☎ 94.07.08.08

■ **Ramatuelle**

Tourist Office
1 Av. Clémenceau
☎ 94.79.26.04

 Exploring

■ **From Cannes to Fréjus** ★★

From Cannes, we suggest a **scenic tour** which can be done in a day and will return you to Cannes. The road takes you full-circle, starting by the seaside road (N 98) to Saint-Raphaël and Fréjus. To return to Cannes, you will traverse the Massif de l'Estérel via N 7. If you like sunsets over the sea, reverse the circuit.

Théoule-sur-Mer

Théoule-sur-Mer is a small, peaceful seaside resort right next to Cannes. Its main attraction is the Parc Forestier de la Pointe de l'Aiguille close by, in the Massif de l'Estérel. This park is particu-

larly spectacular in that it stretches along the coast and offers magnificent views and possibilities for pleasant hikes (see p 282).

Next, the road goes through small villages which all allow easy access to l'Estérel by walking trails. From **Miramar**, you can make a quick climb towards l'Esquillon and enjoy a spectacular view.

Further on at **Trayas**, you can enjoy other trails which feature several lookout points over l'Estérel and the sea. Trayas is the heart of the **Corniche d'Or** ★★.

Not far past Trayas, near Pointe de Maubois, another trail leads towards **Pic du Cap Roux**. The climb to the peak can prove to be difficult for some, but is really worth the effort.

Saint-Raphaël ★

The noteworthy beginnings of this seaside village go back to the 11th century, when its port became more important than that of Fréjus. However, its original settlement dates back even further. During the Roman era, Saint-Raphaël was already a residential suburb of Fréjus.

The city's attractions include seaside resorts, a casino and a marina. The resort was developed mostly during the 19th century, as evidenced by the few remaining villas which attracted artists and the high society. The *belle époque* era did indeed bestow a certain charm upon the city.

Fréjus ★★

Spend your time here visiting the old city. Its origins go back to Roman times

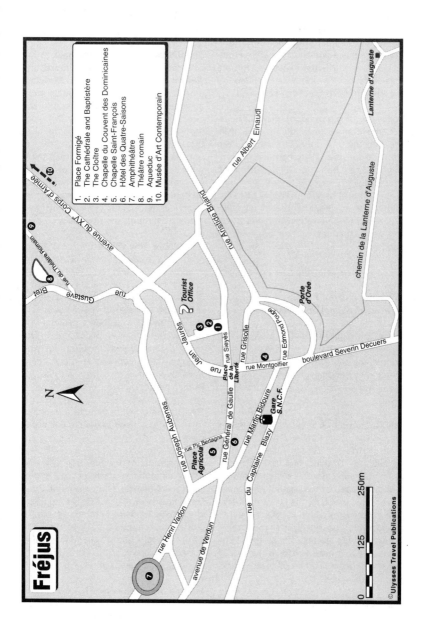

Fréjus

1. Place Formigé
2. The Cathédrale and Baptistère
3. The Cloître
4. Chapelle du Couvent des Dominicaines
5. Chapelle Saint-François
6. Hôtel des Quatre-Saisons
7. Amphithéâtre
8. Théâtre romain
9. Aqueduc
10. Musée d'Art Contemporain

Tourist Office

Lanterne d'Auguste

chemin de la Lanterne d'Auguste

rue Albert Einaudi

rue Aristide Briand

Porte d'Orée

rue Jean Jaurès

rue Sieyès

rue Grisolle

Place de la Liberté

rue Montgolfier

rue Edmond Poupé

boulevard Séverin Decuers

rue du XV° Corps d'Armée

rue du Théâtre Romain

rue Gustave Bret

rue Joseph Aubenas

rue Pic Bertagna

Place Agricola

rue Général de Gaulle

rue Martin Bidouré

rue du Capitaine Blazy

Gare S.N.C.F.

rue Henri Vadon

avenue de Verdun

N

0   125   250m

© Ulysses Travel Publications

when the Forum Julii (Julius market), located on Voie Aurélienne linking Rome and Arles, was an important stopping place for the Romans. From AD 374 onward, the town became an episcopal city which was fortified at the beginning of the 14th century.

Following this period of glory, Fréjus became a small insignificant city until the beginning of the 20th century. At the end of the 19th century, Saint-Raphaël had been at the forefront of the evolving tourism industry. Only since the end of World War II has this city began to regain some of its stature, as development has intensified, but the consequences of this are controversial.

This tour begins at the heart of the old city. Follow the many signs indicating the city centre. There is a parking lot nearby where you can leave your car.

Place Formigé (1) is the site of the cathedral, baptistery, and cloister. It is named for the architect who directed major restoration work on the baptistery and the cloister between 1920 and 1930.

The **Cathédrale ★★ (2)** *(8 AM to noon and 4 PM to 7 PM; ☎ 94.51.26.30)*, built on the site of an ancient Roman temple, is Gothic, but nevertheless presents many Roman characteristics. It is composed of two naves. The main nave dates back to the 13th century. The other nave, which supports the bell tower, dates back to the 11th century but was only completed in the 12th century. Most noteworthy in this building are the exquisitely sculpted wood Renaissance-style doors.

We strongly recommend the guided tour of the baptistery and the cloister.

You will learn a wealth of fascinating historical details.

The **Baptistère ★★**, dating back to the 5th century, is especially interesting since it is one of Gaul's oldest Christian monuments. Pillars and capitals from ancient Roman sites were used in the construction of this building with octagonal walls. It's interesting to note that the entrance to the baptistery is not the original doorway. Instead there were originally two doors on either side: one small door, by which those to be baptised entered, and a large one by which they exited, since they had "grown" through their baptism.

The **Cloître ★★ (3)** *(in winter, Wed to Mon 9 AM to noon and 2 PM to 5 PM; in summer, Sun and Sat 9 AM to 7 PM)* also incorporates several elements from old Roman buildings. It opens up to two floors of galleries around a well in the centre. The wooden ceilings are painted with Apocalyptic scenes. The small archaeological museum, on the second floor, contains a magnificent mosaic which comes from an opulent Roman palace.

Finally, the city hall is also located in this square, housed in the old episcopal palace.

In the streets of the old city, are several other architectural treasures, namely the **Chapelle du Couvent des Dominicains ★ (4)**, on Rue Montgolfier, the **Chapelle Saint-François ★ (5)**, a Gothic church dating back to the early 16th century, and the **Hôtel des Quatre-Saisons ★ (6)**, on Rue du Général De Gaulle.

Visit the **Amphitheatre (7)** *(Wed to Mon 9:30 AM to noon and 2 PM to 6:30 PM; in winter, until 4:30 PM; ☎ 94.17.05.60)*, slightly to the west of the city-centre, and be transported back to Roman times. The amphitheatre is actually an arena since it forms a complete circle. It dates back to the beginning of the first millennium and has fallen to ruins over the centuries, its materials having been used in other constructions. The site is now being restored and hosts outdoor shows.

The ruins of the **Théâtre Romain (8)** can be found to the northeast of the city. Only vestiges of the stage and of the supporting walls of the stands remain.

Nearby, the ruins of the city walls, dating back to the first century BC are visible. These once completely surrounded the city-centre. They stretched all the way to the Amphitheatre, which was built outside of the walls.

Still on the same site, the **Aqueduc (9)**, also dating back to the 1st century BC, carried water to Fréjus from La Siagnole over an approximate distance of 40 km.

There is a lot to do in this area, starting with a visit to the **Musée d'Art Contemporain** ★★ **(10)** *(25 F; Tue to Sun 2 PM to 7 PM; ☎ 94.40.76.30; to get there: N 7 towards highway A 8, then follow the signs to the Capitou industrial zone)*. Set up in an old factory, the museum offers high-calibre temporary exhibits in wide, well-lit spaces.

Return to Cannes via highway A 8 or, if you have the time, by N 7, which passes through the beautiful landscape of Massif de l'Estérel. On the way, take D 237 and stop in the charming little village of **Les-Adrets-de-l'Estérel**, in the heart of the mountain range. This could be an interesting stop for travellers seeking the tranquillity of the Provençal countryside, since it is home to a few good hotels and restaurants.

■ **From Fréjus to Saint-Tropez** ★

The segment of the N 98 that runs along the sea between Fréjus and Saint-Tropez, via Sainte-Maxime and Port-Grimaud, offers fewer points of interest than the road between Cannes and Fréjus.

Port-Grimaud ★

A modern 20th century "Venetian" city, Port-Grimaud is the brainchild of architect François Spoerry. Canals spanned by bridges replace roads in this city. No cars are allowed, so visitors must leave their vehicles in the pay parking lot at the entrance to the village.

The market square and the Place du Sud are the two busy centres of this town, whose charm is the product of clever design from the ground up. Fortunately, the passing years are managing to give a more authentic look to the architecture.

Port-Grimaud is nonetheless a financial success for the investors and speculators who took an interest in the project since land prices have increased considerably since the village was created.

The village has an abundance of little restaurants and businesses of all kinds. At the bottom of the village, a large beach borders the sea.

A small **tourist train** *(adults 30 F, children 15 F; stops at Les Prairies de la mer camping ground, at Port-Grimaud's main entrance and at Place de l'Église in Grimaud; information: ☎ 94.56.30.60)* links Port-Grimaud to the old village of Grimaud.

Grimaud ★★

This typically Provençal village is worth taking the time to stroll through and explore. The ruins of the **château ★** dominate the village. Built in the 11th century, the castle was surrounded by three walls. It was torn down in 1655 under the orders of Cardinal Mazarin.

Most of the narrow streets are for pedestrians only. The great variety of plants and flowers that adorn the houses and gardens makes this village one of the most picturesque in the region.

Along Rue des Templiers you'll find the **Maison des Templiers ★**, a Renaissance-style building which is also called the *Maison des Arcades*. It stands facing the **Église Saint-Michel ★★** which was built in the 11th century in a purely Romanesque style.

Towards the cemetery, you'll see the restored **Moulin de Grimaud**, a mill dating back to the 12th century, as well as an 11th century chapel.

Finally, try, **Les Santons**, a Grimaud restaurant whose gastronomical delights should not be missed (see p 288).

Saint-Tropez ★★★

Despite all the clichés, Saint-Tropez really is one of the most beautiful and charming spot on the Côte d'Azur. It is situated on a magnificent bay, and its old town is authentically preserved thanks to careful renovations.

Is it any wonder that the Ligurians, the Celts, the Greeks and the Romans were attracted by the natural beauty of this little piece of paradise?

Since AD 739, the history of Saint-Tropez has been punctuated by constant wars, destruction and pillaging that persisted for several centuries. The tower of Château Suffren, at the far end of the port, was constructed at the end of the 10th century. It stands as testimony of the village's defence.

In 1441, the city was established once and for all with the arrival of Genoese families, and subsequently became a small independent republic. It was Colbert, France's centralizer, that put an end to this special status in 1672.

In the centuries that followed, fishermen and merchants transformed the village into a flourishing commercial centre. The 19th century brought on the Industrial Era, after which Saint-Tropez began to decline.

Fortunately, the development of the tourist industry near the end of the 19th century saved the city. Several artists settled here including Franz Liszt and Signac, followed by Matisse and Picabia. Writer Colette took up residence in a superb house near the Place aux Herbes, and later Anaïs Nin, Henry Miller's companion, came here to write the "Tahitian" chapter of her life.

Every summer from 1950 onward, the great stars of Paris such as Greco, Sagan, Vian and Prévert moved to "Saint-Trop."

Saint-Tropez always brings to mind Brigitte Bardot. Since she moved here in the 60s, the city has indeed become world-famous. Her reputation, even today, precedes her such that none can remain indifferent.

Despite the German bombings which destroyed the port in 1944, Saint-Tropez shines today in all its splendour

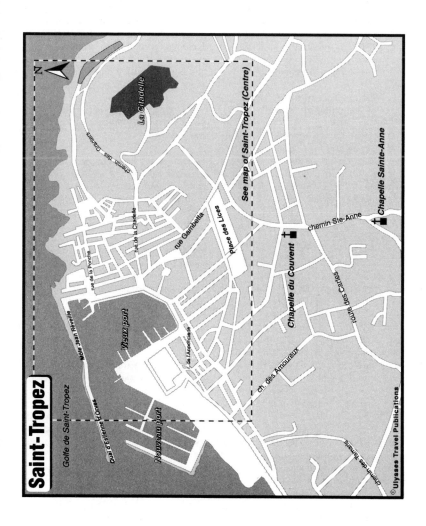

Saint-Tropez

Golfe de Saint-Tropez

Quai d'Estienne d'Orves

Môle Jean Réveille

Vieux port

Nouveau port

La Citadelle

chemin des Graniers

rue de la Citadelle

rue de la Ponche

rue Gambetta

Place des Lices

R. de l'Annonciade

See map of Saint-Tropez (Centre)

Chapelle du Couvent

chemin Ste-Anne

Chapelle Sainte-Anne

route des Carles

ch. des Amoureux

Chemin des Tamaris

© Ulysses Travel Publications

thanks to well-planned reconstruction. The hoards of tourists that invade the streets in July are a price to be paid for all that glory. For as the city bulges with all those people, much of the town loses its charm and its traditional appeal. Postpone your visit to the winter or spring, when the special light enhances the city's true splendour.. it is truly a wonder to behold!

Walking Tour of Saint-Tropez
(see map of the city)

Leave your car in one of the parking lots next to the new port or on Place des Lices. Don't waste your time and energy trying to find a parking spot near the old city, especially during the peak tourist season.

The tour begins at the southwest point of the Vieux-Port.

The old Notre-Dame de l'Annonciation chapel built in 1568, was transformed into a museum in 1955: the **Musée de l'Annonciade** ★★ **(1)** *(admission charge; summer, Wed to Mon 10 AM to noon and 5 PM to 7 PM; rest of year, 10 AM to noon and 2 PM to 6 PM; closed Nov; Place Grammont,* ☎ *94.97.04.01)*. The rooms are stunning. The museum contains, among other things, Georges Grammont's prestigious personal collection, which he bequeathed to the city in 1963.

The Musée de l'Annonciade is a dazzling reminder that Saint-Tropez was one of the most active centres of the artistic avant-garde at the beginning of 20th century, a status it owes mostly to the presence of neo-impressionist painter Paul Signac. Enchanted by the site and the exceptional quality of its light, he bought a house here at the end of the last century. Matisse, Derain and Marquet were likewise seduced. The collec-

tions are remarkable as much for their quality as for their homogeneity. The artists whose works are exhibited were inspired by the light and colours they found, each rendering them in their own style while remaining faithful to the subject. The museum's collection includes works from several of the great artistic movements that marked the beginning of the century including pointillism, fauvism and nabis.

Take Rue des Charrons from Place Grammont, take the first left and then the first right.

Maison des Papillons ★ **(2)** *(same schedule as Musée de l'Annonciade; 9 Rue Étienne Berny,* ☎ *94.97.63.45)* contains over 4,500 butterfly specimens, some of which are quite rare or on the verge of extinction.

Go back towards the port and walk along the docks.

Countless pleasure boats, some quite luxurious, are lined up along the docks. In front of Quai Suffren stands the **statue of Bailli de Suffren (3)**. Nearby, an archway leads to the fish market.

Continue along the docks and you will soon come to the tourist office, which marks the beginning of Quai Jean Jaurès. Hidden behind it is the very picturesque **Place aux Herbes** ★ **(4)**, where the lively fruit and vegetable markets fill the morning air with activity.

At the end of the dock, to the right, stands the **Tour Suffren** ★ **(5)**, dating back to the 10th century, and which played an important role in the city's history.

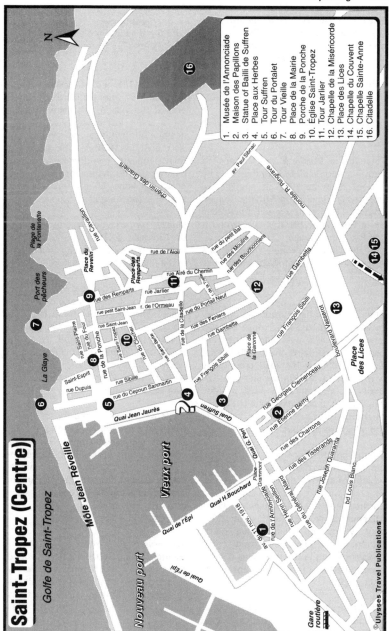

Saint-Tropez (Centre)

Golfe de Saint-Tropez

1. Musée de l'Annonciade
2. Maison des Papillons
3. Statue of Bailli de Suffren
4. Place aux Herbes
5. Tour Suffren
6. Tour du Portalet
7. Tour Vieille
8. Place de la Mairie
9. Porche de la Ponche
10. Église Saint-Tropez
11. Tour Jarlier
12. Chapelle de la Miséricorde
13. Place des Lices
14. Chapelle du Couvent
15. Chapelle Sainte-Anne
16. Citadelle

© Ulysses Travel Publications

Rue Portalet leads to **Tour du Portalet ★ (6)**, which was built in the 15th century and was part of the fortifications. From this vantage point, there is a good view of the **Tour Vieille ★ (7)**, another 15th century construction, which is at one end of the fishing port of La Ponche.

Go back towards Tour Suffren to get to Quartier de La Ponche.

Place de la Mairie ★ (8) features an amazing door sculpted, so they say, by natives from Zanzibar. It opens onto the lovely Rue de la Ponche, where another 15th century tower, the **Porche de la Ponche ★ (9)** stands, beyond it lies Place du Revelin. This square shelters the Hôtel La Ponche. The hotel's restaurant terrace at the back overlooks the fishing port of La Ponche (see p 285).

The fortifications surrounded the old town. The **Église Saint-Tropez ★ (10)**, inside the walls, was built in the 18th century. It contains the bust of Saint Torpès, which is paraded around the town during the processions of **Le Bravade**, a celebration held in May since 1558 to commemorate the arrival of the body of patron Saint Torpès to the village in his boat.

To the south, there is a fourth 15th-century tower, the **Tour Jarlier ★ (11)**, which housed the prison.

Further south, the **Chapelle de la Miséricorde ★ (12)**, built in the 17th century can be visited. Rue de la Miséricorde passes through the chapel's flying buttresses. This gives it a very medieval look that is absolutely charming.

The **Place des Lices (13)**, a very popular spot, is the site of a bustling market on Tuesday and Saturday mornings. It is a pleasant place to meet with its cafe terraces offering a wonderful view of the *pétanque* games.

Of the two churches — **Chapelle du Couvent (14)** and **Chapelle Sainte-Anne ★ (15)** — located to the far south end of the village, the second makes for a more interesting visit. It is a designated historical monument that was built in 1618 by the people of Saint-Tropez to give thanks for having been spared during the Plague. Located on Sainte-Anne Hill, it offers a remarkable view of the gulf.

Finally, top off your visit by a tour of the **Citadelle ★ (16)**. This 16th-century building overlooks the city and stands in the middle of a large nature park. For centuries this was the most important element of defence between Antibes and Toulon. It remains one of the only monuments of its size on the Côte Varoise. The dungeon houses the **Musée Naval** *(Wed to Mon, 10 AM to 5 PM; in summer, until 8 PM; closed from Nov. 15 to Dec. 15;* ☎ *94.97.06.53)*, where historical Saint-Tropez is recalled.

A pleasant walk on the top of the hill offers an exceptional view over the gulf and of Old Saint-Tropez. From this vantage point, visitors can appreciate how the city maintains its genuine cachet despite the throngs of tourists. The urban planners left enough natural growth so that you never feel "trapped" in a living museum.

Walkers might want to catch the **Sentier des Douaniers** trail down towards the sea by the naval cemetery. It follows the coastline of the peninsula to Cavalaire-sur-mer, where bus transportation back to Saint-Tropez is available.

Saint-Tropez Peninsula

A never-ending paradise! Here you'll find the most beautiful beaches in the Côte d'Azur overlooked by gorgeous hills offering a magnificent view over the sea and the Maures. The two charming medieval villages of Ramatuelle and Gassin add to the undeniable beauty of the site.

Suggested Tour (50 km):

From Carrefour de la Foux (between Port-Grimaud and Saint-Tropez), take D 559 and then D 89 to Gassin.

Gassin

Here is a wonderful place to stop and relax, away from the hustle and bustle of Saint-Tropez. This medieval village offers a panoramic view of the Côte d'Azur that spans all the way to the Îles d'Hyères.

From Gassin, go towards Ramatuelle and follow the signs for Moulins de Paillas. Keep going until you reach Ramatuelle.

Ramatuelle

Here rests the body of the great actor Gérard Philippe. Ramatuelle is also where you will find one of, if not the most beautiful beach on the Côte d'Azur: the Plage de Pampelonne. This village is surrounded by numerous vineyards and hosts a theatre festival every summer.

Leave the village in the direction of the beaches.

One possibility is a visit to the lighthouse, the Phare du Cap Camarat. The D 93 provides access to the many beaches strung one after the other all the way to Saint-Tropez. The most famous are the Pampelonne, Tahiti, des Salins and, finally, Canebiers beaches, site of La Madrague, Brigitte Bardot's estate.

Massif des Maures ★★★

The Massif des Maures spans over 60 km between Fréjus and Hyères, and is 30 km wide. Its peaks are nearly 800 m high. The mountain range is crossed by several roads and numerous walking trails offering spectacular views of a landscape that has remained virtually untouched.

We propose an 85 km drive starting from Saint-Tropez which will allow you to discover some of its charms.

Leave Saint-Tropez by D 14 in the direction of Grimaud and Collobrières.

About 5 km before Collobrières, don't miss the **Chartreuse de la Verne ★★** *(admission charge; 10 AM to 6 PM, closed Tue, Oct* ☎ *94.96.05.02).* A designated historical building since 1921, la Chartreuse's history goes back to 1170. Since 1982, la Chartreuse has been a monastery occupied by a group of nuns, the *Sœurs de Bethléem*. It is presently being restored.

Collobrières

Capital of the Maures, this village is one of the most picturesque and most authentic of the Var. The huge forests surrounding the village and the small wild river running through give it a tangibly rustic feeling. You should make a short stop, time enough to go to the Confiserie Azuréenne to buy a few *marrons glacés*, candied-chestnuts. Chestnuts are the hallmark of this little village.

If you wish you can continue through some of the scenic country roads up to Pierrefeu-du-Var where there is a lovely estate called L'Aumérade, which sells its own wine.

Outdoor Activities

Beaches

The coastline between Cannes and Saint-Raphaël is a rather sudden drop to the sea, although a few small sandy bays can be found here and there. At Saint-Raphaël, Fréjus and Saint-Aygulf, the beaches are pleasant and sandy. Up to Sainte-Maxime, the coastline again becomes very rocky and the few beaches along here are not recommended as the water does not seem very clean. Between Sainte-Maxime and Saint-Tropez, the beaches become increasingly beautiful, their beauty and cleanliness culminating beyond Saint-Tropez.

Saint-Tropez

Numerous sandy beaches. Spectacular!

Golf

Saint-Raphaël

Golf 9 Trous de Cap Estérel (9 holes; 120 F, 2 rounds: 150 F; B.P. 940, 83708 Saint-Raphaël, ☎ 94.82.55.00, ⇄ 94.82.58.73). The course offers a spectacular view of the sea.

Sainte-Maxime

Golf de Sainte-Maxime (9 holes: 180 F, 18 holes: 250 F; Route du Débarque-ment, 83120 Sainte-Maxime, ☎ 94.49.26.60, ⇄ 94.49.00.39). The course winds through the mountain, offering superb panoramic views.

Hiking

Fréjus - Saint-Raphaël

You can bask on the beaches or go on walking tours in the nearby Massif de l'Estérel. Here are a few suggestions for walking tours. However, it is best to get a good map that indicates the various walking trails. The tourist office can certainly be of help here. If you expect to do several hikes during your stay on the Côte d'Azur, we suggest you purchase a guidebook (only available in French) that describes 150 walking expeditions: Au Pays d'Azur by L. Touchaud.

Note: Camping, fires and even smoking are prohibited in the Massif, as is picking plants. Make sure you bring drinking water.

The Office National des Forêts (O.N.F.) manages the forests. You'll see different coloured markings as you stroll through the woods. Beware! These markings are not necessarily direction indicators, and to follow them blindly could get you lost in the forest.

Finally, if you're leaving a car behind, don't tempt thieves by leaving things in it.

If you want to see the site of the old Malpasset dam, which tragically broke in 1959 killing more than 400 people, a trail starts where the old D 37 stops. The elevation is not too high, only 300 m. This hike takes at least 4 hours.

Mont Vinaigre ★★ looms over the Massif at an elevation of 614 m. The view from the summit is dazzling. It can be reached from a trail that starts at Pont de l'Estérel on the N 7. Allow at least 4 hours for this hike.

Pic de l'Ours and **Pic d'Aurelle** ★ offer splendid views over the coastline. These can be accessed from the train station at Trayas, which is on the coast between Cannes and Saint-Raphaël. The elevation is almost 500 m.

Finally, many other hiking trails are accessible from parking areas along the forest road that runs through the Massif. The paths can often be seen winding up the hillsides. Short or long hikes are possible along these trails.

Saint-Tropez

Hiking enthusiasts can take a trail that starts from the port of Saint-Tropez, follows the coastline of the peninsula and ends at Cavalaire-sur-mer. The landscapes are lovely. The length of the hike can be adapted to the time available. From Saint-Tropez to Baie des Cannebiers takes 50 minutes. It then takes 1 hour and 45 minutes to reach Plage des Salins, and another hour from there to Plage de Tahiti.

Cavalaire is approximately 25 km from Plage de Tahiti.

You can return to Saint-Tropez by bus if you wish. Enquire with the tourist office for schedules.

 Water Sports

Saint-Tropez

Saint-Tropez offers water sports galore.

Club des Loisirs des Jeunes (sports and activities for ages 6 to 16)
Plage de la Fontanette, La Ponche
☎ 94.97.60.20 or 94.97.00.13

Ramatuelle

Club Water Sports (parasailing, jet skiing, water skiing, wind-surfing)
Route de l'Épi, Plage de Pampelonne
☎ 94.79.82.41

 Sailing School

Baies des Cannebiers (road to des Salins, in the direction of Cap des Salins, east of the old city)

 Scuba Diving

☎ 94.56.05.76, 94.97.08.39 or 94.79.27.77

 Accommodation

■ **Anthéor Cap-Roux**

Halfway between Cannes and Saint-Raphaël, on the edge of Massif de l'Estérel, you'll discover the **Auberge d'Anthéor** *(780-1,070 F bkfst incl.; pb, tv, C in a few rooms, ≈, △, ℜ; closed Nov and Dec; ☎ 94.44.83.38, ⇄ 94.44.84.20)*. This is a remarkable place, directly on the sea. Although the hotel has no beach, there is a small cement dock from which you can dive into the sea. If that doesn't appeal to you, there is a beautiful swimming pool. This modern-Provençal style hotel is one of the *Châteaux et Demeures Traditionel* of France. All the rooms are very clean and modern, and look out onto the sea. There is also a sauna and a games room.

Meals *($-$$)* are served in a beautiful Provençal-style dining-room or on the lovely terrace that looks out onto the sea. Seafood is their speciality.

■ Agay

Around 5 km east of Saint-Raphaël, at the entrance to the village of Agay, a very modern vacation complex sits on a little hill overlooking the sea. The complex, built by "Pierre et Vacances" includes the hotel **Cap de l'Estérel**. The view, which encompasses the Massif de l'Estérel as well as the sea, is superb. This is ideal for families and older people who prefer spending their vacation in one place. Everything is available on site including an abundance of restaurants (11 in all), a huge swimming pool, tennis courts and a small golf course. There is also a medical clinic and a massage service available.

■ Les Adrets de l'Estérel

If you prefer the tranquillity and beauty of nature, and the intimacy and simplicity of small villages, this village in the Massif de l'Estérel, between Cannes and Fréjus, near the N 7 and Lac St-Cassien is a must.

Hôtel de la Verrerie *(310 F; ps, tv;* ☎ *94.40.93.51)* is a small seven-room hotel in a large Provençal-style villa. It is perched on a hillside, slightly off the beaten path, but the way is clearly indicated. Guests can enjoy the tranquillity

of nature and have breakfast in the garden while admiring the magnificent view of l'Estérel. The rooms are modern and sunny. This hotel is a very good value.

Les Logis des Manons *(230-280 F; pb, tv; closed mid-Oct to mid-Nov;* ☎ *94.40.98.38,* ⇄ *94.40.94.57)*, is also located inland between Cannes and Fréjus. Recently built, this Provençal-style bed and breakfast has a garden planted with trees and offers a splendid view of the surrounding area.

The restaurant *($-$$)* offers traditional Provençal cuisine as well as seasonal specialities.

■ Fréjus - Saint-Aygulf

Saint-Aygulf is 6 km from Fréjus, on the N 98 towards Saint-Maxime. There you will find **L'Escale du Soleil** *(260-310 F; for three people, 380-400 F; ps; closed Nov to Mar; 75 Av. Marius-Coulet,* ☎ *94.81.20.19)*. This is a small, pleasant hotel offering simple comforts. It is very clean and good value. Located in a peaceful spot, 50 m from the sea, this hotel has a shaded terrace and parking space for the guests. Ask for a room on the top floor. The owner is very friendly.

■ Grimaud (village)

Around 3 km west of the village, on the road to Collobrières, **La Boulangerie** *(670-790 F, 920 F for triple occ.; 1,390 F for the suite; pb, ℝ, tv on request, ≈, tennis; closed mid-Oct to Easter;* ☎ *94.43.23.16,* ⇄ *94.43.38.27)* is a small and charming hotel nestled in a very pretty garden. At the back, a swimming pool surrounded by a terrace offers a view of the foothills of the Massif des Maures. It is an ideal place to spend a relaxing day or simply to have breakfast. This hotel is a peaceful spot where you will feel like a guest at a large private villa. It offers great comfort and a warm welcome.

If La Boulangerie has no vacancies, try **Le Verger** *(600-850 F; ps or pb, ≈; Route de Collobrières, ☎ 94.43.25.93)*, on the same road. This is another country inn in the middle of a large park with garden and swimming pool that will surely win you over. The owner, who is also the chef, places much importance on the cuisine *($$)*. He uses the freshest ingredients seasoned with herbs from his own garden. Guests can dine indoors or on the lovely terrace with its pastoral decor. Here, once again, tranquillity reigns.

■ **Saint-Tropez**

At the heart of Vieux Saint-Tropez, on a small side-street at the end of the port (near Tour Suffren), visitors can stop at a small modest hotel, **La Michaudière** *(250-450 F; shared shower or pb for the most expensive room, C; 8 Rue Portalet, ☎ 94.97.18.67)*. The owner, Monsieur Thomas, will only be too happy to share with you his vast knowledge of the village's history, customs, activities and restaurants. Note, however, that cheques and credit cards are not accepted.

Can you imagine spending the night in a mythical place reminiscent of And God Created Woman, a place where Romy Schneider often stayed and where Françoise Sagan came to write? Then you must spend some time at **La Ponche** *(950-1,350 F, 1,350 F for a suite, 2,100 F for a suite with terrace overlooking the sea; ps or pb, ℝ, tvc, ℜ; 3 Rue des Remparts, Port des Pêcheurs, ☎ 94.97.02.53,*

⇄ *94.97.78.61)*. The hotel is located in the heart of the old village; it is therefore best that a valet take care of your car when you arrive. The rooms are superbly decorated in soft, calm colours and are equipped with extravagant marble bathrooms.. The room Françoise Sagan used to stay in is available for any visitors looking to tune in some artistic vibes. Its blue walls contain many memories and the terrace is magnificent. Dispersed throughout the hotel are paintings by a local artist, Jacques Cordier. The friendly reception is the epitome of excellence. The two owners, Madame Duckstein and her charming mother, are living history books. They will be happy to recount the thousand and one stories that make up the history of this establishment. There is also a restaurant, see p 287.

■ **Ramatuelle**

Around 5 min (by car) from Saint-Tropez, we recommend **La Ferme d'Augustin** *(620-1,000 F, 1,100-1,500 F for ≡ with garden terrace, 1,800 F for the suite with solarium-terrace offering a double view over the sea; pb or ps, salon, ℝ, tv, ≈, ℜ; closed mid-Oct to Easter; Plage de Tahiti, ☎ 94.97.23.83, ⇄ 94.97.40.30)*. This luxury farmhouse-style hotel is surrounded by a magnificent garden with a very beautiful swimming pool and tennis courts. It is only a few steps away from Saint-Tropez's beautiful beaches. In short, guests can stay in a corner of paradise at a reasonable price. The subtle charm of this farm, furnished with Provençal antiques, won us over instantly. There is also a restaurant where you can dine outdoors.

The hotel **Les Bouis** *(1,050-1,150 F, extra bed 250 F, 350 F supplement for* a double bed; pb, tv, ℝ, private terrace, closed Nov to mid-Mar; Route des Plages, Pampelonne, ☎ 94.79.87.61, ⇄ 94.79.85.20) is located around one kilometre from the sea and six kilometres from Saint-Tropez. Surrounded by an umbrella-pine forest, this peaceful spot offers an exceptional view. The hotel, built a few years ago in Provençal style, has everything you'll need for a most pleasant stay, including a large swimming pool.

■ Gassin

Le Petit Castel (280 F, triple 350 F; ps; closed depending on Véronique's (the owner) mood; ☎ 94.56.14.17) is a very pleasant, simple and affordable hotel. According to the business card, this is a hotel that reflects all your needs. In any case, it is a peaceful spot and you will surely have a few laughs with Véronique as she is quite a character! Never at a loss for words, she loves to talk. She is a great story-teller with a wide repertoire, including recommendations for good restaurants in the area. This is a friendly spot.

■ La Croix-Valmer

On the Saint-Tropez peninsula, the **Parc Hôtel** (360-530 F, 540-660 F for three people, 610-710 F for four people; ps or pb, tv in a few rooms, tv-lounge, ≈, ℜ; closed Oct to Easter; Av. Georges Selliez, ☎ 94.79.64.04, ⇄ 94.54.38.91) would be our first choice for a hotel in the belle-époque palace style. Beyond the gate lies a beautiful garden with a large swimming pool and palm trees. This enchanting and majestic site offers a view over the sea stretching to the Îles d'Hyères. Inside, there is a large salon with a grand piano, and the rooms are spacious and sunny. This hotel is an excellent value. The reception is quite

friendly and the young owner is most dynamic. She is forever looking for ways to improve her establishment, which is clean as clean can be. The only disadvantage might be that it is approximately 3 km from the sea. But, in our opinion, this matters little as the site has everything. After all, 3 km by car or by bicycle is really nothing. There is also a restaurant with a grill, where light meals and snacks are served. The hotel staff will also be able to recommend restaurants in the area that offer more complete menus.

There is a very beautiful neo-Provençal style hotel overlooking the sea from the top of a hill: **Le Souleias** (620-1,480 F, 1,320-1,710 F for three people; pb, tv, ≡ in most rooms, ≈, ℜ; closed Nov to Easter; Plage de Gigaro, ☎ 94.79.61.91, ⇄ 94.54.36.23). You will feel like you are on a small island in the middle of a very beautiful park with a large swimming pool. Most of the rooms look directly out onto the park, and others have balconies. They are very comfortable and most face south, towards the sea. The beach is five minutes away by car or can be reached on foot by a path which is uphill coming back. The large restaurant ($$-$$$) offers a most refined cuisine in a decor that is complemented by natural lighting and a spectacular view.

 Restaurants

■ In the Massif de l'Estérel

Cosima and Alexis de Megvinet welcome you at the **Auberge des Adrets** ($$; closed Oct to Mar; R.N. 7, ☎ 94.40.36.24). If you are going on an excursion in the Massif de l'Estérel, stop and sample the cuisine served at this inn located 16 km from Cannes and 18 km from Fréjus. The lovely dining room is tastefully furnished with antiques. In the summer, it opens up onto a large terrace offering a superb view of the Baie de Cannes. Carefully selected rural dishes are on the menu.

■ Fréjus

Chez Vincent *($; 19 Rue Désaugiers,* ☎ *94.53.89.89)* is a small charming restaurant nestled in a tiny street behind the town hall near the cathedral. It features fine cuisine and comes highly recommended by the locals. The dining room at the back offers a medieval setting.

■ Saint-Aygulf/Fréjus

Le Jardin *($; 583 Av. de la Corniche d'Azur,* ☎ *94.81.17.81)* offers tasty little dishes at reasonable prices, including grilled food, pizza and home-made ice cream. This little restaurant is located near l'Escale au Soleil (see p 284).

■ Saint-Tropez

Le restaurant de l'hôtel La Ponche *($$)* is really worth trying, whether you are staying at the hotel or not. In summer, meals are served on a very beautiful terrace that looks out onto a small busy square of the old village, near the old port. The meat and fish dishes are skilfully prepared and the desserts are divine. The local wines are excellent, so you need not look any further. The service is friendly and efficient. The owner, Madame Duckstein, will take your order and, if you wish, will introduce you to the illustrious history of this "almost sacred" spot. Picasso and many others would come for a

drink here, in this establishment which originally was no more than a meeting place for the local fishermen. For description of the rooms see p 285.

L'Auberge des Maures *($; Rue Dr. Boutin)* is a very nice out-of-the-way spot in a tiny side-street. Its large shaded terrace will delight you: it's an ideal place to take shelter from the summer heat and spend a relaxing moment. The decor is rustic with an attention paid to detail. Provençal cuisine is their speciality.

Le Café des Arts *($; on Place des Lices,* ☎ *94.97.29.00)* is famous for its excellent Provençal cuisine. Not to be confused with the Brasserie des Arts!

A very "in" spot in the city centre, **Chez Fuchs** *($$; 7 Rue des Commerçants,* ☎ *94.97.01.25)* offers Provençal cuisine in a "cantina" setting. Highly recommended by local connoisseurs.

Another place recommended by the locals: **L'eau à la bouche** *($$; Rue Porte neuve)* specializes in Caribbean dishes, for a change from Provençal cuisine.

Finally, if your pocketbook allows: **La Ramade** *($$$; Rue du Temple,* ☎ *94.97.00.15)* is famed as being the region's best restaurant for fish. In summer, guests are served in the garden.

■ Saint-Tropez (beaches)

On Plage de Tahiti, 6 km from Saint-Tropez, **Chez Camille** *($$)* serves bouillabaisse *(280 F for two people)* and other fish dishes. Connoisseurs agree that it is a fine restaurant.

■ **Grimaud**

If you appreciate fine dining, don't miss **Les Santons** *($$; closed Wed and Nov to mid-Mar, except during the Christmas holidays)*. Treat yourself for an evening! It starts with Madame Girard's warm welcome, followed by Monsieur Girard's exquisite cuisine, served in the finest Provençal decor where each element has been tastefully selected. A mere glance at the menu tells you you're in for an evening of delights and you won't be disappointed! As an appetiser, you may choose the *bouquet de salade printannière avec saumon mariné* (spring salad with marinated salmon), *ravioles de homard sauce divine* (lobster served with a truly divine sauce) or *bourride de poisson* (fish with a delicate sauce). For your entrée, the *selle d'agneau de Sisteron* (saddle of lamb roasted with thyme) is a memorable choice. There is a well-stocked wine cellar and the pleasant sommelier can offer excellent advice, so your wine choice will be made easy. True, the prices are on the steep side, but the exceptional quality of the food and the impeccable service more than justify the expense. In short, an unforgettable experience. Simply divine!

■ **Gassin**

Judith, la Dame de Coeur *($; 13 Rue Longue, ☎ 94.56.50.13)* is a quaint little restaurant in a vaulted cellar in the heart of the village. The house specialities are meat and game grilled over the fireplace. The menu changes every day, according to the mood of the owner-cum-chef. Reservations are strongly recommended.

■ **Collobrières**

La Petite Fontaine *($; Place de la République, ☎ 94.48.00.12)* is a wonderful place for lunch. You can eat outdoors on a peaceful terrace which looks out onto a small shaded square with a fountain. The restaurant serves Provençal specialities. The portions are generous and it is an excellent value. Note that credit cards are not accepted.

 Entertainment

■ **Saint-Raphaël**

Compétition Internationale de jazz de New Orleans. A New Orleans-style jazz festival in the streets, early July.

Fête des Pêcheurs A fishermen's festival with traditional celebrations, local music, competitions, dance. At the port, one weekend in early August.

Grand Casino
slot machines 11 AM to 4 AM; gambling 8 PM to 4 AM, in summer until 5 AM
Square de Gand
☎ 94.95.01.56.

■ **Fréjus**

Salon de l'Automobile Car show at the amphitheatre; four days, end of September.

■ **Saint-Tropez**

Discotheque **L'Esquinade** *(with one drink 80 F; every night 11 PM to 4 AM; Rue du Four, behind Place de la Mairie, ☎ 94.97.00.04)*.

Discotheque **Le Papagayo** *(with one drink 90 F; every night 11 PM until dawn; Résidence du Port;* ☎ *94.97.07.56)*. Super atmosphere...

Discotheque **Le Pigeonnier** *(with one drink 70 F; every night 11 PM; 13 Rue de la Ponche;* ☎ *94.97.36.85)*. Gay bar.

Discotheque **Stéréo Club** *(every night 10 PM; 6 Rue de Pullis;* ☎ *94.97.06.69)*. Gay bar.

■ Ramatuelle

Jazz at **Théâtre de Verdure**; mid-July.

Temps Musicaux: Festival de Musique Classique classical music festival, Théâtre de Verdure; second half of July.

Festival de Théâtre theatre festival, Théâtre de Verdure; first half of August.

Shopping

■ Saint-Raphaël

Le Salon des Antiquaires Antique show at the Palais des Congrès, Port Santa Lucia, ☎ 94.83.15.15; second half of February.

■ Fréjus

Art Tendance Sud - Salon des Métiers d'Art Port Fréjus; three days in the middle of May.

Marché Artisanale Arts and crafts market at Port-Fréjus; every Sunday afternoon; information: ☎ 94.82.63.00.

■ Saint-Tropez

You'll find some fine antique pieces and high-quality knick-knacks at **Château Suffren** *(Place de la Mairie,* ☎ *94.97.85.15)*.

Salon des Antiquaires Antique show, end of August and beginning of September.

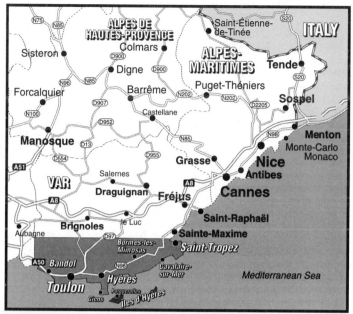

BETWEEN SAINT-TROPEZ AND BANDOL ★★

Heading west from Saint-Tropez, the glittering part of the Côte d'Azur that made it one of the world's greatest resort destinations soon fades. The jet-set lifestyle disappears, the beaches are less attractive, and more than anything, the largest city, Toulon, offers very little for the visitor. Toulon was heavily destroyed during World War II and rebuilt with buildings which are, quite frankly, ugly. The passage of time has not improved the city's allure either, which is too bad considering its wonderful location.

However, this is no reason to be discouraged. This part of the Côte d'Azur is fabulously endowed with natural beauty and tourist attractions.

The Iles d'Hyères (Hyères islands); the magnificent hill range called the Massif des Maures; Bandol and the Ile de Bendor opposite its port, and the delightful villages set back from the sea, La Cadière-d'Azur and Le Castellet for example, are all full of charm.

Considering that the sea is so omnipresent, numerous water activities await visitors. The area inland, known collectively as the *arrière-pays*, or back-country affords countless opportunities for gentle walks and serious hiking. Let's not forget that the area is a reputed wine-producer, and thus the promise of relaxing evenings tasting local bottles is always an agreeable possibility... And last but not least, there are the culinary wonders that await.

Finding Your Way Around

■ **By Plane**

The largest regional airport is located at Hyères, 18 km east of Toulon. Connections are made with all the major French cities. The passenger boarding pier for the Iles d'Hyères is just 5 km from the airport. International flights land at the airports of Marseille (50 km from west of Bandol) or Nice (100 km east of Toulon).

■ **By Train**

The train network operates between Marseille and Toulon. From Toulon, the railroad follows the north side of the Massif des Maures and heads directly to Fréjus. Therefore, apart from a small line linking Toulon with the Hyères airport, there is no coastal train between Hyères and Fréjus. It is therefore impossible to reach Saint-Tropez by train.

■ **By car**

Due to the deficiencies in the rail network in this area, it is probably wisest to rent a car upon arrival.

The road network is well-developed. The **A 50** highway links Marseille, La Ciotat, Bandol, Toulon and Hyères. Leaving Toulon, the **A 57** rejoins the **A 8 - E 80** and continues eastwards towards Fréjus, Cannes and Nice.

The national and departmental roads are very well maintained and pass through some magnificent countryside. The two main routes are the **D 559**, which follows the seaside, and the **N 98**, which is farther north. Crossing through Toulon is now easier than ever,

due to a new road which, unfortunately, cuts the city in two. This does nothing to improve Toulon... but at least it allows cars to pass through this unremarkable place as quickly as possible!

■ **By bus**

A number of bus excursions are possible. Departures can be made from the majority of villages along the coast. Local tourist offices provide all the necessary information.

■ **By boat**

Boating plays an important role in this region, due to the importance of the many islands here. Most of these boats are *vedettes* (modern launches) or sometimes smaller and somewhat antiquated vessels which make regular trips between the islands and mainland.

Iles d'Hyères

Most departures are made from the far end of Presqu'Ile de Giens, situated south of Hyères and the Toulon-Hyères airport. The islands can also be reached from Toulon, from the Port-de-Miramar (13 km east of Hyères), from Lavandou and from Cavalaire-sur-Mer (18 km west of Saint-Tropez).

Ile de Porquerolles

Departure from Port de la Tour-Fondue (☎ *94.58.21.81)* at the far south end of the Presqu'Ile de Giens. At least five return trips a day are made during low season, and 20 a day during July and August.

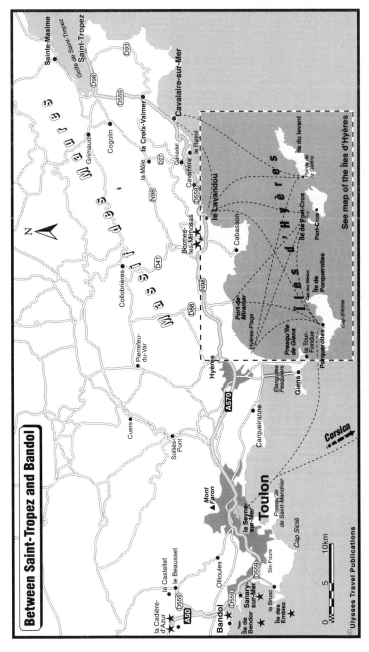

Between Saint-Tropez and Bandol

© Ulysses Travel Publications

Ile du Levant and Ile de Port-Clos

Departures are made from Lavandou (the shortest and least expensive), from Port-de-Miramar, from Hyères-Plage or from the Presqu'Ile de Giens. By choosing this last option, the boat passes by Ile de Porquerolles.

Three Island Circuit ★★

A circuit running in high season two or three times a week allows passengers to visit the three islands in the same day. Departures are at 9:15 AM from Port de la Tour-Fondue, and return at 4 PM. For less active types, this is an ideal way to see the area, for there is little time to visit the islands by foot. Count about 150 F per person.

 Practical Information

■ Le Lavandou

Tourist Office
Quai Gabriel Péri
☎ 94.71.00.61

■ Bormes-les-Mimosas

Tourist Office
9 Place Gambetta
☎ 94.71.15.17

■ Hyères

Tourist Office
Avenue de Belgique
☎ 94.65.18.55

Landing Stage of Hyères Harbour
☎ 94.57.44.07

■ Ile de Porquerolles

Tourist Office
Carré du Port
☎ 94.58.33.76

Room and Apartment Rentals
Le Clos des Galejades
☎ 94.58.30.20 ⇄ 94.58.33.22

■ Toulon

Tourist Office
8 Avenue Colbert
☎ 94.22.08.22 ⇄ 94.22.30.54
Guided walking tours are organized by the tourist office, Wednesday at 9:30 AM, only if arranged in advance.

Taxi (24 hours/day)
☎ 94.93.51.51

SNCF Train Station
Place Europe
Information: ☎ 94.22.90.00
Reservations: ☎ 94.91.50.50

Mont Faron Téléférique
☎ 94.92.68.25

■ Bandol

Tourist Office
Allée Viven
☎ 94.29.41.35

Bicycle Rental
Holiday Bikes
127 Route de Marseille
☎ 94.32.21.89

■ La Cadière-d'Azur

Tourist Office
Place Roger-Salengro
☎ 94.90.12.56

Exploring

We will start the description with the Corniche des Maures, which follows shore between Saint-Tropez and Hyères. The Iles d'Hyères will follow, and the last section will cover the area between Toulon and Bandol, including the villages found inland. The chapter finishes with a **"Dream Tour"** covering the entire region.

Leave Saint-Tropez by the D 559 towards La Croix-Valmer, until Lavandou, then take the D 41 towards Bormes-les-Mimosas.

■ **Bormes-les-Mimosas ★★**

This village will enchant you with its old pink-tile houses built on different levels on the cliffside, its sloping roads, along with the remains of its fortress walls and imposing castle.

A Ligurian tribe from Italy called the Bormani first settled on the coast around 400 BC. For a long time they were fishermen, but in the 9th century they emigrated to the hills to defend themselves against incessant attacks by Saracens. The village wasn't built until the 12th century, and despite the construction of the ramparts, its inhabitants suffered new invasions.

In 1913, the community lost a great part of its territory and its population when the Lavandou district separated in order to develop its maritime activity.

In 1968, a decree officially recognized the appellation Bormes-les-Mimosas, due to the presence of the flowering mimosa tree, part of the acacia family. A festival attracting thousands of visitors occurs the third Sunday in February to celebrate this tree, which is the community's symbol. The event's highlight is the parade of floral-decorated floats. Since 1970, Bormes-les-Mimosas obtained the distinction *"quatre fleurs"* (four flowers), as one of the most flowery village in France, the first village worthy of such an honour.

The interesting parts of Bormes are limited to the old village and Cabasson. The port is horrible. Take the time to stroll through the very pretty roads of the old village, where the charming houses are decorated with fresh flowers and plants.

At the top of the village, only the ruins of the **Château de Bormes** remain. Built between the 13th and 14th centuries, it burnt down in 1589. Today, it is private property and can not be visited. Nevertheless, there is a panorama overlooking the plain and the sea.

Along the Rue Carnot in the old village is the **Musée d'Arts et d'Histoire ★** *(summer, Wed to Mon, except Sun afternoon 10 AM to noon and 4 PM to 6 PM; winter, Wed 10 AM to noon and 3 PM to 5 PM, Sun 10 AM to noon)*. Created in 1926, the museum's collections retrace the history of Bormes, Collobrières, Brégançon and of the Chartreuse de la Verne. Paintings from the 19th and 20th centuries.

Continue below the old village towards Cabasson.

Cabasson is an ideal spot to go walking or cycling. What's more, the village is not always accessible by car. This is the place for nature-lovers, as the forest, vineyards and the sea surround the village.

Head west to Hyères by the N 98.

■ Hyères

The glory days of this seaside resort occurred during the second half of the 19th century. It was visited by many artists and members of high society, most of whom were English. Among those who fell under Hyères' charms were Queen Victoria, the queen of Spain, Tolstoy and Victor Hugo.

Unfortunately, few traces of this glorious past are visible today. In the 20th century, Hyères lost its worldly status to Cannes and Nice. However, it has once again become a popular seaside resort in the past few years. An old villa now houses a **casino**. A glassed-in addition has been integrated into the original building creating a rather spectacular piece of architecture.

There is little to see, apart from the **vieille ville ★★**, or old town. The covered passages and medieval houses confer a certain charm, and traces of the old ramparts can be spotted here and there.

The ruins of a château which was destroyed during the Wars of Religion are found at the top of the village. Admirers of 30s architecture will enjoy the **Villa Noailles ★** *(Chateau Saint-Bernard, summer 8 AM to 7 PM, otherwise 9 AM to 5 PM; Montée de Noailles;* ☎ *94.35.90.65)*. Located below the château ruins, this house was built by the famous architect Mallet-Stevens. The owners, wealthy patrons of the arts, entertained numerous cultural figures there, among them Man Ray, Giacometti, Bunuel and Cocteau.

To reach the landing stage for the Iles d'Hyères, pass through the Presqu'Iles de Giens. The temptation is high to turn towards one of the beaches to enjoy a dip in the sea! There is a rather spectacular road, the D 97, on the west side of the peninsula. This narrow road is delineated by the Salins des Pesquiers on one side, and the sea on the other.

Boats depart from La Tour-Fondue, at the tip of the peninsula, for Porquerolles only. However, the three islands may be reached from Hyères-Plage. See p 292.

■ Iles d'Hyères ★★

These islands were called the "Iles d'Or" (islands of gold) during the Renaissance. But a more interesting legend exists about their creation. Many ages ago, the King Olbianus and his four beautiful and adventurous daughters lived in this land. The princesses adored swimming and their passion took them far and wide. But alas, one day, they were hunted down by pirate ships. Happily, the gods intervened and before the nasty pirates could catch them, the four water-princesses were transformed into the Iles d'Or! This "no doubt" explains the existence of the fourth island — the tiniest one facing Port-Cros and called Ile de Bagaud.

More realistically, these islands have successively endured many influences: Ligurian, Etruscan, Greek and Roman, before being regularly ravaged by the Saracens. It seems like these islands continued to share the same fate as the legendary princesses...

Advice: To really appreciate the flora and fauna of these islands, it is preferable to visit in the spring or autumn. Summer is not the best season, as the flowering vegetation is past its prime and most of the birds have migrated elsewhere.

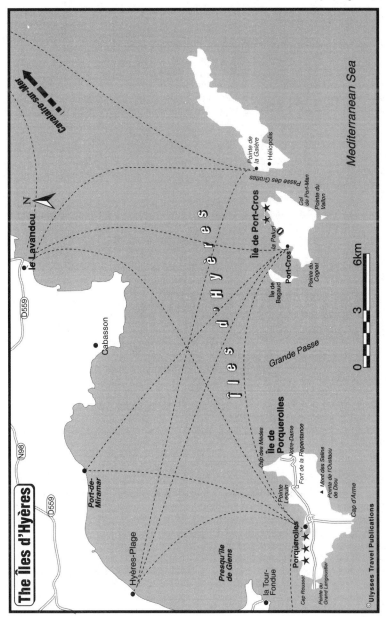

The Îles d'Hyères

Cavalaire-sur-Mer

le Lavandou

D559

N98

D559

Presqu'île de Giens

la Tour-Fondue

Hyères-Plage

Port-de-Miramar

Cabasson

N

Cap Rousset

Pointe du Grand Langoustier

Porquerolles

Cap des Mèdes

Notre-Dame

Fort de la Repentance

▲ Mont des Salins

île de Porquerolles

Pointe Lequin

Pointe de l'Oustaou de Dieu

Cap d'Arme

Grande Passe

île de Bagaud

Port-Cros

la Palud

île de Port-Cros

Pointe du Cognet

Col de Port-Man

Pointe du Vallon

Passe des Grottes

Pointe de la Galère

Héliopolis

Mediterranean Sea

Îles d'Hyères

0   3   6km

© Ulysses Travel Publications

■ **Porquerolles** ★★★

In the beginning of the 19th century, this island, the largest of the three, was not at all known by tourists. It was primarily used as a convalescent centre for soldiers returning from colonial wars. It was at this point that the *Génie Militaire*, military engineers, decided to create the village.

At the turn of the last century, a rich businessman bought the whole island just to enchant his young bride. Imagine that! After his death, the French state purchased the land, except for a few properties which stayed in the hands of the descendants of this family. The owner of the chic hotel Le Mas du Langoustier is the granddaughter of that rich businessman.

Since 1988, the island has been officially recognized as a national site. With its attractive sand beaches and superb viewing points along the southern cliffs which dominate the shimmering sea, Porquerolles is a favourite spot for walking and bicycling.

As the island is only around 8 km long and 2 km wide, it is recommended to rent a bicycle (about 60 F a day). They can be rented from a number of shops found at the port entrance.

Fort Sainte-Agathe *(May to Oct 10 AM to 5:30 PM;* ☎ *94.65.32.98)* was constructed in the 16th century to defend the island. An exhibition on the national park as well as archaeological objects found underwater are presented. A panoramic view of the island is possible from the fort's tower.

The island also contains the **Conservatoire Botanique National** *(May to Sep, 9:30 AM to noon and 3 PM to 6 PM;* ☎ *94.58.31.16)*. The gardens and orchards which shelter different types of fruit trees can be visited.

■ **Ile de Port-Cros** ★★

Due to its classification in 1963 as a national park, this island has remained untouched by man. Lovely walks lead to **Fort de l'Estissac**, which holds small exhibitions in the summer. The **Sentier Botanique** ★★, a botanical trail, begins below the fort and leads to the **La Palud** beach.

This beach is the site of an **underwater path** ★★★ *(a mask and flippers usually available at desk, check first)*. This is truly something out of the ordinary: a path in shallow water (less than 5 m deep) where guides help visitors discover the many beautiful types of fish and plant life. There is even a type of algae which, once calcified, ressembles coral. The experience encourages close encounters of the underwater kind, in our case a jelly-fish insisted on "making contact" with us...

■ **Ile du Levant** ★

Ile du Levant is known especially for the **Héliopolis**, a small paradise for nudists covering the southern part of the island. Small wild paths cross wooded spaces and run alongside the cliffside above the sea. However, the main "occupant" of the island is the *Marine Nationale* (navy). It uses 90% of the territory.

Beaches here are not ideal — there is only one which is sandy. Access to the water is possible by jumping from the rocks along the coast, but beware of sea urchins; there are loads of them.

The tour continues with Toulon. From Hyères, take the N 98 then the A 570 highway. If you are coming from Tour-Fondue, cross the Étang des Pesquiers dune, and follow the D 559.

■ **Toulon**

The city has an exceptional geographical position between Mont Faron and a wide harbour which prides itself on being the prettiest in Europe. It was occupied as of antiquity by Celto-Ligurian fishermen. In the 5th century, the city developped rapidly thanks to the establishment of a bishop's residence here. The inhabitants' livelihood was made from fishing, tanneries, the wine trade, salt and also... piracy.

Toulon became strategically important only after 1481 when the Count of Provence left Provence to the King of France in his legacy. In 1514, the Tour Royale was constructed to defend the harbour entrance, called La Petite Rade. In 1595, Henry IV created the *Arsenal Maritime*, whose main task was to build the royal fleet of galleys. The naval shipbuilding industry has developed ever since, making Toulon the number one military establishment in France.

Upon mounting the throne, Louis XIV asked Vauban to build fortifications capable of defending Toulon by land and sea.

In the 18th century, Toulon reached the apogee of its maritime power and became the most important European port. After having been taken by the English and the Spanish in 1793, the port was reconquered by Bonaparte.

After years of decay, Toulon only refound its prosperity under the Second Empire. The opening of the Suez Canal in 1869 reinforced the city's strategic position.

Up until World War II, the navy was omnipresent. However, the city was half-destroyed during the war and by consequence Toulon carries the scars of history and of its destiny as a strategic military port.

In 1974, after an interruption of 181 years, Toulon became the police headquarters for all of the Var department. Since the 80s, the city has put a lot of effort into revitalising its image and it is currently making major changes in its infrastructure.

City Tour

Leave your car in the public parking lot at Place d'Armes. Head towards the port.

The **Porte de l'Arsenal** ★★, a classified historical monument, comes quickly into view. Its four columns support the statues of Mars, the god of War, of Minerva, the goddess of the Infantry, plus those of the Arts and of Intelligence. They are the works of Puget. The gate shelters the **Musée de la Marine** ★ *(adults 24 F, children 12 F; Wed to Mon 10 AM to noon and 1:30 PM to 6 PM; Place Monsenergue, ☎ 94.02.02.01)*. Where more than two centuries of French maritime history are evoked through the use of models, maps, photos, paintings, etc.

A stroll along the piers is recommended. The Quai Stalingrad leads to a number of small restaurants with terraces. Note the **Atlantes de Puget**, which date from 1657 and grace the Mairie d'Honneur (civic hall).

Head towards Cours Lafayette in the old town.

The Provençal market is held on the Cours Lafayette, which is lined with plane trees. As well, the local history museum is found here, the **Musée de Vieux Toulon** (*free admission; open everyday except Sun 2 PM to 6 PM;* ☎ *94.92.29.23*).

The old town still possesses some charming spots. Some old roads shelter medieval houses. The **Cathédrale Sainte-Marie-Majeure ★** is found on Place de la Cathédrale. This old Romanesque church dates from the 11th century and was enlarged in the 17th century. Behind the classical façade, hides a fine Baroque altar in stucco and marble, made by Veyrier (a student of Puget) and a number of paintings, including one by Puget.

Head northwest towards the opera house.

The Place Puget and its famous Fontaine des Trois-Dauphins are found here. Admirers of fountains may in fact follow a circuit which passes by a number of the city's finest. For more information, contact the Mairie d'Honneur in the port.

In the neighbouring streets, there are two or three pleasant hotels (*see p 305*).

A bit farther west, on the Place Victor-Hugo lies the **Opéra-Théatre Municipal** (☎ *94.92.70.78*), a splendid structure built in 1862. The statues outside are the work of Toulonnais sculptors and represent, for the most part, the muses of the arts. This opera house is renowned for its fine acoustics. The interior is richly decorated with paintings, stucco effects and Napoléon III-style bronzes.

Head west along the Boulevard de Strasbourg, which is found behind the opera house.

The **Musée de Toulon** (*free admission; 1 PM to 7 PM; 113 Boulevard Maréchal Leclerc,* ☎ *94.93.15.54*) is a Renaissance-style structure, built in 1887. It houses a library, contemporary art collection and some paintings from the Provençal school covering the period between the 17th and 20th centuries. The building also holds the **Musée d'Histoire Naturelle** (*free admission; everyday 9:30 AM to noon and 2 PM to 6 PM, except Sun 1 PM to 7 PM;* ☎ *94.93.15.54*).

■ **Mont Faron Excursion ★★**

If travelling by car, follow the directions towards Mont Faron which appear upon leaving the SNCF train station. A winding road leads all the way to the top, where there are beautiful lookout points. The summit can also be reached by **téléférique** (*Tue to Sun 9:30 PM to noon and 2:30 PM to 7 PM; Boulevard Amiral-Vence,* ☎ *94.92.68.25*). **Attention:** the téléférique is not in service when there are high winds.

On top, at an altitude of 500 m, there is a wonderful view overlooking Toulon and its harbour. A magnificent wooded park is perfect for a relaxing stroll, there are well-kept pathways, picnic tables and children's play areas.

There is also a **Zoo** (☎ *94.88.07.89*) concerned with the raising of fawns and a **Mémorial** to the *Débarquement en Provence*, the historic landing of the Allied Forces in 1944 along the coast of Provence (*entry charge; Tue to Sat 9:30 AM to noon and 2:30 PM to 7 PM;* ☎ *94.88.08.09*).

Leave Toulon by the D 559 in the direction of Bandol.

■ **Ile des Embiez ★**

Park your car in the small Le Brusc district. Take the small shuttle boat *(adults 25 F return trip, children 18 F; 10-min trip departures every 30 min;* ☎ *94.74.99.00)*

This charming little island is perfect for walks along the flower-lined paths or on the rough seacoast which hides small inlets suitable for swimming. Equally, there is a small tourist train *(adults 19 F, children 12 F)* which guides visitors across the island.

The Fort Saint-Pierre houses the **Institut Océanographique Paul Ricard ★** *(adults 12 F 50, children 5 F 50; 10 AM to noon and 1:30 PM to 5:45 PM;* ☎ *94.34.02.49)* which includes a Mediterranean aquarium and library. Temporary exhibitions with conferences and films are presented for the public with the aim of increasing their awareness of marine issues.

■ **Bandol ★**

Bandol's history started in 1594 when Henry IV had a fort built here, opposite the Ile de Bendor.

In the 19th century, the village was populated primarily by coopers, the barrel-makers who produced the famous Bandol wine. The port served as a loading centre. Unfortunately, the arrival of the train and the diseases which struck the vines then devasted this flourishing port.

Today, Bandol has become the most important seaside resort on this part of the coast. It considers itself a little Saint-Tropez, although it really hasn't

yet attained this status. The village, however is not devoid of charm: behind the port hide some pretty, narrow streets. On the tiny square where the market is set up is the **Église Saint-François-de-Sales**, built in the middle of the 18th century.

Lovely walks remain the primary interest in Bandol. By climbing the Allée Alfred Vivien, there is a very pretty view over the **Anse de Renecros**, a small bay with a beach which is found on the other side of the port.

Walkers will enjoy the **picturesque trail ★** which follows the coastline and ends at the Les Lecques beaches.

Leave Bandol by the A 50, exit at La Cadière. Or take the more scenic D 559.

■ **La Cadière-d'Azur ★★**

What a pretty name! Built high on a hill (144 m), La Cadière-d'Azur's construction dates from the Middle Ages, as the labyrinth of narrow streets attests. What's even more remarkable is that the village has been able to preserve its ages-old charm.

There is a panoramic view around the village. Under the exceptional light of Provence, the azur sky allows you to discover the luxuriant countryside of the Paluns plain and beyond towards the Sainte-Baume massif. From the other side of the highway, its twin village can be seen: **Le Castellet ★**, a tiny, charming village. To the south, the Grand Vallat stream flows lazily through the plain and vineyards up to the Bandol beach. Such luminosity, unhindered by fog and mist, has been immortalized by many famous painters, including Van Gogh.

Finally, to visit La Cadière without stopping at the **Hostellerie Bérard** *(see p 307 and 308)* would be a sin. This exceptional place pairs culinary art with the beauty of Provence.

  Outdoor Activities

Hiking

La Croix-Valmer

Park your car at the Gigaro beach. A magnificent hike towards two capes situated southwest of the Presqu'Ile de Saint-Tropez, **Cap Lardier** and **Cap Cartay**, can be made from this spot. Small creeks and beaches can be discovered along the shoreline path. Allow about a half-day.

Bandol - Ile de Bendor

The tourist office hands out maps showing the different hiking trails in the area: the coastal path towards Les Lecques, the Gros Cerveau, the Massif de la Sainte-Beaume, the Gorges d'Ollioules, to name a few.

Let's not forget the marked paths and trails officially designated *Grand Randonnées* (GR 9, 90, 98, 99, 51 and 49). GR hiking guides, available in specialty bookshops, provide extensive details.

 Cycling

Le Lavandou

Many beautiful cycling or walking trips in this area around this seaside resort in the direction of Cap Bénat are possible. Contact the tourist office for details. Bicycle rental: Fun Bikes *(Avenue des Ilaires,* ☎ *94.71.00.61).*

**The Dream Tour ★★★
departing from Saint-Tropez:**

Day one: Follow the sea towards Cavalaire-sur-Mer and Le Lavandou. Visit **Bormes-les-Mimosas.** Embark for Ile de Porquerolles during the afternoon. Tour the island by foot or bicycle. Spend the night here in one of the suggested hotels.

Day two: Leave Porquerolles for **Ile de Port-Cros.** Try out the many walking trails across this national park. Leave in the afternoon to return to the mainland and visit **Bandol.** Finish the day at **La Cadière-d'Azur.** Dine and spend the night at the Hostellerie Bédard *(see p 307 and 308).*

Day three: Take the highway towards Hyères or the N 8 towards Toulon, then pick up the N 98 eastbound. Next take the D 41 towards Collobrières. Visit the **Chartreuse de la Verne** (D 14, then D 281). Head next towards **Grimaud.** Visit the village and make another culinary stop at the Les Santons restaurant *(see p 288).*

Ile de Porquerolles

This island was made for cycling. It's also a great way to reach the wonderful beaches and partake in various water sports, notably scuba diving and snorkeling. Bicycle rental, from the landing stage of the island:
Locavélo: ☎ 94.58.33.03
La Méduse: ☎ 94.58.33.03

 Golf

Le Lavandou

Golf du Lavandou *(350 F; Route du golf, ☎ 94.05.80.19)*.

 Scuba Diving

Ile de Porquerolles

Club de Plongée du Langoustier
Carré du Port
☎ 94.58.34.94 ⇄ 94.58.34.87

 Snorkeling

Bandol - Ile de Bendor

Centre International de Plongée
Ile de Bendor
☎ 94.29.55.12

Centre de Plongée
2 Boulevard Victor Hugo
☎ 94.29.41.57

 Deep-Sea Fishing

Bandol - Ile de Bendor

Sport Fishing Club
Hookipa Sport & Pêche
3 Rue Pierre Toesca
☎ 94.29.53.15 or 94.29.66.96

 Boating

Bandol - Ile de Bendor

Société Nautique de Bandol
☎ 94.29.42.26

Centre International de Funboard
Ile de Bendor
☎ 94.32.46.56

 Accommodation

■ Aiguebelle - Le Lavandou

The hotel **Le Grand Pavois** *(450-500 F; pb or ps, tv on request, ℜ, ≈; Plage d'Aiguebelle,* ☎ *94.05.81.38)* was recently taken over by a dynamic young manager. Although the hotel doesn't directly overlook the sea, an underground passage links it to a sandy beach. This is well-appreciated by those visitors travelling with children. In any event, the small road infront of the hotel is a dead-end so clients can enjoy relative tranquillity facing the sea. The Provençal meals are prepared by the owner himself.

■ Le Lavandou

Even though this large coastal town with its heavy traffic is uninspiring, there is one place of great merit:

Auberge de la Calanque *(550-1,050 F, 170 F extra bed, half-board 920-1,420 F; pb, mini-bar, ℜ, ≈; 62 Avenue du Général de Gaulle, ☎ 94.71.05.96; ⇄ 94.71.20.12).* Perched up high, this grand hotel has spacious sitting rooms with views overlooking the sea. The bedrooms are very pretty and its flower garden includes a large swmming pool. Clearly, caring managers with an eye for detail are in charge here. As the hotel is just a few minutes from the sea, there is a risk of hearing noise from the night-clubs in the area, especially during high season when bedroom windows are open. The restaurant *($$-$$$, closed Wed)* has a good reputation. Seafood is the specialty.

■ **Bormes-les-Mimosas**

North of the village, perched up high, is the **Grand Hotel** *(230-380 F, extra bed 80 F; pb, tv 20 F/day, C, ℜ; 167 Route du Baguier, ☎ 94.71.23.72, ⇄ 94.71.51.20).* This establishment has been completely renovated and offers a very pretty view over the Côte d'Azur. Just a few minutes from the village, an old-fashioned cosy atmos-phere reigns in this haven of peace and calm. It is good value and there is an excellent welcome. If you a part of a group, ask for the large room under the roof.

■ **Hyères**

A reasonably-priced hotel is found in the heart of the city, along a pedestrian street: **Hôtel du Portalent** *(150-240 F, 280 F for three with a small terrace; ps, tv in some rooms; 4 Rue de Limans, ☎ 94.65.39.40, ⇄ 94.35.86.33).* In the heart of the medieval district, this hotel is being renovated by its new owners who are putting their hearts and pocket books into the changes.

There is no restaurant, but the owner's son is very knowledgeable about the best addresses in the area, so don't hesitate to ask.

L'hôtel du Soleil *(160-380 F, half-board 400-640 F; ps or pb, tv in some rooms; Rue du Rempart, ☎ 94.65.16.26)* is very close to the city-centre but in fact is quite peaceful due to its location on the hillside (access from Place Clemenceau). The hotel is simple but clean and offers good value. Some rooms can accommodate up to six people *(80 F to 100 F per person; ps or pb).*

Our favourite address in Hyères is the **Hostellerie Provençale la Québécoise** *(230-350 F, half-board obligatory in Jul and Aug 550-730 F; ps or pb, ≈, ℜ; 20 Avenue de l'Amiral-Costebelle, ☎ 94.57.69.24, ⇄ 94.38.78.27).* It is located 3 km south of the city-centre, direction Almanarre, towards the D 559. Halfway between Hyères and the sea, there is a sign marking the way to this lovely hideaway. The owner — no prizes for guessing that she's from Québec — greets guests with a warm welcome. Rooms are pretty and very clean. Meals are served on a large terrace next to a magnificent over-grown garden with a swimming pool and the sound of birds singing. This is an ideal spot to relax for a few days. What's more, it is a good base from which to make excursions in the area, notably the Iles d'Hyères. Excel-lent value.

■ **Iles d'Hyères**

Ile de Porquerolles

We visited three hotels. The **Hôtel Sainte-Anne**, while it is ideally-located on a large square, didn't entirely win us over. So just two others are described here. Both are rather expensive but represent the going rate for the chance to stay on such a beautiful island.

L'Auberge des Glycines *(half-board 650-850 F for three people; pb, ≡, tv, ₵, ℜ; Place d'Armes, 94.58.30.36, ⇄ 94.58.35.22)* is next to the church. Most remarkable here are the beautiful rooms and modern bathrooms. The public sitting rooms are decorated with lovely Provençal furniture. There is a cute terrace, where meals are served. The hotel is sheltered from tourists and the heat. Its **restaurant** specializes in grilled fish, roasted sardines, pasta and pistou soup.

For those interested in the ultimate in luxury, head for **Le Mas du Langoustier** *(full board 2,200-3,200 F; 1,660 F for a small room; 4,762 F for 5 day half-board package; ps or pb, ℜ; ☎ 94.58.30.09, ⇄ 94.58.36.02)*. This beautiful establishment, entirely renovated, is located at the end of the island in an area where the beauty of the forest and sea mixes with gentle breezes to create a dreamy spot. A car service operates between the port and hotel. The scenic landscape may be visited by foot or by bicycle; the hotel itself has a tennis court and a beach. The owner, Madame Richard, is full of stories about the history of Porquerolles, as it was her grandfather who bought it just before the turn of the century. Meals are served in the park or, if the weather forbids it, in a large glassed-in veranda. The **restaurant** *($$-$$$-$$$$)* serves Provençal cuisine.

■ Ile du Levant

The best bargain here is probably the hotel-restaurant called **Chez Valéry** *(690 F half-board; pb; ☎ 94.05.90.83 or 94.05.92.95)*. This establishment includes eight comfortable rooms, a large terrace and a flower garden. It is located in the heart of the island and is peaceful. Although guests must accept the half-board condition, this is hardly penance because the quality of the cuisine is truly remarkable. Fish and seafood are the strong points in the **restaurant**, which considers itself "semi-gastronomic". The welcome, service and quality of the dishes served are entirely worthy of this description.

Moving to a superior class, is the **Héliotel** *(1,000-1,400 F in Aug, 700-950 F in low season; ps or pb, tv in the public sitting room, ≈; ☎ 94.05.90.63, ⇄ 94.05.90.20)* which benefits from a superb site and the warm welcome of its hosts. Surrounded by a forest of pine trees, three-sides of the hotel enclose a very beautiful and large swimming pool. A somewhat isolated independent suite for two people *(1,250 F in Aug, otherwise 750 F)* has its own private swimming pool. The owner herself is in charge of the **panoramic restaurant** *($$-$$$)*.

■ Toulon

This is not the most interesting city in which to pass the night, but prices are lower than in the seaside resort villages.

L'hôtel Molière *(180 F; pb, tv; 12 Rue Molière, ☎ 94.92.78.35)* is an excellent address in its price category. This pleasant and welcoming hotel is found in the city-centre, in the heart of the pedestrian zone on the Place de l'Opéra. It is in good condition, and offers a comfortable sitting room for guests. Another important point is that cars may be parked near the hotel, at an affordable rate.

Followers of 30s style will enjoy the **Saint-Nicolas** *(185-235 F, 258 F four people; pb, tv; 49 Rue Jean Jaurès, ☎ 94.91.02.28)*. The hotel's decor, entirely renovated in 1989, is quite charming. Thanks to its strategic position in the city-centre and the calm found there despite the hustle and bustle surrounding it, this hotel is good value.

If the former hotel is full, try the **Hôtel du Dauphiné** *(225-275 F, 315 F three people; pb, tv; 10 Rue Berthelot, ☎ 94.92.00.08, ⇄ 94.62.16.69)*. It is found in the city centre on a pedestrian street a few steps away from the opera house. The hotel is soberly decorated, well taken care of and pleasant. The opera house's general manager keeps a room here year-round.

Here's a nice spot: the **New Hôtel-La Tour Blanche** *(395-495 F, extra bed 100 F, free for children under 16 years; pb, tvc, ℜ, ≈; Boulevard A. Vence, Mont Faron, ☎ 94.24.41.57, ⇄ 94.22.42.25)*. The hotel is located at the side of the téléférique, which climbs to the summit of Mont Faron. Naturally there is a wonderful panoramic view and absolute calm. The pretty terrace surrounds a modest-sized swimming pool. Many activities are available, including ping-pong and billiards. A golf course is close-by. The **restaurant** *($-$$)* is light and airy, and overlooks a large terrace. Quality cuisine and the dishes are well presented.

■ **Bandol**

We strongly recommend **Les Galet** *(580 F half-board; pb, tv, ℜ; closed Nov to Mar; Montée Voisin, ☎ 94.29.43.46, ⇄ 94.32.50.39)*. Situated on high ground at the village entrance, the hotel has a magnificent view over the sea. The decor is Provençal, the atmosphere is very pleasant and the owners welcoming. Meals are served on a large terrace touching the sea. The beaches and the Casino are nearby.

For a hotel directly on the beach, try the **Splendid** *(280-320 F, 560-600 F half-board; pb, tv, ℜ; closed Nov to Mar; Plage Rénecros, ☎ 94.29.41.61, ⇄ 94.65.92.75)*. This hotel has good, clean rooms and offers good value. A glassed-in restaurant overlooks the sea. About 5 minutes to the city-centre.

Some visitors might enjoy staying in a private villa: the **Catel Myrto** *(2,500 F per week May to Sep; pb or tv, C, ≈; 50 Avenue Général Leclerc, ☎ 94.32.43.36)*. The owner proposes three studios, each with a separate entrance. The villa is located on a quiet street and dates from the 1930s. It is surrounded by a large garden and swimming pool; there are sea views as well. The city-centre is just 5 minutes away and the beach is just two minutes away. Very good value.

The **Master Hôtel** *(780-1,040 F half-board usually obligatory in summertime; ps, pb, tv, ≈, ℜ; Rue Raimu, ☎ 94.29.46.53, ⇄ 94.32.53.54)* is the old villa of the well-known French actor Raimu. It is 5 minutes from the city-centre and overlooks the sea. A beautiful garden provides direct access to the sea.

Travellers who enjoy the finer things in life will adore the **Ile Rousse** *(1,200-1,800 F half-board; pb, tv, mini bar, ≈, ℜ; 17 Boulevard Louis Lumière, ☎ 94.29.46.86; ⇄ 94.29.49.49)*. Situated on the Presqu'île de Bandol peninsula close to the city-centre and port, the hotel is built in a modern 60s architecture which has been well maintained. The sea can been seen from everywhere! Everything is spacious and bright. Rooms are luxurious (bathrobes are offered) and have terraces. A private beach is located below the salt-water swimming pool. The hotel's restaurant has a wide terrace overlooking the sea.

Along *la route des vins de Bandol* (Bandol wine route), 3 km from the beaches, is the **Auberge des Pins** *(490-550 F; pb, tv, ℜ; closed Jan; 2249 Route du Beausset, tl ☎94 29 59 10, ⇄ 94 32 43 46).* This pleasant country hotel has seven bedrooms and was recently renovated. The hotel's half-board rate, while not obligatory, does allow guests to dine on a lovely shaded terrace.

■ La Cadière d'Azur

The real gem of the region is the **Hostellerie Bérard** *(415-720 F; pb, tv, mini bar, ≡, ≈, ℜ; closed Jan to mid-Feb; ☎ 94.90.11.43 or 94.90.14.98, ⇄ 94.90.01.94)* which lies in a magnificent site in this beautiful Provençal village. The Bérard family has transformed an old convent into a place of dreams. The charming ambience is reflected in the Provençal decor with its many antiques, fine fabrics and colourful clay tiles which set the tone and identify each different bedroom. The welcome is very warm and the surroundings are impressively calm. Rooms are cosy, while some are truly spacious. Others lead directly onto a small garden and swimming pool. The joys of Provence are felt everywhere in this hotel — a sensation reinforced by the presence of the owner, Madame Bérard, who is an expert on the region. Guests will no doubt feel doubly passionate about Provence after meeting her and listening to her recount stories about old Provençal customs

and traditions. You'll remember a visit here for a long time to come *(see p 308).*

 Restaurants

Please consult the "Accomodation" section, where some restaurants belonging to hotels are described.

■ Hyères

Les Jardins de Bacchus *(32 Avenue Gambetta; closed Sun night and Mon; ☎ 94.65.77.63)* Provençal cuisine.

Le Bistrot de Marius *(1 Place Massillon, ☎ 94.35.88.38)*

Le Chaudron Magique *(8 Place Massioon, ☎ 94.35.38.45)*

For crepes and home-made ice cream: **La Bergerie** *(16 Rue de Limans, ☎ 94.65.57.97)*

■ Toulon

Along the port, there are a number of restaurants which, while not outstanding, are nevertheless perfectly all right, especially considering their reasonable prices.

One of these is the trendy **Le Grand Café de la Rade** *($; 224 Avenue de la République, Carré du Port, ☎ 94.24.87.01).* Especially good is the copious *Flammenküche* (one portion is ample for two!). Otherwise, try the *choucroute alsacienne* (Alsatian sauerkraut). There is a large terrace over-looking the port and the service is efficient and courteous.

■ Bandol

Hidden away in the city-centre along a small side street, west of the Place de l'Église is **Olivio** *($; 68 F midday menu and 100 F dinner menu; closed Sun; 1 9   R u e   d e s   T o n n e l i e r s ,* ☎ *94.29.81.79)*. A friendly ambience reigns in this pleasant bistrot run by its owner Véronique. This is one spot to recommend to all those who would like to get to know the charm of the Var people. It is well away from the touristy parts of town and the prices offer good value.

For fish and seafood, try **Au Fin Gourmet** *($; 16 Rue de la République,* ☎ *94.29.41.80)*. The midday menu includes two courses for 60 F and *moules-frites* (mussels and fries) are 45 F. The chef will even prepare bouillabaisse if ordered ahead of time.

Auberge du Vieux Port *($-$$)* overlooks the port. This spot is highly recommended by locals and by Bandol's culinary connaisseurs.

■ La Cadière d'Azur

If travelling inland between Toulon and Bandol, **under no circumstances** should visitors pass up the opportunity to enjoy a meal at the **Hostellerie Bérard** *($-$$; closed Sun PM and Mon, during summer closed Mon midday only;* ☎ *94.90.11.43)*. The restaurant proposes four set-price menus: *"marché", "saison", "gourmand"* and *"truffes" (350 F, four courses)*. Monsieur Bérard prepares a cuisine of the highest quality, where the flavours of only the finest ingredients reign. Among the house specialities are a Barigoule of purple artichokes, John Dorry roasted in its skin and perfumed with aniseed, a millefeuilles of beef with fried foie-gras and truffle juice and finally, a rack of young rabbit stuffed with olives. Desserts include a strawberry, Champagne and Séchuan pepper gratin, tiramisu and a selection rightly called *assiette gourmande*. The dining room's pleasant decor and large picture windows assure an evening to remember! You can also stay the night too (see p 307).

Future chefs take note!

The adorable owner of this establishment, Madame Bérard, proposes a **Provençal cooking course** *(package includes five nights accommodation with four days of classes; mid-Oct to mid-Dec and during Mar)*. Students go fishing, visit the markets together, collect herbs on the hills and learn to prepare the authentic cuisine of the region. Also a special course in January on cooking with truffles. *(Information from: Hostellerie Bérard, 83740 La Cadière d'Azur,* ☎ *94.90.11.43,* ⇄ *94.90.01.94.)*

 Entertainment

■ Le Lavandou

Festival Summer Jazz *(mid-Aug,* ☎ *94.05.15.76)*

Le Flamenco *(with one drink 100 F; every night 11 PM to 5 AM; Boulevard du Front de Mer)*. Discotheque. Plus, live entertainment around 1 AM is often presented.

■ Bormes-les-Mimosas

Soirées Musicales de Bormes *(Jul,* ☎ *94.71.15.08 or 94.71.15.17)*

■ Hyères

Festival de Jazz *(late Jul, Pinède de l'Hippodrome;* ☎ *94.35.90.81)*

Journées Médiévales *(early Jul;* ☎ *94.35.90.81)*

Le Blue Bell *(with one drink 80 F; every night 10 PM, off-season only Fri to Sun; Route de Giens;* ☎ *94.58.92.99).* Discotheque with large dancefloor. Plus, roller-skating rink (equipment hire available).

La Grotte *(with one drink 70 F; open in season every night 11 PM to 4 AM, low season Sat and Sun; la Madrague de Giens,* ☎ *94.58.22.21).* Discotheque. Note: this nightclub is sometimes rented to groups and is closed to the public at these times.

The Midnight *(open every night 9 PM to dawn; 6 Rue Général Brosset;* ☎ *94.65.54.21).* Discotheque; except Wed and Sat when there is a band.

The New Rêve *(open every night 10 PM to 4 AM, in season, otherwise open Fri, Sat and Sun; Port de la Capte;* ☎ *94.58.00.07)* Discotheque with theme nights and snack bar.

■ Toulon

Festival International de Musique *(Jun; details from the tourist office)*

Café des Artistes *(dinner 100 F with orchestra; closed Mon and Tue; RN 8, Entrée des Gorges d'Ollioules;* ☎ *94.63.04.33).* Wed: special theme night based on a different country each

week. Thu: jazz night. Fri, Sat and Sun: orchestra.

Clés d'Or *(with one drink 80 F; open Thu to Sun 10 PM to 4 AM; 2 Rue Corneille* ☎ *94.92.34.33).* Discotheque.

Métro Blockos *(entry 50 F, Sat 80 F, 50 F for second drink; closed Mon and Tue; reservations advised: Port de Plaisance;* ☎ *94.42.35.95).* Fashionable nightclub. Live entertainment. Shows every Wed.

La Scala *(entry 50 F weekdays, 80 F Fri to Sun; 11 PM to dawn, closed Mon and Tue; 5 Avenue de l'Elisa;* ☎ *94.27.37.49).* Discotheque-night club. Wed: theme nights. Sun: special evening with live entertainment, fashion shows... A meeting place for trendy types, in an old theatre.

Le Pussycat *(entry with one drink weekdays 50 F, Sat 60 F; 11 PM to dawn, closed Mon and Tue; 655 Avenue de Claret;* ☎ *94.92.76.91).* Popular club-discotheque for gay clientele. Live entertainment.

■ Bandol

Le Stars' Circus *(Mon free; every night from 11 PM to 5 AM; Casino de Bandol, Quai Général de Gaulle;* ☎ *94.32.45.44).* Discotheque, popular with a lively young crowd from the region.

Casino *(4 PM to 4 AM;* ☎ *94.32.45.44):* Roulette, black jack and craps are available. Plus, two bars and a restaurant.

Shopping

■ Hyères

Foire aux Santons (Santons Fair) *(mid-August; Salle d'Honneur of the Park Hotel).*

■ Toulon

Salon de l'Habitat *(late Sep to early Oct; Palais Neptune;* ☎ *94.22.08.58).*

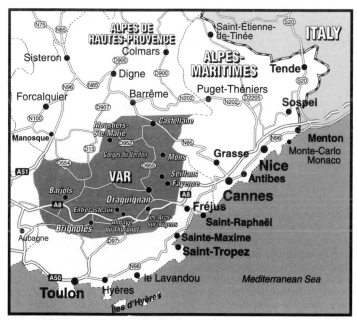

THE VAR DU NORD

The Var covers a large part of Côte d'Azur. Since highway A 8 is an east-west axis that cuts through the area, separating it into two equal parts, we have defined two regions according to this division: The Var du Nord in the north, and The Var du Sud in the south.

The Var du Nord is defined by the Verdon river, by the wild beauty of its gorges, Grand Canyon and impressive cliffs known as the Falaise des Cavaliers. The Verdon empties into a huge artificial lake whose brilliant colour wavers between emerald green and turquoise. An entire village was sacrificed for this lake, which is actually a reservoir built to provide the region with a supply of potable water.

But the Var de Nord is also the Provençal countryside, or *Provence Varoise*, characterized by the serenity of its cultural heritage sites, of which the Abbaye du Thoronet is undoubtedly the most important.

 Finding Your Way Around

The train isn't the best way to get to the Var du Nord. It stops in only two cities, Draguignan and Brignoles. The diversity and vast beauty offered in the Var can best be appreciated by car. Rentals are available in any large city on the Côte d'Azur (see "Practical Information" section for each city).

There is, of course, bus service to link the villages, most of these leave from Draguignan or Brignoles. However, If you choose this option, you will be at the mercy of fixed bus schedules and limited to the routes available.

We propose a tour by car that covers the entire region. This tour, in the form of a loop, begins in the east, climbs north, traverses the Alpes-de-Haute-Provence from east to west and then descends southwards again. This tour will take about three days to complete, depending on how much time you wish spend on outdoor activities when you get to the Verdon's gorges and Lac de Ste-Croix.

■ By Car

The Var can be reached easily from anywhere in Provence or the Côte d'Azur. The **A 8 - E 80** highway crosses the entire territory and connects Menton to Aix-en-Provence. The suggested itinerary begins in the small village of Les Arcs, which has its own highway exit.   From here, a multitude of small departmental roads lead to just about everywhere in the territory.

■ By Train

There are only two SNCF stations in the territory:

Gare S.N.C.F de Draguignan
Av. du Maréchal-Gallieni
☎ 94.91.50.50

Gare SNCF de Brignoles
Av. de la Gare
☎ 94.69.11.95

■ By Bus

The two main transfer points are at Draguignan and Brignoles. These two cities provide access to a vast network of routes, served by numerous operators. The only disadvantage is that, although Draguignan and Brignoles are the largest cities in the territory, they have little to offer. It can be somewhat tiresome having to pass through these cities to get to the other places that are worth visiting.

In any case, get a **bus schedule**, called the *Indicateur des Lignes Routières Départmentales du Var,* which is available at the tourist office in any of the towns or villages that the bus serves. It contains all the information you need to plan your trip.

Finally, there are direct coach services from Draguignan to Nice or Toulon airports (*information in Draguignan:* ☎ *94.68.15.34*).

❓ Practical Information

■ Draguignan

Tourist Office
9 Bd. Clémenceau
☎ 94.68.63.30
⇄ 94.47.10.76

Here you can pick up all the information you need for your trip, including lots of pamphlets that cover the entire region. The friendly, courteous staff know the city and the area very well, and are extremely helpful.

Emergency Medical Service in Draguignan - 24 h
☎ 94.67.01.01

■ **Fayence**

Tourist Office:
Syndicat d'initiative
☎ 94.76.20.08
⇄ 94.76.18.05

■ **Castellane**

Tourist Office
B.P. 8 Route Nationale
☎ 92.83.61.14

■ **Moustiers-Ste-Marie**

Tourist Office:
Syndicat d'initiative
June 15 - September 15 (morning and evening)
☎ 92.74.67.84

Rest of the year: Town Hall 2 PM to 4 PM
☎ 92.74.66.19

■ **Aups**

Tourist Office
Place Frédéric Mistral
☎ 94.70.00.80

 Exploring

This tour begins at the exit for "Les Arcs" on A 8.

■ **Les Arcs sur Argens** ★

This quaint Provençal town is located between the Mediterranean and the Alps. The town lies in the shadow of the old medieval village, perched high upon its rocky peak. Traces of that medieval era still remain, including the surrounding wall and the old 12th-century castle with its impressive watchtower. Today, the old castle is a hotel with lots of character.

Explore the narrow streets and vaulted staircases of the old village, where there are many gorgeous houses. Fans of painter Ludovic Bréa will find a Gothic reredos by this artist in **Église Saint-Jean-Baptiste**.

Leave the village by D 91, towards Sainte-Roseline.

■ **Sainte-Roseline**

The **Château Sainte-Roseline** is a vineyard that produces Côtes-de-Provence wines. Wine-tasintgs are even possible here.

The history of the château goes back to the 12th century, when it was an abbey. At the beginning of the 14th century, and for about two centuries, it became the only Carthusian charterhouse for women in the Var. Only the **chapel** ★ *(Wed and Sun 3:30 PM to 6 PM, also open Sat in Jul and Aug; closed Jan-Feb)* is open to visitors. It houses Ste-Roseline's tomb, as well as the works of several artists, including a mosaic by Chagall, a bronze lectern by Giacometti and stained-glass windows by Raoul Ubac and Jean Bazaine.

Continue along D 91 to N 555, which leads to Draguignan.

■ **Draguignan**

This city's origins are said to date back as far as the 2nd century BC. In AD 843, Provence was annexed to the Holy German Empire, and Draguignan subsequently became a *cité comtale*. At the end of the Middle Ages, it acquired royal status after France took control of Provence.

The city itself is not so attractive, but it does have a nice museum. The **Musée des Arts et Traditions Populaires de Moyenne Provence** (*20 F, children 8 F; Tue to Sun 9 AM to noon and 2 PM to 6 PM except Sun morning; 15 Rue Roumanille, ☎ 94.47.05.72*), a museum of the arts and popular tradiotions of central Provence. It is located on an ancient religious site, and is dedicated to preserving the Provençal heritage. Regional history will unfold before your eyes when you see, among other things, the reproduction of an oil mill and of a Provençal kitchen.

For an enchanting walk, leave Draguignan by D 955 towards Callas. Take D 25, a pretty road that leads to Bargemon, and then follow the D 19 towards Seillans and Fayence. If you're in a hurry, take D 562 instead to D 563, which goes to Fayence.

■ Seillans ★

The road between Bargemon and Seillans is spectacular and leads to one of the most beautiful hillside towns in the Fayence area. An air of mystery surrounds the town. It could be its picturesque streets lined with high narrow houses, its church or its castle that give this impression, but it's like travelling through time into the Middle Ages. The **Église Saint-Léger** and the castle date back to the 11th century, which is also when the first houses began to appear around the castle.

■ Fayence ★

Fayence was home to the bishops of Fréjus from the 18th century up until the French Revolution, when they relinquished their seigneurial rights over the village. The old village is still a maze of narrow streets, leading up to the bishops' castle at the top of the hill. Below the village, a 13th-century fortified door called the **Porte Sarrasine** still stands.

Because of its geographical location overlooking the plain, Fayence became a gliding centre after World War II. It now enjoys international fame.

For a short hike, head from Fayence towards its twin village **Tourettes**. Just before Tourettes is the **Église Saint-Jean-Baptiste**. This church, built in 1750, has a beautiful high altar of pink, grey and white marble. In Tourettes itself stands **Notre-Dame-des-Cyprès**, a pretty 13th-century Romanesque chapel.

Leave by the D 563 towards Mons.

■ Mons ★

The Fayence region's most northern hillside village, **Mons** is also the village with the highest elevation in the Var (800 m). It was completely repopulated by the Genoese after the plague of 1348 wiped out the entire population.

Église Notre-Dame was built in the 13th century beside the seigneurial castle, which was later destroyed. It's worth visiting this church to see its three reredos.

Place Saint-Sébastien, at one end of the village, offers a lovely panoramic view. The tourist office is also located here.

Get back on D 563 northbound to Route Napoléon, or N 85, which leads to Castellane.

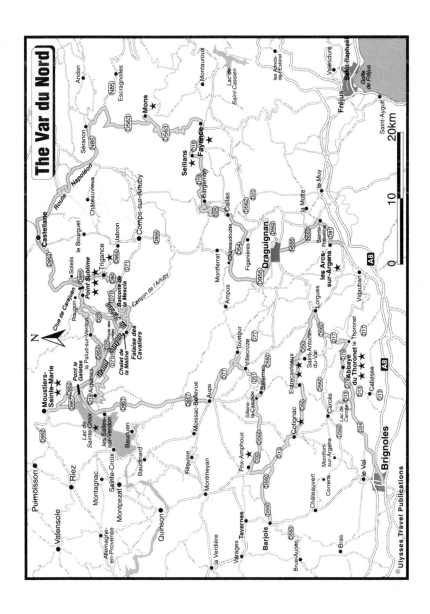

The Var du Nord

Route Napoléon

Andon
Escragnolles
N85
Séranon
Châteauvieux
Castellane
Clue de Carejuan
Soleils
le Bourguet
Jabron
Trigance
Point Sublime
Rougon
la Palud-sur-Verdon
Balcons de la Mescla
Aiguines
Grand Canyon du Verdon
Chalet de la Maline
Falaise des Cavaliers
Canyon de l'Artuby
Comps-sur-Artuby
Mons
Montauroux
Lac de Saint-Cassien
Seillans
Fayence
Bargemon
Callas
le Muy
la Motte
Châteaudouble
Montferrat
Ampus
Figanières
Draguignan
Sainte-Roseline
les Arcs-sur-Argens
Vidauban
Moustiers-Sainte-Marie
Pont le Galetas
Lac de Sainte-Croix
les Salles-sur-Verdon
Baudinard
Bauduen
Sainte-Croix
Montpezat
Quinson
la Verdière
Montmeyan
Régusse
Moissac-Bellevue
Aups
Villecroze
Tourtour
Salernes
Sillans-la-Cascade
Cotignac
Entrecasteaux
Saint-Antonin-du-Var
Lorgues
Abbaye du Thoronet
le Thoronet
Cabasse
Carcès
Lac de Carcès
Montfort-sur-Argens
Puimoisson
Riez
Montagnac
Allemagne-en-Provence
Valensole
Bras
le Val
Brignoles
Châteauvert
Correns
Bruc-Auriac
Barjols
Varages
Tavernes
Fox-Amphoux
Saint-Raphaël
Valescure
Fréjus
Golfe de Fréjus
les Adrets de l'Estérel
Saint-Aygulf

20km

10

0

A8

© Ulysses Travel Publications

■ **Route Napoléon**

Napoleon and his army travelled this road on foot to get from Golfe-Juan on the Côte d'Azur to Grenoble, in the Isère. There are few points of interest along this segment of the road.

■ **Castellane**

This town is in the department of Alpes-de-Haute-Provence, halfway between the Mediterranean and the Alps. Castellane, a stone's throw from the Gorges du Verdon, is a typically Provençal village with its narrow streets, small squares, fountains and main square shaded by century-old plane trees. The town is dominated by a gigantic rocky peak, from which the Notre-Dame chapel seems to keep a benevolent watch over the village. The sight is quite stunning. It is undoubtedly because of these features that Castellane is counted among the *Villages et Cités de Caractère*.

The **Église St-Victor**, with its strikingly simple and modest façade, was built in the 12th century. The church's architecture is an interesting example of the transition between Romanesque and Gothic art. It was designated as a historical monument in 1944.

The rocky peak can be reached by a footpath that begins behind the church. The path is easier than it looks. It winds among the remains of the ancient fortification walls that surrounded Castellane in the 14th century and leads to **Chapelle Notre-Dame-du-Roc**, which has been a pilgrimage site since ancient times. Each year, on August 14th, the townspeople hold a *Veillée aux Flambaux*, a spectacular illuminated evening procession to the chapel.

Castellane is also epitomized by the untamed nature that surrounds it and protects it from pollution and noise. There is nothing but fresh air, open spaces, sunlight and the fragrant clear air. Hiking, horseback riding, hunting and fishing are only some of the activities that can be enjoyed.

Leave via D 952 towards Gorges Du Verdon to Point Sublime on the north bank of Gorges du Verdon.

■ **Point Sublime** ★

Point Sublime offers a striking view of the entrance to Verdon's Grand Canyon. This site offers the most facilities for tourists to the immediate area. There is parking, telescopes, documentation as well as an inn. From here you can get to the **Sentier Martel**, a trail considered the *grande classique* (great classic) of hikes. It is 14 km and about eight hours on foot to the Chalet de la Maline. It's a good idea to do it the other way around. For a shorter hike, try the **Sentier du Couloir Samson**, which goes down to the bottom of the Gorges and can be completed in two hours. This trail gives a good perspective of the Gorges.

■ **Gorges du Verdon** ★

The Gorges and their Grand Canyon are two of Europe's largest natural sites. They are must-sees. There are trails on the north and south banks. No matter which side you choose, the view is equally spectacular and both trails end at Moustiers-Ste-Marie. We recommend the south bank, even though it offers fewer spectacular vantage points, because it allows the possibility of visiting Trigance and Aiguines. Of course, you could always cover both sides by going full circle on the trails. This 130 km trip takes an entire day and can even begin from Nice or Cannes, since the Gorges are only one and a half hours away by car.

To do the north rim tour, go up to the D 952.

The **north rim tour** starts at the Auberge du Point Sublime on D 952. At the beginning of the tour, a secondary road leads to **Rougon**. Going up to the village guarantees an exceptional view of the Verdon. Back on D 952, there is an intersection just before La Palud. Take this road, the D 23 or Route des Crêtes. There are several lofty viewpoints in succession along this road, that form a loop which ends at La Palud, an ancient supply-village with a few stores and hotels. The Refuge de la Maline, along this road is the suggested departure point for the hike along the Martel trail to Point Sublime.

To finish the tour, take D 952 again; there are panoramic views all the way to Moustiers.

End of the north rim tour.

The south rim tour starts with a tour of the village of Trigance. To get there, take D 955 at Pont-de-Soleils, and then follow D 90.

■ Trigance ★

This old village was built way up high on the rocky spur of a mountain at an elevation of 800 m. It is dominated by a fortress that dates back to the 11th century, which is now a hotel belonging to the *Relais et Châteaux* association.

Stroll through the village and discover its vaulted passageways, sculpted-stone lintels and 12th-century Romanesque church.

The ancient fortress is only open to guests who are staying there. You can nevertheless enjoy a drink on the terrace, which offers a gorgeous view of the area, or if you prefer, you can eat in the castle's beautiful vaulted medieval dining room. Of course, some may find it a bit expensive!

Trigance is a good place to stay overnight since both rims of the Gorges du Verdon can be easily reached from here.

Take D 90 south to D 71, which leads to the south rim of the Gorges.

The **south rim tour** is called the Sublime Corniche. It begins with the **Balcons de la Mescla**, where the Verdon and Artuby rivers meet. The view is spectacular. The road continues in a succession of magnificent lookouts culminating at the **Falaise des Cavaliers**. This is most impressive. The **Hôtel de Grand Canyon**, has the advantage of a captivating view over the Gorges, from the rooms and from the restaurant. Several hiking trails on both the north and south rims can be reached from this point via a footbridge. On the other side is the Refuge de la Maline and the trailhead of the famous Sentier Martel.

The trail follows the Gorges and ends at Aiguines. End of south rim tour.

■ Aiguines

At an elevation of over 800 m, Aiguines offers a spectacular view of **Lac de Saint-Croix**, the 3,000 ha artificial lake that provides Aix, Toulon and Marseilles with drinking water. The main attraction in this village besides its church and private castle is the

Musée des Tourneurs de Bois, a lathe artisans' museum.

Take D 19 towards Lac de Sainte-Croix, then D 957 to D 952 leading to Moustiers-Ste-Marie.

■ Lac de Sainte-Croix ★

Route D 19 which descends towards the lake offers superb panoramic views. At the lake, the scenery becomes even more spectacular, especially where the Verdon flows into the lake. The water takes on every shade ranging from emerald to turquoise.

■ Moustiers-Ste-Marie ★

Moustiers is also called the pearl of Provence and the doorway to the Gorges of the Verdon. This village, famous for its earthenware, has a serene and remarkably vast landscape.

The village, divided in two by a rushing mountain stream, embraces the mountain on each side. The exposed rock of the mountain and the bridges that span the torrent as a constant reminder of the rushing water, make it an interesting place for a stroll. Most of the houses along the narrow village streets date back to the 18th century. There are also many restaurants and boutiques which sell, among other things, the village speciality: world-famous **Moustiers** earthenware. Pottery-lovers will want to visit the **Musée de la Faïence** (*Apr to Oct, Wed to Sun 9 AM to noon and 2 PM to 6 p.m; in the crypt near the church*), an earthenware museum.

In the village, **Église Notre-Dame** is worth seeing. It dates back for the most part to the 12th century. The highlight is its Romanesque Lombard-style bell tower.

Those up for more of a challenge can walk up to the **Chapelle Notre-Dame-de-Beauvoir**. Overlooking the village, the chapel offers a magnificent view of the rooftops. It includes a Romanesque section with a single nave, built in the 12th century, to which two Gothic bays were added in the 16th century.

Take D 957 towards Aups.

■ Aups ★

Even though this town is located in the lower foothills of the Alps, **Aups** is only 60 km from the sea. This is a good place to stop a while and stroll through the old picturesque streets and discover many of the characteristic features of Provençal towns, such as the old wash house, the fountains, plane trees, sundials, and the clock tower.

Gourmets shouldn't miss the **Marché aux Truffes Noires**, the truffle market held in Aups every Thursday morning between November and February. The truffles are sniffed out by well-trained dogs.

Leave the town by D 7 towards Tourtour.

■ Tourtour ★

The road to Tourtour is splendid. From a rocky peak, the village looks over a sea of hills. In the 12th century there was a castle, now in ruins, and like all medieval villages, a church. **Église St-Denis** replaced the medieval church and offers a superb view of the entire area, stretching all the way to the coast.

Tourtour is a nice place for a quiet walk, but offers no other points of interest. You can take a leisurely stroll and even relax on one of the terraces on the main square in the centre of the village.

Leave by D 51 towards Villecroze.

■ Villecroze

The village is in the lower foothills of the Alpes de Provence at an elevation of 350 m. Its narrow streets and picturesque archways preserve **Villecroze**'s medieval character.

Overhanging a beautiful park are the **caves** ★, which are definitely worth a visit. The villagers used to take shelter here whenever there was an invasion. There is even a subterranean lake that provided them with water.

Continue on D 51 towards Salernes, then take D 560 towards Sillans-la-Cascade (famous for canoeing and rafting), and continue towards Fox-Amphoux, accessible via D 32.

■ Fox-Amphoux ★

This charming old village has remained virtually unchanged. Tucked out-of-the-way, perched high up on a ridge, it has been spared the usual invasion by the tourist industry. The little shaded square is truly adorable. It also has a hotel that offers a pleasant place to stop, with absolute tranquillity, and good cuisine (see p 327).

The village's setting remains untamed and natural making it a nice spot to explore on foot.

Go back on D 560 to get to Barjols.

■ Barjols

The **Collégiale Notre-Dame-de-l'Assomption** is a designated historical monument. Dating back to the 11th century, this church was built in a Gothic-Provençal style. Behind the Collégiale is the residence of the Pontevès, the entrance of which is marked by a **stone porch** (another historical monument), built in 1532. This town has no fewer than 22 fountains and 16 wash houses.

Leave by D 560 towards Cotignac, then take D 50 towards Entrecasteaux.

■ Entrecasteaux ★

Entrecasteaux is an authentic Provençal town with a small river winding its way through the lush, gently rolling hills.

The enormous **château** ★ *(10 AM to noon and 2 PM to 5 PM, in summer until 6 PM, in winter afternoons only;* ☎ *94.04.43.95)* looms over the valley below. It was built in the 11th century, but has undergone several transformations. By 1974, when it was purchased by an Englishman in an effort to save it, the centuries had left it dilapidated and near ruin. Today it stands magnificently restored and houses permanent and temporary exhibits of oil paintings and period furniture. The owners offer two exceptional guest rooms furnished with period pieces (see p 324). There is also a French Garden, which was designed by Le Nôtre, creator of the gardens of the Palais de Versailles.

The town, a designated historical site, is a beautiful little collection of old houses with high narrow façades, pretty 17th-century porches and vaulted passageways. The Saint-Sauveur fortress-church dates back to the 13th century.

For a walk in the refreshing country air, follow the marked trails.

Leave via D 50 towards Lorgues.

■ Lorgues

This town, which dates back to the 6th century, offers all the charm of a picturesque old Var village. Nine of the 12 towers of the old town wall are still standing. The town also houses the Collégiale Saint-Martin, an imposing classical church containing a beautiful high altar of multicoloured marble decorated with *putti* attributed to Puget.

Leave via D 562 to D 17, which leads to Thoronet. From there, D 79 leads to the Thoronet abbey. The directions are clearly indicated.

■ Abbaye du Thoronet ★

If there is one religious site that has to be seen, this is it. This magnificent **abbey** (*in summer 9 AM to 7 PM, off-season 9 AM to noon and 2 PM to 5 PM; service Sun noon; ☎ 94.73.87.13*) is one of Provence's most important cultural and historical sites. Built in 1160 in the wooded interior of the Massif de Maures, it is one of the purest and most moving architectural works of the Romanesque era in Provence. The astonishing serenity of this Cistercian abbey is a reflection of the serene lives of the founding monks, who were strict followers of Saint-Benoît.

To make the most of your visit to this area, we strongly suggest you take a guided tour. The guides have a vast knowledge and love of this place. Tours begin several times a day between April and September.

The **church ★**, a site of most complete austerity, is absolutely overwhelming, and imparts an incredible sense of inner peace, a deep emotional feeling. The quality of the light inside the church is extraordinary. Heavenly! Every year the abbey hosts a music festival where Gregorian chants take on extraordinary dimensions thanks to the excellent acoustics of the building.

The chapter house, cloister and the **Pavillon de la Fontaine** are also open to visitors. The pavilion's washbasin, with its 16 faucets, was used by the monks before they entered the adjoining refectory, which has since disappeared.

 Outdoor Activities

The region is perfect for nature and sports enthusiasts, who will find lots to do in the Gorges du Verdon and Lac de Ste-Croix. The Verdon is a favorite spot for hiking, canoeing and kayaking, and Lac de Ste-Croix is also great for water sports.

To take full advantage of the Verdon, there are four main starting points: the Point Sublime and the Refuge de la Maline, on the north side of the gorges; Falaise des Cavaliers, on the south side; and Lac de Ste-Croix, at the mouth of the Verdon.

 Hiking

In the Verdon, the **Sentier Martel** is the classic hiking tour. This 14 km trail, usually an eight hour walk, takes you from Refuge de la Maline to Point Sublime (the recommended direction). Of course, the return trip has to be considered, and people travelling in groups usually make arrangements to leave a car at each end of the trail.

Near Point Sublime, you can walk to the bottom of the canyons via the **Sentier du Couloir Samson**. This trail takes two hours there and back. It gives a good overall impression of the Gorges and is a fairly easy hike. Bring a flashlight though, because at one point, the trail goes through a tunnel.

From Falaise des Cavaliers, hikers can easily access the trails that run along either rim of the gorges. At the bottom of the gorges in this location, a foot bridge connects one bank to the other. The Refuge de la Maline is on the other side, near the trailhead of the famous Martel trail. The **Sentier de l'Imbut** follows the south bank but is considered difficult and dangerous. It qualifies as an expert trail, with sudden steep slopes, and is not recommended for children or dogs.

The overall quality of the walking trails is worth mentioning. The difficult sections are equipped with cables anchored along the rock faces, providing hikers with a secure handhold.

Hikers should exercise caution at all times in order to prevent avoidable setbacks or accidents. Wear appropriate footwear, bring a sweater, a flashlight and, most importantly, make sure you bring enough drinking water (springs are rare or often dried up). Hikers are cautioned not to leave the marked trails or cross the Verdon. Finally, check the weather report before setting out, because storms take on a whole other dimension at the bottom of the gorges.

 Kayaking

Experienced whitewater kayakers will want to try running the Verdon from the Pont de Carrejuan (to the east of Point Sublime) to Lac de Ste-Croix, 24 km downriver. It takes two days to go down the river if all goes well. This trip requires a great deal of strength and attention to technique, so appreciating the scenery is only possible with frequent stops. The journey also involves several difficult portages. Going with a guide or a Verdon "veteran" is strongly recommended. Make sure you take enough supplies and extra clothes because once you start you can't go back.

Finally, there is an easier, less challenging route that takes you from Castellane to Point Sublime ending at the beginning of the Grand Canyon.

Whether you're hiking the trails or paddling the river in the Gorges du Verdon, the beauty of the landscape will leave you spellbound. Enjoy yourself, but **be careful!**

In case of accident:
• don't attempt to move the injured person from the accident site
• note which river bank you are on, the precise location, and the type of accident
• alert the village's fire department ☎ 18
• contact the Gendarmerie ☎ 17

 Accommodation

■ **Les Arcs-sur-Argens**

Located at the very top of the charming medieval village of Les Arcs, **Le Logis du Guetteur** (*450 F, extra bed 50 F, 880 F for mandatory half-board during peak season; pb or ps, ℝ, tv, ≈; ☎ 94.73.30.82, ⇄ 94.73.39.95*) is a wonderful place to stop in the country-side. This hotel, built on the site of an ancient castle fortress, offers a breath-taking panoramic view of the entire region. The rooms have an ancient charm and are very comfortable. The terrace and the beautiful swimming pool, with their splendid view over the surrounding area, are most relaxing. The hotel also has a restaurant, see p 325.

■ Draguignan

Quiet hotels are rare in Draguignan. For this reason, it may be best to find lodgings in the nearby villages.

If you do want to spend the night in Draguignan, look for the **Hostellerie du Moulin de la Foux** (280 F; pb, tv; Route de Lorgues, ☎ 94.68.55.33), located in a huge garden. The hotel is just out of the city centre, and not very well indicated, but worth looking for. See the description of the restaurant, p 326.

■ Callas

On a 32 ha estate, **Les Gorges de Pennafort** (600-900 F, 900-1,350 F for half-board; pb, tv, ≈; closed mid-Jan to mid-Mar; ☎ 94.76.66.51, ⇄ 94.76.67.23) offers you Var in all its splendour. Here you will experience Mediterranean hospitality at its best in a peaceful, luxurious setting, where nature and elegance live side by side. The rooms are tastefully decorated and have magnificent bathrooms. You are guaranteed a most delightful and restful stay. See the description of the restaurant, p 326.

■ Fayence

La Sousta (240 F, 340 F for four people; ps, C without , tv available; Place du Paty, ☎ 94.76.02.16) is the kind of small hotel that you'll want to come back to because of its service and personal welcome. The friendly owner is like a mother who takes care of everything so that her guests feel right at home. Each room is equipped with a small kitchenette. Room No. 5 is very much in demand as it's the only one with a terrace, and it has a beautiful view. All in all, this charming old house has a pleasant, family atmosphere that is worth visiting.

■ Mons

For a quiet place to stay, stop at the **Petit Bonheur** (140-230 F, half-board available; pb; Place Frédéric Mistral, ☎ 94.76.38.09). The hotel offers a Provençal atmosphere and a beautiful view over the surrounding area. The village is charming and the hotel rates are quite reasonable.

■ Trigance

At the entrance to the village, you'll find **Le Vieil Amandier** (250-290 F, half-board 520-600 F; ps or pb, tv, ℜ, ≈; Montée St-Roch, ☎ 94.76.92.92., ⇄ 94.47.58.65). The owners are dynamic people, ever concerned with improving the quality of their establishment. The rooms are very beautiful and some open onto a small private poolside terrace. See the description of the restaurant, p 326. Note: half-board is preferred as the restaurant is the owners's main income.

To experience the atmosphere of a medieval castle, stop at (or rather climb up to) the **Château de Trigance** (550-900 F, extra bed 100 F, half-board 1,200-1,400 F; pb, ℝ, tv, ℜ; closed Nov to mid-Mar; ☎ 94.76.91.18, ⇄ 94.47.58.99). The owners, Monsieur and Madame Thomas, welcome you to this castle at the very top of the village. The ancient 9th-century fortress was completely rebuilt and set up as hotel about 30 years ago. Each room has a large bed with a medieval-style canopy, and is carefully and tastefully decorated with antique furniture. This is a peaceful, restful site that offers a most spectacular panorama. Member of the *Relais et Châteaux*. See the description of the restaurant, p 326.

■ Gorges du Verdon

The **Hôtel-Restaurant Du Grand Canyon** (*300-460 F, half-board 500-700 F; ps or pb, tv; Falaise des Cavaliers, D 71, Aiguines,* ☎ *94.76.91.31,* ⇄ *94.76.92.29*) takes full advantage of the Gorges du Verdon, one of the Var's most magnificent sites. At an elevation of 800 m, you can enjoy an exceptional panorama over the gorges from the restaurant or terrace. The hotel's greatest advantage is its proximity to the hiking trails that start right next to it. In addition, the rooms are quite comfortable. The owner will be glad to share his advice on hiking in the area. Always remember that nature reigns here. See the description of the restaurant , p 327.

■ Moustiers-Sainte-Marie

At the entrance to this superb village, you'll find **La Bonne Auberge** (*210-280 F, extra bed 50 F, half-board 580 F; ps or pb; Route de Castellane,* ☎ *94.74.66.18*). Good, friendly service in a modest and very clean setting. The hotel has sixteen rooms but it is best to make reservations because there are rarely any vacancies, even off-season. See the description of the restaurant, p 327.

■ Tourtour

La Petite Auberge (*350 F, apt. 430 F, extra bed 80 F, half-board 610-690 F; pb,* ℜ, *tv,* ℝ, ≈, △; *94.70.57.16,* ⇄ *94.70.54.52*) belongs to the *Relais du Silence* chain. Located at the bottom of the village, on the hillside, it offers a lovely view over the surrounding countryside. The rooms are quiet and well equipped. This establishment also has rooms (*150 to 300 F; ps or pb, wc*) available in an annex located in the heart of the village, near the church. See the description of the restaurant, p 327.

L'Auberge St-Pierre (*350-500 F, half-board 750-900 F; pb, shared tv lounge,* ≈; ☎ *94.70.57.17,* ⇄ *94.70.59.04*) is located outside of the village, right in the countryside. This hotel, formerly a 16th-century residence has been run by the same family for 30 years. The son now runs the kitchen. The owners are very proud of their Provençal roots, and with their attention to detail have created a rustic and authentic Provençal decor. The rooms provide all the necessary comforts, and some have terraces that open out onto the lovely swimming pool. The hotel grounds offer a pleasant place to take a stroll in a pastoral setting. See the description of the restaurant, p 327.

The *Relais et Châteaux* chain has one hotel in this village, **La Bastide de Tourtour** (*550 F, 710- F with a beautiful terrace; pb,* ℜ, *tv,* ℝ, ≈; ☎ *94.70.57.30,* ⇄ *94.70.54.90*), which is only a short walk from the small St-Denis church. This is an old, carefully tended Provençal country house where you will find tranquillity and fine dining in a luxurious decor. The rooms are well equipped, even the less expensive ones. Some even have pretty terraces that look out onto a most peaceful panorama. Surrounding the hotel is a magnificent park perfect for a quiet walk. See the description of the restaurant, p 327.

■ Fox-Amphoux

The first-class **Auberge du Vieux Fox** (half-board 600-750 F; ps or pb, ℝ, tv, closed Dec. 20 to Feb; ☎ 94.80.71.69, ⇄ 94.80.78.38) is shaded by the trees of a small square. This village has a population of... 15! Established in the old priory of a 12th century Romanesque church, this hotel is a wonderful place to stop. Each room has a different personality and each is decorated with original furniture representing Provence in all its warmth and hospitality. The bathrooms are very modern but the tilework does reflect the Provençal style. The lounges and dining room are also decorated with local antiques. You might want to play a few chords on the beautiful Pleyel grand piano. See the description of the restaurant, p 327.

A stay in this hotel is an experience you will never regret. The value is excellent. To avoid disappointment, make your reservations early, especially during peak season.

■ Cotignac

A most beautiful garden lies beyond the gates of **Hostellerie Lou Calen** (270-590 F, half-board 616-936 F; ps or pb, tv, ≈; closed Jan to mid-Mar; ☎ 94.04.60.40, ⇄ 94.04.76.64). This hotel has an undeniable charm and guarantees a most pleasant stay. Lounge in the garden, by the pool side or simply enjoy the comfort of your room. The more expensive rooms are especially comfortable. The beautiful antique furniture lends all the rooms a truly charming and rustic appeal. See the description of the restaurant, p 328.

■ Entrecasteaux

An old country house that still has its stables, the **Hostellerie de Pardigon** (230-270 F; ps, tv in the spacious lounge; Route de Carcès, ☎ 94.73.84.00, ⇄ 94.60.11.17) will welcome you at the heart of a shaded park, on the outskirts of the village. This site has lots of character with its blend of stone, wood and Provençal tilework. The hotel's few rooms offer every comfort and are tastefully decorated. See the description of the restaurant, p 328.

Treat yourself to life in a castle at the **Château d'Entrecasteaux** (950 F, 1,250 F for a suite; pb; ☎ 94.04.49.62, ⇄ 94.04.48.92) overlooking the village. Guests may choose between two rooms with completely different personalities, straight out of a fairy tale. It is not an easy choice. The first, on two floors, has a fireplace. The second, the Marquise's room, is decorated with 18th-century antiques and has a huge white-marble Palladian bathroom. This is a once-in-a-lifetime opportunity. Such decors can usually only be viewed in museums, behind velvet ropes. We suggest arriving as early as possible to take full advantage of this unique environment. The rates are clearly justified since they are by far more reasonable than those of many of the palatial hotels on the Côte d'Azur. If you're going to treat yourself only once during your trip, this is the place to do it!

Note: the establishment only accepts previously confirmed reservations, no smoking, no pets allowed.

■ **Lorgues**

With its shaded park and regional cuisine, the **Hôtel du Parc** (*180-270 F, 350-430 F for three or four people; ps, tv; closed Nov. 15 to 30; 25 Bd Georges Clémenceau,* ☎ *94.73.70.01*) promises a most pleasant stay. This hotel takes you back in time to the France of the '50s and '60s. But most pleasant of all is the old-time charm that permeates the hotel, and the rooms decorated with ancient furniture. Ask for room No. 7 or 8 (with sloping ceiling). They both have a lovely view of the park. See the description of the restaurant, p 328.

 Camping

■ **Castellane**

There are no less than sixteen campgrounds in Castellane and the surrounding area. The region is very popular because of its proximity to the Gorges du Verdon. These are just a few of the campgrounds:

Castillon de Provence (nudist centre) (*100 camp sites, trailer rentals; s,* ≈, ℜ; *La Grande Terre, La Baume,* ☎ *92.83.64.24*). This nudist camp is located 11 km from Castellane, near Lac de Castillon. It offers fishing and canoeing.

Camping Le Frédéric Mistral (*60 camp sites; s; Bd Frédéric Mistral, Castellane,* ☎ *92.83.62.27*). This is the only campground that is open year-round. It is located only 100 m from the city centre, on Route Gorges du Verdon. However, it has few sports activities to offers.

Camping des Gorges du Verdon (*195 camp sites, bungalow and trailer home rentals; s,* ℝ*, tv,* ≈*; Route des Gorges du Verdon, Castellane,* ☎ *92.83.74.72*). This campground is located 9.5 km from Castellane, towards Gorges du Verdon. A very pleasant and friendly place with coordinators who organize lots of sports activities.

■ **Aups**

Aups has three campgrounds. This could be a good place to stop because it is very close to Gorges du Verdon. We recommend the **Camping International** (*150 camp sites; s, supplies,* ℝ*,* ≈*;* ☎ *94.70.06.80*).

 Restaurants

The hotels in this area generally have very good restaurants.

■ **Roquebrune-sur-Argens**

La Femme en Toque (*$$; closed Wed;* ☎ *94.45.73.47*) is located on CD 7, which leads towards the village. It is a country restaurant where meals can be enjoyed outdoors, surrounded by flowers. Provençal specialties are served, including *brioche de poisson avec sa rouille* (fish with sauce), among others. This is a very pleasant place to dine, and the food comes highly recommended by the locals.

■ **Les Arcs-sur-Argens**

The **restaurant** of the **Logis du Guetteur** (*$-$$*) (see p 321) serves a full-flavoured cuisine. A little Provençal flavour here, a touch of exotic tastes there; in short, a gastronomic delight.

The specialties are mostly meats including rack of lamb and beef filets. The vegetables are carefully prepared. As appetizers, we particularly enjoyed the *fleurs de courgettes à la ricotta en beignets* (squash with cheese) and the excellent *marbre de foie de canard à l'artichaut* (duck liver paté with artichoke). Finally, the cheese and rosemary sherbet, served with peaches and red wine, deserves a special mention — a delicately flavoured, unique dessert to end a wonderful meal. Unforgettable!

All in all, this restaurant is an absolute must! And in summer, it is made all the more pleasant because meals are served on the terrace.

■ Draguignan

La Mangeoire (*$; 18 Rue Pierre Clément*), is a little restaurant near the tourist office which serves Italian specialties in a rustic and friendly setting. There are a few tables in a small enclave that opens onto the street. A pitcher of wine (750 ml) is only 35 F, an inexpensive complement to the meal.

The **restaurant** of the **Hostellerie du Moulin de la Foux** (*$*) serves, among other things, home-made foie gras and smoked salmon. See the description of the rooms, p 322.

■ Callas

The **restaurant** of the **Gorges de Pennafort** (*$$; closed Sun evening and Mon off-season*) will enchant you with its Provençal dishes. See the description of the rooms, p 322.

■ Fayence

Here are a few restaurants that were recommended by the locals:

Le Patin Couffin (*$*), gets its name from a Provençal expression that means "to skip from one subject to another." This restaurant has a very special atmosphere, and it is a meeting place for many of the locals, who put this quaint expression into practice.

L'Entracte (*$*) is a creperie, ideal for a simple lunch or a light evening meal.

Le Bleu Marine (*$*) is located next to a fish store belonging to the same owner. The fish is guaranteed to be fresh. You can even order to go.

L'Auberge du Château (*$$*) is more upscale, but the food is excellent. Regional cuisine.

■ Trigance

The dining room of the **Vieil Amandier**, with its sobre yet elegant decor, will delight you with its cuisine from the south of France (*$-$$*). You can even savour a plate of truffles (*$$*) that come from the area. A stop at this hotel guarantees tranquillity and a warm welcome at a very reasonable price. See the description of the rooms, p 322.

The **restaurant** of the **Château de Trigance** (*$$*) serves fine gastronomic cuisine. Its specialty is warm *Sauternes foie gras*. The dining room is spectacular. It is nestled in a stone vault, lending it a truly medieval atmosphere. But if you prefer to eat by daylight, you can also choose the terrace. The view is lovely. See the description of the rooms, p 322.

■ **Gorges du Verdon**

The **Hôtel-Restaurant Du Grand Canyon** (*$-$$*) offers simple to more elaborate cuisine. The *soupe au pistou* (vegetable soup with basil and garlic) is recommended. See the description of the rooms, p 323.

■ **Moustiers-Sainte-Marie**

The **restaurant Les Santons** (*$$; closed Dec and Jan, Mon and Tue off-season; Place de l'Église;* ☎ *92.74.66.48*) overlooks the mountain stream that flows through the village. The setting is very pretty, and the food is good. This restaurant's good reputation has spread far and wide throughout the region. Local cuisine that is not pretentious.

Another restaurant, **La Belle Vue** (*$; closed Tue off-season and Nov and Dec;* ☎ *92.74.66.06*), has a particularly interesting terrace, which gives the impression of floating on an island. The interior, however, is rather dull. The restaurant serves Provençal specialties and game meats in season.

Finally, the old-fashioned **restaurant** of **La Bonne Auberge** (*$*) offers among its specialties *civet de porcelet* and *pieds paquets* (Provençal-style tripe). See the description of the rooms, p 323.

■ **Aups**

The **Framboise** (*$*) restaurant seems to be "the" place to stop. Seated on the terrace, you can enjoy pasta and traditional local dishes. This restaurant has an excellent reputation.

The locals also recommended **Le Chalet** (*$; closed Tue*), located next to Place Général Girard.

■ **Tourtour**

For a simple light lunch, away from the action of the village's main square, stop at **L'Alechou** (*$*) for crepes and salad in an intimate setting. There are a few tables on the little terrace. A very good selection of delicious salads. The only disadvantage is that the restaurant is right next to the road. It can be noisy in summer at the height of tourist season.

The **restaurant** at **La Petite Auberge** (*$*) serves Provençal home-style cooking made with only freshest ingredients. The dining room features a beautiful fireplace. See the description of the rooms, p 323.

The **restaurant** of the **Auberge St-Pierre** (*$*) takes pride in using only farm products that contribute to its healthy, natural appeal. The specialties are, of course, traditionally Provençal. Note: credit cards are not accepted. See the description of the rooms, p 323.

The **restaurant** of **La Bastide de Tourtour** (*$$*) offers a lunch menu that is very reasonable *(every day except Sunday)* considering the quality of the establishment. See the description of the rooms, p 323.

■ **Fox-Amphoux**

The **restaurant** of l'**Auberge du Vieux Fox** (*$$*) will enchant you with its simple, old recipes and aromas to make your mouth water. Worth mention is the *Galette du Berger*, an original lamb specialty. The dishes are garnished with carefully presented vegetables. The dining room opens out onto the garden where guests can dine peacefully in warm weather. The dining room that opens out onto the back of the hotel offers a splendid view over the surrounding countryside. See the description of the rooms, p 324.

■ Cotignac

The magnificent **garden-restaurant** at **Hostellerie Lou Calen** serves Provençal cuisine and features *Lotte à la Raimu* (devilfish). See the description of the rooms, p 324.

■ Entrecasteaux

Next to the château, way up on the hill, is **La Fourchette** (*$*), a restaurant that exudes tranquillity. It offers a very attractive set menu for 115 F. Guests may eat on the terrace, which looks out onto the Provençal countryside.

The dining room of the **Hostellerie de Pardigon** (just outside the village) serves Provençal specialties on the garden terrace, in season. In winter, the fireplace adds warmth to the already cosy, rustic atmosphere. The prices (*$-$$*) are very reasonable considering the quality of the food. See the description of the rooms, p 324.

■ Lorgues

The **Tric-Trac** (*$; Place Georges Clémenceau*) is a little creperie with a terrace that looks out onto Lorgues' very pretty main square. This is a perfect place for a lunchtime stop. In a pleasant atmosphere, the restaurant serves a wide variety of sweet or savoury crepes as well as salads, all at reasonable prices.

The **restaurant** of the **Hôtel du Parc** (*$-$$*), with its garden terrace, specializes in game meats, namely wild boar and rabbit, and in truffles, in season. This hotel is a very pleasant place to stop. See the description of the rooms, p 325.

 Entertainment

■ Draguignan

Draguifolies Various shows, jazz, rock, classical, traditional music (*free; Wed, Fri and Sat 9 PM; mid-Jul to end of Aug;* ☎ *94.68.63.30*).

L'Eté Contemporain Shows, exhibitions, events in 14 different locations throughout the city (*Mid-Jun to end of Aug;* ☎ *94.68.63.30*).

■ Entrecasteaux

Festival International de Musique de Chambre chamber music festival (*70-90 F; in Aug, reservations;* ☎ *94.04.44.83*).

 Shopping

■ Draguignan

Marché de Noël: local arts-and-crafts. (*Place du Marché, before Christmas to Dec 31;* ☎ *94.47.07.47.*)

■ Fayence

Salon de Antiquaires (antique show) End of June to beginning of August.

■ Moustiers-Ste-Marie

You simply cannot leave this magnificent village without browsing through the many shops that sell locally produced earthenware.

■ Aups

The beautiful **La Tonnelle** store offers a wide variety of Provençal products.

FRENCH GLOSSARY

GREETINGS

Hi (casual)	*Salut*
How are you?	*Comment ça va?*
I'm fine	*Ça va bien*
Hello (during the day)	*Bonjour*
Good evening/night	*Bonsoir*
Goodbye, See you later	*Bonjour, Au revoir, à la prochaine*
Yes	*Oui*
No	*Non*
Maybe	*Peut-être*
Please	*S'il vous plaît*
Thank you	*Merci*
You're welcome	*De rien, Bienvenue*
Excuse me	*Excusez-moi*

I am a tourist.	*Je suis touriste*
I am American (male/female)	*Je suis Américain(e)*
I am Canadian (male/female)	*Je suis Canadien(ne)*
I am British	*Je suis Britannique*
I am German (male/female)	*Je suis Allemand(e)*
I am Italian (male/female)	*Je suis Italien(ne)*
I am Belgian	*Je suis Belge*
I am French (male/female)	*Je suis Français(e)*
I am Swiss	*Je suis Suisse*

I am sorry, I don't speak French	*Je suis désolé(e), je ne parle pas français*
Do you speak English?	*Parlez-vous anglais ?*
Slower, please.	*Plus lentement, s'il vous plaît.*
What is your name?	*Quel est votre nom?*
My name is...	*Je m'appelle...*

spouse (male/female)	*époux(se)*
brother, sister	*frère, soeur*
friend (male/female)	*ami(e)*
son, boy	*garçon*
daughter, girl	*fille*
father	*père*
mother	*mère*
single (male/female)	*celibataire*
married (male/female)	*marié(e)*
divorced (male/female)	*divorcé(e)*
widower/widow	*veuf(ve)*

DIRECTIONS

Is there a tourism office near here?	*Est-ce qu'il y a un bureau de tourisme près d'ici?*
There is no..., we have no...	*Il n'y a pas de..., nous n'avons pas de...*
Where is...?	*Où est le/la ... ?*

straight ahead	*tout droit*
to the right	*à droite*
to the left	*à gauche*
beside	*à côté de*
near	*près de*
here	*ici*
there, over there	*là, là-bas*
into, inside	*à l'intérieur*
outside	*à l'extérieur*
far from	*loin de*
between	*entre*
in front of	*devant*
behind	*derrière*

FINDING YOUR WAY AROUND

airport	*aéroport*
on time	*à l'heure*
late	*en retard*
cancelled	*annulé*
plane	*l'avion*
car	*la voiture*
train	*le train*
boat	*le bateau*
bicycle	*la bicyclette, le vélo*
bus	*l'autobus*
train station	*la gare*
bus stop	*un arrêt d'autobus*
The bus stop, please	*l'arrêt, s'il vous plaît*

street	*rue*
avenue	*avenue*
road	*route, chemin*
highway	*autoroute*
rural route	*rang*
path, trail	*sentier*
corner	*coin*
neighbourhood	*quartier*
square	*place*
tourist bureau	*bureau de tourisme*

bridge	*pont*
building	*immeuble*
safe	*sécuritaire*
fast	*rapide*
baggage	*bagages*
schedule	*horaire*
one way ticket	*aller simple*
return ticket	*aller retour*
arrival	*arrivée*
return	*retour*
departure	*départ*
north	*nord*
south	*sud*
east	*est*
west	*ouest*

CARS

for rent	*à louer*
a stop	*un arrêt*
highway	*autoroute*
danger, be careful	*attention*
no passing	*défense de doubler*
no parking	*stationnement interdit*
no exit	*impasse*
stop! (an order)	*arrêtez!*
parking	*stationnement*
pedestrians	*piétons*
gas	*essence*
slow down	*ralentir*
traffic light	*feu de circulation*
service station	*station-service*
speed limit	*limite de vitesse*

MONEY

bank	*banque*
credit union	*caisse populaire*
exchange	*change*
money	*argent*
I don't have any money	*je n'ai pas d'argent*
credit card	*carte de crédit*
traveller's cheques	*chèques de voyage*
The bill please	*l'addition, s'il vous plaît*
receipt	*reçu*

ACCOMMODATION

inn	*auberge*

youth hostel	*auberge de jeunesse*
bed and breakfast	*gîte du passant*
hot water	*eau chaude*
air conditioning	*climatisation*
accommodation	*logement, hébergement*
elevator	*ascenseur*
bathroom	*toilettes, salle de bain*
bed	*lit*
breakfast	*déjeuner*
manager, owner	*gérant, propriétaire*
bedroom	*chambre*
pool	*piscine*
floor (first, second...)	*étage*
main floor	*rez-de-chaussée*
high season	*haute saison*
off season	*basse saison*
fan	*ventilateur*

SHOPPING

open	*ouvert(e)*
closed	*fermé(e)*
How much is this?	*C'est combien?*
I would like...	*Je voudrais...*
I need...	*J'ai besoin de...*
a store	*un magasin*
a department store	*un magasin à rayons*
the market	*le marché*
salesperson (male/female)	*vendeur(se)*
the customer (male/female)	*le / la client(e)*
to buy	*acheter*
to sell	*vendre*
T-shirt	*un t-shirt*
skirt	*une jupe*
shirt	*une chemise*
jeans	*un jeans*
pants	*des pantalons*
jacket	*un blouson*
blouse	*une blouse*
shoes	*des souliers*
sandals	*des sandales*
hat	*un chapeau*
eyeglasses	*des lunettes*
handbag	*un sac*
gifts	*cadeaux*
local crafts	*artisanat local*

sun protection products	*crèmes solaires*
cosmetics and perfumes	*cosmétiques et parfums*
camera	*appareil photo*
photographic film	*pellicule*
records, cassettes	*disques, cassettes*
newspapers	*journaux*
magazines	*revues, magazines*
batteries	*piles*
watches	*montres*
jewellery	*bijouterie*
gold	*or*
silver	*argent*
precious stones	*pierres précieuses*
fabric	*tissu*
wool	*laine*
cotton	*coton*
leather	*cuir*

MISCELLANEOUS

new	*nouveau*
old	*vieux*
expensive	*cher, dispendieux*
inexpensive	*pas cher*
pretty	*joli*
beautiful	*beau*
ugly	*laid(e)*
big, tall (person)	*grand(e)*
small, short (person)	*petit(e)*
short (length)	*court(e)*
low	*bas(se)*
wide	*large*
narrow	*étroit(e)*
dark	*foncé*
light (colour)	*clair*
fat (person)	*gros(se)*
slim, skinny (person)	*mince*
a little	*peu*
a lot	*beaucoup*
something	*quelque chose*
nothing	*rien*
good	*bon*
bad	*mauvais*
more	*plus*
less	*moins*
do not touch	*ne pas toucher*

quickly	*vite*
slowly	*lentement*
big	*grand*
small	*petit*
hot	*chaud*
cold	*froid*
I am ill	*je suis malade*
pharmacy, drugstore	*pharmacie*
I am hungry	*j'ai faim*
I am thirsty	*j'ai soif*
What is this?	*Qu'est-ce que c'est?*
Where?	*Où?*
fixed price menu	*table d'hôte*
order courses separately	*à la carte*

WEATHER

rain	*pluie*
clouds	*nuages*
sun	*soleil*
It is hot out	*Il fait chaud*
It is cold out	*Il fait froid*

TIME

When?	*Quand?*
What time is it?	*Quelle heure est-il?*
minute	*minute*
hour	*heure*
day	*jour*
week	*semaine*
month	*mois*
year	*année*
yesterday	*hier*
today	*aujourd'hui*
tomorrow	*demain*
morning	*le matin*
afternoon	*l'après-midi*
evening	*le soir*
night	*la nuit*
now	*maintenant*
never	*jamais*
Sunday	*dimanche*
Monday	*lundi*
Tuesday	*mardi*
Wednesday	*mercredi*

Thursday	*jeudi*
Friday	*vendredi*
Saturday	*samedi*
January	*janvier*
February	*février*
March	*mars*
April	*avril*
May	*mai*
June	*juin*
July	*juillet*
August	*août*
September	*septembre*
October	*octobre*
November	*novembre*
December	*décembre*

COMMUNICATION

post office	*bureau de poste*
air mail	*par avion*
stamps	*timbres*
envelope	*enveloppe*
telephone book	*bottin téléphonique*
long distance call	*appel outre-mer, une longue distance*
collect call	*appel collecte*
fax	*télécopieur, fax*
telegram	*télégramme*
rate	*tarif*
dial the regional code	*composer le code régional*
wait for the tone	*attendre la tonalité*

ACTIVITIES

recreational swimming	*la baignade*
beach	*plage*
scuba diving	*la plongée sous-marine*
snorkelling	*la plongée-tuba*
fishing	*la pêche*
recreational sailing	*navigation de plaisance*
windsurfing	*la planche à voile*
bicycling	*faire du vélo*
mountain bike	*vélo tout-terrain (VTT)*
horseback riding	*équitation*
hiking	*la randonnée pédestre*
to walk around	*se promener*
museum or gallery	*musée*
cultural centre	*centre culturel*
cinema	*cinéma*

TOURING

river	*fleuve, rivière*
waterfalls	*chutes*
viewpoint	*belvédère*
hill	*colline*
garden	*jardin*
wildlife reserve	*réserve faunique*
peninsula	*péninsule, presqu'île*
south/north shore	*côte sud/nord*
town or city hall	*hôtel de ville*
court house	*palais de justice*
church	*église*
house	*maison*
manor	*manoir*
bridge	*pont*
basin	*bassin*
dam	*barrage*
workshop	*atelier*
historic site	*lieu historique*
train station	*gare*
stables	*écuries*
convent	*couvent*
door, archway, gate	*porte*
customs house	*douane*
locks	*écluses*
market	*marché*
canal	*canal*
channel	*chenal*
seaway	*voie maritime*
museum	*musée*
cemetery	*cimitière*
mill	*moulin*
windmill	*moulin à vent*
lighthouse	*phare*
barn	*grange*
waterfall(s)	*chute(s)*
sandbank	*batture*
neighbourhood, region	*faubourg, quartier*

NUMBERS

1	*un*
2	*deux*
3	*trois*
4	*quatre*
5	*cinq*
6	*six*
7	*sept*
8	*huit*
9	*neuf*
10	*dix*
11	*onze*
12	*douze*
13	*treize*
14	*quatorze*
15	*quinze*
16	*seize*
17	*dix-sept*
18	*dix-huit*
19	*dix-neuf*
20	*vingt*
21	*vingt-et-un*
22	*vingt-deux*
23	*vingt-trois*
24	*vingt-quatre*
25	*vingt-cinq*
26	*vingt-six*
27	*vingt-sept*
28	*vingt-huit*
29	*vingt-neuf*
30	*trente*
31	*trente-et-un*
32	*trente-deux*
40	*quarante*
50	*cinquante*
60	*soixante*
70	*soixante-dix*
80	*quatre-vingt*
90	*quatre-vingt-dix*
100	*cent*
200	*deux cents*
500	*cinq cents*
1 000	*mille*
10 000	*dix mille*
1 000 000	*un million*

INDEX

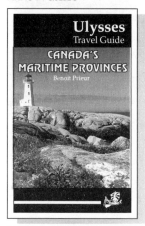

■ ULYSSES TRAVEL GUIDES

☐ Affordable Bed & Breakfasts
   in Québec .... $9.95 CAN
                        $7.95 US
☐ Canada's Maritime
   Provinces .... $24.95 CAN
                        $14.95 US
☐ Dominican Republic
   2nd Edition .... $22.95 CAN
                        $14.95 US
☐ Guadeloupe .... $22.95 CAN
                        $14.95 US
☐ Honduras .... $24.95 CAN
                        $16.95 US
☐ Martinique .... $22.95 CAN
                        $14.95 US
☐ Montréal .... $19.95 CAN
                        $12.95 US
☐ Ontario .... $14.95 CAN
                        $12.95 US
☐ Panamá .... $22.95 CAN
                        $14.95 US
☐ Provence -
   Côte d'Azur ...... $24.95 CAN
                        $14.95 US
☐ Québec .... $24.95 CAN
                        $14.95 US
☐ El Salvador .... $22.95 CAN
                        $14.95 US

■ ULYSSES GREEN ESCAPES

☐ Hiking in the Northeastern
   United States .... $19.95 CAN
                        $12.95 US
☐ Hiking in Québec .... $19.95 CAN
                        $12.95 US

■ ULYSSES DUE SOUTH

☐ Cartagena (Colombia) .. $9.95 CAN
                        $5.95 US
☐ Montelimar (Nicaragua) $9.95 CAN
                        $5.95 US
☐ Puerto Plata - Sosua - Cabarete
   (Dominican Republic) .. $9.95 CAN
                        $5.95 US
☐ St. Barts .... $9.95 CAN
                        $7.95 US
☐ St. Martin .... $9.95 CAN
                        $7.95 US

■ ULYSSES TRAVEL JOURNAL

☐ Ulysses Travel Journal . $9.95 CAN
                        $7.95 US

QUANTITY	TITLES	PRICE	TOTAL
		Sub-total	
		Postage & Handling	3.00 $
		Sub-total	
		G.S.T. in Canada 7 %	
		TOTAL	

Name :_____

Address :_____

City : _____

Postal Code :_____

Payment : ☐Money Order ☐Visa ☐MC ☐Cheque

Card Number :_____

Expiry Date :_____

Signature :_____

ULYSSES
TRAVEL PUBLICATIONS

4176, Saint-Denis
Montréal, Québec
H2W 2M5
Tel : (514) 843-9882
Fax: (514) 843-9448